THE BOOK OF GOD

THE BOOK OF GOD
A Response to the Bible

GABRIEL JOSIPOVICI

YALE UNIVERSITY PRESS
NEW HAVEN AND LONDON 1988

Set in 11/12 Linotron Goudy Old Style by Best-set Typesetter Limited, Hong
Kong, and printed and bound in the United States of America by Murray
Printing Company, Westford, Massachusetts.

Designed by Robert Baldock

Library of Congress Cataloguing-in-Publication Data

Josipovici, Gabriel, 1940–
    The book of God: a response to the Bible/Gabriel Josipovici.
        p.   cm.
    Bibliography: p.
    Includes indexes.
    ISBN 0-300-04320-1
    1. Bible as literature.   2. Bible – Criticism, interpretation, etc.
3. Bible – Language, style.   I. Title.
    BS535.J67   1988
    220.6 – dc19   88-14038
                                                                CIP

FOR MY MOTHER

CONTENTS

ILLUSTRATION

Moses receiving the Tables of the Law (facing page 3)

from a late 17th-century Ethiopic MS of the Octateuch, Four Gospels and Synodos (British Museum, Oriental MS 481. f.4v)

PREFACE

'Oh word, thou word that I lack!' cries Moses in Schoenberg's opera, *Moses und Aron*, and with that cry the work comes to an abrupt end. The composer had written the libretto for a third act but was never able to compose the music for it, and one can see why. His hero's lament is that of Schoenberg himself, and it echoes the cry of many artists in the past hundred and fifty years, who recognized the truth of the Romantic claim that we no longer live within a sustaining tradition, yet lacked the Romantic faith in the ability of human subjectivity to replace it. Once Shelley had proudly asserted that poets were the unacknowledged legislators of mankind, but now Prufrock can only wrily imagine himself as a latter-day Lazarus, come back from the dead to tell what he has seen, or as a John the Baptist uttering his fiery prophecies – and just to imagine this is to recognize the distance that separates him from these biblical characters:

> But though I have wept and fasted, wept and prayed,
> Though I have seen my head (grown slightly bald) brought in upon a platter,
> I am no prophet – and here's no great matter;
> I have seen the moment of my greatness flicker,
> And I have seen the eternal Footman hold my coat, and snicker,
> And in short, I was afraid.

If you are a student of literature or a cultural historian you can say that this is one of the great topics of modern literature: today art is impossible because the artist lacks authority, and to pretend otherwise, to go on as though nothing had happened, is a betrayal not only of artistic but of human values. And you can say that every major work of modern art has sprung Phoenix-like from such ashes. But if you are a simple reader or a writer, then these matters will seem more than merely interesting, and each true work wrenched from such circumstances will seem a miracle.

To try and explain this situation to myself I wrote a book, *The World and the Book*. I felt that the modernist crisis, to use an ugly shorthand phrase, could perhaps best be understood by seeing it in the context not just of nineteenth-century art and culture, but of that culture which so much modern art seemed to look back to as a period at ease within the tradition, free of anxiety. I thought one should take seriously Eliot's love of Dante and Proust's of medieval cathedrals, and I argued that in writers like Rabelais, Swift and Sterne we see not a turning away from the Middle Ages but the most self-conscious attempts by post-Renaissance writers to grasp what it was they had gained and lost by the transition from an Age of Faith to an Age of Reason.

Dante's *Commedia*, though, and the medieval cathedrals, were themselves modelled on a book, the Bible, as that had been mediated to the West by the Church. And as the thinkers of the German tradition, such as Hegel and Nietzsche, understood, the fortunes of art in our time go hand in hand with the fortunes of theology. If one takes the Renaissance Humanist perspective one can rejoice at the ending of the Dark Ages and feel that human creativity had then at last come into its own after centuries of obscurantism and repression; but one can also take another perspective, and argue that once Luther took his stand on his own conscience alone, once Zwingli asserted that the bread and wine of the Mass were purely symbolic, we had already crossed the threshold into the modern crisis of authority. The power and significance of the writings of Kierkegaard and Nietzsche are then seen to stem from the fact that both men recognized that questions of faith and questions of artistic form and content are inseparable, though it was left to a Frenchman to encapsulate their insights in one witty phrase: 'Dieu n'est pas un artiste,' wrote Sartre in an early review, 'M. Mauriac non plus.'

God's existence and place in our lives may be the subject of debate by theologians, but the God of the Jews and Christians is to be found, along with Moses, John the Baptist and Lazarus, in that quaintly named book, the Bible. Like many people of my generation I had grown up with the Bible stories and I had no difficulty in picking up Eliot's references. But I did not 'know' the Bible in the way I did the works of Chaucer or Shakespeare or Proust or Eliot. And when I turned to it I found myself faced with two very striking things: the first was that this book, though supremely authoritative for Jews and Christians, did not, when one actually read it, appear anything like as authoritarian as the *Aeneid* or *Paradise Lost*. It seemed much quirkier, funnier, quieter than I expected. The second was that it contained narratives which seemed, even in translation, as I first read them, far fresher and more 'modern' than any of the prize-winning novels rolling off the presses. Far more 'modern', even, than any of the attempts to rewrite those narratives and fill them out, of which the most weighty was no doubt Mann's *Joseph and His Brothers*.

This aspect of the Bible was not something that either traditional scholarship or traditional theology seemed to have been much concerned with. Indeed, the interested reader of the book of Genesis, or Samuel, or Mark's Gospel, turning to the scholars and theologians for enlightenment in the way one might turn to Chaucer or to Shakespeare critics and scholars after being moved by a reading of *The Canterbury Tales* or a performance of *King Lear*, was bound, I discovered, to be disappointed. Not that traditional biblical scholarship and theology were not fascinating; but they were fascinating, so to speak, in their own right. One learned a great deal from them about the history of the ancient Near East, about hypothetical scribes and redactors, about *kerygma* and *heilsgeschichte* and why it was necessary to use Greek and German words like these, but one learned nothing about why the Bible often showed Jacob and David in such a poor light or how to account for the speed and directness with which Mark tells his story.

Did this mean that the Bible derived its authority in spite of its narratives? That its mode of narration was quite unrelated to its status? Why did scholars and theologians not at least consider the possibility that, on the contrary, the two were interrelated, and that the Bible had kept its pre-eminent place in our culture because of rather than in spite of them?

Forty years ago one would have looked in vain for even an awareness that this might be a genuine issue. Today, however, it's a different matter. In the years following the publication of Erich Auerbach's *Mimesis* (the German edition came out in 1946, the English translation in 1953), with its two wonderful opening chapters comparing the Old Testament with Homer and the New Testament with the Roman historians, the academic world in America and England seemed to have woken up with a start to the fact that the Bible was, among other things, a book which could be explored and examined, and whose special qualities could be brought to light, in the same way as one could examine and bring to light the qualities of *The Canterbury Tales* or *King Lear*. In the past few years leading literary critics, like Northrop Frye, Frank Kermode and Robert Alter, as well as a number of younger scholars like Meir Sternberg and Joel Rosenberg, have produced distinguished books on the subject, and there have been hundreds of articles in learned journals, as well as the emergence of wholly new periodicals devoted to exploring the Bible from points of view which are neither those of traditional scholarship nor of theology.

Most of this work has been devoted, like the opening chapters of *Mimesis*, to a study of biblical narratives. Of course these narratives account for a large part of the Bible, and such concentration, in the hands of subtle and erudite critics like Alter and Sternberg, has yielded rich results. But it has also had the effect of splitting the Bible in two – into a narrative portion, with which the critic is concerned, and the rest, with which he isn't. Of course this latter portion may itself be split again, into poetry, which the critic wishes to study, and non-poetry. But the message is the same: there are parts of the Bible which should never have dropped out of the consideration of students of literature, and there are other parts, such as laws and religious instructions, which can be left to theologians and scholars. But this is certainly not the way earlier readers thought about the Bible. For them it was all one book, with Psalms calling out to Genesis and Job to the Gospels, Paul to Leviticus and Ecclesiastes to Kings. In other words, the question the new criticism implicitly raises – it is the question begged by the titles of Robert Alter's splendid books, *The Art of Biblical Narrative* and *The Art of Biblical Poetry* – is this: is the Bible the repository of some marvellous stories and poems, or is it a whole, perhaps a narrative or a poetic whole? Is it, in short, a book or a ragbag?

The implications of the new criticism, whether its authors mean it like that or not, are that it is the latter. But this conclusion is particularly surprising in view of the fact that theologians, for their part, have begun to show a new interest in story and poetry, and even to argue that a significant aspect of God's message is that it should be delivered as story and poem, and that we cannot understand it at all unless we accept this fact. It is odd, therefore, that the new critics have not at least addressed themselves to the question: one story or many?

To be fair, Northrop Frye's *The Great Code*, which picks up and develops themes already adumbrated in his many earlier books, does address itself directly to the artistic shape of the whole. What is curious is that in the course of his book Frye has very little to say about individual stories and characters. Does this suggest that we must choose? That we must either talk about the richness, complexity and multiplicity of narratives *in* the Bible, or about the story shape *of* the Bible, but not both? And if that is the case, why is it so?

Frye says explicitly that he is dealing with the Christian Bible as it has been known to the West since St. Jerome produced the Vulgate, and more particularly the English Bible, as it was known to Milton and Blake. Alter and Sternberg, on the other hand, are concerned only with the narratives of the Hebrew Bible. Could this have anything to do with their different perspectives? And, if so, might it not be worth asking what is the effect on the narrative or narratives of the Hebrew Bible of the addition to them of the New Testament? Does it totally alter our understanding or only modify it? The New Testament claims both to continue the Hebrew scriptures and to transform them totally. Are the two claims compatible? Are we faced with two notions of narrative in basic agreement with each other or in fundamental conflict? And, since the mode of narration of the Gospels seems to have so much in common with that of Genesis and Samuel, does the division, if division there is, occur between the two Testaments, or between the Gospels and the Epistles?

These are some of the questions which surfaced as I read or reread the Bible and examined some of the products of the new biblical criticism. As I pondered them I began to realize two things. The first was that there was no short-cut to the answers: one could not arrive at them theoretically, but only by immersing oneself in the book, much as anyone seeking answers to the problems posed by *The Canterbury Tales* or *King Lear* would expect to do. And secondly, that the implications of this were indeed daunting. For however dissatisfied one might feel with the answers provided by traditional scholarship and theology, it was clear that they could not simply be ignored. Those critics who, fired by enthusiasm for the biblical narratives, felt they could comment on them by reading them in translation and responding to them as they would to a modern novel, were unlikely to produce work more interesting than might be produced by a non-English speaker, wilfully ignorant of the Middle Ages, writing on Chaucer. On the other hand, to be adequately equipped to comment on even a single verse of the Bible one would ideally have to know half a dozen ancient languages, be familiar with developments in archaeology, palaeography and textual criticism, and have a thorough grasp of the changing historical and cultural conditions of the ancient Near East from prehistoric times to the fall of the Jerusalem Temple in 70 ACE. But even to sketch in answers to some of the questions I found myself asking would entail thinking about the entire Bible as well as about the history of Western civilization with which the changing fortunes of the Bible were so tightly bound up. This was clearly a task well beyond the capacities of any single human being, even one who was willing to devote a lifetime to the project.

But even this was not the most daunting aspect of the whole enterprise. If there is something faintly absurd about the plethora of academic books on *King Lear* and Beckett's *Trilogy*, was this not still more true of the Bible? This book had *mattered* in the past, and mattered intensely. People had died to defend a phrase in it; they had felt that their eternal salvation depended on their responding properly to what it said; in their moments of deepest tribulation they had found comfort in it. How could one possibly engage with it if one's own stakes were not correspondingly high?

At this point I decided it would be wiser to forget the whole thing. I would go on reading the Bible and perhaps allow myself to think a little about its nature and its relation to those books which meant most to me, but that would be all. Unfortunately the questions wouldn't let me go. They came back at me, demanding to be answered, no matter how inadequately. In the end it became clear to me that I would have to throw discretion to the winds and try to answer them to my own satisfaction and in the only way I knew – by writing about them. Otherwise, I sensed, I would never have the peace again to write the narratives *I* wanted to write.

I have tried in this book to tread a path between complete irresponsibility and total submersion under the weight of secondary reading. It is quite likely therefore that at every stage in my argument I have merely repeated in my own words what has been better said by others elsewhere; if that is the case I ask their forgiveness and only hope that there is something in the overall argument which has not been said or not said in that way before, and which will stimulate those more learned and intelligent than myself to move in new directions.

This is a book in the end as much about the nature of reading as about the Bible. As such its greatest debt is to Proust, both to À la recherche and to the earlier essays. That debt will be evident to anyone who reads the following pages. But my understanding of these problems has been coloured by my unprofessional reading of the later Wittgenstein. And it was Buber rather than Auerbach who first gave me a glimpse of how it might be possible to illuminate the Bible by looking at what it said rather than at what lay behind it.

The list of people who have at some time or other in the past twelve years helped me to formulate a problem or see a solution is so long that if I were to put them all down the world, I sometimes feel, could not contain the book their names would fill. Let me single out my four dedicated teachers of Hebrew: Michael Wadsworth, who first insisted I learn the language and introduced me to the concept of midrash; Francis Landy, who not only guided me through the labyrinths of biblical semantics but also gave me a glimpse of what a true inwardness with the Bible could be, and who, at a late stage in the writing of this book, painstakingly went through two-thirds of it and saved me from many errors; and Eti and Effi Paz, who made me see how the Bible could be a living presence without ever becoming an oppressive one. Bernard Harrison, Charles Martindale, Tony Nuttall, Stephen Medcalf, Tony Thorlby, and Jonathan Wittenberg read some of the chapters in early drafts and were generous in sharing with me their understanding of the Bible. John Drury, Harold Fisch and Gerry Webster read the whole book in typescript and made many shrewd and valuable comments. Catharine Carver worked devotedly preparing the typescript for press. I am grateful to all of them for the time and effort they gave to someone else's work. I am grateful too to Jonathan Magonet, not only for his help with more technical points of Hebrew and Bible, but also for annually inviting me to talk to his students at Leo Baeck College in London: I learned much in the preparation of these talks and even more in listening to the audience afterwards. I am also grateful to Michael Wadsworth for inviting me to contribute to Ways of Reading the Bible, and to Frank Kermode for inviting me to contribute to The Literary Guide to the Bible, and for their comments on my contributions. None of these people, it goes without saying, is responsible for any of the errors and weaknesses of this book, for I have rejected advice as often as I have accepted it. Finally, since this is a book about continuities, family stories and trust, it can only be dedicated to one person, who should have written it herself, but whose modesty made such a solution unthinkable.

Lewes, Sussex
March 1988

ACKNOWLEDGEMENTS

I should like to thank the Leverhulme Foundation for their award of a grant which made it possible for me to start writing this book.

I should also like to thank the editors and publishers of the books and journals in which early versions of some of the arguments in this book first appeared: 'The Bible: Dialogue and Distance' in *Ways of Reading the Bible*, ed. Michael Wadsworth (Brighton, Sussex: Harvester Press, 1981); 'The Irreducible Word' in *European Judaism*, XV, no. 1 (Summer 1981); 'Joseph and Biblical Revelation' in *Salmagundi*, no. 66 (1985); 'The Epistle to the Hebrews and the Catholic Epistles' in *The Literary Guide to the Bible*, ed. Robert Alter and Frank Kermode (Cambridge, Mass.: Harvard University Press, and London: Collins, 1987).

AUTHOR'S NOTE

Quotations from the Bible are taken for the most part from the King James Bible or Authorized Version of 1611. Where it is necessary for my argument to grasp nuances not conveyed in the AV, I have made my own versions from the Hebrew or the Greek, but it is always obvious where this occurs.

In places it has helped my argument to transliterate the Hebrew or the Greek. I have tried to keep these transliterations as simple and uncluttered as possible, even at the cost of strict accuracy. Only a few signs need decoding: *ch* in the Hebrew transliterations should be pronounced as in Scottish 'loch', and *ō* and *ē* in the Greek transliterations as in 'snow' and 'hay'; ' and ' stand for the Hebrew *aleph* and *ayin*.

Biblical terms appearing frequently are occasionally abbreviated, as, e.g., 'OT' for Old Testament or 'LXX' for Septuagint, but any such usage is always made clear at the outset. The name of God is given throughout as 'YHWH', except in quotations from authors who vocalize it as 'Yahweh' or 'Jehovah', etc.

G. J.

One

THE READER AND THE BOOK

The words were spoken as if there was no book,
Except that the reader leaned above the page,

Wanted to lean, wanted much most to be
The scholar to whom his book is true, to whom

The summer night is like a perfection of thought.
The house was quiet because it had to be.

WALLACE STEVENS

Moses receiving the Tables of the Law (British Museum, Oriental MS 481. f.4v)

I

THE READER

I begin with an image. It is a full-page illustration from a late Ethiopic biblical manuscript. It shows Moses receiving the Tables of the Law. He is sumptuously dressed in an embroidered cloak of red, blue and yellow. His large naked feet rest on the frame as he faces right, the head in three-quarter profile. His hands protrude from the sleeves of the cloak and hold the bottom of a large square book, which is being held at the top by the hand of God, emerging from a blue cloud outlined in yellow, which takes up the top right-hand corner of the picture. Moses, with bluish hair and beard and a splendid yellow halo, has turned the pupils of his eyes as far to the right as they will go, not looking at the hand but at the book.

This image, it seems to me, is, in essentials, the one that first springs to the minds of most people when the word 'Bible' is mentioned. Whether we read the Bible or not, whether we regularly attend services in synagogue or church, our instinctive sense of the Bible is of a book handed by God to us, the place where, for a moment, God's hand and ours almost touch. Whether we are fundamentalists or atheists, whether we have only vaguely heard of Joseph and Moses and Pontius Pilate, or are acquainted with scholarly controversies over the origins of the Pentateuch and the Gospels and the complex history of their transmission, we tend to think of the Bible as essentially different from all other books, though we may see it daily on our shelves in the midst of other books or even hold it in our hands and turn its pages as we would those of the latest novel or biography.

It is the nature of this difference I will be exploring in the course of this book. Is the difference absolute or relative? Is it inherent in the Bible or merely the result of extrinsic cultural factors? Might it be a mixture of both? To answer such questions we will have to look not only at the Bible itself, but also at ourselves, as readers today and as the recipients of this book in previous centuries. But I want to begin not with reading but with listening, and not with the past of the Western world but with the past of our own lives. For the sense we have of ourselves as like the Moses of the Ethiopic manuscript was not always with us. Once the Bible was not a book but stories told us by our parents.

When stories are read to us in childhood we accept them without question. Spoken as they are by someone we trust and who forms part of the world into which we have come, they seem to us as natural and inevitable as that world itself. As we grow up we leave many of these stories behind us, never to be thought of again until perhaps we in turn read them to our children. A few, though, we return to, by chance perhaps, or out of some lingering curiosity. One day we find ourselves reading them on our own, in the silence of the bedroom or study, or the bustle of a train or café. When that happens it is sometimes difficult to relate the pages before us to our memories of the stories. The tales of Arthur and his knights, it turns out, all fit together in a book called the *Morte Darthur*, written by a fifteenth-century Englishman, Thomas Malory, but drawn by him out of the stock of medieval French tales about Arthur; the stories of Scheherazade and Sindbad the Sailor come from an Arabic book called *The Thousand and One Nights* or *A Thousand Nights and a Night*; the stories of Moses and the plagues, of Jesus and Judas, come from a book with the strange title of 'the Bible'.

Our relation to these stories can no longer be the unproblematic one of childhood. Because we now read instead of simply listening, because we can pause, turn back, put down the book and take it up again, a whole set of questions arises which never troubled us before: Did King Arthur really exist? If so, when and where did he live? Who was Moses? Did the plagues really occur? Was Jesus really the son of God? Did he really appear to his disciples after his death?

Some readers become obsessed by these questions and will not rest till they have found an answer that will satisfy them; others follow them up passionately for a little while and then lose interest; still others, wishing to maintain their relation to these books but sensing that such questions are not likely to lead very far, relegate them to the margins of their consciousness and discover that others are more productive. As they grow more confident in themselves, both as adults and as readers, they discover that there is a constant see-saw movement at work in our relations to the books that matter to us: we are drawn to them because they seem to speak to our condition, and we seek to make them more and more our own: but we are also drawn to them because they seem to be *other* than us, because they guide us out of ourselves into what we feel to be a truer, more real world.

This double process is easier to discern in its aberrations than in its normal functioning. Clearly a book is being misread if the reader as-similates it so entirely to himself that he palpably distorts what it is saying in order to make it fit in with his own needs and desires; equally clearly it is being misread if it is so emphatically placed in its historical and cultural context that any link with our present needs and desires is rigorously denied. The reader of *Hamlet* who asserts that Claudius is the real hero, or that all that is wrong with Hamlet is that he is suffering from an Oedipus complex, is obviously not reading the play before him. Claudius is clearly guilty by the end of the play of not one but many murders, and Gertrude is also at least partially implicated in his actions. But the person who maintains that we cannot identify with Hamlet at all because we cannot will ourselves to believe in ghosts or Hell or Purgatory is also misreading. The play does seem to touch on primal fears and desires, and the history of its reception suggests that it has the power of affecting audiences who no longer believe in the supernatural or in Christian notions of the after-life. Whether it has the power of affecting audiences *whatever* their beliefs is not a question we need pursue here.

How then, it might be asked, are we to decide what is the right interpretation? The question looks perfectly natural, but it isn't. It is the sort of question that is asked when one is only theoretically interested in a work, not when one is actually involved with it.[1] By asking it we give the wrong impression of what happens when we read. Consider what does happen. Because *Hamlet* has captivated us we read more and more plays by Shakespeare and his contemporaries. And the more we read and live the fuller and richer will any re-reading of *Hamlet* be, and the more of its elements will fall into place. Of course the process is not that of a steady advance. It may be a long time before we experience the play again with the clarity and power we for some reason had when we first saw or read it. And of course a wide range of reading and a long life are no guarantees of a better reading. Keats lived less long and must have read a good deal less than most scholars and critics, but no one who knows his letters and poems can doubt that he made up for this by the intensity of his response to Shakespeare and the power and richness of his mind. Shakespeare spoke to him, we might say, and he knew how to listen (and then how to articulate what he heard).

Thus, though questions of the kind – what is *Hamlet really* about? – may trouble philosophers and philosophically-inclined critics, they will trouble few viewers and readers of the play. It is not that we are unconcerned about meaning; it is that, as it stands, the question is too stark, too naked. What Northrop Frye says about value and literary works is just as true of meaning: 'The critic', writes Frye (I would say 'the reader'), 'will find soon, and constantly, that Milton is a more rewarding and suggestive poet to work with than Blackmore. But the more obvious this becomes, the less time he will want to waste in belaboring the point.'[2] In the same way we do not try to decide exactly what *Hamlet* means; we keep re-viewing it and re-reading it, and, if we are so inclined, reading those critics and scholars we have discovered will enhance our enjoyment and understanding of the play.

And the same is true of Malory. Though questions about 'the real Arthur' may be fascinating in themselves, we soon find that they do not help us with the *Morte Darthur*. Questions about Malory's French sources may be nearer the mark, since by reading them we will discover how Malory employed them for his own ends; but there will also be questions about the unfolding relationships of Arthur, Guinevere and Lancelot, about Malory's reticent style, about the way he builds up a sense of the doom that is to overtake the Round Table. These questions can only be answered from within the book and through comparison with similar and contemporary works. No amount of outside information will help us here. We know that the only way to 'find out' is to read the *Morte Darthur* as often and as attentively as possible, and then perhaps to read those books which formed the horizons of Malory's world.

But at this point you may want to stop me. It's all very well to talk about *Hamlet* and the *Morte Darthur* in this way, you will say, but it just won't do for the Bible. Here questions about what it really means, and about the truth or otherwise of the events it narrates simply will not go away. And proof that there is some substance to such claims is to be found in the fact that when we turn to popular introductions to the Bible we find ourselves faced with works that are very different in kind from the equivalent publications connected with Shakespeare and Malory. These popular introductions to the Bible seem to be concerned almost ex-clusively with the question of whether or not Abraham, Moses, David and Jesus existed, with historical reconstructions of the exodus from Egypt or the Passion, with the archaeology of the Holy Land, and possibly with how and where the biblical books came into existence and how they have been handed down to our own day.

All this is fascinating, but it is clear that it provides a kind of service very different from that to which the reader of Shakespeare and Malory is used. One would understand it if in addition there were books like Bradley's *Shakespearian Tragedy* or C. S. Lewis's *Preface to 'Paradise Lost'*, but this does not appear to be the case. Why?

An obvious answer would seem to be that the Bible is a sacred book and the works of Malory, Shakespeare and Milton are not. But this is less satisfying than it might at first appear. It is worth remembering that the Bible is not quite unique in the *kind* of interest it seems to arouse. Popular introductions to Homer also seem to be more concerned with whether the Trojan War ever took place than with Homer's poems. It may therefore not be primarily because the Bible is a sacred text that it is looked at in this way, but because, like Homer, it is a very ancient text which has, miraculously, survived to our own day. Yet Homer too was once a sacred text to the Greeks. But the fact is that it is not sacred to the West and that nevertheless, since the eighteenth century, Homeric and biblical scholarship has run on roughly parallel lines.[3] For the moment, however, a sufficient answer to my question, Why?, would seem to be the fact that the Bible has for centuries been the sacred book of our culture.

Is it an answer, though? For what do we mean by 'a sacred book'? To the ancient rabbis it was, quite simply, a book which, if touched, caused pollution. 'All the Holy Scriptures render the hands unclean,' says the Mishnah. 'R. Judah says: The Song of Songs renders the hands unclean, but about Ecclesiastes there is dissension. R. Jose says: Ecclesiastes does not render the hands unclean.'[4] It is worth noting that these comments do not occur in a discussion of the canon of Scripture but in a treatise on what does and does not pollute. We are on slightly more familiar ground with some remarks made by Josephus, the first-century Jewish historian, in his defence of the Jews against attacks made upon them by the Alexandrian scholar, Apion:

> We have given practical proof [says Josephus] of our reverence for our own Scriptures. For, although such long ages have now passed, no one has ventured either to add, or to remove, or to alter a syllable; and it is an instinct with every Jew, from the day of his birth, to regard them as the decrees of God, to abide by them, and, if need be, cheerfully to die for them. . . . What Greek would endure as much for the same cause? Even to save the entire collection of his nation's writings from destruction he would not face the smallest personal injury. For to the Greeks they are mere stories improvised according to the fancy of their authors.[5]

Few people today would think of the sacred as the physically polluting, and few too would think of dying to uphold the truth of their sacred books. Yet most people would admit to feeling some sort of awe in relation to the Bible. Yet when one asks *why* they should feel that awe they have no ready reply. A few, it is true, respond by saying that the Bible is the Word of God and everything in it is true. But what does that mean? Swift long ago parodied such naïve fundamentalism by asserting that no one should ever use toilet paper, since it is written: 'he which is filthy, let him be filthy still' (Rev. 22:11).[6] We laugh, but a sound principle is being asserted here: all language requires interpretation; there is no such thing as a literal meaning which can be assimilated without the mediation of human beings – without, that is, a grasp of the conventions of grammar and context.

However, few of those who feel that the Bible is essentially different from *Hamlet* and the *Morte Darthur* are naïve fundamentalists. Yet they treat the Bible with an awe which they withold from all other books, even if they are not practising Jews or Christians. Again, why?

A number of mutually reinforcing elements are at work here. First of all we have to note that the Bible is unique in that it is the only book in our culture where the child's relation to books is perpetuated into adulthood. Because the Bible is used for public worship the transition we all experience in our lives from an oral to a written culture is blurred. Think how it would affect our response to the stories of Arthur and his knights if we lived in a community which recounted such stories in public every week.

But, it might be argued, is not school just such a community? Might not the child's experience of Shakespeare at school precisely parallel his experience of the Bible in synagogue or church? How one answers this will clearly be coloured by one's view of both school and church, but even to a dispassionate observer there are clear differences. At school the child is in a class with only those of his own age-group, and he has been forced to go there in order to learn. The teacher tells him that Shakespeare is a great writer and his most likely response is to shut his mind to Shakespeare for the next half-hour and concentrate with his neighbour on something more interesting. The congregation that fills the synagogue or church on the other hand is made up not only of those of his own age but also of his family and relatives, and he is not made to learn lessons but to take part with them in a service. In the Jewish tradition the fact that the focus of worship is the home makes the contrast with school even greater and links up even more strongly with the childhood experience of being told stories by one's parents.

Much of course depends on whether the community of worship is to be equated with the whole village, town or country, or only with a fragment of it in a hostile or indifferent larger whole. Clearly the smaller the group that meets to worship and the more embattled it feels itself to be, the sharper will be the child's response and the greater the likelihood that he will identify strongly, either with those inside against those outside, or with those outside against those inside. Nevertheless, even allowing for such variations, the sacred text is identified with the community in ways no other text ever is. And this is true whether we are talking about Jews in sixth-century BCE Babylon, Catholics in Elizabethan England or Anglicans in the England of today.

Our sense of awe in relation to the Bible, then, has little to do with any innate fundamentalism and much to do with the fact that here, uniquely, our childhood way with books is prolonged into adulthood. But this is reinforced by another fact, less easy to acknowledge, which is, quite simply, the size and diversity of the Bible. Think of the person who decides to find out for himself what the Bible is really about. He is tired of the way it is taken for granted by his parents and in the religious community to which they belong. Or perhaps he is tired of the way it is dismissed by his parents. He is going to find out for himself, as he found out about Shakespeare, satisfied himself that Shakespeare was or was not the genius people made him out to be. He did this by reading the *Complete Works* of Shakespeare. But when he tries to do the same thing with the Bible he discovers that with the best will in the world he cannot do it. There is too much of it, a great deal of it unreadable and a great deal else seeming to belong to a world which makes no sense to him. And when he turns to books on the Bible to help him, he finds, as we have noted, that they do not so much do that as lead him off into the highways and byways of ancient history, or else preach at him from already fixed positions.

He is likely to come away from this encounter with the feeling either that the whole thing is a waste of time, or that there are enough points at which the Bible has touched him for him to give it and the religious community whose sacred book it is the benefit of the doubt. In neither case will anything have been resolved by his decision to read for himself and see.

But here it may be argued that my assumption that the Bible is a single, though enormously varied and complex, book is itself only an assumption, and that my hypothetical reader would simply recognize what scholars have for long been arguing, that the Bible is not a single book at all but a multiplicity of different ancient documents only put together as a single book by the arbitrary decision of a group of religious leaders in some ancient far-off time and place. After all, the name itself comes from the Greek, *ta biblia*, 'little books'. Isn't it absurd to think of it as one? And even the notion of a collection of little *books* is misleading. As James Barr has pointed out:

> In biblical times the books were separate individual scrolls. A 'Bible' was not a volume one could hold in the hand, but a cupboard or chest with pigeonholes, or a room or cave with a lot of individual scrolls. The boundary between what was scripture, and what were other holy books, was thus more difficult to indicate, and so was the order of the books and the organization (if any) of the canon.[7]

How then are we to think of the Bible? It's clearly more diverse than the collected plays, or even the collected works of Shakespeare, for it consists of history, romance, law, poems of praise and vituperation, aphorisms, proverbs, love-songs, visions, and much else besides. Should we think of it then as 'ancient Hebrew literature plus some rather later literature from the Eastern Mediterranean'? Should we, that is, think of it as we would of a book which brought together all that survives of ancient Greek or medieval English literature?

This seems wrong for two reasons. First of all there is the testimony quoted from the Mishnah and Josephus. It is true that the Mishnah refers to an argument about whether or not Ecclesiastes should be included in the canon, and that Josephus refers to 'our own Scriptures' (*tois idiois grammasi*) in the plural. But he does say that this is a single body of writing, to which 'no one has ventured either to add, or to remove, or to alter a syllable', and for which Jews would be prepared to die. There may therefore be a debate about what goes in and what stays out, but what is inside, once it is there, forms a unity of some sort. Josephus, having given a summary of the books to be included in the canon, goes on to say that 'From Artaxerxes to our own time the complete history has been written, but has not been deemed worthy of equal credit with the earlier records, because of the failure of the exact succession of the prophets'.[8] In other words, what is considered Scripture is also considered inspired, however we understand the term, and this sharply differentiates it from all other writings.

Although the writings that make up the Bible are the only ones that have come down to us from ancient Israel, we know that there were a number of other books about, since they are explicitly referred to in the Bible. Numbers, Joshua and Samuel mention the Book of Yashar and the Book of the Battles of YHWH, and Kings refers to the Book of the Chronicle of the Kings of Israel. We also have a number of gospels, acts of apostles, and apocalypses, which were excluded from the New Testament, but survived. Decisions have therefore been taken about what goes in and what stays out, which means that there has always been a sense of the boundaries of Scripture. Thus the analogy with ancient Greek literature or medieval English literature breaks down.

However, it is still possible to argue that these decisions are arbitrary political and social acts which tell us nothing about the unity or otherwise of the book itself. This seems to be the line taken by Barr, when he argues that the Gospel of John, for example, would look quite out of place if a decision hadn't been taken to include it in the canon. If that Gospel had been left out, he suggests, we would have found very good reasons for justifying its exclusion.[9]

We are touching here on something very complex and puzzling, but I think it's something we understand a little better today than people did a hundred and fifty years ago. As so often happens in discussions of the Bible, Barr is arguing from what seems to him like common sense, but really from a notion of what constitutes unity that has its roots in the eighteenth and nineteenth centuries. Valéry once remarked that a poem is never finished, only abandoned. What he was implicitly criticizing was the view that a poem is there inside the poet, waiting to be let out, and that once it has been fully let out the act of creation is over. Instead, Valéry was suggesting, we need to realize that even a lyric poem depends on a series of decisions taken by the poet, none of which has any absolute status or authority. Often a phrase or word stands only because the poet

couldn't think of anything better, and it is a Romantic myth that the
work of art possesses an innate being which can be released from the
unconscious of the poet like a *jinn* from a bottle. Every work of art is
what it is only because of the decisions of a committee, even if in most
cases that committee only exists inside the head of the artist.

Anyone who has ever looked at the facsimile edition of *The Waste
Land* drafts, or read the notes to the 1954 Pléiade edition of *À la
recherche du temps perdu*, which show how much Proust was still adding
to his novel even when it was in proof and he on his death-bed, will
know what Valéry means. But he will also know that that poem and that
novel, far from being patchworks with no inner coherence, are among
the most unified works in our culture. It is simply that, in the light of
modernism, we must revise our notions of what constitutes unity. Or
rather, we must recognize that the notions of unity prevalent in the
nineteenth century, which are still taken for granted by the majority of
those who write about the Bible, themselves have a history, but a very
brief one: it is doubtful if Shakespeare, let alone Chaucer, would have
made much sense of them.

To be fair, there is a growing awareness among scholars that conventional ideas about the canon and its formation derive not from the
Bible itself or even from early Jewish and Christian discussions, but
rather from post-Reformation and post-Tridentine formulations of the
issue by Protestant and Catholic theologians alike. They stress the more
complex attitudes to the problem of the early rabbis and Church Fathers,
and the importance of the sense of a shared tradition in the gradual
coming together of the elements which make up the Bible.[10] Nevertheless, the impression one still gets from most contemporary discussions of
the matter is that a book (or poem) is *either* a unity *or* an arbitrary construct. It is difficult for most writers on the subject to conceive of the
Bible as both at once, or not quite either.

The second reason why we have to think of the Bible as more like a
book than like an anthology is obvious. The books which make up the
Bible, various though they are in style and content, do seem to be related
to each other in ways which the plays of Shakespeare certainly aren't,
and which the whole of ancient Greek or medieval English literature
obviously isn't. The books that deal with the history of the world from
the Creation onwards follow each other in roughly chronological order;
the prophets sometimes appear in the historical books and often mention
events that are dealt with more fully there; the Psalms refer to the
Creation, the crossing of the Red Sea and the Jerusalem Temple; the
Gospels, Acts and the Epistles frequently refer to the earlier books and
the last two of course refer constantly to the Jesus we have encountered
in the Gospels; and Revelation picks up images from Daniel and else-

where and weaves them into something new. As in any narrative, the
same protagonists, God, man and Israel, run through the entire story.

Earlier generations saw the Bible as even more of a unity that that. As
Auerbach and Frye have helped us to understand, and as Patristic
scholars like Jean Daniélou have long been arguing, the events of the
New Testament were once seen as prefigured in the Old, or the Old
foreshadowing the New: the twelve tribes and the twelve apostles, the
forty years in the wilderness and the forty days, the sacrifice of Isaac
and that of Jesus – these are merely the most obvious signs of such
foreshadowing.[11] And, as Frye has repeatedly argued, earlier ages saw the
whole book as essentially a romance, covering the whole of history from
Creation to Last Judgement, where the first Adam is exiled from a garden
because of a serpent and the second Adam, by slaying the serpent, makes
it possible for mankind to enter the garden again, but transformed now
into a gleaming city. We find traces of this romance in Dante and we find
it full-blown in Spenser and Milton.

But, even as Spenser and Milton were writing, the Bible was ceasing
to be seen in this way. One way of understanding what happened to
men's perceptions is to go back to my contrast between the child's
perception of a story and the adolescent's. We can then see that the
men, women and children who were firmly ensconced within the rituals
and traditions of Judaism until the time of the Enlightenment, and the
men, women and children who filled the medieval churches and looked
up at the stained-glass windows as they listened to the preachers, were
living out an elaborated version of the childhood experence. The revolution caused by the Reformation and the Enlightenment can then
be seen as the natural reaction of the adolescent to this, his natural
desire to *find out for himself*.

Of course this revolution cannot be dated to any one event, to
Luther's 'Here I stand', or to Spinoza's *Tractatus Theologico-Politicus*, or
to the decisions of kings and princes. Already in the Middle Ages there
were many who wished to read the Bible for themselves, and now, long
after Luther, there are many who retain the old attitudes towards it.
Nevertheless, once Luther stood up and asserted the need to speak the
truth as he saw it and not pay lip-service to tradition, things could never
be quite the same again. We tend to see Luther's break with the medieval
church, like Spinoza's with Jewish tradition, as the triumph of light and
integrity over the forces of obscurantism and hypocrisy; but this is to see
it from their own point of view. It is important, however, to grasp what
gets lost as well as what is won in such revolutions, and this the analogy I
have suggested can help us to do.[12]

As far as responses to the Bible are concerned, the Protestant revolution
led in two opposite but complementary directions, which we might

describe as towards total subjectivity and towards total objectivity. In both cases the sense of the Bible as a unity was destroyed.[13]

On the one hand it led to a personal reading of the Bible and a personal response to it, which has dominated theology ever since and been responsible for the remarkable writings of Kierkegaard, Barth, Bultmann and their followers. This is the response which says, in effect: On this book depends my life; it is too important a matter to leave to others; if I am to read it as it asks to be read I must shed not only my literary preconceptions but also every attachment I have to the world; for only by giving up everything will I be in a position to find again that everything which Christ offers.

The other response has been that of scholarship. The Bible began to be seen as a collection of documents written by men at different times and in different places. It began to be felt that if we would get to the truth of it we would have to grasp just what documents it does consist of, and discover, if possible, what the author or authors of each document were trying to say. To carry out this exercise it would be vital to get as much help from historians and archaeologists as possible. That is why popular introductions to the Bible have so much to tell us about Bronze Age Palestine and the digs at Jericho and Jerusalem. That is why the results of two centuries of analysis of the texts in order to determine how they have been put together are still presented as the ultimate achievement of biblical scholarship.

Increasingly in recent years, though, both the subjective and the objective approaches have come under fire from those within their own ranks as well as from without. In both cases the feeling has grown that the criteria of subjectivity and objectivity are no guarantee against arbitrariness, and that the fragmentariness forced upon the Bible as a result of applying those criteria is in the end counter-productive. Paul Ricoeur must have spoken for many readers of the Bible when he reproached Bultmann for so increasing the subjective role of the reader that the text was in danger of disappearing altogether:

> A theory of interpretation which at the outset runs straight into the moment of decision moves too fast. It leaps over the moment of meaning, which is the objective stage, in the nonworldly sense of 'objective'. There is no exegesis without a 'bearer of meaning' which belongs to the text and not to the author of the text.

What Ricoeur accuses Bultmann of here is a charge that could be levelled at Protestant interpretation since Luther. Obsessed as it is by the scene of Augustine's conversion in the garden in Milan, or perhaps by Paul's even more dramatic conversion on the road to Damascus, that interpretation has tended to see all genuine response to the Bible as abrupt and violent. Ricoeur points out the inadequacy of the Pauline model, how much of the Bible it leaves out. His critique is the more powerful because he is basically sympathetic to the Protestant existentialist enterprise, but he feels that it is part, and only part, of the process of reading:

> It is the objectivity of the text, understood as content – bearer of meaning and demand for meaning – that begins the existential movement of appropriation. . . . If there is no objective meaning, then the text no longer says anything at all; without existential appropriation, what the text does say is no longer living speech. [14]

Ricoeur, though a formidably learned man, is no Bible scholar, and he leans heavily in his argument on Gerhard von Rad's monumental *Old Testament Theology*. This is a striking attempt to read the Bible in such a way as to retain the central Protestant insights about the importance of saving history and the primacy of event, while insisting that these themes must be seen to emerge out of the Old Testament as a whole. Von Rad wants to draw us away from purely existentialist as well as purely historical and archaeological considerations and back to a reading of the text. He faces the central paradox that the Bible asks to be taken as historical truth yet loses everything that is distinctive about it if we try to substitute history for its own mode of narration. He recognizes that it is important to know about the society from which the Bible springs and to which it refers, but he insists that one of the central historical *facts* about the ancient Hebrews is that they elaborated stories about themselves and their relation to their God, in marked contrast both to their Near Eastern neighbours and to the ancient Greeks. [15]

Von Rad's work seems to have touched a chord in many readers who have grown disenchanted with the extremes of existentialism and traditional biblical scholarship. Yet to the student of literature who turns to the Bible from Chaucer and Shakespeare, von Rad will still seem to be in the grip of certain assumptions about the text which are both puzzling and unhelpful. Chief among these is his unquestioning acceptance of the so-called 'documentary hypothesis'. This is the notion that the Pentateuch is made up of four strands, the Jahwist, the Elohist, the Priestly and the Deuteronomist (abbreviated to J, E, P and D), each in turn made up of many minor ones, and that it is the task of the biblical critic to separate them out.

It is not that the documentary hypothesis is necessarily wrong in substance; Genesis is clearly made up of a number of traditions which have been combined at different stages. But is it not the task of the critic to try and come to grips with the final form as we have it, and to give the final editor or redactor the benefit of the doubt, rather than to delve behind his work to what was there before? The inventors of the documentary hypothesis believed that by trying to distinguish the various strands they were getting closer to *the truth*, which, in good nineteenth-century fashion, they assumed to be connected with origins. But in practice the contrary seems to have taken place. For their methodology was necessarily self-fulfilling: deciding in advance what the Jahwist or the Deuteronomist *should* have written, they then called whatever did not fit this view an interpolation. But this leads, as all good readers know, to the death of reading; for a book will never draw me out of myself if I only accept as belonging to it what I have already decreed should be there.[16]

Let us take a simple example. Von Rad, in his commentary on Genesis, remarks about the opening of chapter 12: 'The transition from primeval to sacred history occurs abruptly and surprisingly in verses 1–3'.[17] Why does he find the transition surprising? First of all because he relegates the last two verses of chapter 11 to the Priestly writer and the start of chapter 12 to the Jahwist; secondly because he holds – this is another dogma of nineteenth-century scholarship – that Genesis is made up of a 'primeval' and a 'sacred' history, which meet precisely here in chapter 12; and finally because he is so busy trying to assign each verse to its own strand that he seems never to have attended to the rhythm of the whole.

But any open-minded reader who has moved through Genesis from the beginning to this point will know that the Bible does not advance in the manner of a nineteenth-century novel or work of history. Chapters of straight though compressed narrative are followed by chapters devoted almost entirely to genealogies, which are then followed by other narratives, related to the earlier ones. This passage is no exception:

> Now these are the generations of Terah: Terah begat Abram, Nahor, and Haran; and Haran begat Lot. And Haran died before his father Terah in the land of his nativity, in Ur of the Chaldees. And Abram and Nahor took them wives: the name of Abram's wife was Sarai; and the name of Nahor's wife, Milcah, the daughter of Haran.... But Sarai was barren; she had no child. And Terah took Abram his son, and Lot the son of Haran his son's son, and Sarai his daughter in law, his son Abram's wife; and they went forth with them from Ur of the Chaldees, to go into the land of Canaan; and they came unto Haran, and dwelt there. And the days of Terah were two hundred and five years: and Terah died in Haran. Now the Lord had said unto Abram, Get thee out of thy country, and from thy kindred, and from thy father's house, unto a land that I will shew thee: And I will make of thee a great nation, and I will bless thee, and make thy name great.... So Abram departed, as the Lord had spoken unto him.... And Abram took Sarai his wife, and Lot his brother's son, and all their substance..., and they went forth to go into the land of Canaan....
>
> (Gen. 11:27–32/12:1–5)

It could have been Nahor who was called, but it wasn't. The point is that before it happened there was no way of knowing. And the Bible does not speculate on why it was Abraham and not either of his brothers.

Some later remarks, though, suggest to us at least how Abraham was seen in the tradition. In Joshua 24:2 the Israelites are reminded that 'Your fathers dwelt on the other side of the flood in old time, even Terah, the father of Abraham, and the father of Nachor: and they served other gods'. This suggests that Abraham is seen as a sort of proto-Moses, leading the people to freedom from the yoke of false gods by crossing a river. This is perhaps reinforced by Genesis 15:7, where God says to Abraham: 'I am the Lord that brought thee out of Ur of the Chaldees, to give thee this land to inherit it'. The Hebrew word translated 'brought you out' is *hotzetikha*, which seems to have the meaning 'to save' in Exodus 20:2: 'I am the Lord thy God, which have brought thee out [*hotezetikha*] of the land of Egypt, out of the house of bondage'.

At the same time another motif has been introduced in verses 29 and 30 of Genesis 11. Almost incidentally we are told that Sarah, Abraham's wife, was barren. Thus when in the following verses (assigned by von Rad to a different strand) we are told that Terah took his son Abraham and his grandson Lot and they went to dwell in Haran, and when this is followed by God's promise to Abraham that he will make him a great nation, a tension is set up in us: Abraham is old, his wife is barren, how can he inherit? Will it not rather be Lot who inherits? The issue will not be resolved till the birth of Isaac in chapter 21, though it is immediately afterwards called into question once more by God's command to Abraham to sacrifice Isaac.

Thus to split the last two verses off the end of chapter 11, as von Rad does, and then to start a whole new section of commentary at 12:10, calling it 'The Biblical Patriarchal History', is to deny the reader the right to experience this as a growing narrative. It is true that the role of Sarah is nowhere commented upon in the text; it is true that after a series of summary verses the narrative expands at the start of chapter 12. But that is the Bible's way of working. Its mode of procedure may seem odd to those whose norms of literary coherence derive from nineteenth-century art, but that does not mean that it does not know what it is doing or that it is made up of a collection of fragments clumsily stitched together by a distracted editor.[18]

Much the same point is made by Robert Alter in the first chapter of *The Art of Biblical Narrative*. Here he demonstrates that chapter 38 of Genesis, which tells the story of Judah and his daughter-in-law Tamar, far from being an incoherent interpolation into the Joseph story, is in fact marvellously tied in with it. It is true that the story of Joseph does not move forward in a straight line, but why should it? There are many ways to develop narrative, and that of the classical novel is only one. Chapter 38, Alter shows, functions partly as a set of variations on the flanking chapters, picking up their themes (lies and truth, the covering up of crimes), and their 'props' (Joseph's coat of many colours, the cloak he leaves in the hands of Potiphar's wife, and Judah's staff, bracelet and signet ring); and partly provide an oblique motivation for the change that comes over Judah between chapters 37 and 44. Alter quotes from an essay by Joel Rosenberg which helps one to understand why the term 'interpolation' has a pejorative ring only for those with a very limited notion of what unity should consist of in the first place:

> It may actually improve our understanding of the Torah [writes Rosenberg] to remember that it is *quoting* documents, that there is, in other words, a purposeful documentary *montage* that must be perceived as a unity, regardless of the number and types of smaller units that form the building blocks of its composition. Here, the weight of literary interest falls upon the activity of the *final* redactor, whose artistry requires far more careful attention than it has hitherto been accorded.

This should not be too difficult for the reader in the age of *Ulysses* to grasp, but one suspects that biblical scholars are far too busy reading each other to have time to read *Ulysses*. Indeed, Alter adds:

> The last clause if anything understates the case, since biblical critics frequently assume, out of some dim preconception about the transmission of texts in 'primitive' cultures, that the redactors were in the grip of a kind of manic tribal compulsion, driven again and again to include units of traditional material that made no connective sense, for reasons they themselves could not have explained.[19]

In effect the charge Ricoeur makes against Bultmann, and that which scholars as diverse as Cassuto and Alter make against von Rad and the historico-critical school of biblical scholarship, is the same: it is that they all misread the Bible because they ask too much of it. Both groups want certainty, either the certainty that the Word of God is striking me here, now, or the certainty that what I am reading has been traced back to its original writer, or, failing that, to its original context. But, as every reader of Shakespeare knows, such rocklike certainty is simply not attainable. Moreover, at least since Nietzsche, we are coming to see that the drive to attain it is not in itself purely natural but has got strong historical and cultural roots. Yet that drive is coming to be questioned in the field of Shakespearian and Homeric scholarship, and even in the natural sciences, suggesting that perhaps, slowly, an era is coming to an end, and that we may be reaching a point where it is possible for us to understand the nature of pre-Romantic art and thought.[20]

The history of biblical interpretation provides some good examples of this process at work. Almost as soon as there began to be such a thing as a sacred text for the Jews, it became imperative to translate it for Jews no longer living in Palestine, or to provide paraphrases for those Jews who still spoke something like the original language, but a version of it which had naturally changed over the generations and so moved further and further away from that of the sacred text, which remained, of course, static and unalterable. These translations and versions naturally made every effort to be faithful to the sacred text, but inevitably, in the course of translating and paraphrasing, subtle changes occurred. Some were the result of conscious attempts to make sense of what looked like a puzzle, while others may have been purely unconscious.[21]

Chapter 11 of Genesis, for example, is partly concerned with the descendants of Shem, and it has close parallels with Genesis 5, which deals with the descendants of Adam. However, where each paragraph of the earlier chapter records the number of years of the father's life and ends with the words, 'and he died' (except in the case of Enoch, where a parallel expression is used), in chapter 11 this ending is left out in all instances except for that of Terah:

> And Nahor lived nine and twenty years, and begat Terah: And Nahor lived after he begat Terah an hundred and nineteen years, and begat sons and daughters. And Terah lived seventy years, and begat Abram, Nahor, and Haran. Now these are the generations of Terah: Terah begat Abram, Nahor, and Haran; and Haran begat Lot. . . . And the days of Terah were two hundred and five years: and Terah died in Haran.
>
> (Gen. 11 : 24–32)

The Samaritan recension of the Torah, however, gives the number of years at the end of each paragraph in chapter 11 as well as in chapter 5. This harmonizes the two chapters, but at the cost of losing the special significance which seems to be attached to Terah, the father of Abram.

A much more striking case is to be found in Isaiah. Chapter 19 contains a series of eschatological pronouncements made to Egypt, and it ends:

> In that day shall Israel be the third with Egypt and with Assyria, even a blessing in the midst of the land: Whom the Lord of hosts shall bless, saying, Blessed be Egypt my people, and Assyria the work of my hands, and Israel mine inheritance.
>
> (Isa. 19 : 24–25)

This is indeed amazing. Egypt, the oppressor of Israel, is now called 'my people'! Neither the Septuagint (LXX) translators nor the Targum paraphrasers could believe that this was possible, so they renationalized the text with the minimum of alteration: '. . . saying, Blessed be my people which is in Egypt and in Assyria and Israel my inheritance'.

This is a clear instance of a reader simply unable to read what is in front of him because it goes so much against the grain of his expectations. His response is to say that 'obviously' there has been a mistake, and that the text 'really means to say' something more in keeping with those expectations. The idea that God might call even Egypt 'my people' was just something the LXX translator could not conceive – there had to be a textual corruption. We, though, respecting the text, may feel that what is happening here can be brought into the orbit of our expectations, though it does give those expectations something of a jolt. Isaiah here opens up to us quite a new dimension of the Hebrew God, and makes us understand that he had of course always been much more than merely the national God of Israel.

But what of the first case? Is the text really saying something about Terah's special status? Aren't we in danger of making too much of what might after all be some sort of textual confusion? The sceptic could well take this line and argue that if we insist on every detail in a text making sense we are in danger of quite fanciful readings. He would find support for this in some of the interpretations proposed by traditional exegesis, both Jewish and Christian. For the rabbis who pored over the text in the early centuries ACE and whose writings are enshrined in the Talmud and the various midrashes, as well as for the Church Fathers, the entire book was written by God and so must be significant. This remained the position till the close of the Middle Ages. Rashi, the great Jewish commentator (1040–1105), basing himself on Jewish tradition, argues, for example, that the line 'the pit was empty, there was no water in it' (Gen. 37:24), at the start of the Joseph narrative, indicates that the pit must have been full of serpents and scorpions, otherwise the statement would be tautologous. Or again, he explains that the line 'And Pharaoh rose up in the night, he, and all his servants, and all the Egyptians' (Exod. 12:30), means that Pharaoh was the first to rise from his bed and went in person to wake his servants, otherwise the word 'he' would be redundant. Even odder from the modern reader's point of view is the rabbinic comment on Genesis 32:4: 'Thy servant Jacob saith thus, I have sojourned with Laban, and stayed there until now.' The Hebrew for 'I have sojourned' is *garti*, a word whose numerical value is 613 (every Hebrew letter doubles for a number, thus encouraging this kind of exegesis), indicating that 'I sojourned with Laban, yet observed the 613 precepts of the Torah and did not learn from his wickedness'.[22]

This last example, we feel, is obviously crazy. Jacob lived long before any precepts and any Torah were ever thought of, and besides, the Bible is just not encoded like that. But of course with someone for whom the Torah is timeless and written by God himself, neither of these counter-arguments carries much weight. Our sense that it can't be like that derives from a feeling that we would lose too much of what is important to us about this book were we to read it in this way. But what about the other two examples? Is Rashi being particularly acute here? I think not. I think we feel him to be wrong because he is explaining what does not need explaining. Familiarity with the Bible, even in translation, makes us aware that it is natural for phrases to be repeated in parallel: 'The heavens declare the glory of God; and the firmament sheweth his handy-work' (Ps. 19:1). 'The pit was empty, there was no water in it' and 'Pharaoh rose up, he, and all his servants' both conform to this model. Rashi appears to be reading carefully, but such careful reading is bad reading, since it ignores what a more superficial reading would pick up. We could say that Rashi is reading but not listening. He knows that this is a sacred text and he decides that he had better account for every word, since it's inconceivable that every word should not count in a sacred text. And of course every word does count, we cannot simply remove half of each sentence. But they count as words do in any well-told story and not as they do in crossword puzzles.

It has to be said, though, that if this kind of problem arises with all narrative, it seems to arise with particular frequency in this particular book. Again we have to ask: is this something inherent in the mode of narration, or is it the result of the Bible's being regarded as a sacred book? There is no reason, of course, why it should not be a combination of both. The Bible's mode of narration is such that we keep being forced to ask questions of it, and its sacred status makes it particularly important that these questions should be answered.

Let us look at a slightly more extended example. In Judges 16 we read that Delilah was promised eleven hundred pieces of silver by each of the Philistine leaders if she delivered Samson into their hands. In the next chapter, in what appears to be a totally disconnected story, we are told about a certain Micah, who stole eleven hundred shekels of silver from his mother and then gave them back to her, so that she could use them to make images of gold and silver. Are we to understand that Delilah and Micah's mother are in fact one and the same person? But if they are, why does the Bible not say so? And if they are not, why is the sum the same in both cases? Yet is it? We are told, not that Delilah was offered eleven hundred pieces of silver for handing over Samson, but that she was offered that sum by each of the Philistine leaders. So perhaps there is no connection at all and the coincidence of numbers is just that and no more. But can we really accept this?

One possibility may be that what we have here is simply a standard figure for 'a very large sum'. If it is, it is certainly not one that figures very prominently in the Bible, and the first century ACE retelling of the story by Pseudo-Philo, in *The Biblical Antiquities*, makes no bones about identifying Delilah and Micah's mother. Michael Wadsworth is con-vinced that Pseudo-Philo is right and that, given this clue, we can begin to discern a whole web of correspondences between two seemingly dis-tinct episodes: 'Blood money, stolen money, money for idols, money accursed – the chain is complete.' Surely if we follow Alter in recogni-zing the links between Genesis 38 and the chapters on either side of it we should follow Pseudo-Philo in recognizing links between chapters 16 and

17 of Judges. And yet doubts remain. For instead of the simple graven and molten images of Judges 17:3, Pseudo-Philo has 'three images of boys, and of calves, and a lion and an eagle and a dragon and a dove . . . and his [i.e. Micah's] iniquity was of many shapes and his impiety was full of guile'. Does this not come dangerously close to the kind of misreading and over-reading we found in Rashi? The question is a delicate one, and it arises whenever we come across a midrashic elaboration of a terse or laconic biblical text. Wadsworth, after quoting Auerbach's remarks about Homer filling in the background to his stories while the Bible leaves these in darkness, and about Homer making sure his narrative forms a seamless web while the Bible works by leaving large gaps, concludes: 'Like a footballer looking for an opening, therefore, the midrashist spots a gap and goes through it'.[23] But if the way to score goals is to go through a gap when one presents itself, is that the way to read?

To take another example from Genesis: when Jacob sends Joseph after his brothers he at once leaves home and reaches Shechem.

> And a certain man found him, and, behold, he was wandering in the field: and the man asked him, saying, What seekest thou? And he said, I seek my brethren: tell me, I pray thee, where they feed their flocks. And the man said, They are departed hence; for I heard them say, Let us go to Dothan. And Joseph went after his brethren, and found them in Dothan.
>
> (Gen. 37:15–17)

Who is this man? What is he doing in the field? One is driven to ask such questions because he does not appear to have any narrative function. The story would have been perfectly intelligible if the verses in which he appears had dropped out, and there is no narrative reason why Joseph should be seen to delay in getting to his brothers. Nor does the man ever reappear.

The question obviously disturbed the rabbis. Some say the man is the angel Gabriel, others that whoever he is he is meant to show the difficulties Joseph had to overcome before reaching his brothers. Philo suggests he is the inner voice of conscience. Josephus takes the easy way out by omitting the incident altogether. In our own day Thomas Mann, who has a penchant for such figures, turns the man into Hermes Psychopomp. Which, if any, of those readings is right?

I think the reader feels that the man's presence does something to the narrative, but that as soon as he is identified clearly with an angel or some moral message, interpretation has gone wrong. It is not easy to see why this happens. I will come back to the episode in a later chapter; suffice it to say here that our unease over too precise an identification has something to do with it suggesting that behind this narrative another is pressing closely upon it, and that this is contrary to our feeling about the way this narrative proceeds.

One final example: At the end of chapter 6 of 2 Samuel we are told how David came dancing before the ark as it was brought in triumph to Jerusalem, and how his wife Michal, Saul's daughter, rebuked him for this, saying sarcastically: 'How glorious was the king of Israel to day, who uncovered himself to day in the eyes of the handmaids of his servants, as one of the vain fellows shamelessly uncovereth himself!' (6:20). David, however, is unrepentant:

> And David said unto Michal, It was before the Lord, which chose me before thy father, and before all his house, to appoint me ruler over the people of the Lord, over Israel: therefore will I play before the Lord. And I will yet be more vile than thus, and will be base in mine own sight: and of the maidservants which thou hast spoken of, of them shall I be had in honour.
>
> (2 Sam. 6:21–22)

The next sentence reads literally: 'And to Michal daughter of Saul there was not to her a child till the day of her death'. The Authorized Version (AV), however, reads: 'Therefore Michal the daughter of Saul had no child unto the day of her death' (23). To the AV translators it was obvious that Michal's childlessness was the result of her criticism of David. They knew that the Hebrew conjunction *wa* covers a far wider spectrum than does the word 'and' in English. They must have known that Hebrew has a term for 'therefore', *al ken*, but that it is used much more rarely than in English and that there are many places where the meaning hovers between 'and' and 'therefore', where Hebrew would use *wa*. Nevertheless the difference in the present case is surely important. Our sense of what kind of a God this is partly depends on it. If he has made Michal barren because she rebuked his anointed one we will naturally think of him quite differently from the way we would think of him if he had not stooped to such (as we might think) petty revenge.

The fact of the matter is that there is no way to tell which the Hebrew means. And this is better brought out in English by 'and', which is also suitably ambiguous. What 'not being able to tell' means, of course, is something quite different from 'we will never know'. The latter implies that now, because of circumstances beyond our control – the death of the author, for example – we will never know. The former suggests that even if we had the author in front of us and asked him, he would not be able to answer us. The *wa* suggests that there is a connection between Michal's childlessness and her attitude to David, since the two are conjoined. But it also leaves us pondering the fact that there might have been quite other reasons for it, which she might have mistaken, for example, as divine anger. The presence of the Lord hovers over the entire passage, but is never explicitly linked with it. *How* we are to read it will depend on how we have learned to read the whole book. But in the whole book, as here, the issue of causality and responsiblility, in

God, in man, will be raised again and again, but will never be settled in such a way that we can shut the book and say: now I know.

The question seems to be: how are we to retain our sense of the Bible as a single whole while doing justice to its peculiarly fragmentary and elliptical mode of narration? Or, to return to the point from which we took off, can we give evidence that the Bible is a unity and not a random collection of books or traditions without forcing that unity upon it?

As must be patently obvious by now, this is not a question that can be settled in the abstract. It is, in fact, the central question to which this book will address itself. What needs stressing is that it is not a question we can settle simply by 'looking at the facts before us' either. The reader is implicated, whether he likes it or not. The temptation is always there for him to take short-cuts, either by insisting that whatever seems to make no sense as it stands must be an interpolation, or by giving it a sense through imaginative elaboration. He must also accept that, as with any ancient text, there are always likely to be corruptions due to transmission errors and the like; but these are rarely likely to make reading impossible, and in the few cases where they do he simply has to accept it. The temptation to be inflexible assails us whenever we read a book, and the experienced reader is the one who knows how to deal with it.[24]

Once again, though, the reader may interrupt me, saying: All this is very well, you have almost hypnotized me into accepting your premises. But though all this talk of reading the Bible just as one reads other books may help me to appreciate some of the Biblical narratives, that is not in the end what the Bible is about. It may contain fine stories and I may have enjoyed these as a child, but I cannot accept that we should treat the Bible simply as literature in this way.

This kind of response is worth taking seriously, if only because some of the finest writers of what for want of a better term we may as well call 'literature' have in recent times reacted in just this way. In an essay published in 1936 Eliot himself insisted that 'the Bible has had a literary influence upon English literature *not* because it has been considered as literature, but because it has been considered as the report of the Word of God'. Twenty-two years later C. S. Lewis made much the same point: 'Those who talk of reading the Bible "as literature" sometimes mean, I think, reading it without attending to the main thing it is about; like reading Burke with no interest in politics or reading the *Aeneid* with no interest in Rome.'[25] Such remarks by committed Christians who are also distinguished writers have found echoes recently in the work of Jewish and Christian scholars. Thus James Kugel writes towards the end of his book on biblical poetry: 'We have shuddered to hear Joseph called "one of the most believable characters in Western literature", and not just because this statement puts the Bible on the wrong bookshelf'.[26]

And James Barr, in a lecture entitled 'Reading the Bible as Literature', has insisted that 'the Bible must be read in a theological mode', which means, he says, 'as a source of true knowledge about the objects described in the Bible – about God, about the creation of the world, about his redemption of mankind, about sin and salvation, about the possibility of a future life'. Originally, Barr reminds us, the Bible had an informational function, and we simply misread it if we ever forget this. In a more recent book he returns to the subject and argues that the Bible must not be seen as a book but as a window on people, events and teaching. It was not a book to Jeremiah or St. Paul, he asserts, and it must not be a book to us. Why are theology and literature not the same thing? he asks. Because theology does not depend on a book but on the relation of that book to a reality outside itself.[27]

Now no one would dispute the criticisms of Eliot, Lewis, Kugel and Barr. Editions of the Bible entitled 'The Bible Designed to be Read as Literature' and essays on the character of Joseph do indeed make one feel uneasy. But not because they traduce the Bible but because they traduce *literature*. While Eliot would no doubt feel that a mistake had been made if someone were to compare his poems to the Bible, he would also feel *he* had not been understood if they were described as 'literature', with the implication that they were 'mere' literature. C. S. Lewis admits as much when he brings the *Aeneid* into the argument, for no one would read that poem 'with no interest in Rome', and yet no one would deny that it was a poem and not a sacred text. Indeed, he goes on to qualify his earlier remarks by saying: 'But there is a saner sense in which the Bible, since it is after all literature, cannot properly be read except as literature'. When Eliot, early in his article, criticizes people who 'enjoy these writings *solely* because of their literary merit', one has to ask what criticism worth its salt ever treats its subject as providing only 'literary' satisfactions?[28] When Barr says that theology is interested not in the Bible as a book but as saying something about reality, one has to ask whether that is not just as true of good criticism of Homer, Dante, Shakespeare, Proust and Eliot. No one imagines that these writers are meaningful to us because of their 'beautiful language' or their 'exquisite form'.

In other words, every reader knows that a book which means something to him is more than a book. But when we go on to ask: what is it then? we have great difficulty in answering. Falstaff and Swann are clearly more than just words on paper. Yet that does not mean that we feel the need to discover who 'the real' Falstaff and Swann 'really' were. Indeed, when scholars painstakingly reveal that Sir John Oldcastle was the model for Falstaff or Charles Haas for Swann, we feel that they have added nothing to our understanding either of these characters or of the works in which they appear.

But though Eliot and Lewis and perhaps even Kugel and Barr would assent to this, I suspect they would still want to say that *somehow* the Bible is different. Barr, in his lecture, makes determined efforts to come to grips with this issue, and it is instructive to see what little headway he makes. He begins by pointing out that

> [t]he decades from the thirties up to the sixties, was also the time of a marked revival of biblical influence and authority within Christian theology; and in this revival one of the opinions most strongly held was that the Bible had authority not for what it was in itself, least of all for its literary qualities, but because it testified to the great truths of God and his work in history for the salvation of mankind.

He then proceeds to embark on his own analysis of the situation:

> It would indeed be a thin and no doubt a useless reading of the Bible that did not recognize its profoundly religious and theological character; indeed it is almost fantastic to suppose that one might read it without recognizing that it is written not out of joy in the sonorousness of its own language, out of pleasure in its own literary quality, but because it wanted to say something about God and his works, God and his dealings with man.

This is still very much Lewis's point, and, as we have seen, it applies to all books, which want to do more than take pleasure in the sonorousness of their language.

Barr, however, seems to want to advance beyond this: 'The recognition that the Bible is a religious text, that it is concerned to speak about God, is not the same thing as an acceptance that its religious teaching must be right, a willingness to read it as a source of authority for me today'. This distinction, between a Christian's reading of the Koran and a Moslem's, for instance, is clearly important. But it is blurred by Barr's language. What does he mean by 'its religious teaching', for example? Is it one thing? If so, why have there been so many Christian sects? Why, come to that, do both Jews and Christians look to the Bible as their sacred text? If what Barr really wants to say is that the Anglican should conform to the precepts of the Anglican Church, then why bring the Bible into it at all? Then again, what does he mean by 'an acceptance that its religious teaching must be right'? Even if we could isolate such a thing as the Bible's 'religious teaching', we would have to ask: right in what sense? As we feel Proust is right about memory or Tolstoy about war? And how, finally, does one link this with 'a source of authority for me today'?

Barr is clearly uneasy with his formulation because he immediately tries to rephrase it:

> The recognition that the Bible is dominated by a religious concern is no obstacle to the reading of it as literature; but the idea that its religious teaching must be right and must be accepted as authoritative does constitute

in the minds of many people a serious block to the enjoyment of it as literature.

But this is no more satisfactory than the previous way of putting it. Once again we have the notion of 'its religious teaching', and once again 'must be right' is asserted without any indication of what this can mean, and elided with 'must be accepted as authoritative', as though the two were the same thing. Once again too we have the tell-tale phrase 'the enjoyment of it as literature', as though literature were merely there to provide a pleasant way of passing an evening.[29]

What seems to lie behind all these remarks, those of Eliot, Lewis and Kugel as well as Barr, is the assertion of the Bible's authority. For some, of course, that authority will depend on the decrees of Church Councils, for others on tradition, and for others it will have no outward mark but will depend on an inner, existential response. But, given such varied attitudes, the reader who has come to the Bible from the works of Homer or Dante will want to ask: does not every major work or writer speak with authority?

A hallmark of the post-Romantic crisis in the arts is that the issue of authority has become central, from Beethoven and Keats to Kafka and Thomas Mann. Even writers like Eliot and Kafka, who continually insist in their work that they have no authority, are thereby merely asserting their concern with this issue. And it is the very seriousness of their concern which ensures that we go back to their work long after their more popular contemporaries have been forgotten. We return to it not because we 'enjoy it as literature' but precisely because it now strikes us as speaking authoritatively – about the nature of authority.

As cultural critics like Erich Heller have pointed out, the Romantic crisis of authority itself has roots in the sixteenth century,[30] in the moment – if one wants a symbolic moment – when Luther raised the question of the authority of the Church and in his wake Zwingli raised the question of whether the bread and wine of the sacrament were 'really' the body and blood of Christ, or only 'symbolically' so. It has become fashionable in recent years to raise this issue of authority in relation to the so-called canon of authoritative works in our literature. This has had the virtue of bringing into the foreground the question of the nature of artistic authority. Is Shakespeare, to take a prime example, the national poet of England for some intrinsic reason related to the quality and nature of his work, or because those in power have, for their own ends, decided to make him so? No one who has been to Stratford can doubt that it has been extremely useful as well as profitable for some to develop a myth about Shakespeare and English national culture; just as no one can doubt that at various times the Church has used various myths about the Bible for purposes that have little to do with either that book or the teachings of Christ. But that does not automatically mean that Shakespeare and the Bible are nothing but the product of such myths. Frye's remarks about Milton, in the passage I quoted earlier, apply here just as well: Shakespeare is a more rewarding poet to read than Drayton, but the more obvious this becomes the less time will one want to spend trying to prove it.

And the same is true of the Bible. It may be that it is only in our predominantly secular age, an age where religious authority has lost its hold on all but a very few, that this truth can become evident. But if that is the case then we will need to heed the words of Wittgenstein when he says:

> The aspects of things that are most important for us are hidden because of their simplicity and familiarity. (One is unable to notice something – because it is always before one's eyes.) The real foundations of his enquiry do not strike a man at all. Unless *that* fact has at some time struck him. – And this means: we fail to be struck by what, once seen, is most striking and most powerful.[31]

For James Barr authority is something distant and impersonal. What Wittgenstein suggests is that it is in fact close and personal. The Bible once struck us as authoritative because its stories were recounted to us by our parents. These stories were not enjoyable 'as literature', and even 'enjoyable' seems an inadequate term. They just were. Going back to them in later life we have somehow felt that there must be a reason for their authority, that we must get behind them to find out what they were really about, to find out if perhaps we have been taken in. But, as we are beginning to see, it is the idea of testing and of being taken in that really needs to come under scrutiny, not the book itself.

But where does that leave us? 'The confusions which occupy us arise when language is like an engine idling, not when it is doing work,' Wittgenstein wisely points out.[32] And the same is true of our relations to books – to *The Wind in the Willows*, *The Trial*, the Bible. We feel ourselves driven to ask questions about 'the authority' of the Bible, or what happens when we read the Bible 'as literature', but these questions have to be resisted. Instead we have to trust the book itself and see where it will take us.

As I have suggested, the Bible is a book which seems to resist our best efforts. It is too vast, too varied, too ancient. There is, however, something about it which can help us to overcome many of these difficulties. This is that, unlike the *Iliad* and *War and Peace*, but like Dante's *Commedia* and *À la recherche*, it is actually *about* many of the critical and hermeneutical issues I have touched on in this chapter. After all, I began with an episode in the Bible: Moses receiving the Tables of the Law from the hand of God. I later suggested that existentialist theologians were perhaps too obsessed with the drama of St. Paul's conversion on the road to Damascus. Do we not in the story of Adam's expulsion from Eden find a dramatization of that transition from childhood to adolescence about which I have made so much? And may we not see in Saul's desperate calling up of Samuel from the dead, and in the irony of the old prophet's ghost being able to tell Saul only what he already knew, an image of those scholars who would penetrate behind the veil of the Bible's words to the truth beneath, only to find there what they knew already?

These are not games and fantasies. They rest upon the simple fact that the Bible recognizes no sharp divisions between our attitude to the world and our attitude to books and stories. The issue of whether the Bible is a unity or a series of fragments, and, if it is a unity, of what kind, is not a purely literary question. How we answer it depends on how we answer similar questions put to the world. By exploring how men do indeed answer such questions, and by dramatizing their errors, the Bible guides us, if we will only let it, towards the answers it contains but can only show, not tell.

I began with an image. I suggested that it was a picture of how, half-consciously, we conceive our relation to this book. I suggested that it was a potent image but a misleading one. We now need to supplement it, not with another image, which would be equally misleading, but with an episode which also occurs in this book, yet cannot be figured. I refer to Jacob's struggle with the angel.

When Jacob finds himself engaged in a fight in the middle of the night with a 'man' who is also 'God', he does not say to him, as he would in a fairy-tale: 'I will not let you go till you tell me your name'. Instead, surprisingly, he says: 'I will not let you go till you bless me'. Whereupon the 'man' asks Jacob *his* name, and, when told it, announces that henceforth Jacob will have a new name, Israel.

Our task is to wrestle with this book as Jacob wrestled with the 'man', in pitch blackness, and not for the mere sake of the contest or in order to wrest the book's secret from it, but in order that we may hear it utter its blessing upon us. But that, we must not forget, is what we would expect of our encounter with any great book.

II

THE BOOK

The Bible, for most of us, is distinguished from other books first of all by its physical appearance.[1] It is a book bound in black leather, its pages edged with gold or red, printed on very thin paper in double columns, with numbered verses and headings to each chapter or page, and sometimes with medial margins crammed with references in tiny print to other verses in the book. The reason for the double columns and the thin paper is simply that it is a very long book and that, unlike the *Complete Works* of Shakespeare, it is meant to be carried about, so it can't be too large. The paraphernalia is there to help us find our way about its labyrinthine recesses. But so strongly does habit colour our responses that a major reason why the New English Bible was greeted with such a chorus of disapproval was surely that in most editions it was designed to look just like any other book.

Was this a valid reason for disapproval? Our first instinct is to say that of course it wasn't. But let us pause a little and ponder the fact that books, as well as being windows *on to* the world, are also objects *in* the world.

In the Foreword to his little book on Proust Beckett explains that all his references to *À la recherche* 'are to the abominable edition of the *Nouvelle Revue Française* in sixteen volumes'.[2] Most readers are, I suspect, a little shocked to find such a remark in a work of literary criticism. But Beckett was not only perfectly correct in his description of the first edition, his remark was also particularly appropriate to the work of an author who has himself written so well about the subtle ways in which the appearance and feel of a book colours our response to it. Everybody knows Marcel's marvellous evocations of the pleasures of childhood reading; less well known but even more instructive for our purposes is the passage in *Contre Sainte-Beuve* where Proust discusses M. de Guermantes's relation to his favourite author, Balzac:

> In the little library on the second floor where, on Sundays, M. de Guermantes hurries off to take refuge as his wife's first visitor rings the door-

bell, and where, at tea-time, his fruit juice and biscuits are brought to him, he has all the works of Balzac in a gilded calf binding with a green leather label from M. Bechet or Werdet.

The Duke knows every Balzac novel as well as he knows his own biography, and every character is an old friend. When his brother comes to visit him their conversation often turns to Balzac, 'for it was part of their upbringing; they had read those volumes in their father's library, precisely the one which was now owned by the Count, who had inherited it'. Their taste for Balzac, Proust notes, was forever coloured by those early readings, 'before Balzac had become a great writer and, as such, been subjected to the vicissitudes of literary taste'. Thus not only is M. de Guermantes fonder of little-known Balzac than of the more famous works, but his instinctive taxonomy stands sophisticated literary response on its head. For, as Proust goes on to tell us, the Duke would often cite works by Balzac's now totally forgotten contemporaries, such as Roger de Beauvoir and Celeste de Chabrillion, with no apparent awareness that these were not by Balzac himself, for the simple reason that on his library shelves all three authors' works were bound in the same way.

> When one opened them and the same flimsy paper covered with large print introduced one to the heroine's name exactly as if it were she in person who was introducing herself to you in this portable and commodious form, accompanied by a faint smell of glue, dust and age which was like the emanation of her charm, it was very hard to establish between these volumes a purportedly literary distinction that was artificially based on notions foreign both to the plot of the novel and to the physical aspect of the volumes.

Is Proust having us on? Or is he satirizing the innate philistinism of aristocrats and bibliophiles? The answer is that he is doing neither, although the first-person narration of the story – for even *Contre Sainte-Beuve* is more story than literary criticism – doesn't quite allow us to rule out irony. He is, however, making a point which is close to his heart, for he goes on: 'And I sometimes wonder if even today my way of reading is not more like that of M. de Guermantes than that of contemporary critics'.[3]

One of the things that emerges from this passage is that the distinction I was drawing in the last chapter between listening and reading, child and adult, is not as clear-cut as I was making it. The first books a child reads for himself he still responds to with that total sense of trust which coloured his response to stories read to him. And that sense of trust, that sense of the book as a world which one enters without question and where the material and spiritual (if one may use the word) aspects of the book are inseparable, survives even the doubts of adolescence. The physical appearance and even the smell of the books we first read remains for us an essential part of what those books are, and we are always a little disconcerted to find ourselves reading as adults a book we read as children, but in another edition. That is why to ask someone to discard their little leather-bound childhood Bible for the large cloth-bound *Reader's Bible*, for example, because in that way he will be reading it 'as it was meant to be read', or 'untroubled by such extraneous issues as the smallness of the print or the thinness of the paper', is actually to ask for rather a lot. Much more than asking someone to switch from a cheap *Complete Shakespeare* to the Arden edition of one of the plays – though who is to say how much of a wrench it is to switch from a much-loved and much-used *Complete Shakespeare* to one of the Ardens?

It could therefore plausibly be argued that a proper reading of the Bible will have to be a reading of the book we are all familiar with, and that urging us to read a Bible printed and presented just like any other book is a bit like urging us to go back to some hypothetical 'pristine' text – it would be very nice if we could but it is highly unlikely that we can. If we are to understand the Bible today, the argument would go, we must read it as it has traditionally been read, and that means reading it in that little black leather-bound double-column volume. But if we accept this argument (and I hope I have given good reasons for suggesting that we cannot dismiss it lightly), we should at least be aware of what it is we are doing, be like Proust himself rather than like M. de Guermantes. As with all appeals to tradition we have to ask: what tradition? M. de Guermantes's father, we are given to understand, was a contemporary of Balzac and bought his books as they came out, before he became famous, the Balzac of the histories of literature. But neither our fathers nor our grandfathers were contemporaries of the authors or redactors of the Bible. The Bible was a sacred and special book long before that little black leather-bound volume appeared, long before the age of printing even.

The only complete manuscripts of the Bible date from the Middle Ages, and medieval Bibles, while usually more sumptuous than other books, were sumptuous only as all books were in a manuscript culture where an ordinary book might cost as much as a four-poster bed. Dante makes a distinction between a *libro*, which is any book, and a *volume*, which is a special and authoritative book. But for him the *Aeneid* is as much a *volume* as the Bible.

What immediately distinguishes medieval Bibles from modern ones is the way text and commentary are related, in both the Jewish and the Christian traditions. Often the text almost disappears under the weight of the various marginal and interlinear glosses and commentaries; and one of the key motives of the Reformers was to remove these glosses and allow readers to read the Holy Book for themselves, without the constant nudgings of commentaries which they felt had been imposed by the

Church and had no warrant in the text. As has often been pointed out by historians, there is a close connection between the rise of printing and the spread of Protestantism. It was the growing impetus towards making each Christian read for himself or herself the Word of God which encouraged the development of printing, as much as the development of printing helped to disseminate the Word. We have often been told about the interconnection between the rise of Protestantism, the development of privacy, leisure and better lighting, and the rise of the novel. Equally significant is the matrix of self-reinforcing elements which led to the privatization of the Bible, to its gradually becoming a book to be owned and read rather than one to be listened to in church or used only for devotional purposes.

However, it is important to remember that the Christian in the Middle Ages was not dependent for his knowledge of the Bible solely on church services and sermons. He would also have seen or even participated in the annual pageant of biblical plays on the feast of Corpus Christi, and he would always have had before him what indeed became known as the poor man's Bible, on the walls and in the windows of his churches. That these were likely to inculcate in him a sense of the Bible very different from our own is attested by the Corpus Christi cycles themselves, and by the great Bible-based poems of Dante and Langland.

Technical revolutions, as we know, though they may sweep all before them, take some time to oust attitudes and feelings based on the way life was before they occurred. Thus the first cars were merely faster and smoother carriages and the first printed books merely slightly cheaper manuscripts. But in the long run, perhaps long after Milton, perhaps not till Wordsworth, printing effected its revolution not just in the market-place but on men's sensibilities. And one index of that change is the change in the format of the Bible and in our attitude towards it.

Can we itemize some of the main features of that attitude? First of all there is the sense, which never existed in the Middle Ages, that what we are reading is a translation. For the man of the Middle Ages the Latin Bible, which had been in continuous use by the Western Church since St. Jerome translated it in the late fourth and early fifth centuries, quite simply *was* the Bible. But the first thing the reader of the Authorized Version comes across, after the Epistle of Dedication to the King, is an essay entitled 'The Translator to the Reader'; and though Englishmen have always felt that the Authorized Version was *their* Bible, they have also known that it was not the Bible of the French or the Germans. However beautiful its cadences, however familiar its rhythms and many of its phrases, a slight effort has always to be made to allay the suspicion that the translation may not be wholly accurate or faithful. A sense of defensiveness results from this, which can easily lead to fundamentalist claims; and, perhaps in response to this, more recent translations and editions, such as the New English Bible (NEB) and the Jerusalem Bible (JB), include footnotes where disputed readings are drawn to our attention.

It may be useful to have before us one or two examples of the difficulties that arise in translation from ancient tongues, so as to try and gauge the effect our sense of the existence of such difficulties has on our attitude to the Bible. How, for example, are we to translate the phrase which forms the climax to the episode in which Elijah hears the voice of God (1 Kings 19:12)? Is it a 'still small voice' (AV), a 'low murmuring sound' (NEB), the 'soft whisper of a voice' (Good News Bible), or 'the sound of a gentle breeze' (JB)? The Hebrew, *kol demamah dakah*, means literally 'voice of thin silence'. But what does *that* mean? Do we try to work that out first and then find an adequate English rendering? Or do we adopt the Nabokovian principle that the host language should be twisted and bent by the pressure of the original? 'Still small voice' is magnificent and has existed in the culture for close on four hundred years – but has it won the right to stay? Stephen Prickett has recently argued that it has, and is in fact a more accurate translation of the Hebrew than the more modern translations.[4] But, though he is persuasive, he makes no effort to convey to us just what the Hebrew would have meant to its original listeners – and how could he, since we have nothing else in Hebrew to compare it with or test it against?

Again, do we translate the famous command in Leviticus 19:18, *Ve'ahavta lere'aka kamoka*, as 'thou shalt love thy neighbour as thyself' (AV), as 'you shall love your neighbour as a man like yourself' (NEB), as 'You must love your neighbour as yourself' (JB), or as 'You shall treat your neighbour kindly for he is a human being like yourself', as suggested by Edward Ullendorf?[5] The AV and JB translations give the usual Christian interpretation of the phrase, but whether we are aware of it or not the JB and NEB translations alter its impact by turning 'thou' and 'thy' into 'you' and 'your'; while Ullendorf's suggestion is more of a paraphrase than a translation. However, it may be that here only a paraphrase will bring out the real meaning. There is of course a world of difference between loving someone as much as you love yourself and being kind to someone because he is after all a human being like yourself. If the text means the latter, as Ullendorf suggests, then it cannot mean the former.

I am not here concerned to adjudicate between translations, even if I had the competence to do so. I only wish to draw attention to the effect on us as readers of knowing that what we are reading is only a translation. But if it makes us feel a little uneasy that does not mean that the reader without Hebrew or Greek should give up right at the start. Who is to say that the Greekless Keats did not absorb more of Homer from Chapman's translation than most Greek scholars get from the original? There is obviously a great advantage in being able to read the Bible, or any other book, in the original, but simply knowing Hebrew will not ensure that we 'grasp' *kol demamah dakah* or Leviticus 19:18. Rather, it is the ability to respond to the whole book to the limits of our capacity – which is, as I suggested in the previous chapter, a very different proposition.

And if the example of Keats seems too exalted, there is always that of Erich Auerbach. His marvellous chapters at the start of *Mimesis* on the way biblical narrative functions have been, as I have said, the inspiration behind the renewed interest in the narrative style of the Bible.[6] Yet Auerbach finds no difficulty in making his points without recourse to the original languages, and his essays suggest what any good reader of the Bible would have suspected, that the problem of translation here is not essentially different from what it is in Dostoevsky or Kafka. Most of us have first read those writers in the translations of Constance Garnett and the Muirs. More recent translators, such as Magarshack and the Sterns, may alert us to the fact that the two writers are funnier and their dialogue sharper and more ironic than we had realized; but that does not alter our basic sense of the 'feel' of Dostoevsky or Kafka. I imagine that their uniqueness, the 'voice' of each author, would emerge whatever the translation. And the same holds true of the Bible. Once again it is our anxiety in relation to this particular book that makes us concentrate on whether we are accurately understanding the details while ignoring the challenge of responding to the whole.

There are other things that colour our response to the whole. There is, for example, the fact that it is divided into verses in a way no other book is. This seems so much part of what it is that we question it as little as we do the use of knives and forks. But in fact, like the use of the fork, the division into verses is a comparatively recent phenomenon, and the division into chapters only a little older.

The division into chapters was made by Stephen Langton, later to become Archbishop of Canterbury, when he was a doctor at the University of Paris towards the end of the twelfth century. The division into verses was first made, for the Old Testament (OT), by Rabbi Nathan, in 1448, as a help in Jewish debates with the Christians, and the OT was first printed in this form in Venice in 1524. Robert Estienne (Stephanus) took up the idea in the Graeco-Latin New Testament (NT) he printed in 1551. His Latin Bible of 1555 was the first to show verse divisions in both Testaments, and this was introduced into the English Bible published in Geneva by exiles from Mary's England (NT, 1557; whole Bible, 1560). Thus it was that both chapter and verse divisions found their way into the AV of 1611.

Pre-Reformation Bibles, as I've said, contained more commentary than text; those which followed the Reformation, while ostensibly getting rid of glosses, in fact retained a small number of them, using them usually in an openly polemical way. King James therefore wisely stipulated that the AV should contain no such glosses and so bear the mark of no single party. However, whether we realize it or not, our Bibles today nearly always bear the traces of commentary, which influences our reading all the more for being so nearly concealed. I am referring to the headings to be found at the start of each chapter in some Bibles, or, more frequently, at the top of each page.

Let us look at one or two examples to see how these affect us. Judges 13–19 contains first the often mysterious story of Samson, and then, as we saw in the last chapter, the possibly related story of Micah, his mother and the idols. My edition of the AV, published by the British and Foreign Bible Society and reprinted in 1958, gives the following headings to these pages: 'An angel foretelleth the birth of Samson/Samson killeth a lion/His marriage feast/The exploits of Samson/He is enticed and betrayed by Delilah/His death/Micah's Gods/The Danaites search the land, rob Micah, and take Laish'. The NEB, with its policy of making the Bible look as much like a classical novel as possible, has just one heading for the chapters dealing with Samson: 'Israel oppressed by the Philistines', followed by one heading for the remainder of the book: 'Years of lawlessness'. The JB, with its policy of making the Bible as much like a newspaper as possible on the assumption, presumably, that newspapers are the only forms of print the buyer of such a book would otherwise encounter, divides the entire book of Judges into four large sections: 'First Introduction', 'Second Introduction', 'The Story of the Judges Told in Episodes' (each episode being given a letter of the alphabet), and 'Additions'. The chapters we are concerned with thus belong to III. L and IV. They carry the following subtitles, which appear not at the top of but in the middle of the page, often two or three to a page: 'Samson's birth foretold/The angel appears a second time/Samson marries/Samson's riddle/Samson sets fire to the crops of the Philistines/ The donkey's jawbone/The gates of Gaza/Samson is betrayed by Delilah/Samson's revenge and death'. Then come the 'Additions', and under 'A', called 'The Sanctuary of Micah and the Sanctuary of Dan', we find: 'The household shrine of Micah/The Danites go in search of a territory/The migration of the Danites/Laish taken. Dan and its sanctuary founded'.

Clearly each edition guides one towards reading the text in a particular way. If we are told the Micah story is an 'addition', then it is going to be impossible to take in any links it might have with the Samson story. If, as the NEB presents it, the stress is on the historical 'facts', then it is going to be very difficult for us to think about Samson himself and the strangeness of his story. If, on the other hand, the personal aspect of Samson's story is stressed to the exclusion of all else, as it is in the AV, then we will fail to see the story in its context. Most important of all,

though, is the fact that all three editions give us the sense of a text which
has already been mastered and understood. Any impression we might
have received from the text that what we were reading was strange,
elusive and problematic is banished from the outset.

The contrast between the signals being emitted by the AV and the JB
is even more striking when we get to the Psalms. The page on which we
find Psalm 24, for example, is headed 'King of Glory' in the AV, while
the psalm itself is presented by the JB as an 'Antiphonal psalm for solemn
entry into the sanctuary'. Turning to the New Testament, and taking
Mark 14 as an example, we read in the AV: 'The betrayal/The last
supper/The sorrow in Gethsemane/Jesus condemned and mocked'. The
NEB simply calls the last three chapters of Mark 'The Final Conflict';
while the JB, as usual, goes into more detail than any other edition.
There, the last three chapters form section V of the whole gospel:
'Passion and Resurrection'. This is particularly misleading, since the
'resurrection' element of this gospel is confined to 16 : 9–20, which, as a
JB footnote indicates, 'many MSS omit', and which modern scholars, in
the light of both this fact and internal evidence, tend to discount. The
JB subheadings for chapter 14 run: 'The conspiracy against Jesus/The
anointing at Bethany/Judas betrays Jesus/Preparations for the Passover
supper/The treachery of Judas foretold/The institution of the Eucharist/
Peter's denial foretold/Gethsemane/The arrest/Jesus before the Sanhed-
rin/Peter's denials'. Once again the effect in all three editions is to turn
the narrative into a series of tableaux and to drain it of any element of
the puzzling and the problematic.

Some editions, as I've said, fill the margins between the two columns
of text with references to other places in the Bible where the same words
occur. Though these may be useful for the student or the scholar and can
even be of interest to the layman, they reinforce the impression of the
text as spread out in a timeless continuum before us, and make us think
of connections between parts of the book entirely in terms of words and
phrases and not of any larger configurations. They thus help to fragment
and hold down the text and to deny to reading its natural rhythm. We
are constantly aware that every word counts (and has been counted), but
as a result we lose all sense of a context for these words and for the dramas
they embody and convey.[7]

All these are minor matters, though. The editorial intrusions do
influence our reading, but not perhaps all that much. One feature of the
Bible is of decisive importance in our reading, but is so large and obvious
that it is actually quite difficult to get it into focus. I am talking about the
simple and obvious fact that the Bible is both one book and two. I will be
touching on this often in what follows. Here I want to draw attention to
the most obvious and 'objective' features of the ambiguity, to the actual

content and organization of the Jewish and Christian Bibles. But even this, as we will see, will lead us straight into some of the most basic problems connected with this book.

Most people take it for granted that the Christian Bible consists of the Hebrew Bible plus the New Testament. They are also vaguely aware of the fact that certain differences exist between the Bibles of the Catholic, Reformed and Anglican Churches. The first assumption is both true and untrue, and the way it is untrue, as we shall see, has profound implications for our reading of the Bible. The second is relatively trivial, but scholars, who love nothing better than dwelling on details while ignoring large issues, spend a great deal of time on the second and none at all on the first. Let us get the question of the minor differences out of the way.

The Jewish scriptures were finally fixed around the year 100 ACE. The Torah had already for a long time been regarded as fixed and canonical, and it is probable that most of the 'historical' books and the prophetic books had become fixed by about 200 BCE. That left a large miscellaneous group of writings, about which there continued to be some argument. We caught a glimpse of it in the passage I quoted from the Mishnah in the previous chapter: the Song of Songs definitely defiles, but what about Ecclesiastes? The Christians, who were in the first place a Jewish splinter group, adopted the Jewish scriptures, but they also included some books which were finally excluded from the Jewish canon, such as Tobit, Wisdom and Ecclesiasticus. They also adopted different and longer versions of some books, such as Esther, which existed in Greek but not in Hebrew. All this was incorporated into Jerome's Latin Bible, which was in effect the Bible of the West till the Renaissance. The Reformers, with their concern for a return to pure uncontaminated origins, excluded both these uncertain books and the longer versions. The Anglicans compromised as usual, and placed the doubtful books in a sort of appendix to the OT, calling them apocryphal, and meaning by this that they should not be considered sacred but should nevertheless be read alongside the others.

Although there was a great deal of controversy about this at the time, it does not really affect our sense of the Bible as a whole, for the works about which there was disagreement were few in number and didn't play a very important role in the overall structure. Again, a relaxed rather than an anxious attitude to the subject of the canon would have suggested that what we had here was really no problem at all, just as it would make little difference to our sense of Shakespeare were we to learn tomorrow that he definitely had or definitely had not written *Henry VIII*. It is a fine and interesting play, but its inclusion in or exclusion from the *Complete Works* would not really affect our sense of what the other plays add up to. This could not be said of A *Midsummer Night's*

Dream, Hamlet or *The Tempest*. (Could it be said of *Much Ado*? Of *Coriolanus*? A question for the reader to ponder.)

As far as the Bible is concerned, though, much more important than the question of what goes in or stays out at the periphery is the question of the order in which the central books are arranged. For it is a fact of decisive importance that the Christian Bible, though incorporating the bulk of the Jewish scriptures into its Old Testament, drastically alters the order in which they are arranged. Why? And what effect does this have on the material?[8]

Northrop Frye begins his book on the Bible with a clear statement of principle:

> What matters is that 'the Bible' has traditionally been read as a unity, and has influenced Western imagination as a unity. It exists if only because it has been compelled to exist. Yet, whatever the external reasons, there has to be some internal basis even for a compulsory existence. Those who do succeed in reading the Bible from beginning to end will discover that at least it has a beginning and an end, and some traces of a total structure.

But, he goes on,

> For my purposes the only possible form of the Bible that I can deal with is the Christian Bible, with its polemically named 'Old' and 'New' Testaments. I know that Jewish and Islamic conceptions of the Bible are very different, but that is practically all I do know about them, and it is the Christian Bible that is important for English literature and the Western cultural tradition generally.[9]

This is perfectly fair. But if one's interest in the Bible is not so much in it as an influence on later literature but as a book to be read for its own sake, the problems cannot be shrugged off quite so easily. For one can accept that any single book of the Bible should be treated as a unity which has been given its final shape by the last redactor; one can even accept that the whole of the Hebrew and the whole of the Christian scriptures form a unity given its final shape by the custodians of tradition; but if each is a unity what happens to the first when it is subsumed under the second?

The Church Fathers and Christian theologians till well into the eighteenth century were in no doubt as to what happens: the Hebrew scriptures alter in meaning when placed in a sequence which ends with the Christian scriptures. In polemics both with heretics who wished to do away with the 'Old Testament' as being irrelevant to Christians, and with Jews, who regarded their scriptures as the record of the relations of the Jewish people with God, they insisted that the Hebrew scriptures were a prelude, a foreshadowing of Christ, giving meaning to Christ's advent, but also deriving their own true meaning from Christ's advent, death and resurrection.

This view, which they rightly saw as already articulated by Jesus himself and the authors of the Christian scriptures, naturally has far-reaching implications. Not only does it alter the meaning of what is there (something we will be looking at later), but it also exerts an influence on *how* what is there is *organized.*

Let us look again at the book we hold in our hands. It consists of two major sections, the Old and the New Testaments. Each is divided into four parts, though the divisions are not necessarily indicated. First, in the Old Testament, comes the Pentateuch, the five books 'of Moses', which recount the story of the world from the Creation through the choosing of Abraham, the stories of Abraham and his descendants, the bondage in Egypt, the escape under the leadership of Moses, the giving of the Laws in Sinai, the forty years' wandering in the wilderness, and the arrival at the borders of the Promised Land, where Moses dies. This is followed by the historical books, which take the story through the conquest of Canaan, the establishment of the Kingdom with Jerusalem or Zion as its capital, the disintegration of the Kingdom for both internal and external reasons, the great catastrophes when powerful neighbours overrun the land, destroy the Temple and deport the people, then through exile, and the return to the land and the rebuilding of the Temple when the Persians defeat the Babylonians and allow a remnant of the people to go back. A final book in this section, Esther, tells of an intrigue against the Jews at the Persian court and of their eventual triumph over their enemies. The third section consists of the 'poetical' books, Psalms, Job, Proverbs, the Song of Songs and Ecclesiastes, in which God's relation to Israel and Israel's to God is examined from a variety of angles and meditated upon in a variety of modes. The fourth and final part of the Old Testament consists of the prophetic books, starting with Isaiah and ending with Malachi.

The book of Malachi begins with God insisting that he has loved Israel yet been poorly rewarded for his pains: 'I have loved you, saith the Lord. Yet ye say, Wherein hast thou loved us? Was not Esau Jacob's brother? saith the Lord: yet I loved Jacob, and I hated Esau' (1:2–3). The mysterious love of a father for one of his sons at the expense of the other has, however, been forgotten by the beneficiaries of that love. Now sons turn against fathers, priests perform the rites half-heartedly or using unclean animals, they take bribes and think only of their own welfare, and men take as wives women who worship other gods, mere idols; divorce is rife and interfamily quarrels frequent and bitter. Yet when taxed with all this Israel can only answer hypocritically: what have I done? So,

Behold, I will send my messenger, and he shall prepare the way before me: and the Lord, whom ye seek, shall suddenly come to his temple, even the messenger of the covenant, whom ye delight in: behold, he shall come, saith the Lord of hosts.

(Mal. 3:1)

On that day Israel will be purified with a terrible purification: 'But who may abide the day of his coming? and who shall stand when he appeareth? for he is like a refiner's fire, and like fullers' sope...' (3:2). In that day the justice and mercy of the Lord will be fully evident. For those who have not turned aside from his way he will spare, 'as a man spareth his own son that serveth him' (3:17).

So this section and with it the entire Old Testament ends, with a vision of the terrible Day of Judgement, but also with a reminder that, as Moses saved Israel from the Egyptian bondage, so Elijah will return, heralding the final reconciliation of God and Israel:

For, behold, the day cometh, that shall burn as an oven;
And all the proud, yea, and all that do wickedly, shall be stubble:
And the day that cometh shall burn them up, saith the Lord of hosts,
That it shall leave them neither root nor branch.
But unto you that fear my name shall the Sun of righteousness arise
With healing in his wings;
And ye shall go forth, and grow up as calves of the stall.
And ye shall tread down the wicked;
For they shall be ashes under the soles of your feet
In the day that I shall do this, saith the Lord of Hosts.

Remember ye the law of Moses my servant,
Which I commanded unto him in Horeb for all Israel,
With the statutes and judgments.
Behold, I will send you Elijah the prophet
Before the coming of the great and dreadful day of the Lord:
And he shall turn the heart of the fathers to the children,
And the heart of the children to their fathers,
Lest I come and smite the earth with a curse.

(Mal. 4:1–6)

Thus the end looks back to the beginning, and forward into the future.

The New Testament follows immediately after this. Its first section consists of the four Gospels, the first of which, Matthew, begins with a genealogy of Jesus, which takes us back to Genesis: 'The book of the generation of Jesus Christ, the son of David, the son of Abraham. Abraham begat Isaac; and Isaac begat Jacob; and Jacob begat Judas and his brethren...' (1:1–2). In chapter 11 Jesus tells the crowd about John the Baptist and makes the link with the end of Malachi explicit:

But what went ye out for to see? A prophet? yea, I say unto you, and more than a prophet. For this is he, of whom it is written, Behold, I send my messenger before thy face, which shall prepare thy way before thee. Verily I say unto you, Among them that are born of women there hath not risen a greater than John the Baptist. . . . For all the prophets and the law prophesied until John. And if ye will receive it, this is Elias, which was for to come.

(Matt. 11 : 9–14)

Just as Elijah dwelt in the desert in rough clothing, so John; and just as Elijah will return at the end of days to herald the Messiah, so has John heralded me, says Jesus. By chapter 25 there is no longer any room for doubt: the Day of Judgement foretold by Malachi is upon us:

When the Son of man shall come in his glory, and all the holy angels with him, then shall he sit upon the throne of his glory: And before him shall be gathered all nations: and he shall separate them one from another, as a shepherd divideth his sheep from the goats: And he shall set the sheep on his right hand, but the goats on the left.

(Matt. 25 : 31–33)

The next Gospel, Mark's, picks up the themes of Malachi again. After an opening flourish which quotes Isaiah 40 : 3, 'the voice of one crying in the wilderness, Prepare ye the way of the Lord',[10] it plunges straight into the action:

John did baptize in the wilderness, and preach the baptism of repentance for the remission of sins. . . . And John was clothed with camel's hair, and with a girdle of a skin about his loins; and he did eat locusts and wild honey; And preached, saying, There cometh one mightier than I after me. . . .

(Mark 1 : 4–7)

There is no time for a genealogy here, but Luke's, the next Gospel, makes up for it by providing us with a genealogy of both John the Baptist and Jesus. John, we are told, will go before the Lord, 'in the spirit and power of Elias' (1 : 17), while Jesus is traced back beyond Abraham to Adam himself. The last Gospel, John's, caps the whole edifice by opening with an even firmer return to the very beginning:

In the beginning was the Word, and the Word was with God, and the Word was God. The same was in the beginning with God. All things were made by him; and without him was not any thing made that was made.

(John 1 : 1–3)

This first of the four New Testament sections thus echoes the five books of Moses, presents itself as a new Genesis, but also as the fulfilment of the prophecy with which the Old Testament ended, the coming of the Messiah heralded by Elijah and bringing the final Day of Judgement.

The second section, corresponding to the historical books, is the single book of the Acts of the Apostles. This is followed by the Epistles, which correspond to the poetic and meditative section of the Old Testament. Finally the New Testament, and the entire Bible, comes to an end with Revelation and its vision of the heavenly city and the end of time:

> And I saw a new heaven and a new earth: for the first heaven and the first earth were passed away; and there was no more sea. And I John saw the holy city, new Jerusalem, coming down from God out of heaven, prepared as a bride adorned for her husband. And I heard a great voice out of heaven saying, Behold, the tabernacle of God is with men, and he will dwell with them, and they shall be his people, and God himself shall be with them, and be their God. And God shall wipe away all tears from their eyes; and there shall be no more death, neither sorrow, nor crying, neither shall there be any more pain: for the former things are passed away.
>
> (Rev. 21 : 1–4)

All that is left now is for the vision itself to be ratified:

> And he that sat upon the throne said, Behold, I make all things new. And he said unto me, Write: for these words are true and faithful. And he said unto me, It is done. I am Alpha and Omega, the beginning and the end.
>
> (21 : 5–6)

There follows the injunction that no one is to 'add unto these things' or to 'take away from the words of the book of this prophecy' (22 : 18–19), and the book closes with a blessing: 'He which testifieth these things saith, Surely I come quickly. Amen. Even so, come, Lord Jesus. The grace of our Lord Jesus Christ be with you all. Amen' (20–21).

It's a magnificent conception, spread over thousands of pages and encompassing the entire history of the universe. There is both perfect correspondence between Old and New Testaments and a continuous forward drive from Creation to the end of time: 'It begins where time begins, with the creation of the world; it ends where time ends, with the Apocalypse, and it surveys human history in between, or the aspect of history it is interested in, under the symbolic names of Adam and Israel'.[11] Earlier ages had no difficulty in grasping this design, though our own, more bookish age, obsessed with both history and immediacy, has tended to lose sight of it. Neither theologians nor biblical scholars have stood back enough to see it as a whole. Yet it *is* a whole and quite unlike any other book.

If we turn from this, however, to the Hebrew scriptures, we find that though there is no new material, the organization is quite different. Instead of forming a half-arch, hanging in the air and waiting for its mirror image to complete it, the Hebrew scriptures present us with no easily recognizable visual image. To begin with, they are divided into three parts rather than four. And the reason for this would appear to be less the desire to create a pattern than the historical accidents of how and when the scriptures were accorded their sacred and authoritative character. Accident rather than design seems to be the main principle at work. Yet, since there is no such thing as pure accident in the making of any book, let us look a little more closely at what went into the formation of this one.

The first of the three sections corresponds precisely to the Pentateuch. This is the Torah, the oldest and most revered part of the Hebrew Bible, which was already fixed in more or less its present form during the Babylonian exile in the sixth century BCE. Not so the next section, however, This is known as the 'Prophets', and includes not just the books the Christian Bible calls prophetic, but also most of the historical books from Joshua through to Kings, though it does not include Ruth, Esther, Chronicles, nor, among the prophets, Daniel.

There are three points to be made about this, two significant and one crucial. The first concerns the books included in this section. By subsuming the 'historical' books under the general rubric of 'Prophets', the tradition seems to imply that what is important is not so much the historical continuum of conquest, exile and return, as the spiritual link between Moses, the first prophet ('by a prophet the Lord brought Israel out of Egypt,' says Hosea 12 : 13), Samuel, David and Elijah, and the so-called 'writing prophets' like Isaiah and Jeremiah. It suggests that to separate the 'historical' and the 'prophetic', as the Christian Bible does, is to run counter to the intentions of the Hebrew Bible.

The second point concerns the order of the books in this section. While the five books of the Torah were firmly in place in the sixth century BCE, it was probably (as we saw above) not till about 200 BCE that this second group was recognized as absolutely authoritative. And though the books from Joshua to Kings follow chronology, there appears to be considerable variety in the manuscript tradition as to the order in which the writing prophets should appear. Haggai, Zechariah and Malachi are commonly regarded as the last of the prophets, since after them, it was felt, the 'divine spirit' ceased to be active in Israel. As we've seen from Josephus, there was a tradition which affirmed that in the period of the second Temple, as opposed to the first, prophecy had ceased. It is quite possible therefore that the closing verses of Malachi are meant to be an epilogue to the entire collection, expressing the recognition of the cessation of prophecy and the hope of its renewal.[12]

Since the twelve minor prophets always appeared on one scroll, if Malachi ended the entire section, the others must also have come at the end. The sequence in which they appear is the same as in the Christian Bible, though of course Daniel is missing. But the position with regard to the other writing prophets is more problematic. Jeremiah and not Isaiah is often placed first, after Kings, with Ezekiel next and Isaiah last, just before Hosea, the first of the 'twelve'. The rabbis were clearly puzzled by the fact that Hosea comes after Isaiah, but explain this by pointing out that Hosea belongs with the other minor prophets on one scroll. They were also puzzled by the fact that Jeremiah, who is chronologically later than Isaiah, often comes before him, and the Babylonian Talmud explains it thus:

> The Book of Kings ends with a record of destruction; Jeremiah deals throughout with destruction; Ezekiel commences with destruction and closes with consolation, while Isaiah is entirely consolation. Therefore we juxtapose destruction to destruction and consolation to consolation.
>
> (*Baba Bathra* 14b)[13]

This is illuminating precisely because it is not very convincing. After all, Jeremiah deals with comfort as well as destruction and Isaiah with destruction as well as consolation. Nevertheless, what the rabbis were concerned with was to find reasons for the order, and they discovered these in thematic rather than chronological links. In the same vein, it has been suggested that the similarity between Isaiah 1 : 1 and Hosea 1 : 1 explains why Isaiah and the scroll of the Twelve are placed side by side. Finally, the suggestion has been made that as well as being linked through theme and theme-words, the prophetic books reflect an arrangement in descending order of size.[14] Both these notions, of links via theme and via size, shock our aesthetic sensibility, for we want our links to be 'organic' and not 'mechanical'. But these are after all principles of order like any others and, fifty years after *Ulysses*, should surely cause us no surprise.

The most important point about this second section of the Hebrew scriptures, however, is the most obvious. It is that the prophets come *second* and not third and last. In other words the date of canonization and the link between Former and Latter Prophets was felt to be more important than ending with the writing prophets. And yet what could have been more natural? The end of Malachi, as I've said, could well be a deliberate conclusion to the whole corpus of the prophets; and the prophet Elijah, so important for that ending, was of course a central figure in Jewish legend and folk-tale. That, naturally, is why he plays the role he does in the Christian scriptures. But it is not as if he had been taken up by the New Testament and dropped out of Judaism. After all, in the entire Bible only Enoch and Elijah seem not to have died, and this naturally led to a great deal of speculation about their possible return. Even today Elijah has a special chair set out for him at circumcisions, and is always expected on the night of the Passover celebrations. The ending of Malachi hints at the belief that, as Moses led the Jews out of Egypt to freedom, so Elijah will, at the end of days, come back to reconcile parents and children and prepare the way for the Messiah.[15] And yet in spite of all this, no attempt was made, when the canon of the Bible was finally closed, to end with this expression of Messianic hope. The question seems never even to have been raised.

In the Hebrew Bible the 'Prophets' section is followed by one simply called 'Writings', a miscellaneous group which includes Psalms and Job as well as the books of Ruth, Esther, Daniel, Lamentations and the Song of Songs, each of which is recited on a different festival. This section was the last to be incorporated into the canon and, as we saw in the last chapter, there was still at the time of the Mishnah some disagreement about the full canonicity of Ecclesiastes and probably of some other books as well.[16] There seems to have been no fixed order for any of the items in this group, and it is particularly interesting to note that the order which eventually prevailed is almost aggressively achronological. For the Hebrew Bible ends not with Ezra and Nehemiah but with Chronicles, which is chronologically anterior to the other two.

The last words of the Hebrew Bible thus present us with the Israelites in exile, with only the promise of restoration, a promise not enunciated by God or a prophet but by a foreign monarch:

> Now in the first year of Cyrus king of Persia, that the word of the Lord spoken by the mouth of Jeremiah might be accomplished, the Lord stirred up the spirit of Cyrus king of Persia, that he made a proclamation throughout all his kingdom, and put it also in writing, saying, Thus saith Cyrus king of Persia, All the kingdoms of the earth hath the Lord God of heaven given me; and he hath charged me to build him an house in Jerusalem, which is in Judah. Who is there among you of all his people? The Lord his God be with him, and let him go up.
>
> (2 Chr. 36:22–23)

Thus instead of a heavenly city and the end of time we have only a very secular royal proclamation and a very earthly city, along with a simple expression of hope: 'let him go up....'.[17]

There were, as I've said, other arrangements of the books in this last section, but the one ending with Chronicles is the one that prevails in the early manuscripts and that eventually established itself in the Masoretic Text (MT). But it raises once again the question we touched on when looking at the Prophets, namely what principles lay behind the ordering of the entire corpus of the Hebrew scriptures? This question of order is raised in the same section of the Babylonian Talmud as the one we have just looked at, *Baba Bathra* 14b:

> Our Rabbis taught: the order of the Prophets is Joshua, Judges, Samuel, Kings, Jeremiah, Ezekiel, Isaiah, and the Twelve.... The order of the Writings is Ruth, the book of Psalms, Job, Proverbs, Ecclesiastes, the Song of Songs, Lamentations, Daniel, the scroll of Esther, Ezra and Chronicles.

Nahum Sarna, in the essay on the canon and text of the Bible in the *Encyclopedia Judaica*, points out that the notion of an order of the books is puzzling so long as the individual books filled a single scroll, and that the Talmudic comment, not being later than the second century ACE, long antedates the use of codices by the Jews. Thus, he suggests, what we must be dealing with here is methods of storing papyrus rolls and cuneiform tablets which had been common practice in the Mesopotamian and Hellenistic worlds, as well as the requirements of the scribal schools, which 'engendered an established sequence in which the classic works were to be read and studied'. And so 'the reference would be to the order in which the individual scrolls in these two corpora [the Prophets and the Writings] were shelved and catalogued in the Palestinian archives and schools. The silence about the Pentateuch...is due to the fact that its priority in its long fixed order was so universally known as to make it superfluous.' However, Sid Leiman has taken issue with this and suggested that 'the need for an ordering of the biblical books arose out of the economical practice of copying two or more books on the same scrolls.'[18] Whatever the reasons, there is no doubt that the final order as enshrined in the MT was the subject of considerable speculation, and this is only to be expected since the reasons for the arrangement were not as self-evident as they were in the Christian Bible.

It seems clear that we have to look for thematic rather than chronological links. Thus Genesis and Chronicles both begin with the origin of the human race and end with the promise of redemption and return to the land of Israel from exile. Indeed, the two books employ the same key verbs in this connection in their concluding phrases: *pakad* ('visit') and *'alah* ('go up'):

> And Joseph said unto his brethren, I die: and God will surely visit you [*pakod yiphkod etkhem*], and bring you out of this land unto the land which he sware to Abraham, to Isaac, and to Jacob. And Joseph took an oath of the children of Israel, saying, God will surely visit you [*pakod yiphkod elohim etkhem*], and ye shall carry up [*ha'alitem*] my bones from hence.
>
> (Gen. 50:24–25)

> Thus saith Cyrus king of Persia, All the kingdoms of the earth hath the Lord God of heaven given me; and he hath charged me [*vehu phakad 'alai*] to build him an house in Jerusalem, which is in Judah. Who is there among you of all his people? The Lord his God be with him, and let him go up [*ya'al*].
>
> (2 Chr. 36:23)

In the same way the initial chapter of the Former Prophets and of the Latter Prophets, and the closing chapter of the Prophets, as well as the opening chapter of the Writings, all contain a mention of the Torah:

> This book of the law [*sepher hatorah*] shall not depart out of thy mouth....
>
> (Josh. 1:8)

Hear the word of the Lord, ye rulers of Sodom; give ear unto the law of our God [*torat elohenu*], ye people of Gomorrah.

(Isa. 1 : 10)

Remember ye the law of Moses my servant [*torat moshe 'avdi*], which I commanded unto him in Horeb for all Israel, with the statutes and judgments. . . .

(Mal. 3 : 22[MT]; 4 : 4[AV])

But his delight is in the law of the Lord [*torat adonai*]; and in his law [*torato*] doth he meditate day and night.

(Ps. 1 : 2)

What conclusions then are to be drawn from this analysis? First of all that where the Christian Bible moves in a firm arch from beginning to end, the Hebrew Bible is very much more concerned with getting the beginning right than the ending. The possibility was there to shape it so as to end, as the Old Testament does, with a Messianic thrust, but it was rejected, and instead the book ends flatly with a collection of miscellaneous 'writings'. Secondly, whatever órder it has depends in the first place on the historical and contingent fact of when the different sections were canonized, and then on the use of thematic and verbal links.

The Christian order is one we find perfectly natural and easy to understand, partly because we ourselves, whatever our beliefs, have been conditioned by Christian culture, and partly because it corresponds to a profound need in each of us for closure and for a universe shaped according to a clearly comprehensible story. As we shall see in later chapters, these two aspects are by no means unrelated. But just because the Christian pattern is so simple to grasp, it is easy to overlook the extraordinary nature of the Hebrew Bible's *refusal* of such a pattern. For there is little doubt that the original Torah included the conquest of Canaan – included, that is, the book of Joshua. Such a shape, from Abraham's setting out from Haran to the conquest of the land promised him at the start (Gen. 12 : 1–3), is attested in nearly all the recitations of the saving history (Deut. 26, Josh. 24, etc.). Yet, as we have it, the Torah ends with Israel and Moses outside the land and waiting to enter. Why?

J. S. Sanders has argued persuasively that the experience of the Babylonian exile was decisive. It led to a renewed meditation on the nature of Israel's relations to God and to a recognition of the fact that the essential history of Israel, unlike that of the nations surrounding it, was one not of small beginnings leading to a triumphal climax, but of perpetual exile and defeat. The sense of being a chosen people rather than the occupiers of land was what came to be seen as the central feature of Israel's particular destiny. And it was, paradoxically perhaps, this recognition which ensured the survival of Israel's sacred book while those of the surrounding nations disappeared with the empires they had celebrated and had to wait for the archaeologist's spade to make them available to us once more. As Sanders says,

> No longer at the heart of the canon was there any nationalist fulfilment of identity or hope, but rather a service of thanksgiving projected for the time that restoration would take place.... Israel in dispersion could cling for as long and as often as need be to the unifying hope of returning home, once more to be an autochthonous people.[19]

Sanders provides a convincing rationale for the shape of the Torah as we have it, but more than that, for the shape of the entire Hebrew Bible. Each of its three sections was to repeat the pattern of the first, and by so doing provide Jews with a Bible very different not only from the Christian Bible but also from the Old Testament of the Christians.

All this helps to explain one or two further aspects of the different ways Jews and Christians regard their Bible. First of all it is significant that there is no single designation common to all Jews and employed in all periods by which the Jewish scriptures have been known. Though the earliest and most diffuse term was *hasepharim* (the books – see Daniel 9:2), which was the term adopted by the Greek-speaking Jews and translated as *ta biblia*, many other terms are also to be found: *siphrei hakodesh* (holy books), *kitvei hakodesh* (holy writings), *mikra* (reading), and the acronym *tanak*, standing for *Torah, Nevi'im, Ketuvim* (Law, Prophets, Writings). Secondly the titles of the different books of the Pentateuch with which Christian readers are familiar – Genesis, Exodus, etc. – come from the Latin Bible, which is itself based on the Greek. Though such titles survive in rabbinic and medieval Hebrew (The Book of the Creation of the World, The Book of the Exodus from Egypt), the MT designates the books by their opening word or by the first significant word – *bereshit, shemot*, etc. This was the normal practice in the ancient Near East, and it reinforces the sense that no overview is possible, that to read we have to start at the beginning and move forward. With the introduction of titles like Genesis and Exodus we are already on the way to that form of tacit commentary I dealt with earlier.

All this lends force to the claim of some scholars that while the Jews were content to use scrolls for their sacred books, it was the Christians who began to use codices or books.[20] For a book reinforces the sense of unity, of an end already implicit in the beginning, which was precisely the view the Christian scriptures desired to promote – understandably enough, since for the Christians unity had been given to history, and therefore to the book which enshrined that history, by the person of Jesus himself. And what this suggests is that, among the implicit and explicit

arguments about the nature of God and of history in which Jews and
Christians have engaged, there is bound up an argument about the
nature of books and of this book in particular.

In the last chapter I quoted James Barr's somewhat dismissive comment about the Bible needing to be thought of not so much as a book
but as a cave or cupboard in which a miscellany of scrolls has been
crammed. In the light of the present chapter we can perhaps see that our
attitude to such a remark will depend less on 'the facts' and more on our
sense of what constitutes a whole. If the Christian Bible was indeed once
nothing but a bundle of scrolls in a cupboard, there is something within
it which wants to turn it into something else. At the same time we have
come to see that the image might be viewed positively rather than
negatively. A generation which has experienced *Ulysses* and *The Waste
Land* (to say nothing of Butor's *Mobile* and Perec's *La vie mode d'emploi*)
should be able to do this more easily than one whose idea of a book and a
unity was a novel by Balzac or George Eliot.[21] Indeed, many modernist
works might well be described as more like cupboards or caves crammed
with scrolls than like carefully plotted nineteenth-century novels or
even fairy stories and romances. But we should also realize that this is a
feature they have in common with a great deal of ancient literature, but
one upon which the Christian Bible deliberately turned its back.

Thus even before we start to read we are faced with interpretation. The
appearance of a book, the order and arrangement of its parts, the glosses
appended to it, are themselves already interpretation. The advent of
Christ gave meaning to history, says the New Testament. It also gives
meaning to the pages in which that history is narrated. To give meaning,
however, is not a neutral activity; something disappears at the same
time – in this case the spirit in which the Hebrew Bible was written and
put together. We have therefore to start by trying to discover what that
spirit was, and this cannot be done by looking outside the Bible: we
must listen as carefully as possible to what the Bible itself is saying. Only
then will we be in a position to understand and judge the nature of
the Christian transformation. And that means starting with the first
sentence of the first book of the Bible. To this I now turn.

Two

ELEMENTS OF RHYTHM

The Sabbath is not simply a time for rest, for relaxation. We ought to contemplate our labours from without and not just from within.

LUDWIG WITTGENSTEIN

THE RHYTHM ESTABLISHED:
BERESHIT BARA

Beginning at the beginning is what most readers tend to do. As we have seen, the beginning of the Bible is not a title, 'Genesis', or a subtitle, 'The Primeval History', or even a chapter heading such as 'The Creation of the World'. The beginning, in Hebrew, is *bereshit bara elohim et hashamayim ve'et ha'aretz*. In English, as everyone knows, it is: 'In the beginning God created the heaven and the earth'.

But is it? The NEB, for one, has a strikingly different opening: 'In the beginning of creation, when God made heaven and earth...'. It is true that it adds a footnote which reads: 'Or "In the beginning God created heaven and earth".' But can we really rest satisfied with that 'or'? Surely the difference between the two versions is too great to be dismissed with a simple 'or'. These are not alternative ways of translating; they seem to be alternative accounts of the origin of all things. The traditional account says that everything began with God creating heaven and earth; the NEB account suggests that before the creation of the universe there was already something, though we only enter the narrative at the point when God starts to create. In the one case God is the origin of all; in the other the possibility is floated that God himself may have been a part of some primal chaos out of which our world too was made, just as man is later made out of dust.

In grammatical terms the question seems to hinge on whether we take the phrase 'in the beginning' to be absolute or dependent. The reader who is troubled by the casualness of that NEB 'or' will naturally turn to a commentary to find out what the real translation should be. Two of the main such commentaries available in English are the Anchor Bible *Genesis* by E. A. Speiser, and the Old Testament Library *Genesis*, by Gerhard von Rad. However, the reader had better consult both, for, as we might have suspected from the way the NEB hedges its bets, each opts for a different one of the two alternatives. Far from being a cause for despair at this early stage, however, such a conflict of readings may actually help to sharpen our awareness of the way the Bible works.

Speiser translates:

> When God set about to create heaven and earth – the world being then a
> formless waste, with darkness over the seas and only an awesome wind
> sweeping over the water – God said, "Let there be light". And there was
> light.[1]

Von Rad translates:

> In the beginning God created the heavens and the earth. The earth was
> without form and void, and darkness was upon the face of the deep; and the
> Spirit of God was moving over the face of the waters. And God said: 'Let
> there be light'; and there was light.[2]

This corresponds to the AV, though it lacks the latter's dignity:

> In the beginning God created the heaven and the earth. And the earth was
> without form, and void; and darkness was upon the face of the deep. And the
> Spirit of God moved upon the face of the waters. And God said, Let there be
> light: and there was light. And God saw the light, that it was good: and God
> divided the light from the darkness.
>
> (Gen. 1 : 1–4)

This in turn goes back to St. Jerome's Latin translation:

> In principio creavit Deus caelum et terram. Terra autem erat inanis et vacua,
> et tenebrae erant super faciem abyssi: et Spiritus Dei ferebatur super aquas.
> Dixitque Deus: Fiat lux. Et facta est lux. Et vidit Deus lucem quod esset bona.

Where then does Speiser get his reading from, and why does the
NEB seem to prefer it to the traditional one? The answer of course is that
the Hebrew is ambiguous. The Hebrew alphabet consists only of consonants, the vowels being signified by means of accents placed above
or below the letters. The nature of the language makes it possible for
Hebrew words which have the same consonants to mean different things
if the vowels are different. The text of the Hebrew Bible was originally
unaccented ('unpointed' is the technical term), and was given its vowel
marks by the Masoretes, the custodians of the traditional way of speaking
Scripture out loud. The Masoretic Text thus embodies the way in which
the Jewish tradition pronounced its Bible – which in effect means, how
it read it. (There are a few cases where a traditional reading is in conflict
with the pointing, and this is also noted in the tradition, but no
examples of this occur in the lines we are concerned with here.)

How we are to point the consonants 'b', 'r', 'sh' and 't' in the first word
of the Bible was fixed by tradition as *bérēshīt*. Now while *reshit* means
'beginning' and is linked to the word for 'head', *rosh*, *bereshit* cannot
mean 'in the beginning'. The article *ha* would have to show up, and this
would produce the form *bareshit* (from *behareshit*). However, in the
construct state, which is the Hebrew form of the genitive, the vowels are
elided, and the *a* would become *e*, thus giving us what we have at

present: _bereshit_. The word as we have it must mean 'in-the-beginning-
of' – in other words, 'when'. This then is the reason for Speiser's
translation and the NEB's. As Speiser explains in a note: 'The absolute
form with adverbial connotation would be _bareshit_. As the text is now
vocalized, therefore, the Hebrew Bible starts out with a dependent
clause.'[3]

Here Speiser, though in disagreement with the entire Christian
tradition and a good deal of Jewish tradition, does have the support of the
medieval commentator Rashi, who translates: 'At the beginning of the
creation of heaven and earth', and, like Speiser, holds back the main
verb till the third verse: 'God said...'. Such a reading, Speiser insists,
also has the support of the Bible itself, in the second chapter of Genesis,
which he rather tendentiously translates so as to bring out the parallels
with the opening:

> At the time when God Yahweh made earth and heaven – no shrub of the
> field being yet in the earth and no grains of the field having sprouted, for God
> Yahweh had not sent rain upon the earth and no man was there to till the
> soil; instead, a flow would well up from the ground and water the whole
> surface of the soil – God Yahweh formed man from clods in the soil and blew
> into his nostrils the breath of life.
>
> (Gen. 2:4b–7)

Here too, Speiser argues, we start with a dependent clause, 'at the time
when', move on to a hanging parenthetical passage, 'no shrub of the field
being yet...', and finally arrive at the subject and verb: 'God Yahweh
formed man'. This precisely parallels Speiser's rendering of the opening:
'[At the time] when God created...the world being then...God
said...'.

Finally, in case there should still be any doubt about the rightness of
his case, Speiser points out that, as we know, such an opening was
typical of the Creation stories of the ancient Near East. The most famous
of these, the Akkadian epic, _Enuma Elish_, is a good example. The title
comes from the first two words, 'When on high', and though naturally
scholars give slightly different renderings, there seems in this case to be
no disagreement about the syntax. Here is a translation:

> When on high the heaven had not (yet) been named,
> and below the firm ground had not (yet) been given a name,
> when primaeval Apsu, their begetter,
> (and) Mummu-Tiamat who gave them all birth,
> (still) mingled their waters,
> the reed had not yet sprung forth nor had the marsh appeared,
> none of the gods had been brought into being,
> they were (still) unnamed and their fortunes were not determined,
> then the gods were created in their midst.[4]

Here too we find the sequence: temporal clause, parenthetic clauses, main clause. As Speiser triumphantly concludes: 'Thus grammar, context, and parallels point uniformly in one and the same direction'.[5]

Why then, in the face of all this evidence, does the Christian tradition persist with a different reading, and why does von Rad, as learned an Old Testament scholar as Speiser, though without the latter's expertise in Akkadian, follow suit? The answer of course is that more rests on this than simple decisions about grammar. As von Rad puts it:

> We do not follow the old conjecture that v. 1 is not to be understood as an independent sentence but as the introductory clause to v. 2 or even to v. 3 ('at the beginning when God created heaven and earth...'). Syntactically perhaps both translations are possible, but not theologically....If one considers vv. 1–2 or 1–3 as the syntactical unit, then the word about chaos would stand logically and temporally before the word about creation. To be sure, the notion of a created chaos is itself a contradiction; nevertheless, one must remember that the text touches on things which in any case lie beyond human imagination. That does not mean, however, that one must renounce establishing quite definite and unrelinquishable theologumena. The first is that God, in the freedom of his will, creatively established for 'heaven and earth', i.e. for absolutely everything, a beginning of its subsequent existence.[6]

Von Rad would seem to be arguing here for a translation which goes against the natural syntax and grammar of the Bible just because it fits in with certain religious dogmas he accepts independently of the Bible. But this is not quite fair. He backs up his remarks not just by asserting the impossibility on theological ground of any other reading, but also by pointing out how consistently the Bible, particularly in its opening chapters, sets its face against the myths and legends of the ancient Near East, and therefore how unlikely it is that in this first and most crucial sentence it would depart from its principles. Where the gods in the myths of the ancient Near East are a motley crew, born in a variety of ways, and standing for different aspects of the physical world – the sky, the seas or the storm wind – the god of the Hebrew Bible is alone and all-powerful, coming from nothing and bearing no children. And if this is how the Bible sees God, then it would be absurd to try and interpret the meaning of individual phrases in it by appeals to parallels in ancient Near Eastern texts.

Moreover, von Rad points out, the second word, *bara*, is not the usual word for 'make', which is *'assa*, but 'contains the idea both of complete effortlessness and *creatio ex nihilo*, since it is never connected with any statement of the material'. And he concludes his analysis in tones as confident as those of Speiser:

It is amazing to see how sharply little Israel demarcated herself from an apparently overpowering environment of cosmological and theogonic myths. Here the subject is not a primeval mystery of procreation from which the divinity arose, nor of a 'creative' struggle of mythically personified powers from which the cosmos arose, but rather the one who is neither warrior nor procreator, who alone is worthy of the predicate, Creator.[7]

Von Rad does not only speak for Christian readers. Samson Raphael Hirsch, for example, in his edition of the Pentateuch, has no time at all for the views of those who opt for a God who is coterminous with chaos. The construct reading favoured by Rashi and Speiser is, according to him,

> not only a metaphysical lie which has robbed the theories of mankind as to the origin of the world of truth, i.e. of agreement with actuality, but is the much further-reaching pernicious denial of all freedom of will in God and Man, which undermines all morality. If the material was there, was given to the world-former, He would only make the best possible out of that material, but not the absolute best world. All physical and moral evil would then be in the imperfection of the material.[8]

As with von Rad, what leads Hirsch to read the sentence one way rather than another is the sense that his entire view of the Bible and his entire structure of beliefs would collapse if a different translation were allowed. Once grant that God is dependent on matter and where is Judaism, where Christianity? We would be back with the mystery religions and the worship of idols and nature deities from which biblical religion was supposed to have freed us.

It is true that this did not seem to trouble Rashi, who could hardly be accused of subscribing to a mystery religion. Indeed, by making the first phrase dependent on the third he avoided what might be thought an almost equally dangerous heresy (mentioned only to be dismissed by von Rad): the notion that God was the creator of chaos as well as of the world and man. However, both von Rad and Hirsch clearly find this a lesser evil than to accept a God who is not the primal creator of all things. Von Rad even puts forward the daring paradox that 'unless one speaks of chaos, creation cannot be sufficiently considered at all'.[9]

All these theologico-linguistic arguments immediately seem to call forth counter-arguments. Von Rad, as we've seen, puts a great deal of weight on the special meaning of the word *bara*, seeing in its use proof of the Bible's decisive break with ancient Near Eastern ways of thought. But if we read on in Genesis 1 we discover that though God *bara* heaven and earth and the sea monsters, 'and every living creature that moveth... and every winged fowl', and man himself, he only '*assa* or 'made' the animals and reptiles. Does the Bible really mean to distinguish between animals and the rest in this way? Moreover, when, at the end of the sixth day, God looks back on what he has accomplished, he 'saw every thing that he had 'assa, and behold, it was very good' (1 : 31). Does this not suggest that for the author the two words, bara and 'assa, were interchangeable?

This would seem to be the implication of the parallel sentences which round off the entire first week:

> And on the seventh day God ended his work [melakhto] which he had made ['assa]; and he rested on the seventh day from all his work [melakhto] which he had made ['assa]. And God blessed the seventh day, and sanctified it: because that in it he had rested from all his work [melakhto] which God created and made [asher bara elohim la 'assot].
>
> (Gen. 2 : 2–3)

Both words are then repeated in the following verse, which acts as a transition in the narrative: 'These are the generations of the heavens and of the earth when they were created [behibaram], in the day that the Lord God made ['assa] the earth and the heavens' (2 : 4).

On the other hand, von Rad is supported by almost the entire Jewish tradition (though one commentator, Abarbanel, notes that bara is sometimes used in a passage where creation out of nothingness is not explicit, as in verse 21, where the great fish could be understood as having been formed out of the water), and a close look at the opening chapter of Genesis does suggest that the author has been at pains to stress the importance of bara: God is mentioned 28 – that is, 4 × 7 – times; there are 7 days; the word bara occurs 7 times; and when man is the object, in verse 27, bara occurs 3 times.

In the light of all this the reader today cannot but feel sympathy for those modern Nietzscheans who, faced with the confidence of von Rad and Hirsch on the one hand, and of Rashi and Speiser on the other, slyly note that God 'appears to be determined by grammar: only if his action enjoys the status of an independent sentence, and is therefore origina- tive, is he unlimited; if, on the other hand, creation is a dependent clause, then God too is subordinate to necessity'. Andrew Martin, whose remarks I have just quoted, seeks to administer the coup de grâce to those who would anchor both universe and Bible to a totally free and authoritative God, upon whose fiat the entirety of creation depends, by bringing to our attention just one more piece of philology. There is, he points out, a way of taking bereshit as an absolute. But if we do that we have to translate it 'in a beginning', to account for the absence of the definite article in the word. Thus the choice would not actually be between the absolute and the construct, but between a beginning which is only one of many and a beginning which is not really a beginning at all.[10]

The Nietzscheans would appear to have triumphed. But is the issue really quite so clear-cut? I think not, for we have not quite finished with the puzzles generated by that first phrase. If the first word does indeed look as though it had to be a construct, the second is not at all what we would expect to follow a construct. What should follow is a participle, giving us something like: 'at the beginning of the creation by God', or 'at the beginning of God's creating'. And this is in fact what we do find at 2 : 4b: 'At the time of the making by God Yahweh of earth and heaven'. If 1 : 1 were really parallel to this, as Speiser would have us believe, then it would have to read: *bereshit bero elohim*. Instead, as we have seen, it reads: *bereshit bara elohim*. *Bara* is the finite form of the verb, 'he created'. Speiser acknowledges the difficulty, but this time it is he and not von Rad who brushes it aside and insists that it is not damaging to his argument: 'Hebrew usage', he says, 'permits a finite verb in this position.'[11] And he refers us to Hosea 1 : 2, *techilat diber adonai*, 'beginning-of spoke the Lord', where we would expect 'at the beginning of the *speaking* of the Lord'. Here, though, we come up against one of the perennial problems connected with clarifying usage in the Bible: the fact that we have no other available body of Hebrew material against which to check usage. Given that fact, we have to make the best of a bad job, and it has to be said that Speiser's single example is not very convincing proof that the opening phrase is natural. Hebrew may permit a finite verb after the construct, but as we can see from the parallel expression in Genesis 2 : 4b–7, it is hardly natural. And no scholar, as far as I know, has commented on any similar oddity about the opening of *Enuma Elish*.

Where then does all this leave us? Not, I think, in the ironic impasse that Andrew Martin would seem to imply. For what has I hope become clear in the course of this protracted philological excursus is that there is something very strange about the opening sentence of the Bible. And if, instead of opting in desperation for one interpretation or the other, we ask why this should be the case, we may find that it will help us to understand a little better what the whole book is up to.

No one, in the wake of James Barr's *Biblical Words for Time* (1962), can ever again feel at ease in talking about 'the Hebrew mind' or contrasting it with 'the Greek mind'. But that does not mean, as it is sometimes taken to mean, that we cannot talk about a 'biblical' mode of perception or a 'Homeric' mode of expression. After all, that is only saying that major works have their distinctive styles, something surely no one would wish to dispute. And it is also accepted that when we read works in foreign languages, particularly works which are distant from us in time and space, we must take great care not to translate them too quickly into our own idiom. We saw in the first chapter just how difficult this precept was to follow in practice, but this doesn't mean that we shouldn't try.

In the light of this we may feel that Speiser's painstaking analysis of the first sentence (as well as of the parallel sentence from chapter 2), though designed to recreate for us the precise nuances of the Hebrew, suffers from being couched in terms of grammar and syntax derived from the Latin. Thus he argues that we have to begin with 'a dependent clause', treat verse 2 as 'a parenthetic clause', and discover 'the main clause' in verse 3. But the whole notion of subordination and dependence is alien to the Hebrew, as even a clumsy literal translation helps to bring out:

> At the beginning of created [sic] God the heaven and the earth and the earth was *tohu* and *bohu* and darkness on face of deep and the wind of God hovering over the face of waters and God said let there be light and there was light.

I have not tried to find equivalents for the mysterious words *tohu* and *bohu*, translated in AV as 'without form, and void', since no one knows exactly what they mean, and the sound would appear to convey the meaning pretty well (the French, who have what is perhaps the least distinguished vernacular Bible of any of the Western nations, have taken the terms into their everyday vocabulary, and talk unselfconsciously of 'le tohu bohu' to mean a state of confusion). I have also tried to keep the definite article only where it exists in the Hebrew.

What emerges from this is first of all that the opening phrase does indeed baffle the mind, and secondly that what is important in the passage is not this word or that but the overall rhythm established by the simple conjunction 'and' (*wa*). This being the case, the AV does much better, both here and in 2:4b–7, than any other translation, since it retains that rhythm. Readers of the AV, as of the Hebrew, find themselves rocked into a mood both of acquiescence and of expectation, grasping 'what is going on' and assenting to it, long before they have understood precisely what this is. The NEB, as usual, gets the worst of all possible worlds by opting for subordination and then not going all the way with it, deferring the main subject and verb but then cutting the sentence short and starting again with 'God said':

> In the beginning of creation, when God made heaven and earth, the earth was without form and void, with darkness over the face of the abyss, and a mighty wind swept over the surface of the waters. God said...

There is only one other major work known to me which begins with a sentence as grammatically puzzling as the Bible's and that is Proust's *À la recherche du temps perdu*: 'Longtemps, je me suis couché de bonne heure.' How is one to translate that 'longtemps'? 'For a long time' would be a translation of 'depuis longtemps', while 'long ago' would be a translation of 'il y a longtemps'; yet 'long time' does not work in English. In French, however, it seems at once perfectly acceptable and impossible to construe. As a result what it conveys to us is not meaning but the fact that a voice has begun to speak; the fact of utterance precedes meaning. The word lies there, separating what comes after it, the whole book, from everything that came before. And the ensuing pages, with their constant see-saw motion between sleep and waking, past and present, bring us slowly up to the point where most novels begin, with a clear memory, a definite story. That story, however, is forever coloured by its problematic origins, and, in its predominantly iterative procedures, keeps on reminding us of them.[12]

Proust, then, begins his long exploration of time, memory, imagination and the mysteries of the body in a kind of limbo, neither past nor present, neither in this place nor in that, but in a space and time which can only be the space and time of utterance. 'Long...temps' – the word stretches out, miming its meaning, reaching out, as we will discover, to that 'temps' with which the novel ends. Its grammatical oddity is meant to disorientate us, to stop us crossing over too quickly to some 'real' world beyond or behind the book. It holds us within the book and begins to teach us the lesson with which the whole novel will be concerned, that books, like life, are not repositories of meaning but generators of rhythm.

Something of the same sort seems to be going on in the opening words of the Hebrew Bible. They disorientate us just enough to impose their rhythm on us, but not enough to stop us moving forward. But the process is even harder to grasp than in Proust, for the world which those opening words bring into being is not just the world of the book, but (so it is asserted) the very world in which we who are reading the book exist. This is so different from the implications of most other books that we need to explore it a little more fully.

How does one start a story? There would appear to be two basic possibilities: to begin at the beginning or to begin in the middle. Epic chooses to start in the middle, partly because Homer did so, but partly for the deeper reason that epic does not so much tell a story as recount for the community the main features of its world, and it does not therefore much matter where you begin, since any opening will eventually allow you to articulate the whole.

However, before his account can get under way the epic singer has to invoke the Muse to help him:

> The wrath do thou sing, O goddess, of Peleus' son, Achilles, that baneful wrath which brought countless woes upon the Achaeans, and sent forth to Hades many valiant souls of warriors...sing thou thereof from the time when at the first there parted in strife Atreus' son, king of men, and good Achilles.
>
> Who then of the gods was it that brought these two together to contend? The son of Leto and Zeus; for he...
>
> (*Iliad*, tr. A. T. Murray, I. 1 ff.)

Tell me, O Muse, of the man of many devices, who wandered full many ways after he had sacked the sacred citadel of Troy. Many were the men whose cities he saw and whose mind he learned.... Of these things, goddess, daughter of Zeus, beginning where thou wilt, tell thou even unto us.

Now all the rest, as many as had escaped sheer destruction, were at home, safe from both war and sea, but Odysseus...

(*Odyssey*, tr. A. T. Murray, I. 1 ff.)

The pattern is the same in both cases: invocation, a foretaste of the ensuing story, a repeat of the invocation, and then the plunging into the story at a specific point. Virgil remains faithful to this model:

Arms I sing and the man who first from the coasts of Troy, exiled by fate, came to Italy and Lavinian shores; much buffeted on sea and land by violence from above, through cruel Juno's unforgiving wrath, and much enduring in war also, till he should build a city and bring his Gods to Latium.... Tell me, O Muse, the cause; wherein thwarted in will or wherefore angered, did the Queen of heaven drive a man, of goodness so wondrous, to traverse so many perils...?

There was an ancient city, ...Carthage...

(*Aeneid*, tr. H. Rushton Fairclough, I. 1 ff.)

And so does Milton:

> Of man's first disobedience, and the fruit
> Of that forbidden tree, whose mortal taste
> Brought death into the world, and all our woe,
> With loss of Eden, till one greater man
> Restore us, and regain the blissful seat,
> Sing heavenly Muse...

(*Paradise Lost*, I. 1 ff.)

By contrast the novel tells a private story, often in the first person, and, in its classic phase, it tends to start at the beginning. *David Copperfield*, for example, opens with a chapter entitled 'I Am Born':

Whether I shall turn out to be the hero of my own life, or whether that station will be held by anybody else, these pages must show. To begin my life with the beginning of my life, I record that I was born (as I have been informed and believe) on a Friday, at twelve o'clock at night. It was remarked that the clock began to strike, and I began to cry, simultaneously.

The novel, as Sterne sensed, and Dickens demonstrates with his usual wonderful naïveté, lives under the aegis of the clock. The clock starts ticking as the novel opens and does not stop until it closes.

There are, however, two major works of literature known to me which combine the timelessnes of epic with the forward drive of the novel. One, *À la recherche*, we have already glanced at. The other, Dante's *Commedia*, also begins in a strange no man's land between sleeping and waking:

> Nel mezzo del cammin di nostra vita
> mi ritrovai per una selva oscura,
> che la diritta via era smaritta.

Here 'mi ritrovai' functions rather like Proust's 'je me suis couché'. Does the narrator mean that he came to, that he 'found himself' in some metaphorical way, or perhaps that he 'found himself' *again*? As in À *la recherche* the first-person narrator acts upon us in a strange way, forcing us to identify with him partly through the rhythm established by his opening words, and partly by his fluidity, his lack of precise contours. By contrast *David Copperfield*, though written in the first person, could just as well have been written in the third. The hero, who also happens to be the narrator, at once takes on clear outlines, a specific identity. He begins with his birth, and we soon find out enough about him and his background to be able to retell his story in our own words. By contrast, there is no point in asking, with Dante and Proust, what happened before the voice started talking, because everything begins with that 'longtemps', that 'nel mezzo del cammin'.

In Homer, Virgil and Milton we begin with two figures, the poet and the Muse. Both are sharply dramatized, and out of their interaction emerges the third element, the story. In the epic tradition one begins decisively, with the object: *Mēnin aeide, thea* (the wrath sing, Goddess); *Andra moi ennepe, mousa* (the man tell to me, Muse); *Arma virumque cano* (arms and the man I sing); 'Of man's first disobedience...sing, Heavenly Muse'. In *David Copperfield*, though we begin with the birth of the narrator, it is a birth *recounted* by him later in life, when he is in full possession of his language. In Dante and Proust, on the other hand, there are not two elements, fiction and narration, song and poet, but one single thing, the voice which cuts into the envelope of silence, hesitates, gathers momentum, hesitates again, and gradually finds both a body to house the voice and a world in which that body exists. Indeed, the search for a body to house the voice is the central quest of both works, which end when that body has been found. Yet that body is nothing other than the work itself, brought into being by the voice. Thus in contrast to *Enuma Elish*, the *Iliad* and *David Copperfield*, what we witness is not the recounting of a narrative but the coming into being of what, before the work, did not exist. The tense may be past – I went to bed, I found myself – but the voice advances into a future which is always open, never known in advance; and the reader finds himself in the same position, discovering himself as he reads rather than learning the details of a series of anecdotes.

Look again now at the biblical opening. Note how the 'ands' establish themselves as the ground bass, and how the voice moves upon that bass, advancing, retreating, repeating, advancing again: 'In the beginning God created heaven and earth and the earth was...and darkness on . . . and the wind of God hovering . . . and God said, Let there be light, and there was light.' Hovering, *merachephet*, mimes that voice and its to-and-fro movement, caught so beautifully by Yeats in his late poem, 'The Long-legged Fly', with its refrain: 'Like a long-legged fly upon the stream / The mind moves upon silence'. Out of this hovering there emerges, not a story – of the fight between Marduk and Tiamat, of Achilles' anger, of the trials and tribulations of the young David Copperfield – but a world. And that world is one with the confident assertion of speech itself: 'And God said'. We who read or listen find ourselves not merely taking something in, but mouthing those words, actively involved in the first act of creation: 'And God said, Let there be light: and there was light.' There is no referent 'out there' for that first 'light': we speak the word and at its next appearance it does indeed have a reference.

The rhythm of those 'ands', however, has carried us on, rocking us gently towards a further statement which is also a return, a looking back at what has just been achieved by that creative act which came so easily and naturally: 'And God saw the light, that it was good: and God divided the light from the darkness.' It is we who affirm that it was good, as well as hearing that it was, and who, having done so, are now confident enough to accept what is inseparable from creation, division. But no sooner is the word *vayavdel*, 'and he divided', out, than the basic rhythm reasserts itself powerfully, with a new call from God (*kara* is 'to call out', 'proclaim', 'read aloud' – whence 'Koran' – rather than merely 'to name'): 'And God called out to the light: Day! and to the darkness he called: Night! And there was evening and there was morning: first day.'

And so the chapter advances, by means of the basic pattern laid down in the opening: full repetition, partial repetition, innovation – or any combination of two of these three elements. It is so intricately constructed, with that balance of symmetry and dissymmetry which Stravinsky once said was the hallmark of all great art, that it would need a musical analysis to do it justice. Nevertheless, even without using the technical tools of phonetics, and simplifying greatly, we can pick out some of its key elements.

As has often been pointed out, the first 34 verses divide into 3 days plus 3 days plus 1 day, and 7s and 3s play a binding role throughout. But note how day one relates to day two. Day one begins with two introductory verses, then: 'God said . . . God saw . . . God called'. Day two consists of three verses: 'God said . . . God made . . . God called' (6–8). What God says, however, has not got the creative power it had on day one, since it is followed by 'God made', and what God made is not this time called 'good'. As if to compensate for this, though, a new phrase is introduced: 'And it was so.' That phrase is in its turn taken up in the opening of the third day: 'And God said...and it was so' (9). Immediately after this verses 5 and 8 are picked up and verse 4 added as a climax: 'And God called the dry land Earth; and the gathering together of the waters called he Seas; and God saw that it was good' (10).

The fourth day is devoted to the creation of the sun, moon and stars. At the start of the fifth day (21) we get the word *bara* again for the first time since verse 1, followed by the phrase used in verses 4 and 10: 'And God created [*bara*] great whales, and every living creature that moveth...and God saw that it was good.' At once a new term is introduced: 'And God blessed them, saying...' (22). But again as though to compensate for this we get a repeat of verses 7, 13 and 19: 'And the evening and the morning were the fifth day' (23). There follows the making (*'assa* not *bara* this time) of the animals, and then once again at verse 26 a new element is introduced, amidst a sudden flurry of detail: 'And God said, Let us make man in our image, after our likeness: and let them have dominion...' This is the first time God talks to himself rather than uttering his creative word. The variants *tzelem* and *demut* ('image' and 'likeness' will do) hint at a new verboseness after the restraint of what has gone before, where, if two terms were used, they formed a contrast rather than acting as mere synonyms (the only parallel to *tzelem* and *demut*, ironically, is the *tohu* and *bohu* of the opening verse). All this serves to prepare us, to some extent, for the most amazing sentence of the chapter, where the word *bara* is used no less than three times (out of a total of seven): 'So God created man in his own image, in the image of God created he him; male and female created he them' (27). However new this is, though, it still echoes an earlier verse, 21 ('And God created great whales, and every living creature that moveth, which the waters brought forth abundantly, after their kind, and every winged fowl after his kind'), as the next verse echoes 22: 'And God blessed them, and God said unto them, Be fruitful, and multiply...' (28).

The last verse of chapter 1 continues the pattern of repetition and innovation: 'And God saw every thing that he had made, and, behold, it was very good. And the evening and the morning were the sixth day' (31). Day seven then begins by echoing the opening sentence: 'Thus the heavens and the earth were finished...' (2:1). The 'ands' continue, providing the matrix for the introduction of another completely new element: 'And on the seventh day God ended his work which he had made; and he rested on the seventh day.... And God blessed the seventh day, and sanctified it: because that in it he had rested from all his work which God created and made' (2:3). Yet this new word, 'rest' (*shavat*), only articulates the feeling which has been growing in us right through the first chapter, of each new element being made out of a return to a permanent point of rest, a creative centre of stillness. No wonder it is blessed and sanctified; for it is what we have been calling the ground bass of the whole.

'The Sabbath is not simply a time for rest, for relaxation. We ought to contemplate our labours from without and not just from within,' noted Wittgenstein, putting his finger on a point of vital importance.[13] For what the institution of the Sabbath does, like the use of those 'ands' to bind the opening week together, is to make visible the fact that all the separate elements spring from a ground which is prior to each one of them and yet is not utterly distinct from them. And it helps us to understand the centrality of the Sabbath both in the life of Israel and in the life of the Bible. It is one of the two basic elements that make this book what it is, that make it possible at all.

It is a commonplace of Old Testament scholarship and theology that whereas other cultures of the ancient Near East thought cyclically and wrote myths to celebrate the annual return of the spring, the Israelites thought in a linear way and wrote history to celebrate the way their God acted within history.[14] There is some truth in this, as we will see in a later chapter, but as a formulation it lacks suppleness. It does not take into account the fact that in one sense the Hebrew Bible is much more concerned with repetition and return than the other narratives which have come down to us from the ancient Near East. There are three key aspects to those narratives, which we can distinguish for the sake of convenience, though in practice they interact. First of all they are attempts to make sense of the world as it is – to explain why the sky is above the earth, why storms and floods exist, why men do not live forever. In order to do this they posit a number of gods, a storm god, a sea god, an earth goddess and so on. This leads to the third aspect, the fights that take place amongst the gods to determine who will have mastery. Thus the fragments of Canaanite myths which have come down to us deal with the fight between Baal, the God of the Storm, and Mot or Death, whose helpers are the Princes of the River and the Sea. Traces of this struggle can still be found in the Bible, particularly in Isaiah and Job, but also in the whole episode of the crossing of the Red Sea. Again, in the Akkadian epic, *Enuma Elish*, the plot is quite simple: various gods are created or born, they form alliances and fight each other, and the poem ends with the triumph of 'Marduk, who vanquished Tiamat and achieved the kingship'.[15]

Note now the role of the Sabbath in the Bible narrative. Since there is no battle of the gods there can be no dramatic structure. What then stops the narrative just ambling forward until it loses momentum and comes to a halt? In the first place the underlying rhythm and manner of progression. But what makes this underlying rhythm visible, gives it a role in the narrative, is the institution of the Sabbath. The Sabbath makes it clear that life and history are meaningful, not simply a matter of chance or the whim of the gods. God ceases his activity not out of exhaustion or defeat but purposefully, and celebrates by instituting the Sabbath. It is significant too that though the seven days clearly relate to the lunar month, the day of rest is not established on the day of the new or the full moon, so that God's decision is kept free from natural phenomena. In other words the Sabbath *explains* nothing; it *institutes* something. And thus it makes the growth of this book possible, for by instituting a pause it allows the narrative to renew itself. This, though, as we have seen, is only to bring out into the open and give a name to the principle we saw at work in the opening sentence.

Just as God looks back and sees that what he has created is very good, so we, in this moment of rest, can look back and see what a long way we have travelled. As we do so we may ask ourselves where the beginning was, and find that we are unable to answer. The rabbis, who argued at length about the precise meaning of the first verse of Genesis, were nevertheless agreed that the beginning was a mystery which had to be accepted though not understood. The Jerusalem Talmud comes up with a delightful proof of this. The Bible, it says, begins with the letter *beth*, the second letter in the Hebrew as in the English alphabet, and not with the first, *aleph*, because 'Just as the letter *beth* [ב] is closed on all sides and open only in front' – Hebrew, it must be remembered, is read from right to left – 'similarly you are not permitted to enquire what is before or what is behind, but only from the actual time of creation' (*Chagigah* 2 : 1).[16]

In this the Bible is like the *Commedia* and *À la recherche*, but unlike either epic or novel. All three suggest that there is no such thing as 'a' or 'the' beginning, there is only the activity, 'beginning'. When we begin we do not know we are doing so, but when we look back we see that we are on our way. Yet the Bible differs from the two later works in that it combines this view of origins with a sense of authority lacking in them. This is partly due to its being in the third person and not the first, and to the fact that it is impossible to separate the creator God and the narrator. This is something I will come back to. But it is also the result of the continuous confidence the narrative inspires in us. Everything that follows reinforces what has come before. It we lost confidence either in this God or in this narrative we would find, retrospectively, that we had lost confidence in the opening. This means that the rhythm we have been analysing, the see-saw motion of innovation and repetition, must be strong enough and supple enough to accommodate far greater change and variety than we have encountered in the first chapter. It must be able to cope not just with the division of night from day or land from water, but with the division of the actual focus of interest of the narrative, i.e. of man from God.

One of the most valuable results of the growing doubts about the value of the documentary hypothesis and of the new literary interest in the Bible has been that we can now see the opening three chapters of Genesis as a single unit.[17] Yet even here the tendency has been to try simply to make sense of the double Creation rather than to bring out the developing rhythm of the whole. But if what I have been saying is correct, then it is clear that the Bible works by way of minimal units laid alongside each other, the narrative being built up by slotting these together where necessary. This is an extraordinarily simple and an extraordinarily flexible system, which can lead from what could almost be described as shorthand to rich elaboration. Naturally this is made possible or perhaps reinforced by the paratactic nature of Hebrew syntax and by the denial of dualism within the narrative. The three aspects intermesh and create a narrative which can spend nine chapters getting from the Creation to Noah and his descendants, or else cover the ground in just four verses, as in Chronicles: 'Adam, Sheth, Enosh, Kenan, Mahalaleel, Jered, Henoch, Methuselah, Lamech, Noah, Shem, Ham, and Japheth' (1 Chron. 1 : 1–4).

Perhaps, to put it starkly, we need to think of the Bible – the Hebrew Bible at this point – as constructed less like St. Paul's, or even a medieval cathedral, and more like the Centre Pompidou. That is, as a huge and imposing edifice whose skeleton is quite visible and to which more and more parts can be added without altering the basic structure, and whose inner floors can be raised or lowered at will.[18]

This of course is only a rough approximation. A narrative moves in time in a way which can only apply metaphorically to architecture. Each new element in Genesis 1 helps to bring into focus prior elements which we would have overlooked had we not been alerted to them by what follows. In just the same way chapters 2–3 help bring into focus the theme of division in chapter 1. There division is seen as an almost natural and certainly benevolent activity, but that need not always be the case. To divide is to make articulation possible, to bring a world into being, but it is also to destroy a pre-existing wholeness. That is why we need to be hurried forward at the start. Here alliteration reinforces rhythm to keep us moving, while giving us the comfort of security in repetition: *bereshit bara elohim*. The *ber/bar* cuts us off from everything that came before, while the *a/i* of *bara elohim*, picking up the *i* of *bereshit*, opens us to the future. Thus the envelope of silence is cut and we are propelled forward. Further divisions follow, as we've seen, culminating in the creation of man out of the earth, *Adam* from *adamah*. Man is made in God's likeness, the same and yet other, as *bara* was the same as *bereshit* and yet other. And as God talked to himself so now he can talk to man. The narrative progresses, dividing and then healing and then dividing again.

The serpent, both in his appearance and in his function, is the personification of division. He brings real dialogue into the story for the first time, and he brings what has to come with dialogue, the possibility of lies and dissimulation. Through speech he persuades the woman to bypass language and eat of the magic fruit so as to know as much as God knows ('good and evil' are to be taken not as ethical categories but as synonymous with 'everything'), but all she and Adam come to know is that they are naked. We have seen how certain pivotal words in chapter 1 articulate the chain of creation/repetition in that chapter. In chapters 2–3 the pivotal words are *yad'a*, 'know', and *'arum*, which is what Adam and Eve are at the end of chapter 2, but also what the serpent is at the start of chapter 3: 'more *'arum* than any beast of the field' (3:1). Thus knowledge and wisdom, nakedness and subtlety, are all interconnected, and God's creative word turns into the guile of the serpent, which divides man from himself and from the woman, from God and from the Garden.

It is important to realize that the notion of nakedness here probably implies vulnerability more than sexuality. When the word is used elsewhere in the Hebrew Bible it is usually in relation to someone stripped of protective covering, perhaps even of possessions, as in Job's famous words: 'Naked (*'arum*) came I out of my mother's womb, and naked (*'arum*) shall I return thither: the Lord gave, and the Lord hath taken away; blessed be the name of the Lord' (Job 1:21).[19] Secondly we should note that the coming of death, and exile from the Garden, are not so much new and decisive events, as the Christian term 'Fall' implies, as merely further instances of that division which we saw was an essential part of the narrative from the moment the first word cut the envelope of silence. Indeed, if the institution of the Sabbath is the first major element in the structure of this book, the establishment very soon after of death as man's lot is the second. The first, through the institutionalizing of repetition, makes endless development possible; the second provides both the dynamic of change, as generation succeeds generation, and a further instance of benign repetition, as each life conforms to the limitations set upon man at the start.

In the cultures of the ancient Near East, as we've seen, myths were invented to make sense of the universe. As well as depicting the struggles of the gods the myths naturally explored the central fact about man, his mortality. For these myths man's immortality was the equivalent of the triumph of the chief god over his enemies. If, like Gilgamesh, the hero failed in his quest, that was the end of the story. In Homer too death is the end, to be avoided as long as possible, though to die heroically is the essential desire of the fighting man. In Virgil individual death is less important than the establishment of Empire, though, as Book VI of the *Aeneid* demonstrates, this is not an easy lesson to learn, or one about which Virgil feels no doubts. In the classic novel death may overtake any of the characters except, obviously enough, the hero, if the book is written in the first person – but that holds true for most third-person narratives as well. Only in the Bible, as far as I know, and just because it deals with thousands of characters and dozens of generations, does death form part of the natural rhythm of the whole. 'So teach us to number our days, that we may apply our hearts unto wisdom,' say the Psalmist. And it should occasion no surprise that the number of those days equals seventy years ('three score and ten'), since, as we've seen, the primary rhythm is first articulated in terms of threes and sevens: 'The days of our years are threescore years and ten; and if by reason of strength they be fourscore years, yet is their strength labour and sorrow; for it is soon cut off, and we fly away' (Ps. 90:12,10).

It has often been argued (most recently and forcefully by Herbert Schneidau) that the Bible sets its face against the world of the ancient Near East in its refusal of the consolations of myth or culture, of the comforts of annual cycles or of a land that is owned.[20] Again, there is much truth in this, but again the picture is too one-sided. Our analysis of the opening verses of Genesis reveals that such refusals of comfort are only possible because the Bible accepts that there is a deeper rhythm than that of the annual cycle of the seasons, a rhythm that belongs not to nature but to God. We now see that if that rhythm does not belong to the 'natural world', it does seem to belong to man. And, as is often the case, it emerges more clearly in the breach than in the observance, as when men forget the Sabbath or attempt to die like Homeric heroes or bring about the deaths of others long before their years are up. But so firmly has the rhythm been established in the opening verses that these deviations from the norm only reinforce our sense of what that norm should be.

Our sense. Because of course as readers we are privileged to see more, and therefore to understand more, than the people whose lives are recounted in the Bible. The rhythm, which spreads across the generations, is likely to be hidden from them (though, as we shall see in a later chapter, the repeated injunction to recount the old stories is specifically designed to open their eyes to these things); but it is not hidden from the reader. The rhythm, in other words, is revealed not directly, in the world, but in this book.

We move then from the initial division of the envelope of silence, through the articulation of the universe by means of division, to the separation of man from earth, of woman from man, of man and woman from the Garden and from immortality, of brother from brother as Cain asks, 'Am I my brother's keeper?' (Gen. 4:9), of all men from their inheritance as they offend God, and so to Noah, the new Adam 'who, in Gen. 9:1–9, presides over a restored world, a renewal of creation depicted in the terms and imagery of Gen. 1:26–31'.[21] But of course it is not a complete restoration, for Noah too must die, and the rhythm keeps going, as men forget the Lord, do evil, repent, are forgiven, forget again, build the Tower of Babel and are scattered over the earth. At this point the narrative pulls back and focuses on just one group, though never letting us forget that it is only one of many:

> And Abram and Nahor took them wives: the name of Abram's wife was Sarai; and the name of Nahor's wife, Milcah, the daughter of Haran, the father of Milcah, and the father of Iscah. But Sarai was barren; she had no child. And Terah took Abram his son, and Lot the son of Haran his son's son, and Sarai his daughter in law, his son Abram's wife; and they went forth with them from Ur of the Chaldees, to go into the land of Canaan; and they came unto Haran, and dwelt there. And the days of Terah were two hundred and five years: and Terah died in Haran.
>
> (Gen. 11:29–32)

The narrative is free to go on with the genealogy or to stop and pick up the thread at any one of the points left open. In Chronicles it chooses the first option: 'Shem, Arphaxad, Shelah, Eber, Peleg, Reu, Serug, Nahor, Terah, Abram; the same is Abraham. The sons of Abraham; Isaac, and Ishmael...' (1 Chron. 1:24–28). In Genesis it chooses to pause and fill out: 'Now the Lord had said unto Abram, Get thee out of thy country, and from thy kindred, and from thy father's house, unto a land that I will shew thee' (Gen. 12:1).

The Lord had spoken before, to Adam, to Cain, to Noah, even, as we saw, to himself. In all these instances except for his self-communing and his first words to Adam, he had spoken in response to a transgression. To Adam he had given a negative command: 'Of every tree of the garden thou mayest freely eat: But of the tree of the knowledge of good and evil, thou shalt not eat of it' (Gen. 2:16–17). Now, though, we have quite a new kind of command. 'Leave your country, your kindred and your father's house,' God orders Abraham. As with the opening words, *bereshit bara*, an arresting alliterative phrase urges us forward and leaves us no chance to pause or look back: *lekh lekha*, orders God, take yourself and go. It is a phrase which is used only once again in the Bible, also by God and also to Abraham: 'Take your son, your only son, whom you love, Isaac, and *lekh lekha* to the land of Moriah, and offer him there for a burnt offering upon one of the mountains which I will tell you of' (Gen. 22:2).[22] This time the forward thrust of the alliteration is barely reined in by any compensating sense of return: the brevity of the first word, *lekh*, forces the breath to leap on to *lekha*, and the repetition accentuates the urgency, an urgency carried over into the repeated *kha* sounds of the rest of the phrase: *lekh lekha me'arzkha umimoladtakha umibait avikha el ha'aretz asher arekha*.

The command this time is not to refrain but to act. To leave father and family and home and go – where? Into a land Abraham does not

know, a land and a place which God will indicate to him. It is misleading
to talk, as Speiser does, about an 'epic voyage',[23] for that suggests a
voyage which will be sung about in the future in admiration and wonder.
Even Aeneas, who has to leave a burning city and go at the bidding of his
destiny to a land he doesn't know, is, so to speak, protected from failure
and insignificance *by the poem*. It is called the *Aeneid* and from the
opening sentence we know that he is its hero. But for Abraham, as for us
reading about Abraham, there is no certainty that things will work out.
He could, presumably, ignore the voice and stay put. Moreover, he may
not be the important figure he appears to be at this moment. We will see
instances of other figures, such as Lot, Joseph, Saul, who appear to be
central to the unfolding story but who turn out to be marginal. The form
the narrative takes leaves open this possibility, since, if the narrative can
stop at any point and pick up a character or a whole tribe, it can also
abandon them, and no character or tribe can be known in advance to be
more privileged than any other. God speaks to Abraham, that is all.
Lekh lekha, he says. Get up and go.

But once again, as if to compensate for that uncompromising command, we find ourselves back in familiar territory. First of all, we have
heard God speak before, even if Abraham hasn't. Then we recall, though
Abraham cannot: 'And God blessed them, and God said unto them, Be
fruitful, and multiply, and replenish the earth, and subdue it: and have
dominon over the fish of the sea, and over the fowl of the air, and over
every living thing that moveth upon the earth' (Gen. 1:28). God does
not merely tell Abraham to get up and go. He tells him to go 'unto a land
that I will shew thee'. And he goes on: 'And I will make of thee a great
nation, and I will bless thee, and make thy name great; and thou shalt be
a blessing' (12:1–2). If Noah was a second Adam then Abraham too, it
seems, is to be granted something of the same status. Unlike Moses and
the prophets when God first speaks to them, however, Abraham shows
no inclination to argue. He at once does what God orders him to do, and
the narrative, as is its wont, makes no comment either: 'So Abram
departed, as the Lord had spoken unto him; and Lot went with him'
(12:4).

There follow famine, a descent into Egypt, the separation from Lot
(since 'the land was not able to bear them, that they might dwell
together' [13:6]), battles with other groups in the region, renewed
affirmation that Abraham's seed will grow and inherit the land. But now
the theme of Sarah's barrenness, left hanging at the end of chapter 11,
surfaces again and blossoms into the main theme, culminating in the
miraculous birth of Isaac from a mother long past the age of child-
bearing, and then comes that second *lekh lekha* and its equally
miraculous outcome.[24]

Genesis is no doubt made up of many strands of tradition, but what is important is how these have been blended together. To understand how it functions it is necessary to put aside comparisons with myth and saga, short story, drama and novel. Comparisons with specific works, such as *Enuma Elish* or *A la recherche*, as we've seen, prove far more useful. But, it will be asked, are not comparisons of the Bible with Dante and Proust pointlessly anachronistic? I don't think the issue is one of anachronism exactly. Artistic history does not move forward in a straight line, and artists in every age find ways of escaping from the immediate past by going backward in time and outward in space. Virgil escaped from the constraints of his age by going back to Homer, Dante by going back to Virgil, Eliot by going back to Dante. There is nothing inherently surprising in the fact that readers of Proust and Joyce are more at ease with Genesis than readers of Balzac and George Eliot. We must not, of course, become hypnotized by comparisons, but only use them where they will help us.

Well then, it may be argued, what help can the first-person narratives of Dante and Proust be with a book like the Bible which, in its impersonality, is surely closer to ancient epic than to modern narrative? But it is precisely the use of the first person in Dante and Proust that can guide us to an understanding of some of the larger themes and strategies of the Bible. For as every reader knows, the first-person narrator in Dante and in Proust is a problematic figure, quite unlike Robinson Crusoe or David Copperfield. For in both *À la recherche* and the *Commedia* there is a split between the 'I' who undergoes the journey and the 'I' who narrates that journey, a split which in the fiction is almost bridged by the end, and in the work completely bridged, since the first 'I' has so completely become the second that the book itself can be written by him. Another way of putting this would be to say that the second 'I' embodies all the potential that was there in the first but which, for many reasons, was frustrated in him. The baffling thing about this, though, is that the potential is both embodied in and released by the work which recounts those frustrations and the attempts to overcome them.

When we turn to the Bible we soon become aware of a similar kind of division, but this time not between narrator and protagonist, but between Creator and creature. God, in this book, does not have features which can be described, or a biography which can be recounted, as do the gods in ancient Near Eastern myths, and in Homer and Virgil. He appears to be pure potential realized in activity. The book begins with his presence, but it is not a presence which can be seized. Who and what this God is we only learn as the relations between him and Adam and him and Adam's descendants develop; as with the *Commedia* and *À la recherche*, his potential is only realized (in both meanings of the word) in the unfolding narrative.

Yet, as always, if the Bible proves ungraspable by the intellect, it never makes a mystery of its mode of procedure. Nor does God make a mystery of himself.[25] When Moses asks him point-blank who he is, he answers as accurately as he can: *ehyeh asher ehyeh* (Exod. 3:14). Once again the standard English translation, 'I am that I am', derives from the LXX, via the Vulgate, *ego sum qui sum*. As commentators have long pointed out, that way of putting it suggests distinctions in Greek philosophy between essence and existence, being and becoming, which have no place in the Hebrew phrase. YHWH here identifies himself with the verb *haya*, to be, but as an *activity* rather than as an *essence*. YHWH has just said to Moses: 'I will be [*ehyeh*] with you' (3:12), and now he defines himself as the one who will be what he will be. In other words, he explains that he cannot be held by a name or a set of attributes, like Marduk or Juno, but will be understood in his acts and in his relations with Moses. For us this means that we will not find stories *about* him in this book, as we will find stories about Marduk in *Enuma Elish* or about Juno in the *Aeneid*, but that the stories in this book will be our only way of discovering and understanding him. In this sense Abraham and Moses and all the others who encounter YHWH in the Bible will have to respond to him as we respond to anybody we meet: we learn who and what they are over time and through how they behave in different circumstances, and there is always the possibility that we may be wrong.

There is one other aspect of the phrase *ehyeh asher ehyeh* which needs to be noted. This is that it is the almost perfect antithesis of the opening phrase, *bereshit bara*. Where that was all harsh consonants, forcing us forward towards an ever-open future, this is as near as we can get in language to pure breath, non-articulation, non-division. In uttering it God both defines himself as pure potential and repudiates the kind of definition Moses – and we – are looking for. But he also indicates by his palindromic utterance, with its repeated 'h' and 'sh' sounds, that his is the breath that lies beneath all utterance and all action, a living breath which does not move forward yet does not remain static, upholding both speech and the world.

JOSEPH AND REVELATION

C reation, revelation and redemption are the central features of the Bible, according to the theologians. On these three pillars must rest any meaningful biblical theology. In a famous essay on Buber, Gershom Scholem made the point that Buber, having lost the age-old faith in a once-and-for-all revelation, had to try and make up for it by positing a continuous and continuing revelation;[1] what Scholem says holds good for all theology after the great divide of the eighteenth century, or perhaps even, as I suggested in the opening chapter, of the sixteenth century. For the scientific study of the Bible arose at precisely the moment when it became impossible, for one reason or another, to accept that there had been an unproblematic once-and-for-all Revelation, whether on Sinai, in Galilee, or in Jerusalem. And the problem has been there from that day to this – from, let us say, Luther to the Bishop of Woolwich.

As we have seen, though, theological problems tend to melt away, or at least to change their shape, when we examine what actually happens as we read the Bible. I therefore want to read rather carefully a passage where a revelation seems to occur. It is not the revelation of God to man, but of Joseph to his brothers. It may be that coming at the issue from this direction will help us to see just how the Bible tends to work and to alter the framework of our expectations.

The examination of this passage will also have the advantage of allowing us to go on exploring the developing rhythm of Genesis, while transferring our interest from words and phrases to characters.

The episode occurs in chapter 45 of Genesis, and it is worth quoting in full, though it is well enough known, because, as we saw in the previous chapter, there tends to be a large discrepancy between our vague sense of what is in this book and what is actually there. Joseph, now the Pharaoh's right-hand man, has for a number of chapters been toying with his brothers, though they of course are not aware of it. He has made them fetch their youngest brother, Benjamin, against their father's wishes, and manoeuvred them into accepting responsibility for the theft

of a wine cup which he has had placed in Benjamin's sack. Now, feeling
that he has subjected them and his father to enough torments to make up
for his own sufferings at their hands, he decides the time has come to
reveal himself to them:

> Then Joseph could not refrain himself before all them that stood by him; and
> he cried, Cause every man to go out from me. And there stood no man with
> him, while Joseph made himself known unto his brethren. And he wept
> aloud: and the Egyptians and the house of Pharaoh heard. And Joseph said
> unto his brethren, I am Joseph; doth my father yet live? And his brethren
> could not answer him; for they were troubled at his presence. And Joseph
> said unto his brethren, come near to me, I pray you. And they came near.
> And he said, I am Joseph your brother, whom ye sold into Egypt.
>
> (Gen. 45:1–4)

The first thing to be said about this scene is that we respond to it with
the greatest of ease. We have, in a sense, been waiting for it ever since
Joseph was first thrown into the pit by his brothers. Scenes of this kind
have had a central place in Western literature from the earliest times.
What is the *Odyssey*, after all, but the long deferral of just such a
moment? And its implications were explored in the first and perhaps
greatest treatise on poetics, that of Aristotle, whose term for it,
anagnorisis, is more or less accurately defined by Liddell and Scott as
'recognition, as leading to the denouement'. Nor is it only that, as
Aristotle goes on to point out, for in tragedy such denouement involves
reversal or peripeteia. Oedipus or Agave come to know themselves at the
climax as they come to understand what it is they have done, and this
knowledge leads to a dramatic reversal in their fortunes. With this the
play comes to an end.

In comedy too revelation is the linchpin, and here as well it brings
reversal in its wake. In *Twelfth Night*, for example, it finally emerges
that there is not one Cesario, but two, Viola and Sebastian. Once this is
discovered everything falls into place. Recognition here takes the form
of identification ('My father had a mole upon his brow.' 'And so had
mine'), a process parodied by Ionesco in *The Bald Prima Donna*, but
already treated ironically by Euripides in his *Electra*.

In both tragedy and comedy, then, revelation seems to mean the
knitting up of the plot and the discovery of the truth at last. And this
pattern is not confined to drama. The novel too seems committed to it,
the classic form being that of the orphan who discovers his paternity,
which makes marriage and the end of the work possible. In detective
stories it is society, in the form of the detective, which discovers and
removes the murderer, thus allowing normal life to start again and also
bringing the book to an end.[2]

Here the novel, like drama, harks back to Aristotle. But I wonder if the pattern would have retained as firm a hold as it has on the Western imagination had it not been for another, far more influential work, the Christian Bible. For what else do we find there but a pattern in which, after an initial series of revelations of God to his people, all grows murky and confused until He appears again in the form of Jesus, first to John the Baptist, then to the disciples, and finally to the whole world? Appropriately, the book closes with a section entitled Revelation.

What I want to suggest in this chapter is that the effect of all this is not simply to incorporate the Hebrew Bible into the larger Christian Bible, but to blind us to the particular mode of narration of the Hebrew Bible.

The Joseph episodes must not be seen either as distinct from the rest of Genesis or as a closed unit. To start from either of those assumptions is to make it very difficult to see what is there. Yet this is precisely what we find von Rad doing:

> The stories about Joseph are clearly distinguished from those about Abraham and Jacob, and are a real connected narrative and not a compilation of many previously independent traditions. As regards their literary form, they call for a totally different judgement from that passed on the stories about Abraham, Isaac, or Jacob, which are to some extent composed of cultic or local units of tradition. The Joseph stories are didactic narrative, such as we find in the Wisdom literature.[3]

This shows some of the things that happen as we transform ourselves from readers into critics. Von Rad is of course quite right that the Joseph episodes give us a longer sweep than those of Jacob — but then those of Jacob have themselves more continuity than those about Abraham. The Egyptian milieu in which the Joseph stories are mostly set also means that they do incorporate many elements of the Wisdom literature common to the ancient Near East. But does that mean that 'they call for a totally different judgement from that passed' on the earlier stories? Or that we can call them simply 'didactic narrative'?

But if the scholar's concern for sources and origins hampers von Rad's response, that is not to say that the critic concerned to respond to the Bible 'as literature' is any less free of constraining assumptions. Errol McGuire, for example, in an essay on the Joseph story, begins his analysis by saying: 'The drama opens. . . in the midst of both great love and profound hatred, and will ultimately close with all hatred being swallowed up in love'.[4] The model of a play has already made it impossible for him to see what is there before him. For this is not drama but narrative. It does not 'open' at chapter 37, nor, as we shall see, 'close' at chapter 45 (or 50) of Genesis. For Joseph's story is, after all, only an episode in Jacob's story, which begins at chapter 25 and only ends with

Jacob's death in 49. Unless this is understood the story of Judah and
Tamar will not begin to make sense. And even Jacob's story, of course, is
only an episode in the larger story of Israel, which begins in chapter 11
and does not have an end; and that, as we saw in the previous chapter, is
itself only an episode in the larger history of the world, which begins in
chapter 1. To take the episodes in the Bible as individual units and talk
about 'the story of Joseph' or 'the story of David's succession' is already to
make certain assumptions about the kind of book this is – an anthology
– which are totally unwarranted. These assumptions, as we can see, are
to be found both in the scholar who sees every bit of the book in terms of
its sources, and, since these sources are distinct, must then see the stories
as distinct; and in the critic who unthinkingly brings to this book notions
of literary form, such as drama and short story, which really have no
place here.

Genesis 45 is in no sense equivalent to the final scene of a play. What
happens in that chapter is going to be partially completed only in chapter
50. Moreover, the long speech of Joseph's which follows the four verses
already quoted, and which takes up the first half of the chapter, must not
be read as the recital of timeless truths, as the pretext for a sermon or a
theological treatise, but as an individual's *utterance*. Something is going
on here which is not and cannot be entirely expressed in words. The
reader has witnessed the bafflement and fear of the brothers as they are
accused of being spies, have one of their number held back as hostage,
return for a second time, leave, find the silver mysteriously in their sacks
and are once more dragged before the terrifying ruler of the land. The
tension has been gradually building up in us as readers: when, we wonder, will Joseph have done tormenting them? When will he reveal himself to them?

At last, as we have seen, he does so. He can no longer 'refrain
himself'. He calls for the hall to be cleared and finally reveals himself to
his brothers. But, having said: 'I am Joseph, your brother, whom ye sold
into Egypt', he goes on:

> Now therefore be not grieved, nor angry with yourelves, that ye sold me
> hither: for God did send me before you to preserve life. For these two years
> hath the famine been in the land. . . . And God sent me before you to
> preserve you a posterity in the earth, and to save your lives by a great
> deliverance. So now it was not you that sent me hither, but God: and he hath
> made me a father to Pharaoh, and lord of all his house, and a ruler through-
> out all the land of Egypt. Haste ye, and go up to my father, and say unto him.
> Thus saith thy son Joseph, God hath made me lord of all Egypt: come down
> unto me, tarry not: And thou shalt dwell in the land of Goshen, and thou
> shalt be near unto me, thou, and thy children, and thy children's children,
> and thy flocks, and thy herds, and all that thou hast: And there will I nourish
> thee. . . . And, behold, your eyes see, and the eyes of my brother Benjamin,

that it is my mouth that speaketh unto you. And ye shall tell my father of all my glory in Egypt, and of all that ye have seen; and ye shall haste and bring down my father hither. And he fell upon his brother Benjamin's neck, and wept; and Benjamin wept upon his neck. Moreover he kissed all his brethren, and wept upon them: and after that his brethren talked with him.

(Gen. 45 : 5–15)

Before revealing himself to them, we are told, Joseph 'wept aloud: and the Egyptians and the house of Pharaoh heard'. Now at the end of his speech he falls upon Benjamin's neck and weeps some more. He is clearly in a highly emotional state. And what about the brothers? The fascinating thing about this scene is their silence. Even when at the end we are told that 'his brethren talked with him' we are given no indication of what they said. Perhaps because the narrator feels it would be superfluous, since in a sense we can imagine what they felt and need not hear them expressing it.

But can we? Is it not possible to read in their silence something other than total acquiescence in Joseph's mood? As always in the Bible this is mere conjecture from silence. But we are given a hint of what their reaction might have been five chapters later, when we read about Jacob's death:

And when Joseph's brethren saw that their father was dead, they said, Joseph will peradventure hate us, and will certainly requite us all the evil which we did unto him. And they sent a messenger unto Joseph, saying, Thy father did command before he died, saying, So shall ye say unto Joseph, Forgive, I pray thee now, the trespass of thy brethren, and their sin; for they did unto thee evil: and now, we pray thee, forgive the trespass of the servants of the God of thy father. And Joseph wept when they spake unto him. And his brethren also went and fell down before his face; and they said, Behold, we be thy servants. And Joseph said unto them, Fear not: for am I in the place of God? But as for you, ye thought evil against me; but God meant it unto good, to bring to pass, as it is this day, to save much people alive. Now therefore fear ye not: I will nourish you, and your little ones. And he comforted them, and spake kindly unto them.

(Gen. 50: 15–21)

Did Jacob really issue such a command before he died? We will never know. What this tells us though is that the brothers have never ceased to fear that Joseph would revenge himself upon them for what they had done to him. They are so afraid, now that the restraining hand of Jacob has been removed, that they don't even dare speak directly to Joseph, but instead send a message to him. Reading this we recall the opening of chapter 45. Joseph says to them: 'I am Joseph; doth my father yet live?' But 'his brethren could not answer him; for they were troubled at his presence'.

And they are right to be troubled, and to be afraid at Jacob's death. People in this book have long memories, and if Joseph seems emotional and sincere, then after all so does David. Yet David's treatment of Shimei shows that emotiveness and a long memory for injuries received are not incompatible.

Shimei is a man of the house of Saul. When David is leaving Jerusalem in disarray, retreating before the advance of his son Absalom's troops, Shimei comes out of the hills and curses him, calling him a 'bloody man' and a 'man of Belial', and saying:

> The Lord hath returned upon thee all the blood of the house of Saul, in whose stead thou hast reigned; and the Lord hath delivered the kingdom into the hand of Absalom thy son: and, behold, thou art taken in thy mischief, because thou art a bloody man.
>
> (2 Sam. 16:8)

David restrains Abishai, who wants to kill Shimei, and they move on. Later, when he returns to Jerusalem after his victory over Absalom, this same Shimei comes rushing forward to meet him:

> And said unto the king, Let not my lord impute iniquity unto me, neither do thou remember that which thy servant did perversely the day that my lord the king went out of Jerusalem, that the king should take it to his heart. For thy servant doth know that I have sinned: therefore, behold, I am come the first this day of all the house of Joseph to go down to meet my lord the king.
>
> (2 Sam. 19:19–20)

Once again Abishai wishes to kill him and once again David restrains him: 'And David said. . .shall there any man be put to death this day in Israel? for do not I know that I am this day king over Israel? Therefore the king said unto Shimei, Thou shalt not die. And the king sware unto him' (19:22–23).

However, it is always as well to listen carefully to an enemy's oaths. When, years later, David is on his death-bed, he calls his son and heir Solomon to him, 'and he charged Solomon his son, saying, I go the way of all the earth: be thou strong therefore, and shew thyself a man' (1 Kings 2:1–2); and, having urged Solomon always to walk in the Lord's way, David gives him a few last specific instructions. The first concerns Joab, his troublesome military commander, to whom Solomon is to 'Do. . .according to thy wisdom, and let not his hoar head go down to the grave in peace' (6): the second concerns Barzillai, to whom he is to show kindness as Barzillai showed kindness to David 'when I fled because of Absalom thy brother' (7); the third concerns Shimei:

> And, behold, thou hast with thee Shimei the son of Gera, a Benjamite of Bahurim, which cursed me with a grievous curse in the day when I went to Mahanaim: but he came down to meet me at Jordan, and I sware to him by

the Lord, saying, I will not put thee to death with the sword. Now therefore hold him not guiltless: for thou art a wise man, and knowest what thou oughtest to do unto him; but his hoar head bring thou down to the grave with blood.

(1 Kings 2:8–9)

Having thus tidied up the loose threads in his long life, David peacefully passes away: 'So David slept with his fathers,' says the narrative, equally calm, 'and was buried in the city of David' (10).

In the light of this it is surely not unreasonable to suppose that Joseph's brothers are less than convinced by his protestations of love and forgiveness. We need to think again about that bland phrase in Genesis 45: 'and after that his brethren talked with him'. There is no final reconciliation, but only a partial and qualified one, at least on the part of the brothers, and we misread the episode if we imagine we are being presented with a reconciliation scene such as we find at the end of a Shakespeare play, where the King or Duke, going in to supper with his courtiers and such of the protagonists as are still alive (if this is a tragedy), asks to be told in detail about the events which have just occurred.

Joseph's first words to his brothers in chapter 50, 'Am I in the place of God?' (*hatachat elohim ani*), is a verbatim repetition of the phrase once used by his father Jacob at a moment which is closely connected with his own birth. For when Rachel saw that she bore Jacob no children she envied her sister Leah and said to Jacob, with the same utter directness as Esau had earlier employed when asking Jacob for his mess of potage: 'Give me children, or else I die' (30:1). Whereupon 'Jacob's anger was kindled against Rachel: and he said, Am I in God's stead [*hatachat elohim anokhi*], who hath withheld from thee the fruit of the womb?' (30:2). Here Jacob denies responsibility and uses the phrase to protect himself from Rachel's accusation, but also turns it into a reprimand to her: 'Who can see God's ways? We must trust in patience.' So now Joseph, the son who is the fruit of that patience, both accuses the brothers and reassures them: 'Your lives', he says in effect, 'have never been and could never be in my hands, but in the hands of God. Therefore fear not. No one can know God's ways, neither you nor I, but we can trust that he will always be with us.'

And yet Joseph's very next remark at least partially contradicts this, for he proceeds to tell his brothers just what God meant: 'But as for you, ye thought evil against me; but God meant it unto good' (50:20). The Hebrew is even starker: 'And you meant evil upon me, God meant it for good.' This pared-down, reticent style is, we have begun to see, *the* style of the Bible. What it implies is that we can read most episodes in any number of different ways, though always with the sense that other ways are possible. The narrative is not going to help us adjudicate between them. Here, for example, it is possible that Joseph is only pretending to be reconciled to his brothers but that as soon as their father dies he will turn on them and revenge himself for what they once did to him. It is possible that Joseph genuinely thinks he has forgiven his brothers but does not realize the depth of his resentment against them, which the brothers for their part accurately gauge, and that after their father's death he will use any slight excuse to turn against them. It is also possible that Joseph has really forgiven them from the depths of his heart but that their sense of guilt goes on troubling them and will do so for ever.

This does not, of course, exhaust the possibilities. The point is that where in works of art in the West there is usually a place at which interpretation stops and the truth appears, the Hebrew Bible does not seem to work like that. Just as we get parataxis instead of subordination at the level of syntax, so, in the narrative, we are always denied a point of view above the action. When we think we have found at last a place from which to interpret we find that it too is subject to conflicting interpretations.

The narrative, as we have seen, constantly makes use of phrases and incidents which have already occurred in different contexts, but again it doesn't draw attention to this, merely requires that we keep on the alert and make the connections ourselves. So Joseph weeps on three occasions: when he first sees Benjamin among the brothers; when he reveals himself to the brothers; and when he finally insists that all is in God's hands. Each time the tears are, as they are for all of us, a sign of the acceptance of a contradiction in the very fabric of reality. Dante, it will be recalled, made the fact of being unable to shed tears one of the greatest torments of the damned: in the bottom-most pit of Hell it is so cold that the tears freeze on the cheeks of those who try to cry. And this makes us realize how tears normally mediate between inner and outer, between our desires and the reality life deals out to us.

What is it that leads Joseph to cry when he reveals himself? First of all of course it is the sight of his beloved younger brother. Secondly it is the fact that Judah, in his long speech in chapter 44, seems for the first time to be concerned not with saving his own skin but with the terrible effect it would have on their father were Benjamin to be left behind:

> And our father said, Go again, and buy us a little food. And we said, We cannot go down: if our youngest brother be with us, then will we go down: for we may not see the man's face, except our youngest brother be with us. And thy servant my father said unto us, Ye know that my wife bare me two sons: And the one went out from me, and I said, Surely he is torn in pieces; and I saw him not since: And if ye take this also from me, and mischief befall him, ye shall bring down my gray hairs with sorrow to the grave. Now therefore

> when I come to thy servant my father, and the lad be not with us; seeing that
> his life is bound up in the lad's life; It shall come to pass, when he seeth that
> the lad is not with us, that he will die: and thy servants shall bring down the
> gray hairs of thy servant our father with sorrow to the grave.... Now there-
> fore, I pray thee, let thy servant abide instead of the lad a bondman to my
> lord; and let the lad go up with his brethren. For how shall I go up to my
> father, and the lad be not with me? lest peradventure I see the evil that shall
> come on my father.
>
> (Gen. 44:25–34)

As Alter sensitively points out, Judah is here finally acknowledging
the painful truth all siblings have to face: that there is no rhyme or reason
in parental love, or at least none that children can grasp, and that we
cannot blame our parents for loving our brothers or sisters more than
ourselves.[5] Judah, in his speech, recognizing Jacob as a person and not
just his father, is also in a sense accepting responsibility for what all the
brothers have done to Joseph. At this point their punishment is indeed
complete and Joseph can reveal himself to them. But his tears are a sign
too of the ambivalences of love and hate which bind him to his brothers
and all of them to their father.

Yet while tears cannot be counterfeited, there is such a thing as self-
delusion, even sentimentality: there is no end to the layers of the psyche.
And there are aspects of Joseph's self-revelation which should cause us
concern. It is obvious that from the start of his story he at any rate is in
no doubt that he is going to be the hero and saviour. The story of Jacob's
children, in other words, is going to be *his* story. And I use the term
advisedly, for it is not the narrator but *Joseph* who sees their lives in
terms of a story or a drama with an initial prophetic dream, a catas-
trophe, a miraculous recovery, a revelation and a final reconciliation as
all come to accept the truth of the prophetic dream.

Such dreams abolish time. When Joseph dreams at the beginning the
end is already before us:

> And he dreamed yet another dream, and told it his brethren, and said,
> Behold, I have dreamed a dream more; and, behold, the sun and the moon
> and the eleven stars made obeisance to me. And he told it to his father, and
> to his brethren: and his father rebuked him, and said unto him, What is this
> dream that thou hast dreamed? Shall I and thy mother and thy brethren
> indeed come to bow down ourselves to thee to the earth? And his brethren
> envied him; but his father observed the saying.
>
> (Gen. 37:9–11)

If this were a fairy-tale all would be simple. The dream gives validity and
meaning to the story that follows; Joseph dreams it, his father is puzzled
but accepts; his brothers show their wickedness by denying it. But though
the Bible loves to play with the implications of fairy-tale, it does so with

a purpose which is other than that of fairy-tales themselves. Most often the pattern, as we will see in the case of David and Saul, is to start with a fairy-tale opening and then subject it to reality in the form of real failure and death. At other times, as with the episodes concerning Jesus, the relation is more complex and ambiguous. And so it is here.

When they first see Joseph coming to meet them the brothers have a contemptuous phrase for him: *ba'al hachalomot halazeh bah*, they say, 'This Baal of dreams comes' (37:19). The epithet clearly means more than simply 'dreamer', as the AV translates it, though whether we translate 'Baal' as 'man' (JB), or gloss it as 'the one empowered to prophetic dreams' as von Rad does,[6] or read into it the contempt of the prophets for the local Canaanite deities, it is impossible to say – once again we are let down by the paucity of comparative material.[7] But at least dramatically, within the context in which it is spoken, the phrase suggests the anger and frustration of the brothers at Joseph's self-evaluation. It also helps us to gain distance from Joseph's own perspective. If the brothers have come through the first episode as arrogant and confident, Joseph has emerged as insensitive, to say the least, to the feelings of others.

As is the way with narrative, though, the fact that Joseph in the next few episodes is so often in danger of losing his life makes us identify with him and sympathize with him. But do we feel he learns anything from his experiences? There is surely something rather unpleasant about his insistence, in his speech in chapter 45, on his present power and glory. One could of course argue that he needs to let his father know his eminent position in Egypt so that the old man may come down to him with all his household in full confidence that Joseph will be able to support him. Nevertheless, there seems to be an element of pride and triumph in Joseph's words which jars with the idea of reconciliation the chapter appears to be presenting to us: 'Haste ye, and go up to my father, and say unto him…God hath made me lord of all Egypt…. And ye shall tell my father of all my glory in Egypt….' Joseph has not changed.

And yet he should have, for he has undergone fearsome experiences. We learn, for instance, that Joseph cried out and begged his brothers for mercy when they dropped him into the pit. Typically, we are not told this at the time, it is not turned into drama when it happens, but we hear of it in passing, much later, when the brothers begin to reflect on their actions: 'And they said one to another, We are verily guilty concerning our brother, in that we saw the anguish of his soul, when he besought us, and we would not hear; therefore is this distress come upon us' (42:21). Surely Joseph's crying out then, like his tears later, is a sign of deep inner contradiction, very different from his confidence in the opening section. He knows what God has in store for him, yet he is afraid. This is very similar to the contradiction which surfaces in Jesus' cry of fear in Gethsemane; in both cases there are moments when outer reality and the fairy-tale pattern both protagonists are convinced their lives will reveal seem to move too far apart for their comfort or for ours.

Despite this, though, Genesis 45 suggests that Joseph has not really learned anything at all. He is still the hero of his own psycho-drama. He still has in his mind's eye those early dreams, so that when he sees the brothers bowing down before him it is as though time itself had been abolished, and with it any doubts he might have had along the way. But here is where the narrative delivers its final irony, where, having played with our expectations that it would conform precisely to Joseph's dreams, it parts company with them. Indeed, given Judah's admission of guilt and willingness to make restitution, it would be profoundly troubling if it were otherwise.

I said that 'here' the narrative delivers its final irony, but there is no 'here' in this text on which we can take our stand. It is only in the light of what comes later that such a moment and such a place appears. What in fact happens is that if we do not artificially divide Genesis from Exodus and both from Judges and Samuel and Kings, we discover that a pattern is being created to which Joseph is not privy. For the fact of the matter is that it will be Judah's seed which will inherit and not Joseph's. And this is not presented to us in such a way that we are made to exclaim: 'That poor Joseph, so he was fooled all along!' The Hebrew biblical narrative does not work like that. Irony as we conceive it may be used locally, but never in the larger patternings. Instead, as I've said, the events are laid out alongside each other, without comment, and we are never allowed to know whether the pattern we see emerging at one point is the true pattern. Nevertheless, it turns out that David belongs to the house of Judah; and we have seen how Shimei, one of Saul's followers, will come to David as he returns in triumph to Jerusalem, and say: 'I am come the first this day of all the house of Joseph to go down to meet my lord the king' (2 Sam. 19 : 20). And we have seen how David dealt with Shimei. In the light of all this even Genesis 50 has to be thought about again. God *did* mean it for good, but even Joseph could not see what good it was that God meant.[8]

Fairy-tales are the natural expression of our desires. We all believe deep down that we are destined to be the heroes of the drama in which we find ourselves. As Marthe Robert has shown, the classical novel continues the fairy-tale or romance pattern,[9] and the great archetype of such a pattern is the Christian Bible (though, as I've suggested, and as we will see in more detail later, there are elements in the Gospels which function very differently and in fact recall the mode of procedure of the Hebrew Bible). The Hebrew Bible, though, seems to work very differently. Not by simply turning its back on fairy-tale in the name of 'realism', but by first accepting that we all have need of such patterns, and then placing

that need in a larger context which, for want of a better term, we may
call reality. It is in fact those who think they are privy to God's word
– Joseph, Saul, David – who have to learn that this is not the case: no
one is privy to it, not even the reader himself. The narrative refuses its
comforts to Joseph, to David, to Jesus, and to us.

If the Hebrew Bible is, in this respect, doing something very different
from the bulk of Western literature, it does show surprising affinities with
certain modern works, which also seek to place the natural desires of men
for meaning, fulfilment, even immortality, within a context of reality. I
am thinking in particular of the poems of Wallace Stevens and of Proust's
novel. In one of Stevens's late poems, for example, 'The Course of a
Particular', a cry comes to the poet, and he has, in the interests of reality,
both to respond to it and to recognize that it is not addressed to him in
particular:

> The leaves cry. . .One holds off and merely hears the cry.
> It is a busy cry, concerning someone else.
> And though one says that one is part of everything.
>
> There is a conflict, there is a resistance involved;
> And being part is an exertion that declines:
> One feels the life of that which gives life as it is.
>
> The leaves cry. It is not a cry of divine attention,
> Nor the smoke-drift of puffed-out heroes, nor human cry,
> It is the cry of leaves that do not transcend themselves,
>
> In the absence of fantasia, without meaning more
> Than they are in the final finding of the ear, in the thing
> Itself, until, at last, the cry concerns no one at all.[10]

Even more striking is the similarity of Proust's mode of narrating to
that of the Hebrew Bible: a pattern is presented and asks to be read in
one way, but subsequent events show that it should have been read quite
differently; often, further events suggest that the first reading was in fact
the correct one, but there is nothing to assure us that this is the point at
which interpretation must stop. Interestingly, Proust's method of both
dividing and linking his different chapters and books is also very close to
that of the Bible: a section comes to a definite closure and is followed by
another with a clear beginning, often years later and in another place.
Yet gradually, as the new section unfolds, elements of the earlier section
start to be picked up and we are made to sense a continuity between the
two which is deeper than that of mere chronology, alerting us to the fact
that at all times and in all cases chronology is but a weak joiner of two
moments in time. There is thus in Proust, as in the Bible, a sense of the
infinite depths of individual moments, and the awareness of the possibility of the perpetual enrichment of the material from within rather

than by mere extension. And this way of conceiving of both human existence and the material of narrative not as linear but as, so to speak, spherical, is reflected in Proust's actual working methods – which, when one comes to think of it, and making due allowance for the difference between a single author and a body of tradition, are not very different from those which we can imagine the Bible authors to have used.[11]

The Christian Bible leads to the end of time, to the fulfilment of time. When time is fulfilled everything will have been revealed. In Hebrew apocalyptic too there is an urgent desire for this, but by and large the Hebrew Bible chose a different path. It chose to stay not with the fulfilment of man's desires but with the reality of what happens to us in this life. We all long in our daily lives for an end to uncertainty, to the need for decisions and choices, with the concomitant feeling that the choices we have made may have been the wrong ones. Yet we also know that life will not provide such an end, that we will always be enmeshed in uncertainty. What is extraordinary is that a sacred book should dramatize this, rather than be the one place where we are given what we desire. But that is precisely what the Hebrew Bible does.

There is one interesting moment when Joseph does seem to understand that the world and his dreams do not coincide, does seem to see his brothers as themselves and not just his brothers, in the same way as Judah sees Jacob as a man with his own life and not just as his father. This is the strange episode when we are told that Joseph 'heard' his brothers when they, not realizing that the Egyptian prince could speak Hebrew, since he had taken care always to converse with them through an interpreter, speak among themselves in his presence. 'And they knew not that Joseph heard/understood them; for he spake unto them by an interpreter' (Gen. 42:23). Perhaps though it is the presence of this interpreter, who is not really needed, which is necessary if Joseph is ever to understand his brothers. The word shama'a, which means both 'to hear' and 'to understand', is the very word used in the episode of the Tower of Babel: God confounds men's languages so that they can no longer hear/understand one another (asher lo yishme'u ish sephat re'ehu [Gen. 11:7]).[12] Perhaps that is what the narrative is suggesting: that there is no such thing as direct communication, that we always need a decoy in order to listen properly to others, for when we speak to them face to face we are too busy trying to avoid or overcome them. And this may be the function of art: that it is something to which we can really listen because it does not address us directly.

Be that as it may, because there is an interpreter between them, and because the brothers are not speaking directly to him and yet are speaking openly, Joseph for once in his life actually listens to them. For on the whole he does not listen. He is the one who dreams, the one God guides,

the one to whom *others* have to listen. And it is perhaps for this reason
that the Bible posits a break between the first three patriarchs and all
who follow. God is always the God of Abraham, Isaac and Jacob; we
never hear of the God of Abraham, Isaac, Jacob and Joseph. And it is
Jacob the father, for all his gullibility and tendency to overdramatize, to
see himself as part of a drama (a point well brought out by Alter in his
analysis of Jacob's response to the brothers' initial story and the sight of
Joseph's coat[13]) – it is Jacob who has torn out of him, in a moment of
deep crisis, the true response, which Joseph, the interpreter of dreams,
never achieves. When Jacob wrestles with the angel he says to him: 'I
will not let you go till you bless me'. As we have seen, he does not say, as
he would in a fairy-tale, 'I will not let you go till you tell me your name',
but 'till you utter a blessing upon me'. And if there is a climax to this first
book of the Bible it is not Joseph's self-revelation in chapter 45, but
Jacob's blessing in chapter 49, which is in turn taken up and echoed at
the end of the entire Torah, in Moses' final blessing.

Blessing is utterance, not vision or revelation. Just as Genesis began
not with a vision but with a voice: *bereshit bara*, and then God saying:
'Let there be light', so it ends with Jacob saying to his sons:

> Gather yourselves together, that I may tell you that which shall befall you in
> the last days. Gather yourselves together, and hear, ye sons of Jacob; and
> hearken unto Israel your father. Reuben, thou art my firstborn, my might,
> and the beginning of my strength. . . . Judah, thou art he whom thy brethren
> shall praise: thy hand shall be in the neck of thine enemies; thy father's
> children shall bow down before thee. . . .
>
> (Gen. 49 : 1–8)

This is not prophecy, or the telling of a dream; here the act of utterance
helps bring about what is uttered. But Joseph, we can be sure, is not
listening. He is looking at the images of his greatness which pass before
his mind's eye.

In between that first utterance of God and the final utterance of Jacob
there are many revelations, but they are, at best, only partial. God
appears, to order, guide, promise, and argue – but never to explain, to
make everything clear. The Christian Bible, by contrast, ends with the
book of Revelation, which itself ends with a dire warning against those
who would add anything to the book once the final revelation has taken
place: that revelation is indeed to be the last.

On the one hand, blessing; on the other, revelation. If these are the
poles of the Jewish and Christian Bibles respectively, then it is no
wonder they ask to be read quite differently. I suggested early on that the
hold which notions of revelation have upon us may be the result of the
central place of the Christian Bible in our culture. But in the light of
what I have said about Joseph himself we need to revise this view. The
hold which notions of closure, of final understanding, have upon us may

express itself in terms derived from Aristotle or Christianity, but their roots go much deeper. What we have to say is that Christianity expresses profound desires and suggests that these can eventually be fulfilled. The Hebrew Bible refuses that consolation. The deep argument between the two may then rest upon the question of whether that fulfilment is bound to be a fake, a denial of reality, or is the expression of a reality which we persist in refusing to see.

We will return to these deep-seated tensions in later chapters. For the present it is enough to say that there is a certain kind of narration present here which is the expression of a theology. Such a narration, properly understood, is quite different from what we find in classical drama or the classic novel, and we do not simply misread but go against the entire thrust of the narrative if we persist in trying to read it in their terms. But we are also misreading if we try to read it in the open-ended structuralist terms employed by Edmund Leach.[14] For though such terms explicitly reject the notion of closure, they nevertheless suggest that the structuralist can stand on a height overlooking the narrative, and see it from the beginning to the end. But if there is no fulfilment in time in the Hebrew Bible that does not mean that time is annulled. On the contrary, time is perhaps the secret protagonist of the entire narrative, time which was moving on when Joseph was born and which will move on after his death, time which brings with it the unfolding not of a random sequence but rather of a sequence which we in our time-bound state can never grasp. Joseph's dream annihilates time, since it shows him what is to be; but the narrative which tells of Joseph and his dreams, of Ruth and Boaz and David and Solomon, bears witness to what the Psalmist summed up by saying: 'My days are like a shadow that declineth; and I am withered like grass. But thou, O Lord, shalt endure for ever; and thy remembrance unto all generations' (Ps. 102:11–12). That endurance could be described as the triumph of time over the individual; but it is also the fact that underpins the triumph of narrative over dream.

V

BUILDING THE TABERNACLE

Everyone knows the stories of Genesis and of Moses and the escape from Egypt – but what happens after that? Critics like Alter and Sternberg, whose theme is biblical narrative, have little to say about the last two-thirds of the Pentateuch, and neither do scholars like von Rad and G. E. Wright whose notion of Old Testament theology is based on the idea of a 'saving history'. One can easily see why. For the plain fact is that there is very little narrative and very little 'history' between the crossing of the Red Sea and the crossing of the Jordan.

Indeed, so little happens in the interval between these two crossings, and so powerful is the image of transition they represent, that in both the Hebrew Bible itself and in Christianity there is a strong pull towards conflating the two crossings. In Psalm 114, for example, we read:

> When Israel went out of Egypt,
> The house of Jacob from a people of strange language;
>
> Judah was his sanctuary,
> And Israel his dominion.
>
> The sea saw it, and fled:
> Jordan was driven back.

> (Ps. 114:1–3)

There is no space here between the two events: the imagination flies straight from the one to the other, and the insistent parallelism of Hebrew verse even suggests that the events were one and the same. In Christian thought both crossings are assimilated to Christ's baptism in the waters of the Jordan and so spiritualized into a type of baptism in general. St. Thomas uses this to promote 'the river' over 'the sea':[1]

> It should be said that the crossing of the Red Sea prefigures baptism insofar as baptism takes away sin. But the crossing of the River Jordan, insofar as it opens the gates of heaven, which is a more important effect of baptism, can be fulfilled only by Christ. It is more fitting then that Christ should be baptized in the Jordan rather than in the Sea.

> (*Summa Theologica*, III. 39, art. 4, ad. 1.)

Such an assimilation of the two crossings, and the consequent passing over in silence of what happened in between them, is more understandable in Christian writers than in Jewish ones. For, to the latter, the core of the Torah is of course to be found precisely in the time between: the greater part of rabbinic commentary on the Bible is commentary on the laws and commandments which form the bulk of Scripture from the middle of Exodus to the end of Deuteronomy. Surely then this is where a 'literary' reading of the Bible breaks down, where the attempt to see the Bible as a whole is doomed to failure, where the wisdom of the initial decision of Alter and Sternberg, to concentrate on narratives *in* the Bible rather than any narrative *of* the Bible, is made manifest.

There must be something perverse, one feels, in trying to pretend that passages like the following can be read in the same way as *Hamlet* or the *Commedia* or even Genesis:

> If an ox gore a man or a woman, that they die: then the ox shall be surely stoned, and his flesh shall not be eaten; but the owner of the ox shall be quit. But if the ox were wont to push with his horn in time past, and it hath been testified to his owner, and he hath not kept him in, but that he hath killed a man or a woman; the ox shall be stoned, and his owner also shall be put to death.
>
> (Exod. 21:28–29)

> These also shall be unclean unto you among the creeping things that creep upon the earth; the weasel, and the mouse, and the tortoise after his kind, And the ferret, and the chameleon, and the lizard, and the snail, and the mole. These are unclean to you among all that creep: whosoever doth touch them, when they be dead, shall be unclean until the even. And upon whatsoever any of them, when they are dead, doth fall, it shall be unclean; whether it be any vessel of wood, or raiment, or skin, or sack, whatsoever vessel it be, wherein any work is done, it must be put into water, and it shall be unclean until the even; so it shall be cleansed.
>
> (Lev. 11:29–32)

It could perhaps be argued that, read slowly, and read, as they must be, in the light of Genesis 1, both passages are quite readable. One might even argue that the first is amusing and the second wonderfully bizarre. But that is clearly not the line of defence that should be used, for it leads us precisely to the view of the Bible as 'literature' which I criticized in chapter I. No. Any defence of the laws adumbrated in Exodus, Leviticus, Numbers and Deuteronomy as being of interest to other than Orthodox Jews or historians of religion must go about things in a different way, demonstrating that they are a meaningful and necessary part of the whole.

But it is just here that the reader, even with the best will in the world, will balk. What we are presented with in these sections of the Bible, he will feel, are laws which the Israelites felt it important to write down and retain; but no one, apart from historians of law, ever reads Justinian's *Institutes*, so why pretend that these Israelite laws are any different? It is true that these are religious laws which a certain group of people still feels to be binding, but for those of us who don't, what point can there be in struggling through them?

Again, the uncomfortable answer is that, in contrast to the Greeks and Romans and the peoples of the ancient Near East, the Israelites placed their laws within a narrative context, in a book along with stories, genealogies, poems and prophecies, and even, as in Exodus, within the same portion of the book. Are we being good readers when we split up what has been put together in this way? Is it not up to us to try and understand what that putting together might imply? What sort of narrative is it that can include so much that is, to our understanding, non-narrative? Or, to put it another way, what happens to reading and listening when we get to the latter half of the book of Exodus and then to the rest of the Pentateuch?

David Damrosch has drawn attention to the way in which history and law interweave in Leviticus, and how the very theme of the book is to be found in the tension it sets up between the absolutes of law on the one hand and historical contingency on the other. Thus, as Damrosch observes, even the rites are time-bound, and 'reflect different points in the ritual year, and different problems which require the several different types of sacrifice', while 'the variant forms allow for differences in the circumstances of the people making the offerings'.[2] The one clear bit of action in the book, the sudden destruction by divine fire of Aaron's two sons in chapter 10, only serves to bring out the way in which contingency and law interact, and opens the way for chapters 11–25, which have to be understood not as non-narrative but as positively anti-narrative.

For these chapters, argues Damrosch, seek 'to reconstruct a metaphoric wholeness' from the fragmentariness of events and their narrative telling. This wholeness, however, is profoundly ambivalent, for if it harks back to Eden and forward to the Promised Land, it is adumbrated at a point in time between that past and that future, and neither in a garden nor in a city but in the wilderness of the desert. And yet, by a paradox typical of the Bible,

> the place where everything has been lost can prove to be the place where everything is gained. The stark landscape of the Wilderness seems to the people to lack any source of hope, we might say any narrative possibility, to be a dead end: 'and they said to Moses, Was it because Egypt lacked graves that you have brought us out to die in the wilderness?' (14:11) Leviticus sees the Wilderness as the necessary lacuna, between cultures and between past and future history, in which the people can receive the redemptive symbolic order of the Law.[3]

Not everyone will agree with Damrosch's argument, but it is a salutary reminder of how much damage we do to this book by focusing on isolated portions of it without regard to the rest. In this chapter I want to look not at the laws but at the other massive chunk of 'non-narrative' material in Exodus, the description of the Tabernacle which takes up the major portion of the second half of that book.

To make matters worse the description occurs twice. God first tells Moses exactly how he wants the Tabernacle built, how he wants it furnished, what clothes the priests who officiate in it are to wear; and then, after the episode of the Golden Calf, we are told exactly how the Tabernacle was in fact built, what clothes were made for the priests, and so on. Of course this kind of repetition occurs elsewhere, as when a message is sent and we are first told the content of the message as it is delivered to the messenger and then hear from his mouth exactly the same words when he delivers his message. But nowhere else do we get repetition on quite such a scale as here. Reading the instructions once is difficult enough; reading them twice seems to be beyond the powers of even the most dedicated reader. But is this not perhaps the very point the text is making? May it not be that if we ask, not What is the text saying? but What is happening to me as I read? we may be able to understand the function of the descriptions?

The instructions begin with the ark which is to find shelter in the innermost sanctuary of the Tabernacle. God says to Moses:

> And they shall make an ark of shittim wood: two cubits and a half shall be the length thereof, and a cubit and a half the breadth thereof, and a cubit and a half the height thereof. And thou shalt overlay it with pure gold, within and without shalt thou overlay it, and shalt make upon it a crown of gold round about. And thou shalt cast four rings of gold for it, and put them in the four corners thereof; and two rings shall be in the one side of it, and two rings in the other side of it. And thou shalt make staves of shittim wood, and overlay them with gold. And thou shalt put the staves into the rings by the sides of the ark, that the ark may be borne with them. The staves shall be in the rings of the ark: they shall not be taken from it.
>
> (Exod. 25 : 10–15)

Into the ark will be put 'the testimony', the two tablets Moses is to bring down from the mountain. Now follow instructions for the making of the mercy seat, the cherubim, the table for the shewbread and the seven-branched candelabrum. After that come the instructions for the making of the Tabernacle itself:

> Moreover thou shalt make the tabernacle with ten curtains of fine twined linen, and blue, and purple, and scarlet: with cherubims of cunning work shalt thou make them. The length of one curtain shall be eight and twenty cubits, and the breadth of one curtain four cubits: and every one of the

curtains shall have one measure. The five curtains shall be coupled together one to another; and other five curtains shall be coupled one to another. And thou shalt make loops of blue upon the edge of the one curtain from the selvedge in the coupling. . . . And thou shalt make fifty taches of gold, and couple the curtains together with the taches. . . . And thou shalt make curtains of goats' hair to be a covering upon the tabernacle. . . . And thou shalt make boards for the tabernacle of shittim wood standing up. Ten cubits shall be the length of a board, and a cubit and a half shall be the breadth of one board. . . . And thou shalt make bars of shittim wood. . . . And thou shalt make a vail of blue, and purple, and scarlet, and fine twined linen of cunning work: with cherubims shall it be made: . . . And thou shalt hang up the vail under the taches. . . .

(Exod. 26 : 1–33)

Then follow the instructions, equally elaborate, for the clothes of the High Priest, his breastplate, ephod, robe, coat, mitre and girdle:

And thou shalt make the robe of the ephod all of blue. And there shall be an hole in the top of it, in the midst thereof: it shall have a binding of woven work round about the hole of it, as it were the hole of an habergeon, that it be not rent. And beneath upon the hem of it thou shalt make pomegranates of blue, and of purple, and of scarlet, round about the hem thereof; and bells of gold between them round about: A golden bell and a pomegranate, a golden bell and a pomegranate, upon the hem of the robe round about. And it shall be upon Aaron to minister: and his sound shall be heard when he goeth in unto the holy place before the Lord, and when he cometh out, that he die not.

(Exod. 28 : 31–35)

Finally God gives Moses detailed instructions about the sacrifices to be offered in the Tabernacle, ending with precise details about the incense to be burned at the altar:

And the Lord said unto Moses, Take unto thee sweet spices, stacte, and onycha, and galbanum; these sweet spices with pure frankincense: of each shall there be a like weight: And thou shalt make it a perfume, a confection after the art of the apothecary, tempered together, pure and holy: and thou shalt beat some of it very small, and put of it before the testimony in the tabernacle of the congregation, where I will meet with thee: it shall be unto you most holy. And as for the perfume which thou shalt make, ye shall not make to yourselves according to the composition thereof: it shall be unto thee holy for the Lord. Whosoever shall make like unto that, to smell thereto, shall even be cut off from his people.

(Exod. 30 : 34–38)

Traditionally there have been two ways of accounting for these chapters: either to see them, with all their details of pattern and colour, as symbolic; or to see them as the blueprint for the erection of an actual tent which we can, with the help of archaeology and anthropology, reconstruct for ourselves. Those who take the latter view argue, logically enough, that we cannot read the passage properly unless we know just what an ephod is, or what the function of the cherubim was in the cultures of the ancient Near East. But within these two broad groups there are of course many differences of opinion.

There are those, like Josephus, who read the passage as symbolic of the cosmos: 'every one of these objects is intended to recall and represent the universe, as he will find it if he will consent to examine them without prejudice and with understanding.' Thus 'by placing upon the table the twelve loaves, he signifies that the year is divided into as many months'; the seven lamps stand for the seven planets, the tapestries woven of four materials the four elements, and blue when it appears signifies heaven. Then there are those, like Philo, who see it as symbolic of the soul or wisdom: 'Let us look then upon the tabernacle and the altar as ideal, the one being the idea of incorporeal virtue, and the other as the emblem of an image of it, which is perceptible by the inward senses.'[4]

Among those who would see it historically there are some who believe that the Tabernacle cannot belong to the period of Moses but must, for archaeological reasons, belong to that of the second Temple; and there are some who believe that it does indeed belong to the period of Moses and cannot, for good archaeological reasons, belong to any later date. And there are some, like von Rad, who are concerned not so much with the date and provenance of the Tabernacle itself as with the Tabernacle tradition: 'But what theological conclusions can be gathered from the almost wholly technical accounts of P's regulations for the tabernacle?' asks von Rad. 'Since their yield by way of direct theological statement is meagre in the extreme, we shall attempt to approach the question via history.'[5]

Finally we might include two more modern responses. First there are those who believe that since what we have here is no more than a set of instructions to carpenters and weavers, there is little point in reading it or trying to understand what individual phrases mean unless one is thinking of actually putting up the tent oneself. And then there are those who say it doesn't matter what the words or phrases mean and that what is important is simply to roll the sonorous language around on one's tongue.[6]

All these responses leave me uneasy. The traditional ones because they want to move too quickly from the text to another reality, whether symbolic or historical; and the modern ones because they are too cavalier in their dismissal of meaning. All fail to account for the *function* of the passage in the book as a whole, whether we think of that whole as being Exodus, the Pentateuch or the entire Bible.

But how then does it function? Comparison and contrast, Eliot said, are the main tools of the critic, and the student of the Bible, that most complex yet most reticent of books, would do well to take that advice to heart. As far as our passage is concerned, at any rate, there is no paucity of material with which to compare it within the Bible itself. In fact there are at least six other major descriptions of the making of an object of significance within the Hebrew Bible. Let us look at each of these in turn.

The most immediate and obvious comparison has to be with the Golden Calf. The episode of the making of the Calf, after all, occurs precisely between God's giving Moses his instructions about the Tabernacle and the actual making of it, so that it seems likely, to say the least, that the narrator wished us to draw some conclusions from the differences between the two episodes.

God finishes instructing Moses in what is to be done and orders him to appoint a chief builder, Bezaleel, and an assistant, Aholiab, to carry out the work; then he calls Moses up to the top of the mountain to receive the Tablets which are to be lodged in the Tabernacle. Moses goes up, takes the Tablets, and descends again with them. As he re-enters the camp, however, he finds the people worshipping a Golden Calf. In a fit of anger and despair he throws down the Tablets, shattering them, and then sets about destroying the Calf and rebuking the people.

While Moses has been up on the mountain, leaving his brother Aaron in charge, the narrative has switched to the Israelite camp:

> And when the people saw that Moses delayed to come down out of the mount, the people gathered themselves together unto Aaron, and said unto him, Up, make us gods, which shall go before us; for as for this Moses, the man that brought us up out of the land of Egypt, we wot not what is become of him. And Aaron said unto them, Break off the golden earrings which are in the ears of your wives, of your sons, and of your daughters, and bring them unto me. And all the people brake off the golden earrings which were in their ears, and brought them unto Aaron. And he received them at their hand, and fashioned it with a graving tool, after he had made it a molten calf: and they said, These be thy gods, O Israel, which brought thee up out of the land of Egypt.
>
> (Exod. 32:1–4)

Almost every feature of this forms a stark contrast with the making of the Tabernacle. Here it is the people who ask Aaron to make them 'gods which shall go before us', gods, that is, who will be visible to them; in the other it is God who instructs Moses. Here Aaron orders them to break off their golden earrings and bring them to him; in the other God says to Moses: 'Speak unto the children of Israel, that they bring me an offering: of every man that giveth it willingly with his heart ye shall take my offering' (25:2). Here Aaron makes the Calf so quickly that the object is there in less than a sentence (the Hebrew reads: 'And he fashioned it with a graving tool, and made it a molten calf ').[7] By contrast, as we have seen, the narrative lovingly lingers on every detail of the making of the Tabernacle.

When Moses descends and sees the people dancing round the Calf he hurls down the Tablets, shattering them, takes the Calf, burns it, pulverizes it, strews the remains on the water, and forces the people to drink. Only then does he turn to Aaron and ask him why he has 'brought so great a sin [Heb.: 'a great sin']' upon the people (21). Aaron answers, like Adam in the Garden, that it was not his fault but the people's: they asked him to make them a calf and he did: 'And I said unto them, whosoever hath any gold, let them break it off. So they gave it me: then I cast it into the fire, and there came out this calf' (24). Moses does not reply but turns to the people and orders the Levites to put to death all those who were guilty of the offence. Only when this is done and three thousand Israelites have been killed does he go up once again to intercede for the people before the Lord.

Now Aaron is clearly remembered in the Bible as a very different kind of person from the idolatrous monarchs who fill the pages of the book of Kings. He is not punished for making the Calf, and indeed it is from him that the line of High Priests descends. Yet what are we to make of the sudden and surprising death of his two eldest sons a short while later? They die, we are told, because they 'offered strange [*zarah*, 'illicit'] fire before the Lord, which he commanded them not' (Lev. 10:1) In fact God had expressly commanded against this in Exodus 30:9; and because they go directly against such commands 'there went out fire from the Lord, and devoured them, and they died before the Lord' (Lev. 10:2). But the question is, why do they disobey like that?

There are many examples in the Bible of earlier sins catching up with their perpetrators in unexpected – and unexplained – ways. Not only does Shimei's curse rebound upon him, but there is the example of Jacob, who tricked his elder brother out of his birthright and then was himself tricked into marrying an elder sister, while his true love, Rachel, tricked her father and later died by the wayside, an untypical death for the matriarchs and patriarchs in Genesis. Is the death of Aaron's two eldest sons in any way related to his sin in listening to the people and making for them the idol they desired? The Hebrew Bible, as ever, lets us make up our own minds.[8] There is no doubt, however, not just as to the severity of the people's sin in asking for the Calf, but as to the absolute contrast between Calf and Tabernacle in terms both of function and of construction.

There is one other place in the Bible in which a good leader is prevailed upon to make an idol for the people:

Then the men of Israel said unto Gideon, Rule thou over us, both thou, and thy son, and thy son's son also: for thou hast delivered us from the hand of

Midian. And Gideon said unto them, I will not rule over you, neither shall my son rule over you: the Lord shall rule over you. And Gideon said unto them, I would desire a request of you, that ye would give me every man the earrings of his prey.... And Gideon made an ephod thereof, and put it in his city, even in Ophrah: and all Israel went thither a whoring after it: which thing became a snare unto Gideon, and to his house.

(Judg. 8:22–27)

Here too, though the plea comes from the people, the leader immediately acquiesces; and here too the object is no sooner asked for than it is made. The ephod, as we have seen, was the elaborate cloak of the High Priest, so it seems as though Gideon, while refusing the kingship, is nevertheless setting himself up as Judge and leader. He is of course a great hero, singled out by God to save the people against their enemies. But he is also a rather ambiguous figure. The ephod becomes 'a snare unto Gideon, and to his house', and his son, after Gideon's death, makes himself king against the Lord's express command, and immediately shows what a disaster this is by trying to subdue the other Israelite tribes and bringing civil war to the community. The ambiguity surrounding Gideon gives way here to clear-cut condemnation, but what are we to think of Gideon himself, who calls his son 'My father is king' (Abimelech)?

Rather more clear-cut is the episode of the Tower of Babel. Once again it is men and not God who decide to build: 'Go to, let us build us a city and a tower, whose top may reach unto heaven; and let us make us a name, lest we be scattered abroad upon the face of the whole earth' (Gen. 11:4). We are not told how long it took them to build, but we know the tower was never finished, and that God took only a moment to disperse them: 'So the Lord scattered them abroad from thence upon the face of all the earth: and they left off to build the city' (11:8). It thus remains an uncompleted ruin, lying in the plain of Shinar, while the Golden Calf was utterly destroyed, down to the last fragment.

Shortly before the episode of the Tower there is another episode which has a bearing on our theme. The building of the Ark by Noah provides us with what is perhaps the closest parallel to the later making of the elaborate tent. The initial command comes from God: 'Make thee an ark' (Gen. 6:14). There follow precise instructions about the size and shape of the boat, and these Noah takes care to execute to the letter. When it is finally done we are told: 'Thus did Noah; according to all that God commanded him, so did he' (6:22). In the Tabernacle episode God begins by saying to Moses: 'Speak unto the children of Israel, that they bring me an offering: of every man that giveth it willingly with his heart ye shall take my offering' (Exod. 25:2; cf. 35:5). A few verses later God says to Moses, as he did to Noah: 'And let them make me a sanctuary; that I may dwell among them. According to all that I shew thee, after the pattern of the tabernacle, and the pattern of all the instruments thereof, even so shall ye make it' (25:8–9). Finally, when the Tabernacle is completed: 'According to all that the Lord commanded Moses, so the children of Israel made all the work. And Moses did look upon all the work, and, behold, they had done it as the Lord had commanded, even so had they done it: and Moses blessed them'(39:42–43).

In contrast then to the episode of the Golden Calf and of the ephod of Gideon and the Tower of Babel, we have, in both the episode of the Ark and of the Tabernacle, a plan devised by God, passed on to man, and willingly carried out by him in precise accord with the instructions. Medieval artists and commentators were close to the mark when they depicted the Ark as the first Church, sailing on the waters of the world. They read better than later scholars, who have been so busy matching the instructions to archaeological evidence that they have failed to understand the larger function of these buildings within the unfolding narrative.

This comes through even more forcefully when we compare the Tabernacle to Solomon's Temple. By and large the scholarly consensus today is that the description of the Tabernacle in Exodus is a projection backward into the past of the Temple built by Solomon.[9] Yet if we look at the events surrounding the building of the two what strikes us most forcibly are the differences rather than the similarities. God, we are told, 'gave Solomon wisdom and understanding exceeding much, and largeness of heart, even as the sand that is on the sea shore' (1 Kgs. 4:29) The word *hokhmah*, wisdom, is the very word that is applied to Bezaleel, the man appointed by God as the chief maker of the Tabernacle: 'See, I have called by name Bezaleel the son of Uri, the son of Hur, of the tribe of Judah: And I have filled him with the spirit of God, in wisdom [*hokhmah*], and in understanding, and in knowledge, and in all manner of workmanship' (Exod. 31:2–3).

However, the parallel ends there, for Solomon, planning to build, at once sends a message to Hiram, king of nearby Tyre, in which he sounds much more like the young Joseph than like either Bezaleel or Moses:

> Thou knowest how that David my father could not build an house unto the name of the Lord his God for the wars which were about him on every side, until the Lord put them under the soles of his feet. But now the Lord my God hath given me rest on every side.... And, behold, I purpose to build an house unto the name of the Lord my God, as the Lord spake unto David my father, saying, Thy son, whom I will set upon thy throne in thy room [i.e. instead of you], he shall build an house unto my name. Now therefore command thou that they hew me cedar trees out of Lebanon....
>
> (1 Kgs. 5:3–6)

Hiram is delighted with the order and promises to furnish supplies:

> And king Solomon raised a levy out of all Israel; and the levy was thirty thousand men. And he sent them to Lebanon, ten thousand a month by courses: a month they were in Lebanon, and two months at home: and Adoniram was over the levy. And Solomon had threescore and ten thousand that bare burdens, and fourscore thousand hewers in the mountains; Beside the chief of Solomon's officers which were over the work, three thousand and three hundred, which ruled over the people that wrought in the work. And the king commanded, and they brought great stones.
>
> (1 Kgs. 5:13–17)

This massive deployment of a labour force to hew and cut stone is more reminiscent of the Israelites in Egypt than of the willing makers of the Tabernacle.

Again, though, the Bible leaves it to the reader to draw his own conclusions. The description follows of the building 'which king Solomon built for the Lord'. A good deal of detail is given about the building, but it is important to note that it is always Solomon himself who is mentioned as the instigator of the project: 'So he built the house, and finished it; and covered. . .and then he built. . .' (6:9–10). The Temple takes seven years to complete, and if this suggests that a great deal of care and effort has gone into it, it is put into perspective by the information that we are now given: it takes Solomon *thirteen* years to build his own palace.

Eventually, however, both Temple and Palace are finished. 'Then spake Solomon, The Lord said that he would dwell in the thick darkness. I have surely built thee an house to dwell in, a settled place for thee to abide in forever' (8:12–13). To the assembled people he boasts: 'Blessed be the Lord God of Israel, which spake with his mouth unto David my father, and hath with his hand fulfilled it. . .' (8:15). He repeats that David himself had wanted to build a temple but that the Lord had other plans, telling him that it would not be he but

> thy son that shall come forth out of thy loins, he shall build the house unto my name. And the Lord hath performed his word that he spake, and I am risen up in the room of David my father, and sit on the throne of Israel, as the Lord promised, and have built an house for the name of the Lord God of Israel.
>
> (1 Kgs. 8:19–20)

The Lord, however, is not particularly impressed. Earlier he had said to Solomon:

> Concerning this house which thou art in building, if thou wilt walk in my statutes, and execute my judgments, and keep all my commandments to walk in them; then will I perform my word with thee, which I spake unto David thy father: And I will dwell among the children of Israel, and will not forsake my people Israel.
>
> (1 Kgs. 6:12–13)

And this is what he substantially repeats when Solomon has made an end of praising and invoking him before the people. This time he appears to the king and says:

> I have heard thy prayer and thy supplication, that thou hast made before me: I have hallowed this house, which thou hast built, to put my name there for ever; and mine eyes and mine heart shall be there perpetually. And if thou wilt walk before me, as David thy father walked, in integrity of heart... Then I will establish the throne of thy kingdom upon Israel for ever, as I promised to David thy father.
>
> (1 Kgs. 9 : 3–5)

In other words, he accepts the Temple graciously, but stresses that it was Solomon's idea from the start and that what is important as far as he is concerned is not the erection of a house for himself but that Solomon and Israel should 'walk in my way', just as David did. Are we wrong to hear in this speech a gentle rebuke to Solomon for trying to raise himself above his father?

I think not, since by chapter 11 Solomon is already turning aside from God's ways, taking foreign wives and, under their influence, drawing closer to their gods than to that of his fathers. Indeed, all his actions seem explicitly to go against the commands of God who had, in Deuteronomy, said of the king whom the Israelites would eventually set over themselves: 'he shall not multiply horses to himself.... Neither shall he multiply wives to himself, that his heart turn not away: neither shall he greatly multiply to himself silver and gold' (17 : 16–17). No wonder civil war follows, bringing in its wake the division of the kingdom, the looting of the Temple, and the eventual annihilation first of the Northern and then of the Southern Kingdom, the destruction of the Temple and the Babylonian captivity. It is as though the precarious unity achieved by David had not been able to withstand the imposition by Solomon of a concrete symbol of that unity in the form of a building for the Lord and for the King. Both Temple and Palace had been erected by setting the people to what was in effect a new form of slave labour, such as they had experienced only once before, when building the pyramids for the Egyptian Pharaohs. Too much like the Tower of Babel and too little like Noah's Ark, these buildings are in fact vain attempts to create tangible images of unity that will redound to Solomon's own glory. This was hardly what God can have meant by following his statutes and walking in his way.

We come now to the most interesting parallel, that between the building of the Tabernacle and the Creation of the world. The text itself makes the parallel clear in at least three aspects. First of all a direct link is made between Bezaleel and the God of Genesis 1: 'See, I have called by name Bezaleel the son of Uri, the son of Hur, of the tribe of Judah: and I have

filled him with the spirit of God. . .' The phrase 'spirit of God' (*ruach
elohim*) occurs rarely in the Bible, but it does occur, and strikingly, in the
second verse of Genesis: 'And the earth was without form, and void; and
darkness was upon the face of the deep. And the Spirit of God (*ruach
elohim*) moved upon the face of the waters.' It also seems to be the case
(though there is argument among the rabbis over this) that the first week
of Creation is commemorated in the first week of the liturgical year; it is
on the first day of the new liturgical year that the new world emerges
from the waters after the Flood (Gen. 8:13); and that the Tabernacle is
set up and dedicated in the wilderness (Exod. 40:2). Finally, the text
itself makes the link between the Creation of the world and of the
Tabernacle explicit, for after God has given his instructions to Moses and
filled the craftsmen with wisdom, he orders Moses to remind the people
to keep the Sabbath, for 'It is a sign between me and the children of
Israel for ever: for in six days the Lord made heaven and earth, and on
the seventh day he rested, and was refreshed' (Exod. 31:17). The
linguistic parallels too between God looking at what he had done and
Moses looking at the completed Tabernacle are striking: 'And God saw
every thing that he had made, and, behold, it was very good' (Gen.
1:31); 'And Moses did look upon all the work, and, behold, they had
done it as the Lord had commanded, even so had they done it' (Exod.
39:43). 'Thus the heavens and the earth were finished' (Gen. 2:1);
'Thus was all the work of the tabernacle of the tent of the congregation
finished' (Exod. 39:32). 'God ended his work which he had made' (Gen.
2:2); 'So Moses finished the work' (Exod. 40:33); 'And God blessed the
seventh day' (Gen. 2:3); 'And Moses blessed them' (Exod. 39:43).

Of course none of this escaped the ancient commentators. Already in
antiquity, as my earlier quotation from Josephus demonstrates, the
Tabernacle was seen as a model of the cosmos or the heavens. And there
are many examples from the ancient Near East of the temple of the god
facing his heavenly dwelling place and mirroring it.[10] The Epistle to the
Hebrews provides an interesting variant, seeing in the Tabernacle a
shadow of the heavenly sanctuary, though an imperfect one, since in the
heavenly sanctuary Christ will be the High Priest and he sacrificed
himself once only by contrast with the repeated sacrifices performed by
the High Priest of the Jews (Heb. 9).

There are, however, problems with this view. For one thing, as I have
said, throughout the many chapters which describe the making of the
Tabernacle it is nowhere spelled out that its elements must be read
symbolically. As I will try to show, it is when we attempt to move from
the piece-by-piece description of the making to a single overview of what
the Tabernacle is or looks like that we go wrong. But the Bible, here as in
many other places, is both reticent and helpful.

It is clear here that the text wants to make explicit the parallels between the making of the world and the making of the Tabernacle. But it is also clear that it wants to keep us from identifying the two. Look again at the words used to describe Moses and God looking back in satisfaction at their handiwork:

> According to all that the Lord commanded Moses, so the children of Israel made all the work. And Moses did look upon all the work, and, behold, they had done it as the Lord had commanded, even so had they done it: and Moses blessed them.
>
> (Exod. 39:42–43)

The phrase 'and behold' is normally an indicator that we should switch from the viewpoint of the narrator to that of the main character. Thus the narrator tells us that the work was done exactly as Moses had commanded, following God's instructions, and that when it was done he looked at it and it seemed to him that it had been done just as he had commanded; so he blessed the makers. When God, on the other hand, has finished making the world and all its creatures, 'God saw every thing that he had made, and, behold, it was very good' (Gen. 1:31). This is a truly extraordinary moment. The narrator, who has been a sort of absent recorder so far, now separates himself from the maker of the universe, giving us first the objective statement about the completion of the task, and then God's own personal response to it, a response as full of wonder as that of any maker looking at a finished piece of work. Moses merely 'finished the work' on the Tabernacle, but God, looking back, saw and said to himself (this is the significance of that 'behold', *hineh*): it is very good (*tov me'od*).

How does this affect our understanding of the making of the Tabernacle? The author of the most recent full-length study of Temples in ancient Israel, Haran, has to confess, when he comes to the Tabernacle: 'We are faced with a unique combination of long-winded description on the one hand and total omission of various particulars on the other.'[11] But for us by now both these aspects of the description ought to be falling into place. We have already seen that the Tabernacle stands in opposition to Solomon's Temple because it is built at God's express command, following his instructions to the letter. The earthly craftsmen are precisely that: craftsmen, not artists, inventors. What we are presented with here is a dramatization of making, not the description of a finished object. That is why both the believers in symbolism and the believers in archaeology go wrong. When Haran talks about the 'total omission of various particulars', what he means is that we cannot use the passage as a blueprint for erecting our own Tabernacle.

But that is not what the passage is about. At no time does it allow us to stand back and contemplate the finished object. The emphasis is always on making, weaving, joining:

> And every wise hearted man among them that wrought the work of the tabernacle made ten curtains of fine twined linen, and blue, and purple, and scarlet.... And he coupled the five curtains one unto another...and he made...and coupled...and he overlaid...
>
> (Exod. 36:8–38)

We are presented with dozens of elements – coloured cloths, cords, planks – but though we read about the way they are joined together, we never get a chance to see the whole, even when the tent is finally completed:

> Thus was all the work of the tabernacle of the tent of the congregation finished: and the children of Israel did according to all that the Lord commanded Moses, so did they. And they brought the tabernacle unto Moses, the tent, and all his furniture, his taches, his boards, his bars, and his pillars, and his sockets, And the covering of rams' skins dyed red, and the covering of badgers' skins, and the vail of the covering...The ark...The table...The pure candlestick...the golden altar...The hangings of the court, his pillars, and his sockets...The cloths of service to do service in the holy place ...According to all that the Lord commanded Moses, so the children of Israel made all the work.
>
> (Exod. 39:32–42)

It is important too that the object is a tent and not a stone building. It is made of poles and curtains and is only itself when in action, so to speak, as an animal cannot be adequately understood in terms of bones and skin, but needs to be studied in movement, as a living whole. So the tent is always going to be more than the kit that makes up its parts. Each time it is erected, therefore, the process of making is renewed. And it is a process we readily accede to because for us too there has been a process: the process of reading. In neither case – the erecting of the tent or reading – do we have the finished object before us. We cannot contemplate it as the Israelites contemplated the Golden Calf or the men of Gideon the ephod; we can only read, which means experience, it as an *unfolding*. The people cannot bear Moses' absence, they cannot bear not having a tangible visible God to lead them through the wilderness, just as later they will not be able to bear not having a king like the surrounding nations. But the reader is being taught otherwise.

That this is how the episode asks to be read is, I believe, borne out by the importance accorded to the Sabbath in the making of the tent. You must not work for more than six days without resting on the seventh, the Lord says. 'It is a sign between me and the children of Israel for ever: for in six days the Lord made heaven and earth, and on the seventh day he rested, and was refreshed' (Exod. 31:17). It would have been so easy for the text to have stopped after 'rested', but it doesn't. By adding that last phrase it brings home to us wonderfully what the day of rest did for the Lord: it refreshed him. It gave him back his zest for work. It recreated him, in a sense. The Hebrew word *vayinaphash*, 'and was refreshed', is connected with *nephesh*, 'soul', 'living being', 'desire', 'appetite', which we first encounter in Genesis 1:20: 'Let the waters bring forth abundantly the moving creature that hath life' – *nephesh chayah*. Thus God rested on the seventh day and was made alive once more.

In an earlier chapter we noted how the establishment of the Sabbath brought out into the open the underlying rhythm of Creation and established time as a factor in the narrative. By his insistence on its place in the making of the Tabernacle God brings out how it makes of work something other than the forced labour to which the Israelites were subjected in Egypt, and which later they would have to endure under Solomon. Keeping the Sabbath, even in the midst of a vitally important project, implies willing work, work accepted freely, and therefore done with love and care. Such work is not to be understood as individualistic and 'creative', but as the carrying out to the best of one's ability precisely allotted tasks, tasks which have been entrusted to one because of one's skill and long experience. And that of course is a definition of craft.

We can now look for the last time at the words used to describe the chief craftsman, Bezaleel:

> See, I have called by name Bezaleel the son of Uri, the son of Hur, of the tribe of Judah: And I have filled him with the spirit of God, in wisdom, and in understanding, and in knowledge, and in all manner of workmanship, To devise cunning works, to work in gold, and in silver, and in brass, And in cutting of stones, to set them, and in carving of timber, to work in all manner of workmanship.
>
> (Exod. 31:2–5)

The Hebrew phrase for 'to devise cunning works' is *lachshov macha-shavot*, and the word *choshev* can have both a good and a bad meaning, depending on the person involved. In a passage we have already looked at, Joseph says to his brothers *ve'atem chashavtem 'alai ra'ah*, 'But as for you, ye thought evil against me' (Gen. 50:20). However, where craftsmanship is concerned the word clearly has positive overtones. 'To make makings' or 'to encunning cunningnesses' might catch the sense of ancient craftsmanship, so often conveyed in Greek by the Homeric word *poikilos*, which means both 'dappled' and 'cunningly wrought', and in Latin by the Lucretian word *daedalus*, which means 'artificial', 'adorned', but also 'variegated'.[12] In this connection it is worth pointing out that the more precious the hangings in the Tabernacle, the more different-coloured threads they seem to be made out of. In contrast both with the slave work in Egypt and with the making of the Golden Calf, what we have here is a stress on the process of making as itself a sign of God's relation to man and man's to God. And, by extension, it stresses the *process* of reading, not its end. Breath, we recall, is what separates Adam from *adamah*, 'earth', and here making, resting, reading, and even living itself take on a rhythm akin to breathing. The *ruach elohim* which fills Bezaleel is echoed by the *vayinaphash* of God on the seventh day of creation, but also by our own experience as we read.

The Tabernacle is empty and it is portable. It does not contain God, it is only a place he can enter. Each time the people move on they dismantle it and carry it with them; each time they stop they set it up again. It is, as it were, a portable Sinai. In the later history of Israel there will be many attempts to find a centre, mountain or temple, from which authority can radiate downwards and outwards, but all such attempts will end in failure and destruction. There will also be many attempts to find a centre to the book which tells of these things, but they will only reveal how tenacious is our desire for centres. The book will perhaps only survive because it has many centres and none, because it too is, so to speak, empty and portable.

In Leviticus 18 : 2–5 we read:

> Speak unto the children of Israel, and say unto them, I am the Lord your God. After the doings of the land of Egypt, wherein ye dwelt, shall ye not do: and after the doings of the land of Canaan, whither I bring you, shall ye not do: neither shall ye walk in their ordinances. Ye shall do my judgments, and keep mine ordinances, to walk therein: I am the Lord your God.

Egypt and Canaan are always with us. It is not easy to take the way of the desert, the way of the mere sojourner, the *ger*. We need something firm to hold on to, and if it isn't a calf to worship or a king to obey, it is a book to which we can defer. The Hebrew Bible fully recognizes the temptation, and indeed explores its nature exhaustively. But only to point to the other, more difficult way. And yet is it really more difficult? The people have left the safety of servitude and they are heading for a land of promise which is unknown to them. No wonder they grumble and fret, begging to be led by what they can see and touch. On the way they are given two things: a set of laws which must be followed and a set of instructions for the building of a portable tent. The descriptions of the tent and of the making of the tent show us how comforting and pleasurable can be the giving up of oneself to a task in the performance of which one can take pleasure and discover one's potential. All three elements, the wandering, the tent and the laws are indeed remembered together and with pleasure in Psalm 119: 'Thy statutes have been my songs in the house of my pilgrimage' (54).

The episode of the making of the Tabernacle mirrors our own reading of it. We cannot get beyond and above the elements of the unfolding description, for we are only human, with a limited memory and an even more limited capacity for concentrating and imagining. Better in such circumstances to concentrate on the detail of the work in hand than to try and see the whole shape. And when we do this we discover that it is we too who have been the makers of this most elaborate tent. And at each rereading we remake it. It is quite other than we could ever have imagined had we tried to invent it ourselves, and yet without us it would not exist.

THE RHYTHM FALTERS:
THE BOOK OF JUDGES

Later biblical tradition seems to have had no difficulty with the book of Judges. The Jewish author of Ecclesiasticus, for example, wrote:

> And concerning the judges, every one by name, whose heart went not a whoring, Nor departed from the Lord, Let their memory be blessed. Let their bones flourish out of their place, And let the name of them that were honoured be continued upon their children.
>
> (Ecclus. 46:11)

And in the great roll-call of Old Testament figures who 'were commended' 'for faith', which forms chapter 11 of the Epistle to the Hebrews we read:

> And what shall I more say? for the time would fail me to tell of Gedeon, and of Barak, and of Samson, and of Jepthae; of David also, and Samuel, and of the prophets: Who through faith subdued kingdoms, wrought righteousness, obtained promises, stopped the mouths of lions, Quenched the violence of fire, escaped the edge of the sword, out of weakness were made strong, waxed valiant in fight, turned to flight the armies of the aliens.
>
> (Hcb. 11:32–34)

It is true, the author adds, that 'these all', despite 'having obtained a good report through faith', 'received not the promise: God having provided some better thing for us, that they without us should not be made perfect' (39–40). But both authors were in no doubt that the book of Judges presents us with a series of portraits of noble men whose memory must be perpetuated.

In modern times, however, the book has tended to be read less as a catalogue of heroes than as a set of clues to an obscure period of history. For there is no doubt that, despite the massive advances in historical knowledge, the period between the crossing of the river Jordan by Joshua and his men and the establishment of the kingdom of Israel under David, a crucial one for Israel's history, is also one for which little hard historical and archaeological evidence exists.

The story the Bible itself tells is confused in detail but relatively simple in its broad outlines. After the crossing of the Red Sea and the forty years' wandering in the wilderness, Israel finally enters the Promised Land. This, as God had warned, is already occupied by a variety of local tribes who naturally resent the intrusion of a new group into their midst. As well as having to defend themselves from armed attacks by these groups, the Israelites are in constant danger of assimilating to them and thus of abandoning the worship of YHWH for the worship of Canaanite idols. However, through the help of YHWH, and despite frequent backslidings, the Israelites do finally succeed in forging a kingdom for themselves, centred in the fortified city of Jerusalem, under a powerful leader, David.

Nineteenth-century historians and archaeologists accepted this general picture but often reversed the values it implied. Thus Sir Flinders Petrie could write:

> The invasion of the nomad hordes of Israelites on the high civilisation of the Amorite kings...must have seemed a crushing blow to all culture and advance in the arts; it was much like the terrible breaking up of the Roman Empire by the northern races, it swept away nearly all the good along with the evil; centuries were needed to regain what was lost, along with the further gain of a better moral order than that which had been destroyed.[1]

More recently, the whole story as it is presented in the Bible has come under increasing suspicion. The growing scholarly consensus seems to be that far from all Israel going down into Egypt with Jacob, only a small portion of it did so; that when the descendants of this group returned to Canaan it was to a country on the brink of a sort of peasants' revolt; and that what was really going on in the period of the Judges was something more akin to a revolution than to tribal warfare. Out of the ashes of this revolution there emerged, in due time, the little kingdom of Israel.[2]

It will clearly be a long time before historians of the ancient Near East reach agreement on what actually happened in the period between 1200 and 1000 BCE. What is important for our purposes is the way in which, once again, genuine and laudable historical curiosity has diverted attention from what the text is actually saying and doing. So anxious are scholars to peer behind it, to use its every detail as a clue leading to the proof of this or that theory of 'what really happened', that the question of how these details function within the book, or how the book itself functions within the larger whole of which it is a part, is not even asked. When some attention is paid to why the book is as it is the reasons given seem curiously weak.

What we have in Judges, we are told, is the rather crude stitching together of divers legends about different tribal heroes, made into a unity by a final redactor who added a prologue and epilogue and slipped in the

odd remark here and there to bring the account into line with the
teachings of Deuteronomy. Yet a change in attitudes is beginning to take
place, and there have been one or two relatively sophisticated attempts
to come to terms with the book as a whole, notably by Boling in his
edition and by Barry G. Webb – though both still insist on seeing
chapters 17–21 as an appendix, and neither really comes to terms with
the book's most puzzling aspects.[3]

The same is true of the often subtle and sensitive treatments of
individual episodes in the book by recent critics whose interest is not
historical. Robert Alter, for example, has a fine analysis of the story of
the fat Moabite king, Eglon, and his death at the hands of the Benjamite
freedom fighter, Ehud; while Mieke Bal has written interestingly on
Samson from a feminist and psychoanalytical perspective.[4] But neither
critic addresses the question of why these stories should be where they are
in the book or how they function within the larger economy of the
whole.

But, a critic of such an approach might argue, how can one talk of a
larger whole in this instance? Is it not obvious to every reader that the
book of Judges is in fact only a collection of disparate stories and
completely lacks the organization and patterning so obvious in the book
of Genesis or in Samuel? My response to this would be that the book of
Judges is indeed oddly fragmented and jagged, even by the standards of
the Bible, but that this is part of what it is about, not something to be
condemned. To put it in the terms we have been using so far, I would
want to argue that in this book the underlying rhythm, which was established in the very first chapter of Genesis, which was developed in the
stories of the Patriarchs and given a new dimension in the account of
the building of the Tabernacle and the giving of the laws, here comes
under such strain that it almost collapses. I would want to argue further
that it is important for the larger rhythm of the whole book that this
should occur, and that it prepares us for a re-establishment of the
rhythm, after a stutter under Saul, when David appears on the scene, and
for its eventual disintegration under the Kings of Israel and Judah. In
other words, I want to argue that the sense of fragmentation, sometimes
of parody and absurdity, which recent scholars have detected in many of
the episodes of the book of Judges, is not the result of confusion on the
part of authors and redactors, but has to be taken seriously as the central
feature of what the book itself is about.

The book of Joshua ends with a great assembly at Shechem in which
Joshua addresses the tribes and reminds them of who they are and what
the Lord has done for them:

> And Joshua gathered all the tribes of Israel to Shechem. . . . And Joshua said
> unto all the people, Thus saith the Lord God of Israel, Your fathers dwelt on

the other side of the flood in old time, even Terah, the father of Abraham, and the father of Nachor: and they served other gods. And I took your father Abraham from the other side of the flood, and led him throughout all the land of Canaan, and multiplied his seed, and gave him Isaac. And I gave unto Isaac Jacob and Esau.... I sent Moses also and Aaron, and I plagued Egypt.... And I brought your fathers out of Egypt.... And I brought you into the land of the Amorites.... And I have given you a land for which ye did not labour, and cities which ye built not, and ye dwell in them; of the vineyards and oliveyards which ye planted not do ye eat. Now therefore fear the Lord, and serve him in sincerity and in truth....

(Josh. 24:1–14)

And the people in their turn reaffirm the saving history:

God forbid that we should forsake the Lord, to serve other gods; For the Lord our God, he it is that brought us up and our fathers out of the land of Egypt, from the house of bondage, and which did those great signs in our sight, and preserved us in all the way wherein we went.

(Josh. 24:16–17)

These great passages of remembrance form a giant loop, taking us right back to the beginning of the story, to Abraham's setting out at God's command, and they touch on all the major points along the way. With that communal repetition behind us we can move forward once more.

At the end of the book of Judges there is another assembly, this time at Mizpah. But instead of a renewed affirmation of the past, the only subject is the present. And it is a most unexpected present, for what is at issue now is not the common history of the different groups, it is not even how best to fight the common enemy, but how to take revenge on one of the tribes, Benjamin, for an outrage it has committed on all the others:

And all the people arose as one man, saying, We will not any of us go to his tent, neither will we any of us turn into his house. But now this shall be the thing which we will do to Gibeah; we will go up by lot against it.... So all the men of Israel were gathered against the city, knit together as one man.

(Judg. 20:8–11)

What has knit them together is nothing other than their desire to avenge themselves on one of their own. What has happened in the course of this single short book to alter matters to such an extent?

In Deuteronomy Moses had admonished the people:

Ye shall not do after all the things that we do here this day, every man whatsoever is right in his own eyes. For ye are not as yet come to the rest and to the inheritance, which the Lord your God giveth you.

(Deut. 12:8–9)

At the beginning of Judges, though, we learn that 'the children of Israel did evil in the sight of the Lord' (2:11). And as the book nears its end this has become: 'In those days there was no king in Israel, but every man

did that which was right in his own eyes' (17:6). The first part of this
sentence is repeated at the start of chapters 18 and 19: 'In those days there
was no king in Israel', '. . . when there was no king in Israel'; and with the
final sentence of the book the entire sentence returns: 'In those days
there was no king in Israel: every man did what which was right in his
own eyes' (21:25).

We have thus moved in the course of the book from a unified
confederation under Moses' chosen successor to total fragmentation, in
which there are as many views of the world as there are individuals. It is
not surprising that in such circumstances God should seem to withdraw.
At the start God is ready to answer direct questions in a direct way:

> Now after the death of Joshua it came to pass, that the children of Israel
> asked the Lord, saying, Who shall go up for us against the Canaanites first, to
> fight against them? And the Lord said, Judah shall go up: behold, I have
> delivered the land into his hand.
>
> (Judg. 1:1–2)

But at the end God does not answer:

> And the people came to the house of God, and abode there till even before
> God, and lifted up their voices, and wept sore; And said, O Lord God of
> Israel, why is this come to pass in Israel, that there should be to day one tribe
> lacking in Israel? And it came to pass on the morrow, that the people rose
> early, and built there an altar, and offered burnt offerings and peace offerings.
>
> (Judg. 21:2–4)

No amount of human activity, however, can shake off the burden of that
silence.

But the book describes more than God's silence. From the very
beginning it seems to flaunt the loss of any meaningful speech, any
underlying rhythm. The most obvious example is to be found in the place
death has in this book. As we saw in Genesis, the fact of death is early
made a fundamental constituent of rhythm, marking out man's threescore years and ten and making possible the articulation of an idea of
permanence (the family, the tribe) linked to the idea of human limits
(the death of the individual). The book of Joshua ends with the mention
of no less than three deaths and burials:

> And it came to pass after these things, that Joshua the son of Nun, the
> servant of the Lord, died, being an hundred and ten years old. And they
> buried him in the border of his inheritance in Timnath-serah.
>
> (Josh. 24:29–30)

> And the bones of Joseph, which the children of Israel brought up out of
> Egypt, buried they in Shechem, in a parcel of ground which Jacob bought
> of the sons of Hamor the father of Shechem.
>
> (24:32)

> And Eleazar the son of Aaron died; and they buried him in a hill that
> pertained to Phinehas his son, which was given him in mount Ephraim.
>
> (24:33)

As Genesis had ended with the deaths of Jacob and Joseph, and
Deuteronomy with that of Moses, so Joshua ends with the death of
Joshua. All these are 'good' deaths. The Patriarchs die 'old and full of
years', and the rhythm of their long lives is completed by burial with
their fathers. That sense of rightness, of completion, is maintained with
Joshua.

But as soon as we enter the book of Judges we find ourselves in a
different world. Practically all the deaths in that book are unnatural and
none is followed by burial:

> And Ehud came unto him; and he was sitting in a summer parlour, which he
> had for himself alone. And Ehud said, I have a message from God unto thee.
> And he arose out of his seat. And Ehud put forth his left hand, and took the
> dagger from his right thigh, and thrust it into his belly: And the haft also
> went in after the blade; and the fat closed upon the blade, so that he could
> not draw the dagger out of his belly; and the dirt came out.
>
> (Judg. 3:20–22)

Eglon, the fat king of Moab, is taken by surprise because Ehud is left-
handed. Ehud is a Benjamite, and later we hear about 'seven hundred
chosen men lefthanded; every one could sling stones at an hair breadth,
and not miss' (20:16). These men too are Benjamites, descendants of
Benjamin, which in Hebrew means 'the son of the right hand'. I will
return later to the lack of fit in this book between name and person. For
the moment it is worth noting that most of the deaths in the book might
be called by anthropologists 'left-handed' deaths, meaning unnatural,
shockingly unnatural, deaths.[5]

Such a death, for a warrior, would be death at the hands of a woman.
In chapter 4 Sisera, the commander of the army of the king of Hazor, is
killed by a woman, Jael, when he is her guest, by having a nail driven
through his head. A little later we read of Abimelech, who murders his
seventy 'brethren' and sets himself up as king in Shechem. However,
after one victorious siege – against the Shechemites, who have rebelled
against him – he is killed trying to capture Thebez:

> And Abimelech came unto the tower, and fought against it, and went hard
> unto the door of the tower to burn it with fire. And a certain woman cast a
> piece of a millstone upon Abimelech's head, and all to brake his skull. Then
> he called hastily unto the young man his armourbearer, and said unto him,
> Draw thy sword, and slay me, that men say not of me, A woman slew him.
> And his young man thrust him through, and he died.
>
> (Judg. 9:52–54)

Despite his wish, the memory of his death at the hands of a woman is to live on and mock him. When David writes his fateful letter to Joab, instructing him to get rid of Uriah, Joab carries out his instructions and then sends the messenger back with these words:

> And if so be that the king's wrath arise, and he say unto thee, Wherefore approached ye so nigh unto the city when ye did fight? knew ye not that they would shoot from the wall? Who smote Abimelech the son of Jerubbesheth? did not a woman cast a piece of a millstone upon him from the wall, that he died in Thebez?
>
> (2 Sam. 11:20–21)

What is striking is that while Ehud and Sisera were enemies, and thus might be thought to deserve their left-handed deaths, Abimelech is an Israelite. Yet, it might be argued, he is clearly a bad lot. This is not true of Jephtha, the next Judge to whom the text devotes any amount of space, but here too the theme of sinister death persists. Jephtha rashly vows to sacrifice the first thing that comes to meet him on his return if God grants him victory over his enemies, and that thing turns out to be his own daughter. 'And it came to pass, when he saw her, that he rent his clothes, and said, Alas, my daughter! thou hast brought me very low, and thou art one of them that trouble me: for I have opened my mouth unto the Lord, and I cannot go back' (Judg. 11:35). After that we have the even more extended set of episodes connected with Samson, who does not actually die at the hands of a woman, though a woman is responsible for his death. Samson, however, is one of the few characters in the Bible to take his own life.

And so we come to the last of the left-handed deaths in the book, that of the Levite's concubine. To grasp its implications fully, we have to go back to the very first death in the book, which I deliberately omitted in my earlier account:

> And they found Adoni-bezek in Bezek: and they fought against him, and they slew the Canaanites and the Perizzites. But Adoni-bezek fled; and they pursued after him, and caught him, and cut off his thumbs and his great toes. And Adoni-bezek said, Threescore and ten kings [note the number, equivalent to the years in a natural lifetime], having their thumbs and their great toes cut off, gathered their meat under my table: as I have done, so God hath requited me. And they brought him to Jerusalem, and there he died.
>
> (Judg. 1:5–7)

This is bloodthirsty, but again it might seem reasonably fair: a foreign oppressor has done to him what he did to others. What is unnerving is that the theme of cutting up the human body returns at the end of the book, as though to stress in quite a literal way the notion of fragmentation, and this time it is not only done by one Israelite to another, but by a Levite to his wife/concubine.

This Levite has gone south from his home in Ephraim to fetch home his concubine who has run away to her father's house in Bethlehem. After a strange evening with his father-in-law, who seems unwilling to let him go, he collects her and they start back home. They think of spending the night in Jerusalem, at that time a Jebusite city, but decide against it for that reason, and go on to the Benjamite city of Gibeah. There they find no shelter till an old man, himself from Ephraim country, takes them into his house. However, the house is soon besieged by rowdy locals, who demand that the Levite be delivered to them, 'that we may know him'. The old host refuses and offers them his own daughter instead, but they are not interested.

Eventually the Levite pushes his concubine out to them and shuts the door:

> and they knew her, and abused her all the night until the morning: and when the day began to spring, they let her go. Then came the woman in the dawning of the day, and fell down at the door of the man's house where her lord was, till it was light. And her lord rose up in the morning, and opened the doors of the house, and went out to go his way: and, behold, the woman his concubine was fallen down at the door of the house, and her hands were upon the threshold. And he said unto her, Up, and let us be going. But none answered.
>
> (Judg. 19:25–28)

The dead-pan narration leaves many questions unanswered: what was in the man's mind as he pushed out his concubine? What was in his mind as he opened the door in the morning? Did he think she was merely asleep when he ordered her to get up and get ready to go? Of course we will never know, but even the most generous interpretation of his actions and remarks must leave us wondering at his sheer lack of awareness.

Robert Boling, the Anchor Bible editor of this book, tries to tidy things up a little by inserting the phrase 'for she was dead' after 'But none answered'. There is good reason for this, since the phrase is found in LXX. Boling accepts the LXX reading, asserting in his notes that the phrase was obviously 'lost through haplography due to homoioteleuton in MT'. But no reader who responds to good writing could possibly believe this. It seems much more likely that an insensitive translator felt the point needed to be driven home and thus ruined a wonderful sentence, without thereby making the actions of the Levite either more comprehensible or more excusable. The author of this book knew exactly what he was doing, and no amount of smoothing out in the interests of clarity or tact by later translators or editors can conceal this fact.[6]

The Levite proceeds to throw his concubine on to his donkey and resumes his journey:

> And when he was come into his house, he took a knife, and laid hold on his concubine, and divided her, together with her bones, into twelve pieces, and sent her into all the coasts of Israel. And it was so, that all that saw it said, There was no such deed done nor seen from the day that the children of Israel came up out of the land of Egypt unto this day: consider of it, take advice, and speak your minds.
>
> (Judg. 19:29-30)

This gives us a clue as to how we are to read the whole episode, for if the cutting up of the concubine evokes echoes of Adoni-bezek, it alerts us also to the fact that both parts of the story of the Levite have their counterparts elsewhere in the Bible. The first part reminds us of Genesis 19, when two angels come to Sodom and are given hospitality by Lot; the second reminds us of how Saul cut up a yoke of oxen into twelve pieces and sent them to the twelve tribes to urge them to rally round him against the Ammonites. Indeed, so close are the parallels that scholars have often seen the stories as versions of one another.

However, if one is not obsessed with the search for sources what strikes one is precisely the *difference* between what happens here and what happens in the other two stories. Stuart Lasine is one critic who has seen this clearly: 'Judges 19 uses Genesis 19 to show how hospitality is turned upside down when one's guests are not angels, and one lives in an age governed by human selfishness,' he says bluntly.[7] Not that there are not absurd elements in the Genesis episode. Lot offers his daughters to the besieging crowd, the angels have to pull him back from the door, he cannot make up his mind to leave Sodom in spite of the angels' insistence, and at the end of the episode he is tricked into incest by his daughters. But the parallel of course is not between Lot and the Levite but between the angel guests and the Levite. The angels blind the mob and help Lot and his family to escape, while the Levite calmly hands over his concubine to the men and then, the next day, seems completely unaware of the fact that anything unpleasant might have happened to her.

That the narrator of Judges is profoundly critical of the Levite is confirmed by the way in which the second half of the story makes use of the parallels with Saul and the oxen. It is important to notice that the nexus of towns is the same in both cases. The outrage to the Levite's concubine takes place in Gibeah, Saul's city; when the Israelites gather to discuss what should be done to the Benjamites, the only group not to join them is the one from Jabesh-Gilead, and these men are then put to the sword for not joining them. In the parallel story Saul, the newly established king of Israel, cuts up a yoke of oxen and sends a portion to each of the twelve tribes to rally them to him so that he may relieve the besieged city of Jabesh-Gilead. Why does he send the message in this form? Because 'Whosoever cometh not forth after Saul and after Samuel, so shall it be done unto his oxen' (1 Sam. 11:7). The message is understood, the tribes rally round, the city is saved from the enemy, and Saul is firmly established as king.

The action of the Levite, on the other hand, is not a sign at all. Or rather, it is a false sign, for it seems to imply that this is what the men of Gibeah have done to the woman: 'all that saw it said, There was no such deed done nor seen from the day that the children of Israel came up out of the land of Egypt unto this day' (Judg. 19:30). But not only is this not the case, it was actually as a direct result of the Levite's own action that the woman was raped and murdered. It is true that the Levite later explains that it was he who cut her up, but his whole description of what happened is a clear case of special pleading, reminding us of Adam's attempt to shift the blame to Eve over the eating of the fruit, or Aaron's to shift it on to the people for the making of the Calf. 'I came into Gibeah that belongeth to Benjamin,' says the Levite to the assembly at Mizpeh,

> I and my concubine, to lodge. And the men of Gibeah rose against me, and beset the house round about upon me by night, and thought to have slain me: and my concubine have they forced, that she is dead. And I took my concubine, and cut her in pieces, and sent her throughout all the country of the inheritance of Israel: for they have committed lewdness and folly in Israel.
>
> (Judg. 20:4–6)

As Lasine points out, the Levite still seems to be concerned only with himself: 'I came...against me...my concubine...I took...I cut...I sent...' Whether he is telling the story as he genuinely remembers it or is trying to conceal his own less than heroic role in the affair we cannot know. What is clear is that, compared with Saul's firm and clear action, there is a terrible confusion of values here and a frightening lack of correlation between action and meaning. Though he does not make precisely this point, Lasine implies it in his acute observations on the way the theme of blindness and sight in the episode relates to the general theme of the book of Judges, and of the Bible as a whole:

> Both Lot and the old host tell the mob to 'do what is good in your eyes'...to the women they offer (Gen. 19:8; Judg. 19:24). This phrase has extra significance in the book of Judges, which describes a period in which every man does what is good and right in his eyes. In Judges 19 the mob does proceed to do what is good in their eyes to the concubine, while in Genesis 19 the eyes of the mob are 'blinded' by the angels.... Even though the Levite refused to spend the night in a town which did not belong to Israel, neither

he, the old host, nor the base fellows of Gibeah act in accordance with what
is good and right *in Yahweh's eyes* [Lasine's emphasis].[8]

The deaths of Adoni-bezek and of the Levite's concubine enclose the
whole book of Judges. And they serve to alert us to the fact that though
none of the other deaths in the book is quite so gruesome, or demonstrates quite so literally the fragmentation of unity that is consequent
upon men doing what is right in their own eyes, nearly all are sinister.
The whole episode of the concubine also serves to alert us to the fact
that this book operates under the sign of irony, that to grasp its theme
fully we must be aware of the ways in which it distorts motifs and
episodes found in other parts of the Bible. We are so used to thinking of
the Bible as a serious, even a solemn book, that we find it hard to realize
that there are places where the narrative becomes as self-consciously
ironic and satirical as anything in Chaucer. Once we accept this
possibility, though, much else falls into place.

Consider, for example, the call of Gideon, At first sight it fits perfectly
into the pattern of call narratives, of which the call of Moses is perhaps
the best example. But does it?

> And the angel of the Lord appeared unto him, and said unto him, The Lord is
> with thee, thou mighty man of valour. And Gideon said unto him, Oh my
> Lord, if the Lord be with us, why then is all this befallen us?'
>
> (Judg. 6 : 12–13)

Gideon reacts like one of Chaucer's naïve narrators. Instead of saying
'Here am I', he treats the words of the angel as a simple statement of fact,
which he challenges. The Lord (for, as so often, he and his angel merge)
reassures him and says he will save Israel. Gideon, in typical fashion,
protests that he is too lowly and weak, and when the Lord insists he is the
one, asks, like Moses, for 'a sign that thou talkest with me' (17). But
instead of falling silent at this point and waiting for God to do just that,
he goes on: 'Depart not hence, I pray thee, until I come unto thee, and
bring forth my present, and set it before thee.' God, with, one feels, a
rueful shrug of his shoulders, plays along with this: 'And he said, I will
tarry until thou come again' (18).

We are then told how Gideon went indoors, 'made ready a kid, and
unleavened cakes of an ephah of flour: the flesh he put in a basket, and
he put the broth in a pot, and brought it out unto him under the oak,
and presented it' (19). If he thought they were going to have a picnic
together, however, he was mistaken. The angel tells him to set the
offerings on a rock, and causes a flame to come up which consumes them.
Then he departs. But Gideon, apparently only now accepting that this
was indeed God, cries out, 'Alas, O Lord God! for because I have seen an
angel of the Lord face to face.' But the Lord, though no longer visible,

reassures him: 'fear not: thou shalt not die' (22–23). That same night he
tells Gideon what to do. He is to go down to the altar of Baal and cut
down the grove that is there and build instead an altar to the Lord.

But even after he has done this, and after 'the Spirit of the Lord came
upon Gideon' (34), he still seems unconvinced. He now asks God to
perform a further miracle to prove he is in earnest. When Gideon lays his
fleece on the ground in the night God is to make the fleece wet with dew
and leave the surrounding earth dry. Indeed, when Gideon gets up next
day he finds the fleece soaking; but, perhaps realizing that he's asked for
the wrong thing, since it is perfectly natural for the wool to accumulate
moisture and thus no sign at all of God's special concern with him, he
asks for the reverse to occur: 'Let not thine anger be hot against me, and I
will speak but this once: let me prove, I pray thee, but this once with the
fleece; let it now be dry only upon the fleece, and upon all the ground let
there be dew' (39).

In Genesis 18, we recall, Abraham pleads with God for Sodom and
Gomorrah. God says that if he finds fifty righteous men there he will
spare the city. Abraham steadily beats him down, until finally he says:
'Oh let not the Lord be angry, and I will speak yet but this once: Peradventure ten shall be found there. And he said, I will not destroy it for
ten's sake.' (Gen. 18 : 32) The phrases, *al na yichar ladonai va'adabrah
akh hapa'am* in Genesis and *al yichar apkha bi va'adabrah akh hapa'am*
here, are too close for the echo to be a coincidence. But where A-
braham's words were part of a powerful effort to save the cities of the
plain, Gideon's are merely the admission of his own bumbling.

When we compare the call of Gideon and his response with that of
Moses it becomes even plainer that everything is not as it should be
in the Judges episode. Moses too keeps asking God for signs, and is
only satisfied after a long demonstration. But Moses, who has turned
aside to the bush out of amazement at seeing it burn and yet not burn up,
responds at once to God's calling him by name, covering his face in awe
and terror. Though he too says he is not worthy to be sent on the mission
God asks of him, his initial response is 'here am I', indicating an attitude
of concentrated attention. And it is not for himself that he is concerned;
he is only worried that the people will not understand or follow his lead.
Hence his desire for something more from God than the assurance that
he will be with him, his need for some such object as the snake-rod
which God then gives him.

If one had to characterize the call of Gideon one might say that it was
written by someone who was naïvely trying to produce a version of the
call of Moses without fully understanding its implications and with his
head full of other bits of the Bible. But one could also say that, as with
Chaucer, what we have here is a sophisticated author trying to convey
the sense of a strange discrepancy between words and deeds, between

description and event. There is of course no way of telling, but the question which thrusts itself upon us as we meet more and more of these oddities in the course of the book of Judges is, is this like a bit of mad medieval romance or is it like *Sir Thopas*? And then the further question arises: if it is the latter, what is the Bible up to?

The oddities pile up. In the very next chapter, for example, God argues that there are too many Israelites and that if they all engage with the Midianites and defeat them the victory will appear to be the people's and not God's. This is introducing a separation between reality and faith that is quite new to the narrative, and its oddity is enhanced by the extraordinary means God uses to separate out those who are to fight from the others: 'Every one that lappeth of the water with his tongue, as a dog lappeth, him shalt thou set by himself; likewise every one that boweth down upon his knees to drink' (7:5). Since it is those who lap who are chosen, commentators have tried to argue that it really requires more ingenuity to drink in this way than in the other, which is clearly false; or else they have argued that it is the less ingenious who are chosen, precisely so as to demonstrate God's power: he can defeat the enemy with the worst of tools. But when we think of how Jacob is contrasted with Esau, and how often elsewhere in the Bible we are shown that it is the wily and resourceful who are helped by God, we cannot but feel that this episode is at odds with the basic rhythm of the whole.

Shortly afterwards, when Gideon and his men are preparing to fight the enormous forces of the enemy, we learn of a dream which one of the soldiers has had, and which he recounts to a comrade: 'Behold, I dreamed a dream, and, lo, a cake of barley bread tumbled into the host of Midian, and came unto a tent, and smote it that it fell, and overturned it, that the tent lay along' (7:13). The other has no difficulty in interpreting the dream: 'This is nothing else save the sword of Gideon the son of Joash, a man of Israel: for into his hand hath God delivered Midian, and all the host' (14). Just as the action of the Levite made us recall that of the angels in Sodom, and as Gideon's bargaining with God recalls Abraham's over the two cities of the plain, so here we cannot but think back to Joseph's dreams and find this one clumsy and grotesque in comparison with them. It may be, as Boling points out, that the 'barley bread', *lechem se'orim*, is a play on the words *locheme se'arim*, 'gate-fighters',[9] but that does not make the dream any the less ridiculous.

The final words concerning Gideon are the most baffling and contradictory. After his triumphs against the Midianites, as we saw in the last chapter, he made an ephod in Ophrah, which led the people astray and became a snare to his house, though he refused to be made king. Now, as we are told of his death, the final ambiguous statement is made concerning him:

And his concubine that was in Shechem, she also bare him a son, whose name he called Abimelech. And Gideon the son of Joash died in a good old age, and was buried in the sepulchre of Joash his father, in Ophrah of the Abiezrites.

(Judg. 8 : 31–32)

Gideon dies like the Patriarchs, 'in a good old age', and is buried with his fathers. And yet this Gideon, who had refused the kingship, calls his son 'My Father is King'. As usual, though, the narrative shows no sign of being aware of the contradiction.

The episodes concerning Gideon are typical rather than unique. As I have suggested, we seem everywhere to be asked to read Judges as a parody of Genesis and Exodus. Or, perhaps better, to think of the figures as like mechanical puppets with the electricity running down or only functioning sporadically. The episodes concerning Samson bring this out most clearly, and a careful reading makes us aware of the huge gap between the Samson of later tradition, both Jewish and Christian, and the figure actually presented to us in these pages.

Samson's birth, like Gideon's call, seems at first to fit in perfectly with the tradition of the birth of a saviour:

And there was a certain man of Zorah, of the family of the Danites, whose name was Manoah; and his wife was barren, and bare not. And the angel of the Lord appeared unto the woman, and said unto her, Behold now, thou art barren, and bearest not: but thou shalt conceive, and bear a son.

(Judg. 13 : 2–3)

This child, she is told, is to be 'a Nazarite unto God from the womb', and he will 'begin to deliver Israel out of the hand of the Philistines' (5).

Now the basic meaning of the root *nzr* is 'to separate' or 'to keep separated' from profane use; thus, 'to consecrate', and the noun *nazir*, 'one consecrated to God'. Any man or woman could consecrate him or herself to God for a limited period, under the rules given in Numbers 6 : 1–21. During this period the nazir is to abstain from wine and all fermented drinks, allow his hair to grow and avoid contact with a dead body. At the end of the period he is to offer a holocaust, then shave his head and offer his hair to be burned along with the sacrifice. After that he is no longer sacred and can return to normal life. St. Paul completed a vow of this kind at Cenchrea (Acts 18 : 18), and again, along with four other men, at the Temple in Jerusalem (Acts 21 : 23–24). Scholars, referring to Amos 2 : 11–12, often argue that originally the nazirite was not a person who had made a vow but one possessed of a God-given charisma. 'The Nazirite', says Roland de Vaux, 'is a man whom God has consecrated to himself. i.e. . . . a man whom God has separated from the realm of things profane.' But only in Samson, he argues, do we find the full range of features that characterize the original Nazirite: 'His long hair was the sign of this consecration...and the source of his miraculous strength...; God had chosen Samson and given him this extraordinary strength to make him his champion.'[10]

However, de Vaux, like other scholars more concerned with origins and 'the reality underlying the Bible stories' than with what is actually said in the Bible, does not pay enough attention to the ironies and ambiguities which surround the figure of Samson from the time of his birth to his death. First of all, the vow here is not Samson's own but that of his mother, and the special care with which Samson must be protected from pollution results in the angel's telling the mother while Samson is still in her womb that *she herself* must abstain from strong drink and the eating of 'any unclean thing'. Then, in repeating the episode to her husband, the woman adds a phrase that was not in the angel's original command: 'for the child shall be a Nazarite to God from the womb to the day of his death' (Judg. 13 : 7). Now the angel appears to Manoah, who, like Gideon, is slow to recognize him, and repeats his instructions, but still not saying anything about the consecration being unto death. What are we to make of this anomaly?

The text, as usual, goes its way serenely, leaving it to the reader to struggle with the inconsistencies and oddities: 'And the woman bare a son, and called his name Samson: and the child grew, and the Lord blessed him. And the Spirit of the Lord began to move him...' (13 : 24–25). Yet what form does this Spirit take? The next words only deepen our bafflement:

> And Samson went down to Timnath, and saw a woman in Timnath of the daughters of the Philistines. And he came up, and told his father and his mother, and said, I have seen a woman in Timnath of the daughters of the Philistines: now therefore get her for me to wife. Then his father and his mother said unto him, Is there never a woman among the daughters of thy brethren, or among all my people, that thou goest to take a wife of the uncircumcised Philistines? And Samson said unto his father, Get her for me; for she pleaseth me well.
>
> (Judg. 14 : 1–3)

What are we to make of this? The narrator seems to help us at this point, only to confuse us further: 'But his father and his mother knew not that it was of the Lord,' we are told, 'that he [i.e. the Lord] sought an occasion against the Philistines: for at that time the Philistines had dominion over Israel' (14 : 4). God, we recall, hardened Pharaoh's heart so as to bring his plan for Israel to pass, but it is baffling that he should use one of his chosen people in this way, and particularly one who has been specially chosen, like the nazirite, Samson. Unlike Moses and

Isaiah, who never lose their own free will and their own consciousness even when speaking for God, and unlike Saul, who fumbles and yet is deeply aware of his lack of direction, Samson appears to be the blind instrument of God's will. And blind is the operative word, for Samson, like the rest of the Israelites in this book, seems to do merely 'what is good in his own eyes': he sees the Philistine woman, desires her, and asks for her. If there is a parallel with Pharaoh, the parallel with Shechem, the son of Hamor the Hivite, is even more striking. When Dinah, Jacob's daughter, wanders out 'to see the daughters of the land', Shechem 'saw her,...took her, and lay with her, and defiled her.... And Shechem spake unto his father Hamor, saying, Get me this damsel to wife' (Gen. 34:1–4).

Nothing that follows in the Samson story makes it any easier for us to identify him with other men specially chosen by God among the Israelites. Going down to Timnath he encounters a young lion which 'roared against him', 'And the Spirit of the Lord came mightily upon him, and he rent him as he would have rent a kid, and he had nothing in his hand' (Judg. 14:6). It is frequently the case that the spirit of the Lord descends on one of God's chosen ones so that he may save his people, but why here, in this private encounter between Samson and a wild animal? The phrase suggests that in this case we are dealing with some sort of fit or physical possession rather than with God's speaking 'with the lips' of an Isaiah. Samson does not seem to be aware of what is happening to him: the fit comes upon him, he acts, then goes his way, untouched by what has just happened:

> And after a time he returned to take her [the Philistine woman], and he turned aside to see the carcase of the lion: and, behold, there was a swarm of bees and honey in the carcase of the lion. And he took thereof in his hands, and went on eating, and came to his father and mother, and he gave them, and they did eat: but he told not them that he had taken the honey out of the carcase of the lion.
>
> (Judg. 14:8–9)

As far as the narrative is concerned it is of course important that Samson say nothing to his parents about the source of the honey, but there is no narrative necessity for the phrase, 'and he took thereof in his hands, and went on eating'. What it does is to reinforce our sense of Samson as a great big simpleton, totally unconscious of his strength or his role in God's plan, simply grabbing whatever sweet thing he desires. And what are we to make of his contact with a dead animal, since such contact is expressly forbidden a nazirite?

One of the most striking things about Samson is that he does not change and develop, as Jacob or Judah or David do. He is just the same at the end of his life as he was at the beginning. Shortly after we are told

that 'he judged Israel in the days of the Philistines twenty years' (15 : 20),
we learn that 'Then went Samson to Gaza, and saw there an harlot, and
went in unto her' (16 : 1). The Philistines besiege him, thinking that at
last they have got him, but once again the spirit of the Lord descends
upon him and he simply walks away carrying the gates of the town with
him. He falls in love with another woman, Delilah, and, as with the
earlier, unnamed woman 'of Timnath', she presses him to tell her his
secret so that she may divulge it to her countrymen, he begins by refusing,
but eventually, worn out by her nagging, gives in. But the greater
elaboration of this episode and its tragic outcome forces us to ask, if
Samson knows why she is asking and knows the danger he is in, why does
he give in at last? Once again we are faced by a gap between action and
meaning.

Mieke Bal tries to resolve the puzzle with a Freudian interpretation.
As in the story of Judah and Tamar, she argues, Samson wants to break
free of his father and mother, but fears the dangers he associates with
women (Judah, she had argued earlier, wants descendants, but fears to
give his third son to the apparently death-dealing Tamar though the law
requires him to do so). The story of Samson shows, says Bal, that he
cannot both ensure his safety and satisfy his natural desires.[11] But though
there is much to be said for such an interpretation, even within its
perspective the differences between the two stories are as striking as their
similarities. Tamar, in Genesis 38, disguises herself as a prostitute and
teaches Judah how wrong he was in his view of her; and from their union
twins are engendered, and the line perpetuated that will eventually lead
to David. In the Samson story there is complete deadlock: without the
woman there can be no continuity, but to surrender to the woman means
death and therefore also no continuity. However we look at the story it
seems to contradict everything we have so far learnt about God's ways
with men.

Nor does Samson's death resolve the ambiguities. The Philistines have
finally captured and blinded him, but his hair begins to grow again. Let
out to perform for them (as the singers in Psalm 137 are asked to perform
before their Babylonian captors), he deliberately destroys both them and
himself. He asks the boy who is leading him to place his hands against
the pillars of the building and then, for the only time in his life, he calls
on God: 'O Lord God, remember me, I pray thee, and strengthen me, I
pray thee, only this once, O God, that I may be at once avenged of the
Philistines for my two eyes' (Judg. 16 : 28). Even here, though, he asks
God to remember him only that he personally may be avenged on his
captors. There is no mention of Israel and no awareness that he has
brought this on himself:[12]

> And Samson said, Let me die with the Philistines. And he bowed himself
> with all his might; and the house fell upon the lords, and upon all the people

that were therein. So the dead which he slew at his death were more than
they which he slew in his life.

(Judg. 16:30)

Why does Samson pray to die? Because he realizes his folly? Because,
without his sight, life no longer means anything to him? However we
read it there seems to be a gulf between what the text presents us with
and the pious remarks of theologians such as Ulrich Simon, who would
have us see the 'abiding theme' of the story as 'the propriety of violence
and the ultimate justification of self-sacrifice'. Simon goes on: 'The
young fighter pilots of England, who were "the few", rose to the sky in
the true spirit which they inherited from the Bible, Shakespeare and
Milton. Without that brand of godly heroism a race is doomed.'[13] Such
rousing stuff makes for good sermons, perhaps, but only at the cost of
removing from the Bible its profound and irresolvable ambiguities.

What we are left with at the end of the Samson episodes, though, is less
a puzzle than a delightfully compressed piece of language: 'So the dead
which he slew at his death were more than they which he slew in his life.'
In Hebrew the word-play is even more striking: *vayihyu hametim asher
hemit bemoto rabim me'asher hemit bechayav*. The root of the word
'death', *mt*, is repeated three times, yet the whole ends with *chaya*, 'life',
which echoes the *yihyu*, 'they were', of the opening. This is a fitting end
to the Samson stories, for if there is one thing which can be said with
certainty about them it is that they abound in word-play. And not just
those stories, though it is most noticeable there; the whole book of
Judges pulsates with riddles, songs, parables and word-play of every kind.
Is there a special reason for this? And can we relate it to the tendency to
fragmentation we have noticed and to the striking disjunction between
action and meaning which seems to be such a feature of the book?

   In Paradise Adam names the animals: God brings them to him and he
gives each one a name, 'and whatsoever Adam called every living
creature, that was the name thereof' (Gen. 2:19). In Paradise too there
is no death. But death, as we have seen, has become a part of life and
must be accepted and integrated into the rhythm of life. That rhythm is
what is disrupted in the book of Judges: the many deaths it recounts are
sinister, they cut men off before their appointed time, and often do so
most horribly; while the lives it describes lack rhythm, lack any sense
of growth and change and development. The scholars have maintained
that what we have here is an accumulation of stories stitched together,
but this is an instance of how apparently neutral and commonsense
observations, when unrelated to any sense of the whole, actually inhibit
understanding. Nor has scholarly explanation had much to say about
the role of language in this book. But could it not be that what we are
witnessing here is an attempt to revert to an Edenic world, a world where

there are no hard choices and no responsibilities? But if that is so, then is such an attempt not doomed, since time and change and responsibility cannot simply be ignored in our world, and we cannot return to Eden simply by doing what is right in our own eyes?

Adam has only to name the beasts and that is what they are. In the book of Judges most of the names mean something: Deborah means 'honey-bee', Gideon means 'hacker', Jephtha means 'the one who opens', Gaal ben Ebed means 'loathsome son of a slave', and Tola means 'worm'. Sometimes, as in the case of Delilah ('flirtatious'), the name matches the person; more often, as with the left-handed Benjamites, there is a clear mismatch. Of course other books in the Bible play with names: Isaac (Yitzhak) is connected with Sarah's laugh, Jacob (Ya'akov) with the heel he grabs, and Hamor is a veritable donkey. But in Judges there seems to be an excess of such names, and their relation to their bearers is more often ironical or problematic. I have already mentioned the left-handed sons of the right hand, but there is also the young man Micayhu ('who is like YHWH?') who steals from his mother, the son of Gideon called Abimelech or 'My Father is King', and Samson, whose name suggests links with the sun, though his actions seem to be conducted in darkness and confusion. Far from guiding us towards an understanding of their bearers, the names seem more often to raise questions in our minds about the precise relation of word to person, language to life.

And there is no other book in which language is thrust at us so aggressively, where it more often seems a barrier to meaning rather than a guide. In chapter 5 the action is interrupted by a long song, in chapter 9 by a long parable. Phrases which one had taken to mean one thing turn out to mean another, as when Deborah tells Barak that Sisera will fall 'into the hands of a woman' (4:9), and we naturally imagine that woman will be Deborah herself, only to find that it is Sisera's apparent ally, Jael. When Gideon tries to calm the Ephraimites he does it not by explaining to them what he has done and why, but by asking them a riddle: 'Is not the gleaning of the grapes of Ephraim better than the vintage of Abiezer?' (8:2). And right through the Samson episodes, of course, we sense a veritable rage for punning and riddling.

No other character in the Bible is so closely associated with riddles. After taking the Philistine woman to wife he offers the young Philistines a riddle at the marriage feast; if they can solve it he will give them a reward. He says: 'Out of the eater came forth meat, and out of the strong came forth sweetness' (14:14). No one can possibly know the answers, but Samson's new bride winkles it out of him and the stage seems set for a climax in which we will hear uttered what we know: that the riddle refers to the honey in the lion's carcase. But instead of coming out with it the Philistines in their turn merely give Samson back a riddle: 'What is sweeter than honey? and what is stronger than a lion?' The lines (14:18) form a nice poetic parallelism: *mah matok midevash umeh 'az me'ari*. Not only that, but there are five *mems* (actually six, for *matok* starts with a double *mem*), and two glottal stops, an *'ayin* and an *aleph*, all in the space of six words. The line rears up between Samson and his triumph, between us and the resolution of the contest: it is as though the young men want to prolong the bout. Samson, however, does not blink, but comes back at them with another couplet, another kind of riddle: 'If ye had not plowed with my heifer, ye had not found out my riddle' (18). Not only do the lines form a parallelism, they also rhyme: *louley charashtem be'eglati/lo metzatem chidati*. Not only does Samson tell them what he thinks of them and of his new bride, he also, in a sense, overcomes them in the language game.

Yet the bout leaves one uneasy. Not only does Samson refuse to face the fact that there is no one to blame but himself if his secret has been found out; not only is the insult to the young men gratuitous, and, as far as we know, unfounded; but, as Mieke Bal points out, something else has been repressed, not necessarily by Samson this time, but by the way the episode is apparently resolved in the riddling game. For the answer to the riddle should surely be that the honey is found *inside* the lion, the sweet in the strong; whereas what the young men answer merely juxtaposes the two elements.[14] Their riddling answer conceals as well as reveals.

Something of this sense, both of pleasure at the skilful deployment of language and unease at the resolution of real-life issues through word games, is to be felt at the very end of the Samson story: 'So the dead which he slew at his death were more than they which he slew in his life.' It is as though the text is satisfied at its resolution in linguistic fireworks, but *we* are left with the feeling that too much has been sacrificed for the sake of the fireworks. We want the narrative to expand, we want people to speak out and say what they mean, we long for the kind of directness which is such a feature of the biblical narratives: Esau's 'Feed me, I pray thee, with that same red pottage; for I am faint' (Gen. 25:30); or Saul's 'Is this thy voice, my son David?' (1 Sam. 24:16). We want this, but we do not get it. Just as walking in God's way seems to have become an impossible task; just as we have the spectacle of a squad of Danites destroying a peaceful Philistine city (Judg. 18:27), or of a struggle among Israelites for the possession of holy men (18:14-21), so we have a narrative which seems unable to speak out honestly, but constantly evades the issue by turning everything into word games, or else reiterates the same phrase again and again: 'In those days there was no king in Israel: every man did that which was right in his own eyes.'

And yet it is language which holds out the only glimmer of hope in this world of inverted values. It is through language that we hear, in a sort of faint echo, the possibility of another world, another way of life. And if the persistent play with language leaves one uneasy, it is also a reminder of a world where men take delight not in destroying their neighbours but in fashioning praises to the Lord who created us and the world and language itself.

It is only a hint, an echo, but it is enough. Our pleasure in the verbal dexterity of Samson is a disinterested pleasure; it is not pleasure in his triumph over his foes but in his revelation of the possibilities inherent in language itself, possibilities lying in wait for each one of us to exploit. Such exploitation does not lead to the destruction of others, as when Samson ties the foxes together, sets them on fire, and lets them loose in the Philistine fields – which shows his strength and ingenuity, it is true, but harnessed to a wild destructive purpose; it leads, on the contrary, to a sense of what it is to *be* another, and so helps us escape from imprisonment in a world where our own eyes are the only arbiters.

Language, responsibly deployed, always gives us back more than we put into it. We thought to say one thing and find we have discovered another. Thus in the narrative in chapter 4 of the defeat and death of Sisera, we are told how the woman Jael invites the fleeing commander into her tent, how when he asks for water she gives him milk, and how, when he has gone to sleep, she drives a nail through his head. When Barak comes rushing up in pursuit Jael is able to take him into her tent and show him his enemy, dead: 'So', says the narrative, 'God subdued on that day Jabin the king of Canaan before the children of Israel' (Judg. 4:23).

What follows, though, and takes up the whole of the following chapter, is a song which tells in its own way the story of that battle and its aftermath. I will discuss in a later chapter the effect throughout the Bible of these large-scale repetitions in a more formal style of what we have just read about as pure narrative. Here I want only to focus on the climax. The verses are well known, but, as always in the Bible, gain from being placed in context:

> He asked water, and she gave him milk;
> She brought forth butter in a lordly dish.
> She put her hand to the nail,
> And her right hand to the workmen's hammer;
> And with the hammer she smote Sisera, she smote off his head,
> When she had pierced and stricken through his temples,
> At her feet he bowed, he fell, he lay down:
> At her feet he bowed, he fell:
> Where he bowed, there he fell down dead.

> (Judg. 5:25–27)

So far we have a reiteration of what the narrative has told us, though its rhythmic nature and the manifold repetitions and partial repetitions give it all a ritualized quality missing from the first account. We can still feel what is going on in human terms, but transmuted almost into a ballet. This is what happened, we feel, but as seen not by men but by God, who can understand Sisera's suffering and Jael's triumph, but who has seen so many murders, for good and bad causes, that he accepts them as part of the pattern of human life on earth.

If the story were not told in such a stylized fashion we might be led to feel that such insight would result in cynicism: we have seen it all before and will see it again. That would be seeing it as men see it, trying but failing to see it from God's point of view. (Is this perhaps how we are to understand Ecclesiastes? As a book about how men *imagine* God sees the world?) What follows, though, explains the difference between the two positions:

The mother of Sisera looked out at a window,
And cried through the lattice,
Why is his chariot so long in coming?
Why tarry the wheels of his chariots?
Her wise ladies answered her,
Yea, she returned answer to herself,
Have they not sped? have they not divided the prey;
To every man a damsel or two;
To Sisera a prey of divers colours,
A prey of divers colours of needlework,
Of divers colours of needlework on both sides,
Meet for the necks of them that take the spoil?
So let all thine enemies perish, O Lord:
But let them that love him be as the sun when he goeth forth in his might.
And the land had rest forty years.

(Judg. 5:28–31)

The common account of this passage is that the singer is ironically invoking Sisera's mother and her attendant ladies in order to gloat over them. 'So let all thine enemies perish, O Lord' is the punch line, and has of course to be understood in the light of primitive cultures, since civilized people cannot condone such sentiments.

Now this may indeed be what the singer intends, but the effect is quite different. Once a verbal object is made it takes on a life of its own and cannot be understood simply in terms of authorial intention. What happens to us as we read, it seems to me, is that the abrupt switch to Sisera's mother and her ladies makes us suddenly aware of the fact that for every victor there is also a vanquished, for every mother who rejoices in triumph there is always one who laments in sorrow. Even if the singer meant to show these women as fiends, his ability to evoke them in their innocence, in the flow of their own lives, makes us experience them as living sentient beings, with their joys and their sorrows, their past and their future.

The singer's reticence has much to do with this. In a comparable scene in the *Iliad* Homer describes Andromache at work weaving in her palace just after he has described Hector's death at the hands of Achilles. He spends eight lines describing the tapestry she is weaving, the hot bath she has her handmaids prepare for Hector on his triumphant return, and then a further seventy lines describing how Andromache eventually receives the news and how she reacts to it, falling in a faint, reviving, lamenting, bewailing the fate that now awaits her and their son. 'So spake she weeping,' ends Book xxii, 'and thereto the women added their laments.'

This is magnificent, but it is not the way of the biblical poet. Homer ends his book with a lament, as he is to end his entire poem, and the lament ensures, in some sense, that we are reconciled even to Hector's death. In the Bible the poet leads us into the world of the dead commander's mother and her women, and then abruptly leaves it before we have a chance to see how they take the news that he is dead, killed by the hand of a woman. As a result the scene we are *not given* hovers behind the concluding words of the song: 'So let all thine enemies perish, O Lord: but let them that love him be as the sun when he goeth forth in his might. And the land had rest forty years.' It hovers there, asking us to imagine other lives and other worlds, ignored by the ringing conclusion, and so in some sense undermines that conclusion and prepares us for what is to happen when those forty years of rest will be over.

The poet has done something we do not find done by any of the characters in the book of Judges: he has given us a sense of the silent victims as well as of the exultant victors. Neither Ehud nor Gideon nor Samson nor the Levite ever seem able to experience what it might mean to be other than themselves. They do what they do and that is that. The words given here to Sisera's mother and her handmaids, and so abruptly cut off, were perhaps called for simply by the exigencies of the song, but they help us to understand what it was we missed so much elsewhere, and what was so peculiarly horrible in the episode of the Levite and his concubine: the woman's silence throughout. [15]

What begins then as the triumphant entry of the Israelite tribes into the land which had been promised them, ends with twelve parcels of flesh and the monotonous repetition of the phrase: 'every man did that which was right in his own eyes'. The problem is to walk in God's way when that way is so badly mapped out. In this book even that underlying rhythm, which had been so firmly established in the very first chapter of Genesis, is felt to falter. And yet, as we read on into Samuel, it starts, miraculously, to reassert itself, at first hesitantly, with the crowning of Saul and his uncertain rule, and then, with gathering confidence, as David moves into the centre of the stage.

David may not be the exemplary figure of later tradition, but he has two essential and inseparable attributes: an instinct for doing the right thing, and the ability to say what he feels. His heart-rending pleas to the ever more hysterical Saul are painful to read, but they are also a welcome relief after the twisted language and the total lack of self-awareness of the characters in Judges. The real turning-point, what persuades the reader that the rhythm has not only returned, but returned with renewed vitality, as if strengthened by its awareness of how close it had been to extinction, comes with David's great lament for Saul and Jonathan, the first extended piece of formal poetry since the song of Deborah. Whatever happens after that will not be the total negativity which lies at the heart of the book of Judges.

Not for nothing is David traditionally recognized as the author of Psalms, the sweet singer of the Lord. It is time to turn then from the underlying rhythm of the Bible to consider the place of speech and song, of all forms of utterance in fact, within it. Only then will we be in a position to understand the role it assigns to David.

Three

ASPECTS OF SPEECH

*It does not abolish the distance
between human beings but brings
that distance to life.*

WALTER BENJAMIN

VII

MEMORY, GENEALOGY AND
REPETITION

I return to the image with which I began: of the Bible as a book handed down by God to man.

Let us begin with a dramatic scene involving a book:

> So the king sent Jehudi to fetch the roll: and he took it out of Elishama the scribe's chamber. And Jehudi read it in the ears of the king, and in the ears of all the princes which stood beside the king. Now the king sat in the winterhouse in the ninth month: and there was a fire on the hearth burning before him. And it came to pass, that when Jehudi had read three or four leaves, he cut it with the penknife, and cast it into the fire that was on the hearth, until all the roll was consumed in the fire that was on the hearth.
>
> (Jer. 36:21–23)

The Book of the Bible is full of references to books. As well as this scroll, containing Jeremiah's words, which is so systematically destroyed by Jehoiakim, king of Judah, there is the scroll God orders Ezekiel to eat, the book eaten by the author of Revelation, which was in his mouth sweet as honey but bitter in his belly, the book with the seven seals, and of course, first and most important, the book of the Law of Moses. And there are many instances of writing: Moses writes what God commands, Joshua writes what Moses commands, Baruch takes dictation from Jeremiah, the mysterious hand writes on the wall of Belshazzar's palace, David writes a letter which sends Uriah to his death, and Jesus writes in the dust at his feet.

Clearly the written word is of paramount importance in this book, and the events surrounding the very first book, the one written by Moses at God's dictation, would seem to bear this out. Already after Moses' first conversation with God on the mountain, 'Moses wrote all the words of the Lord', and, after building an altar and sacrificing thereon, 'he took the book of the covenant, and read in the audience of the people' (Exod. 24:4, 7). The Lord then summons him up again, for 'I will give thee tables of stone, and a law, and commandments which I have written; that thou mayest teach them' (24:12). Moses obeys and God gives him, 'when he had made an end of communing with him upon mount Sinai, two tables of testimony, tables of stone, written with the finger of God' (31:18). However, when Moses descends with the tablets he finds the people worshipping the Golden Calf, and in his anger breaks the tablets. Soon, though, the people make it up with Moses and even, through his intercession, with God, and up he goes once again to collect two new tablets. This time he descends, his face radiant, carrying the tablets, and puts them away for safe-keeping in the ark, where they naturally become Israel's most sacred possession.

In the great summing up which is Deuteronomy, Moses reminds the people of how he broke the tablets the first time and of how he put the second lot in the ark. He tells them to keep the Passover and all the laws, and, after they have crossed the Jordan into the Promised Land, to set up tall stones and write on them 'the words of this law'. He warns them that if they do not keep the words of the law, 'written in this book', they will be scattered for ever (Deut. 28:58). As he prepares to die he commits the law to writing and hands it over to the priests with the injunction that they are to proclaim it in the hearing of Israel every seven years, at the Feast of Tabernacles (31:10–11). Dutifully Joshua, as soon as he has crossed the Jordan, writes upon the stones 'a copy of the law of Moses, which he wrote in the presence of the children of Israel' (Josh. 8:32). When Joshua himself is about to die he calls the people together and orders them to 'keep and to do all that is written in the book of the law of Moses, that ye turn not aside therefrom to the right hand or to the left' (23:6). However, 'there arose another generation..., which knew not the Lord, nor yet the works which he had done for Israel' (Judg. 2:10), and so turns aside from the law of Moses and sets about worshipping Canaanite gods and idols. Thus begins the long history of apostasy followed by divine wrath followed by repentance followed by more apostasy and the return of the whole cycle, which will persist until the Babylonian captivity.

We hear no more about Moses' book as such until a book is found in the Temple as it is being restored at the time of Josiah, many centuries later. However, it turns out that this must indeed be that very book, and in his excitement Josiah calls the people together, reads it out to them, orders Passover to be celebrated and all idol worship, wizards and necromancers to be outlawed, 'that he might perform the words of the law which were written in the book that Hilkiah the priest found in the house of the Lord' (2 Kgs. 23:24).

Sadly, though, the cycle of apostasy and forgetfulness starts up once again, leading in the end to the destruction of the Temple, the exile to Babylon and the new heart-searching such events bring with them. However, all bad, like all good things, come to an end, and the Persians overwhelm Babylon, the Israelites are allowed back to Jerusalem and a new temple is built. 'And all the people gathered themselves together as one man into the street that was before the water gate; and they spake unto Ezra the scribe to bring the book of the law of Moses, which the Lord had commanded to Israel.' Ezra does so and reads it before the people (excluding those children too young to understand), who listen attentively and respectfully, bowing their heads and worshipping the Lord 'with their faces to the ground'. After that the wise men expound the book, helping the people 'to understand the law', and the following day these same wise men gather again, 'even to understand the words of the law'. (Neh. 8:1–13)

This last scene dramatizes within the Bible how the Bible itself will be treated by wise men, both Jewish and Christian, in ages to come. Their explanations and interpretations form the basis of sermons and commentaries right down to the present day. Yet it is not the only way to treat tradition. A counter-theme runs through the Bible, one which puts the stress not on writing and reading but on telling, hearing and repeating. It provides us with an alternative model of our relation to books, to the one we have been examining so far in this chapter, and it is to it that I now wish to turn.

> And it shall come to pass, when your children shall say unto you, What mean ye by this service? That ye shall say, It is the sacrifice of the Lord's passover, who passed over the houses of the children of Israel in Egypt, when he smote the Egyptians, and delivered our houses.
>
> (Exod. 12:26–27)

The command is picked up and repeated in Deuteronomy. It is worth quoting the passage in full because the detail is significant:

> And when thy son asketh thee in time to come, saying, What mean the testimonies, and the statutes, and the judgments, which the Lord our God hath commanded you? Then thou shalt say unto thy son, We were Pharaoh's bondmen in Egypt; and the Lord brought us out of Egypt with a mighty hand: And the Lord shewed signs and wonders, great and sore, upon Egypt, upon Pharaoh, and upon all his household, before our eyes: And he brought us out from thence, that he might bring us in, to give us the land which he sware unto our fathers. And the Lord commanded us to do all these statutes, to fear the Lord our God, for our good always, that he might preserve us alive, as it is at this day.
>
> (Deut. 6:20–24)

The keeping of the Passover service, the observing of statutes, has the simplest of aims: to keep memory alive. To the child they will be a source of puzzlement, since they will differ from the normal pattern of daily activity, but that is precisely the point. They are designed to evoke that puzzlement and thus to elicit from him the question: 'What mean ye by this?'

As we see from the two versions given above, the story can be compressed or expanded; what is important is that it should be told. But it must not be told as a lesson, something the parent simply wishes to teach the child. That is why it is vital that the child be the first to speak: because he asks about something that puzzles him, the story, when it is told, becomes his, does not remain a mere anecdote. These matters are beautifully expressed in the Passover service that still obtains today. Custom decrees that it be the youngest child present who asks his father four questions (and if there is no child you are to ask yourself):

> How does this night differ from all the nights? For on all other nights we may eat either leavened bread or unleavened; on this night, nought but unleavened. On all other nights we eat all manner of herbs; on this night, those only that are bitter. On all other nights we do not steep that which we eat even once; on this night, twice. On all other nights, we eat either sitting or reclining; on this night, all recline.[1]

It is in answer to this fourfold question that the father tells the story of the exodus, beginning with Deuteronomy 6:21: 'We were Pharaoh's bondmen in Egypt'. For this reason, he goes on after he has recounted the story, 'even were we all wise men, all men of understanding, all advanced in years, all men with knowledge of the Torah, it would be our duty to recount the story of the coming forth from Egypt; and all who recount at length the story of the coming forth from Egypt are verily to be praised.'

To bring out the importance of such telling and retelling the service goes on to speak of four sons, a wise son, a simple son, a wicked son, and 'the son who does not even know how to ask a question'. The wise son asks about the meaning of the laws and customs being carried out by his parents, thus giving them a chance to retell the story. The simple son merely asks 'What is this?' and has to be told simply that 'By strength of hand the Lord brought us out from Egypt, from the house of bondage' (Exod. 13:14). The poor son who does not even know how to ask a question has to have everything explained to him, as the Bible enjoins: 'And thou shalt shew thy son in that day, saying, This is done because of that which the Lord did unto me when I came forth out of Egypt' (Exod. 13:8). This formulation stresses the fact that the Lord did this to *me* when *I* came forth out of Egypt – but this is just what the wicked son refuses to accept. For *he* asks: 'What mean ye by this service?' By saying 'ye' he excludes himself from the group, and it is enjoined upon the parents to reply: ' "This is done because of that which the Lord did unto me when I came forth out of Egypt" – unto me, not him; for if he had been there he would not have been delivered.' That is, because he now excludes himself from the story, seeing it as a story about them, not about himself, about *you*, not about *us*, he is excluded from the redemption which forms the climax of the story.

The crucial fact then is that this is more than the mere commemoration of a past event, since it was not some anonymous other who was delivered from Egypt in those far-off days, it was myself. How was it myself? Not through any mystical oneness of all being, but by the simple fact that if my parents had not been delivered then I would still be in bondage.

The Bible is at great pains to stress the way in which lineage functions. At the ceremony of first-fruits, ordained in Deuteronomy 26, the celebrant, bringing his offerings to the sanctuary, must declare:

> A Syrian ready to perish was my father, and he went down into Egypt, and sojourned there with a few, and became there a nation, great, mighty, and populous: And the Egyptians evil entreated us, and afflicted us, and laid upon us hard bondage: And when we cried unto the Lord God of our fathers, the Lord heard our voice, and looked on our affliction, and our labour, and our oppression: And the Lord brought us forth out of Egypt with a mighty hand, and with an outstretched arm, and with great terribleness, and with signs, and with wonders: And he hath brought us into this place, and hath given us this land, even a land that floweth with milk and honey.
>
> (Deut. 26:5–9)

Note the way in which the story moves here from 'my father' to 'us', from the patriarchal origins in Mesopotamia to slavery in Egypt and then the acquisition of the land, and never through our own efforts but always through God's favour. Again, there is nothing mystical in this, no merging of the individual in the community, but rather the simple assertion of unity through lineage and a shared memory.

The two go together. Because of what happened to my father I am where I am; but I can only understand this if I am aware of what happened to my father, and I can only ensure that my son in his turn understands this by telling him the story. Without memory, without the story, there is no meaning to my present life. Yet the story does not *confer* meaning, it only makes it manifest: all the stories in the world would not make sense of my life if I were not my father's son.

The task of the Homeric bard too is to recount their past to the Achaeans. Yet there are differences. For one thing, it is only the past of the aristocrats that he recounts; for another he does so not to show them how things turned out for them but to remind them of the heroic deeds of their ancestors. The Bible does not discriminate in this way either between classes or between good and bad deeds: the sins and errors of Adam and Jacob and David are as important as the humility and obedience of Abraham and Moses. And the reason for this is simple: what is important is to grasp what it means that God created the world and ourselves, and how men have frustrated as well as carried out his designs. Thus everything has to be remembered, and even, as we have seen, the attitude to memory itself becomes something that needs to be recalled.

The verb *zakhar*, 'remember', is one of the most frequent in the Bible. It appears 169 times, nearly always with Israel or God as the subject.[2] This God is neither an impersonal essence nor a figure in a cosmic drama, but the God 'of the fathers', of 'Abraham, Isaac and Jacob'. He is a God who cannot be known in himself but only in his deeds, which of course include his entry into dialogue with men. But the most important of these deeds is his adoption of Israel as his child and his bringing of Israel out of the bondage of Egypt. As Yosef Hayim Yerushalmi puts it:

> 'The heavens', in the words of the Psalmist, might still 'declare the glory of the Lord', but it was human history that revealed his will and purpose.... The pagan conflict of the gods with the forces of chaos, or with one another, was replaced by a drama of a different and more poignant order: the paradoxical struggle between the divine will of an omnipotent Creator and the free will of his creature, man, in the course of history; a tense dialectic of obedience and rebellion.

Yerushalmi reminds us that for the other nations of the ancient Near East there were only two times, a present and a 'dream-time', the time of the gods, which the annual ritual festivals could help to recreate. Such rituals were an abolishing of chaos and chance, and helped to ensure the proper working of the seasonal cycle.[3]

Yet surely Yerushalmi is wrong when he asserts that this primeval dream-time is to be found in the Paradise of Genesis 1–3, which, he claims, is then 'abandoned irrevocably'.[4] For, as we saw in an earlier chapter, that abandonment comes with the very first word, which breaks the envelope of silence: *bereshit*. Clearly, though, the history the Bible is concerned with is not the same as that in which Herodotus, for example, was interested, a history which has to be recorded 'to preserve the memory of the past by putting on record the astonishing achievements both of our own and of the Asiatic peoples'.[5] The Bible's history, as we have seen, is concerned to make manifest not the great and wonderful actions of this nation or that, but rather the underlying rhythms of history, and it develops in a slow and regular rhythm, akin to the breathing of a man, moving forward only as it looks back and looking back only to help it move forward.

Just as the first week includes the seventh day of rest, when God looks back on his work of the previous six days in wonder, so human history is punctuated by moments in which we are required to look back and recall, and by so doing to help those who were not there to realize that had it not been for certain events they would not be here now: 'Remember the days of old, consider the years of many generations: ask thy father, and he will shew thee; thy elders, and they will tell thee' (Deut. 32:7); 'Remember these, O Jacob and Israel; for thou art my servant: I have formed thee...O Israel, thou shalt not be forgotten of me' (Isa. 44:21).

The annual festivals, Passover, Weeks and Tabernacles, are occasions for the ritual recalling of what once happened. But time, the distinction between then and now, is not abolished. It is only through hearing and telling the story that I can identify with my ancestor, experience what he experienced. I am the subject of the story, but not through some existential projection which leaves me naked and bereft in the present and places me in an immediate relation to a past event; it is rather in the much simpler and more obvious way that I am descended from these people, who are themselves descended from others; they are my flesh and blood. I am implicated because if they had not been saved then, I would not be hearing this story now. And, hearing the story, I can wonder at my miraculous existence. It is in this sense that I, who am here now, was already there, then.

But even this fails to catch the full effect of these repeated injunctions to remember. For it is a whole set of events that we are being asked to remember, not a single one: had Joseph not gone down into Egypt, had there not been a famine in Canaan, Moses would not have led the people out. Even had I been there, then, I would not have understood if I had not learned how to remember other events and tell them in my turn. Though the story can be compressed or expanded at will, it is necessary, in the remembering, the retelling, to keep the underlying rhythm, for only in this way does 'remember' become 'know', does the recalling of the past become a way of living in the present.

Northrop Frye once remarked that there are only two kinds of readers, those who skip lists and those who relish them. One of the chief stumbling-blocks for readers of the Bible is no doubt the lengthy genealogical lists which appear so often in the Pentateuch and Chronicles, and also occasionally crop up elsewhere. We are now, however, in a position to understand their function.

The genealogical lists in the Bible do not seek to trace a line back from a present emperor or leader to a god, as happens in other ancient Near Eastern cultures and in ancient Greece and Rome; they are there simply to keep alive the memory of the family. That memory is traced back to Abraham, who was adopted by God. He did not particularly deserve to be adopted, yet once the covenant had been made between himself and God the relationship was sealed, with heavy obligations on both sides. The genealogies, like the narratives, keep alive the memory of these wondrous facts: that Abraham was called; that he left Haran; that Sarah bore a child though she was long past the age for doing so; that Jacob stole the blessing; that Tamar conceived and bore a child to Judah; that God brought the people out of Egypt. Such amazing things cannot be repeated often enough. But they can be repeated as a continuous and continuing story because Jacob is Isaac's son and Judah Jacob's.

Interestingly, the first reference to genealogy in the Bible comes not in Genesis 5, 'This is the book of the generations [*toldot*] of Adam' (5:1), but at the end of the first week of creation: 'These are the generations [*toldot*] of the heavens and of the earth when they were created, in the day that the Lord God made the earth and the heavens' (2:4). So even generation itself has no beginning; it only, as it were, begins again:

> This is the book of the generations of Adam [*sepher toldot adam*]. In the day that God created man [*adam*], in the likeness of God made he him; Male and female created he them; and blessed them, and called their name Adam, in the day when they were created. And Adam lived an hundred and thirty years, and begat a son in his own likeness, after his image [*bidemuto ketzalmo*, cf. 1:27]; and called his name Seth: And the days of Adam after he had begotten Seth were eight hundred years: and he begat sons and daughters: And all the days that Adam lived were nine hundred and thirty years: and he died. And Seth lived an hundred and five years, and begat Enos: And Seth lived after he begat Enos eight hundred and seven years, and begat sons and daughters: And all the days of Seth were nine hundred and twelve years: and he died. And Enos lived ninety years, and begat Cainan. . . .
>
> (Gen. 5:1–9)

In this way Adam is linked to Noah and Noah to Abraham and Abraham to Jacob and Jacob to his twelve sons and each of them in turn to their sons and their sons' sons, and so on down through the time in Egypt, the return, the time of the Judges, the monarchy, the Babylonian exile and the second return.[6]

So, on the one hand there is no going back to any primal time, since the long line of ancestors stretches between us now and those people then; on the other hand it is just because of that long line that I am here now: what keeps me apart from Abraham and Jacob is also what binds me to them. Again and again the Bible reveals the temptation to escape from the present and its discontents, either by looking back nostalgically, hankering after the fleshpots of Egypt, or even further back to a lost paradise; or by looking forward to a time when all will be made clear and simple, when I will be exalted and my enemy laid low, when I will at last have all I desire, both physically and spiritually. Both ways mean the end of memory, the end of story-telling. The Bible has much more sympathy for the second attitude than for the first, and it is often propounded with powerful eloquence by the prophets. But even here it is seen as something to be desired but which will only come about if there is reform in the present. And such reform means facing reality, not evading it, means listening to the past, not trying to forget it.[7]

The primary reality is the fact of death. The Hebrew Bible is in no doubt, until some very late writings, about death being the end of the individual. The Patriarchs may live to be very old, but then they die and are buried with due respect. The fear is not of death itself but of the wrong sort of death, or the lack of a proper burial. Jacob asks that though he die in Egypt he be buried with his fathers, in the cave of Machpelah which his grandfather Abraham had purchased from Ephron the Hittite, when he is 'gathered unto my people'. Abimelech, as we saw in the chapter on Judges, dies by having a stone dropped on his head by a woman and, despite his attempt to avert the disaster, the memory of that shameful death lives on. A few figures, such as Enoch or Elijah, seem to escape death, but for that very reason their end is a perpetual source of wonder and mystery. From the moment Adam eats of the tree, death, as far as the Hebrew Bible is concerned, is there to stay, and must be accepted by all men.

For this reason the Bible views with particular horror the cults of the dead which formed so crucial a role in the culture of the surrounding nations, especially Egypt, which seemed to be a society obsessed with death. As von Rad points out:

> The first datum, or at least the obvious thing to do. . . was to confer a positive sacral value on the dead and on the grave. There was no doubt that the dead lived on – especially so if this was assured by means of rites. Thus the dead man was merely changed, and represented, to a higher degree than while living in the body, a power which had to be reckoned with in a very real way. In consequence, it was of prime importance to regulate the relationship of the living to these dead. The dead could of course do harm. But use could also be made of their higher knowledge. How close Israel stood to these ideas may be seen from the fact that the age of Deuteronomy and Isaiah was still exposed to the temptation to consult the dead (Isa. 8:19; Deut. 18:11). And on one occasion when such a spirit was conjured up, it is still actually designated *elohim* (1 Sam. 28:13).[8]

That occasion was of course the time when Saul consulted the Witch of Endor and she called up Samuel from the dead. But that, we are made to understand, merely showed how far Saul had fallen and what little hope there was for him.

Death then, and the acceptance of death as part of man's lot, is almost *the* essential component of reality in the Hebrew Bible. 'I shall go to him, but he shall not return to me' (2 Sam. 12:23), says David, the great realist, about the son God has taken away from him, and a little later Barzilai, the old man who 'had provided the king of sustenance while he lay at Mahanaim' (2 Sam. 19:32), gives an extended version of this doctrine:

> And Barzilai said unto the king, How long have I to live, that I should go up with the king unto Jerusalem? I am this day fourscore years old: and can I discern between good and evil? can thy servant taste what I eat or what I drink? can I hear any more the voice of singing men and singing women? wherefore then should thy servant be yet a burden unto my lord the king?

...Let thy servant, I pray thee, turn back again, that I may die in mine own
city, and be buried by the grave of my father and of my mother.

(2 Sam. 19 : 34–37)

But if man's life cannot stretch out for ever in time, that does not mean,
as Ecclesiastes suggests, that his life is without meaning. On the contrary, it is death which confers meaning upon life and gives special
significance to genealogy.

God, after all, had first made man, then blessed him and told him to
'Be fruitful, and multiply, and replenish the earth' (Gen. 1 : 28); when he
decides to destroy man because of his sins he saves one man, Noah, and
makes a covenant with him, blesses him, and repeats the command to
him and his sons: 'Be fruitful, and multiply, and replenish the earth'
(9 : 1); when men sin again, trying to build a tower that will reach up to
heaven, he orders Abraham to set out 'unto a land that I will shew thee',
and promises 'I will make of thee a great nation, and I will bless thee,
...and in thee shall all families of the earth be blessed' (12 : 1–3). In the
episodes that follow it is as if the narrator wished to demonstrate in every
conceivable way how, against all the odds, God's promise was kept. Isaac
is born of Sarah despite her great age, and is saved at the last moment by
the angel after Abraham has accepted God's command to sacrifice him;
Jacob tricks Esau out of his birthright and blessing; Tamar tricks Judah
into getting her with child; Joseph is saved at the well and then later in
Egypt, and so is able to save his father and brothers from the famine in
Canaan; Moses is miraculously saved from the waters of the Nile and
leads the Israelites to safety through the Red Sea; Hannah bears Samuel
in spite of her barrenness; Ruth gravitates with unerring instinct towards
Boaz and from their union comes the line of David.

So much is obvious; it is perhaps the most striking theme of the early
portions of the Bible. But it is important to see that what is so often at
issue is not just the triumph of God over nature or of the youngest-born
over his elder brothers, but the relations of fathers to sons, of one generation to the next. Reuben, Jacob's eldest son, sleeps with his father's
concubines; Judah, the next in line since Simeon and Levi have blotted
their book by their slaughter of the Shechemites, is the one to speak out
and suggest that Joseph be thrown into the pit. Yet it is this very Judah
who pleads with his father to allow the brothers to take Benjamin with
them, 'that we may live, and not die, both we, and thou, and also our
little ones', and who pledges himself as a surety for the lad (Gen.
43 : 8–9). Why? James Ackerman has suggested that the answer to this
question is to be found in the episode that occurs between chapters 37
and 43, in chapter 38. He suggests that the trick Tamar, Judah's
daughter-in-law, here uses to acquire her rights, a child by one of the
males of Judah's family, teaches Judah something about the relationship
of parents and children. Having tried to withhold his youngest son from

Tamar, after the mysterious deaths of the two older sons as soon as they have been given to her in marriage, he is forced by her to recognize that we cannot totally control our lives, let alone those of our children. And just as Jacob has to let Benjamin go so that Joseph may be returned to him, so Judah has to let his own sons go that he may be blessed with grandchildren.[9]

And as the children of Jacob and Judah must be allowed their freedom, so must man be allowed his by God. For of course the one relation between fathers and children which towers above all the others in this book is the relation of God to man, and in particular to Israel. And if this God is indeed the god 'of the fathers', he is also not very different in his attitudes from any of the human fathers we meet in this book. After the death of Abimelech in the book of Judges, for example, we are told that 'the children of Israel did evil again in the sight of the Lord, and served Baalim, and Ashtaroth, and the gods of Syria, and the gods of Zidon, . . . and the gods of the Philistines, and forsook the Lord, and served not him' (10:6). So the Lord's anger grows hot against Israel and he gives them over to their enemies. Then 'the children of Israel cried unto the Lord, saying, We have sinned against thee, both because we have forsaken our God, and also served Baalim'. Whereupon

> the Lord said unto the children of Israel, Did not I deliver you from the Egyptians, and from the Amorites, from the children of Ammon, and from the Philistines? . . . . and ye cried to me, and I delivered you out of their hand. Yet ye have forsaken me, and served other gods: wherefore I will deliver you no more. Go and cry unto the gods which ye have chosen; let them deliver you in the time of your tribulation. And the children of Israel said unto the Lord, We have sinned: do thou unto us whatsoever seemeth good unto thee; deliver us only, we pray thee, this day. And they put away the strange gods from among them, and served the Lord: and his soul was grieved for the misery of Israel.
>
> (Judg. 10:11–16)

What we have here is hardly what we might expect of a conversation between God and men; but it is exactly what we might expect of a conversation between a loving father and an ever-naughty but charming child. The last phrase is surely one of the most extraordinary in the whole Bible: *vatiktzar naphsho ba'amal Yisrael*: and his soul was grieved for the misery of Israel. We grope in our minds for a memory of where we might have heard a phrase like that before, and then we suddenly realize that the relation of God to Israel suggested here is very close indeed to that of David to his beloved son Absalom. The pathos of that second relationship stems from the fact that David cannot help loving Absalom, because he is his child, and because, of all his children, he is the most appealing. Unfortunately he is also, partly as a result of this, spoilt, vain and ambitious. Even, perhaps, as is the way with such relationships, desperate to be avenged on David because of the very love David bestows upon him and which he finds an intolerable burden. As for David, Absalom may turn against him in war, may try to seize his throne by force, humiliate him by openly sleeping with his women, and even try to kill him, but in the end David would rather give up his kingdom and even his own life than know the horror of that body swinging lifeless in the branches.

It is a relationship of just this kind which binds God to his own children. The relations that exist between God and man, and in particular between God and Israel, cannot be reduced to any formula or to any set of laws. It is true that God chooses Israel in an explicit and incomprehensible act of adoption, but once that choice has been made a relationship is set in train that will be guided by love and hate, and by all the unconscious forces of desire – desire to be loved, desire to be freed of the burden of love – that always exist in family relationships. When the child learns that but for the miracle of the Red Sea he would not be celebrating Passover, that but for the miracle of Sarah's conceiving when well past the age he would not be there at all, he learns that the God of the Fathers is, whether he likes it or not, his God too.

However, a change comes over this relationship in the New Testament.[10] It is true that continuity is asserted, both formally and substantially, in the genealogies which we find in the Gospels of both Matthew and Luke. Marshall D. Johnson has shown at length how these two genealogies differ in the implicit message each is attempting to convey, how Matthew, who traces Jesus' ancestry back to Abraham, wishes to establish him as the Messiah son of David, while Luke, who traces his family tree back to Adam, is concerned to show that he belongs to the line of prophets, via David's third son, Nathan, taken to be the same as the prophet of that name. Johnson is quite aware of the problem the Gospel writers have of trying to do two contradictory things, to affirm Jesus' continuity with the Old Testament and God's convenant with Israel, but also to affirm Jesus' utter difference from all that has gone before by stressing the Virgin Birth. What he does not see is that the difficulty is compounded by the New Testament's own teachings on the question of the relation of God the Father to his children.[11]

In the third chapter of Luke, John the Baptist harangues his audience, urging them to repent in view of the imminent end. 'O generation of vipers,' he says to them,

> who hath warned you to flee from the wrath to come? Bring forth therefore fruits worthy of repentance, and begin not to say within yourselves, We have Abraham to our father: for I say unto you, That God is able of these stones to raise up children unto Abraham.

(Luke 3:7–8)

Jesus himself, as is well known, repudiates his own family in favour of the larger family of God:

> And it was told him by certain which said, Thy mother and thy brethren stand without, desiring to see thee. And he answered and said unto them, My mother and my brethren are these which hear the word of God, and do it.
> (Luke 8:20–21; cf. Matt. 12:47, Mark 3:32, John 19:27)

It is in keeping with this that Paul writes in chapter 9 of Romans:

> For they are not all Israel, which are of Israel: Neither, because they are the seed of Abraham, are they all children: but, In Isaac shall thy seed be called. That is, They which are the children of the flesh, these are not the children of God: but the children of the promise are counted for the seed.
> (Rom. 9:6–8)

He concludes his argument with two quotations from Hosea: 'I will call them my people, which were not my people; and her beloved, which was not beloved' (9:25; Hos. 2:23); and 'where it was said unto them, Ye are not my people; there shall they be called the children of the living God' (9:26; Hos. 1:10). Paul's argument is that the Jews are labouring under the illusion that they have the advantage of being descended from Abraham, but that this is a dreadful error, since God is able to declare anyone a child of Abraham, and, moreover, not all Abraham's children were Israelites – Isaac was, but Ishmael was not. So, being a physical descendant of Abraham does not necessarily make one a child of the promise: God is not bound by genealogy. As Michael Wyschogrod puts it:

> He can...reject those who are of the seed of Abraham and substitute for them as his chosen people another people who were previously not chosen. This is...the Church, which is not a natural family characterised by descent from a common ancestor but an association of persons from many peoples united by a common faith.[12]

This has of course always been the boast of Christianity, a central reason for its success as a world religion and a source of its polemics against Judaism. It is interesting that we warm to it today whether we are Christians or not, for it seems self-evident that the chance Jesus gives to anyone to become one of God's children is much to be preferred to the exclusivity of Judaism. Yet in the light of what I have said about God's relations with Israel, it will be clear that if there is a gain there is also something that is lost. It may be something we are not sorry to lose, but the reader of Romans who has also read through Samuel, for example, will realize that loss there is. A God who can choose his children, and children who can choose their father, are going to be bound by other bonds than those of normal families. The bonds will be either ethical: by being the kind of person I am I have become a son; or mystical: by taking part in a certain mystery, or through some mysterious prior decision of God's, I enter this family. In such a situation it all rests with me; I have nothing to fall back on; and we can see looming at the end of the tunnel the dreadful Calvinist dilemma: am I one of the saved or one of the damned? Can I really choose my choice?

What this means in psychological terms is that the inner self becomes an object of scrutiny, and that the possibility of the co-existence of contrary emotions is ruled out: love *and* hate; pain *and* trust; jealousy. But contrary emotions are what we normally experience in our lives. The encounter with God thus becomes something separated from our normal lives, and that compartmentalization begins which so many Christian theologians lament today.

Even Paul was forced to admit that the Jews 'are beloved for the fathers' sakes' (Romans 11 : 28; NEB: 'they are his friends for the sake of the patriarchs', though the Greek has *agapeitoi*). Paul acknowledges here that God's love for Israel is not something that depends on the actions and choices of men, though these may sadden and anger him. As Wyschogrod says: 'It is perhaps like the love of a man for a woman who dies and leaves children behind. When the bereaved lover looks at the woman's children, he sees her face and presence in them and cannot help but love them. They remind him of his beloved.'[13] God loved Abraham and Isaac and Jacob, and so he loves their children. This has nothing to do with how they *behave*, though if they behave badly this will sadden and anger him, precisely *because* he loves them. We may dislike our family but we cannot escape it. One can always walk out of a community of faith but one cannot change one's parents. When Jesus says, 'no man cometh unto the Father, but by me' (John 14 : 6), he says something that goes counter to everything in the Hebrew scriptures, as of course he means to do. But by saying this he also thins out the sense of the complexity of life, of emotions and desires beyond the range of the intellect and of language, squeezed together so tight that they cannot be separated out, which is what we find in the Hebrew Bible, and which makes it impossible to reduce its narratives to either an ethical or a mystical meaning.

The injunction to remember and recount, as I have said, is central, and in the end much more important than the injunctions to study, learn and interpret. It is of course a religious injunction, but, as I have tried to argue, it is also something we all do at all moments of our lives. Scholars who have been concerned to find a historical basis for Abraham and Moses, and theologians who have become obsessed with the concept of a saving history, have not perhaps been sufficiently sensitive to the implications of that Passover injunction: 'And it shall come to pass, when your children say unto you: What mean ye by . . . Then thou shalt say . . .'

Once again Proust may help us to see what is at issue here. As every reader of À la recherche knows, Proust makes a fundamental distinction between voluntary and involuntary memory. Voluntary memory is the memory of the historian. It tells us that the French Revolution broke out in 1789; that the First World War lasted from 1914 to 1918; that when I was five years old my family moved from X to Y; that I went to such and such a school, took such and such a job, married such and such a person on such and such a date. For Marcel this kind of memory is worse than useless. For what does it do for me to know such things? Proust would no doubt agree with Nietzsche, who, in an early essay on memory and history, had dealt a body blow to the nineteenth century's obsession with the past 'as it really was'. 'It is possible to live almost without memory,' writes Nietzsche,

> and to live happily moreover, as the animal demonstrates; but it is altogether impossible to *live* at all without forgetting. Or, to express my theme even more simply: *there is a degree of sleeplessness, or rumination, of the historical sense, which is harmful and ultimately fatal to the living thing, whether this living thing be a man or a people or a culture.*[14]

Yet Proust, unlike Nietzsche, was not forced by this insight into the position of having to opt for the memoryless life of the beast. Experience had taught him that there is another kind of memory, quite different from that of the historian, and so important had been this discovery that he made the whole of his giant novel develop out of the insight provided by this involuntary memory.

Involuntary memory is the memory unleashed by eating again in adulthood a biscuit one had tasted as a child, when the taste brings back the entire world of that time, not as something consciously recalled but directly, physically, in an overwhelming flood. It is as if this memory were lodged inside the body yet sealed off until some chance taste, smell or motion releases it, like the genie from his bottle. Thus Marcel, bending down to tie a shoelace, suddenly finds himself re-experiencing the entire scene of which this movement had been an insignificant part, when his grandmother had helped him to dress. And as he experiences the living reality of his grandmother, her death hits him truly for the first time; before, he had only remembered her as the historian remembers; now he experiences her living presence and so her terrible final absence.

But the important point about Proust's novel is that Marcel does not remain the mere passive victim of such occurrences. It is true that they cannot consciously be brought into being, but there does not remain for him, as for Nietzsche, an unbridgeable gap between a consciousness which is devoid of meaning and an unconsciousness which is fully meaningful, 'alive'. What bridges the gap is writing. À la recherche is in the

end less about spots of time or moments of true being than about uniting
the lost fragments of the body through the act of writing which tells of
the dispersal of such fragments. And I would suggest that the liturgy, in
both the Jewish and the Christian traditions, works in rather the same
way: it makes accessible to our daily selves a memory which is alive,
which is quite other than the historian's memory. This, I think, is the
point of Yerushalmi's book, *Zakhor*, which tries to answer the question
of why Jews had to wait till the nineteenth century to manifest any real
interest in history. The reason, he suggests, is that until then they had no
need of history; that it was only with the loss of a traditional way of
acceding to the past that the way of the historian became necessary. And
we can see the same thing happening in the Christian world at the end of
the Middle Ages: the rise of modern historiography goes hand in hand
with the collapse of a communal liturgy.

Liturgy differs from involuntary memory to the degree that it is organized and ritualized. There are set times and places for it and an organized
sequence. Yet the similarities are more important than the differences.
For the point about both is that it is the ordinary, the physical, the
utterly other, which opens a door into the past which the private memory of the individual can never unlock. And this may help to explain
why so many people, Jews and Christians, have felt a profound sense of
loss at the introduction of the vernacular into a liturgy previously conducted in Hebrew or Latin. It is not mere nostalgia for tradition, but the
feeling that the use of the vernacular forces us to think about what we are
saying as we say it, rather than letting meaning come to us in its own
good time. It brings that meaning, in a sense, closer to voluntary than to
involuntary memory.

The liturgy allows the participant to lead his life without falling into
the temptation of either nostalgia for the irrecoverable past or the apocalyptic desire for a sudden end. It has neither the atavistic quality of the
return to a dream time nor the purely intellectual quality of the study of
the past. It allows the individual to age naturally by recognizing that he is
made up of the past and yet exists now, and is always moving into an
open future. We are not Moses and the Israelites crossing the Red Sea,
and we are not Jesus breaking bread or his disciples sharing that bread
with him, yet we accede to these events. Memory and repetition make
the past live again.

But we do not exactly relive it. We live it *as* memory and repetition.
Sensing our limits, our own boundedness in time and space, we sense too
that those ancient events were themselves bounded in space and time,
and we thus experience their painful incompleteness. By this I mean that
neither Moses nor Jesus acted as they did in the full knowledge that their
actions would later be commemorated; they could only hope that they
would be: for them, as for us, the future remained open.

Yet there is a difference between the central saving events of the Hebrew and the Christian Bibles, and how these events are projected into the future. Jesus does not ask his disciples to tell again a wonder they have witnessed; he asks them to perform an action. And in the repetition his followers are both performing a natural social act, breaking bread, and repeating the terrible end of the broken body and the spilt blood. The celebration of the mass is thus both like the celebration of the Passover *and* a return to that ritual enactment of the annual death and rebirth of the god against which the people of Israel had so firmly set their faces. Because it is an act, we can choose to take part in it or not; the choice for the Jew is different: he can deny his past or he can accept it and recount it: 'saying *you* he excludes himself from the group.'

Nevertheless, like the Passover service, the mass celebrates not a fact of nature, the turning of the year, but an event which is unique and unrepeatable. In both cases the event is not left stark but carries with it the injunction to recall, repeat: 'When thy son asketh thee..then thou shalt say. . .' 'Do this in remembrance of me.' The emphasis of Protestant theologians on a saving history, a history of God's miraculous deeds, plays down this crucial dimension. This is only to be expected, since the Protestant emphasis on history goes hand in hand with its rejection of liturgy and ritual, but it is important to see how this distorts the Bible itself. For there is no place in the mental universe of such theologians for a history made up of something besides sheer facts or timeless existential encounters. For them repetition only means a return to the world of pagan myth and ritual, and they can thus find no place for the most natural of human activities, remembering and telling.

But for the reader of the Bible who has begun at the beginning and gone on to the Gospels and Epistles, there are no such fears. He recognizes that in this book, as in life, the movement forward always works in rhythm with the look back, and that this looking is saved from turning into nostalgia or compulsion by being recognized and dramatized. As he reads on he comes to see two things. The first is that events do indeed seem to repeat or half-repeat each other, calling up the past even as they lead into the future. We have seen this happening at the level of words and phrases in chapter 1 of Genesis, but as we read on we find it occurring on an ever-increasing scale (there is of course more to look back to). Noah gets into the Ark and sets forth on the waters, carrying the remnant of mankind with him, and some time later Moses is put into an ark as a baby and then, as an adult, leads the Israelites to freedom across the waters of the Red Sea; Samson breaks his bonds and rises up with renewed vigour, and later Jesus pushes back the stone of the tomb and rises again.

Are these things meant? What does meaning mean? Do we glimpse a plan behind the different events? The Christian Fathers of the Church

clearly thought so, and called these parallels types. Modern scholars have
tried to explain their presence in the Bible by saying that they were
retrospectively introduced precisely to give the impression of meaning
and fulfilment. From our perspective, though, we can see that, within
the book, they work on us in ways rather similar to those in which À la
recherche works on us. When Marcel goes to stay with his childhood
friend Gilberte, now married, he discovers that the two 'ways' of his
childhood, which had seemed to belong to quite different worlds, are in
fact very close together, within easy walking distance of each other. The
extraordinary shock this causes him depends on his having experienced
the two ways separately as a child – and so had we, the readers. So for us
too the discovery leads to a reorientation. The two ways do not merge,
but they cease to be hermetically sealed off from each other. They are
and are not two.

   Similarly, for the reader of the Bible, type and antitype remain distinct and yet are felt to be related.[15] We experience this because, once
we start reading, whatever our prior allegiances and beliefs, we too cannot hold back and say, like the wicked son, 'your story, not mine'. As
we read we become part of the story. And as we do so we realize that the
most extraordinary result of the injunction to remember is this, that the
Bible itself, in its entirety, has been remembered, and passed on. After all,
this did not happen to the many other books we hear about as having
existed among the Hebrews; it did not happen to any of the writings
about Jesus not included in the canon, and of which we possess only
fragments or single copies which have surfaced in the past few centuries.
No less than Proust's giant novel, this is a book which is both about
memory and remembering, and the product of memory and remembering.
Now it is because of the text that there are memories; but it is because of
memories that there is the text.

VIII

THE NEED TO UTTER

We would not have had the Bible had it not been for the injunction to which it bears witness to remember and repeat. But there are other imperatives embedded in the text, less clearly defined than this, but nevertheless present, and which also have to do with speech. At the one pole is the imperative to sing the praises of the Lord, and at the other is the need, when in trouble, to cry out to the Lord in supplication. These would seem to be responses to two quite different situations, and to be quite different in their motivation, one enjoined by religion, the other by sheer human need. But they are not in actual fact so far apart, as Psalm 6, for example, demonstrates:

> Have mercy upon me, O Lord; for I am weak: O Lord,
>   heal me; for my bones are vexed.
>
> My soul is also sore vexed: but thou, O Lord, how long?
>
> Return, O Lord, deliver my soul: oh save me for thy
>   mercies' sake.
>
> For in death there is no remembrance of thee: in the
>   grave who shall give thee thanks?
>
> (Ps. 6:2–5)

Here the plea for mercy, for deliverance from suffering, turns into a subtle form of blackmail: if you let me die, the Psalmist tells God, I will no longer be able to praise you – so, if you want praise, save me. Donne had no doubt meditated on the ironies of such pleas in the Bible, for he finished 'Good Friday, Riding Westward' with a similar paradox:

> O think me worth thine anger, punish me,
> Burn off my rusts, and my deformity,
> Restore thine Image, so much, by thy grace,
> That thou may'st know me, and I'll turn my face.

It is, of course, not just in the book of Psalms that we find prayers in the Bible. Moshe Greenberg, in his excellent little book, *Biblical Prose*

Prayer, gives some interesting statistics: prayers and praying are mentioned some 140 times in the Hebrew Bible outside the Psalms. In a
little over 40 cases only the act of prayer is mentioned, as in Exodus
14:10: 'And the children of Israel cried out unto the Lord.' But in some
97 cases we have actual prayers, 38 by lay and humble people, 59 by
kings, prophets and other important figures. We find these distributed
right through the Bible, from Genesis to Chronicles and in most of the
prophetic books.[1] Such prayers, Greenberg points out, range from the
tiny propitiatory formula of Moses when, God having struck Miriam with
leprosy, Aaron pleads with Moses to intercede on her behalf: 'Heal her
now, O God, I beseech thee' (*El na repha na lah* – Num. 12:13), to the
richly elaborated petitionary prayer of Jacob on his way to meet his
brother for the first time since he stole the blessing:

> O God of my father Abraham, and God of my father Isaac, the Lord which
> saidst unto me, Return unto thy country, and to thy kindred, and I will deal
> well with thee: I am not worthy of the least of all the mercies,and of all the
> truth, which thou hast shewed unto thy servant; for with my staff I passed
> over this Jordan; and now I am become two bands. Deliver me, I pray thee,
> from the hand of my brother, from the hand of Esau: for I fear him, lest he
> will come and smite me, and the mother with the children. And thou saidst,
> I will surely do thee good, and make thy seed as the sand of the sea, which
> cannot be numbered for multitude.
>
> (Gen. 32:9–12)

The basic frame is still the same – 'O God...deliver me, I pray thee,
from...' – but it has been elaborated into an entire mini-narrative, recapitulating God's relations with Jacob. Such a prayer merges into those
recapitulations of the saving history, of God's relations with Israel, which
we were examining in the last chapter, and indeed a full exploration of
that topic would have to include a number of Psalms, such as 78, 105,
114, 135 and 136, as well as Deuteronomy 26 and Joshua 24.

Prayer, then, is a way of *reminding* God, as well as praising and im-
ploring him. But to go deeper into its role in this book we need to look
not so much at isolated prayers as at those narratives in which prayers are embedded. And an obvious place to start is the beginning of 1
Samuel. Hannah's extended prayer in chapter 2 is justly famous, and was
of course taken up by Luke (1:46 ff.) and so into the Christian liturgy:

> And Hannah prayed, and said, My heart rejoiceth in the Lord, mine horn is
> exalted in the Lord [NEB: 'In the Lord I now hold my head high']: my
> mouth is enlarged over mine enemies; because I rejoice in thy salvation.
> There is none holy as the Lord: for there is none beside thee: neither is
> there any rock like our God.
>
> (1 Sam. 2:1–2)

In traditional Bibles this prayer, which goes on for another eight verses, is laid out as prose, but in modern editions, such as the JB, the NEB and the Soncino, it appears as poetry. There has, in recent years, grown up quite a debate about the nature of biblical poetry, with some scholars, notably James Kugel, arguing that there is no such thing as a division between poetry and prose in ancient Hebrew, but only more or less dense forms of writing. According to this sort of argument, the modern editorial decision to put some of the Bible into poetry and leave the rest as prose is misguided and even, some would suggest, the result of the imposition of a poetics derived from the Greek upon the entirely different traditions of Hebrew.[2] This is not a debate we need to enter into, though it does draw attention to something we will see emerging in the course of this chapter, namely the difficulty we have in knowing how to take all formalized utterances.

Indeed, the problem is immediately apparent if we look beyond the extended prayer of 1 Samuel 2; for we discover that there is already a prayer in chapter 1. That chapter tells us about Hannah and her husband Elkanah, and about the fact that Hannah, like so many of the important women of the Hebrew Bible, is barren. Elkanah's other wife laughs at her, just as Hagar laughed at Sarah for a similar failure, and Hannah in turn envies her, just as Rachel envied Leah. She grows more and more dispirited, weeping and not eating. Her husband tries to cheer her up by saying, rather smugly, 'Am I not better to thee than ten sons?' (1 : 8), but she makes no reply. Instead, the narrative continues,

> Hannah rose up after they had eaten in Shiloh, and after they had drunk. Now Eli the priest sat upon a seat by a post of the temple of the Lord. And she was in bitterness of soul, and prayed unto the Lord, and wept sore. And she vowed a vow, and said, O Lord of hosts, if thou wilt indeed look on the affliction of thine handmaid, and remember me, and not forget thine handmaid, but wilt give unto thine handmaid a man child, then I will give him unto the Lord all the days of his life, and there shall no rasor come upon his head.
>
> (1 Sam. 1 : 9–11)

This address, which, we are told, is both a prayer and a vow, has clearly much in common with Hannah's more extended plea in chapter 2. Why then is it left as prose, when that is printed as poetry? The question is addressed not simply to editors but to all readers. We must ask what it does to have a piece of poetry in front of us instead of a piece of prose. Do we read the two differently? And if so, in what does the difference consist?

Before trying to answer that question it is as well to examine another set of examples:

> Then Jonah prayed [*vayitpalel*] unto the Lord his God out of the fish's belly,
> And said, I cried by reason of mine affliction unto the Lord, and he heard me;
> out of the belly of hell [*Sheol*] cried I, and thou heardest my voice.
>
> (Jonah 2 : 1–2)

This prayer too extends for some ten verses, and here too JB, NEB and
Soncino set it out as verse. As with Hannah's second prayer, many
verses in it are identical to those found in the Psalter,[3] and once again it
is preceded by a prayer left in prose by the editors. This time it is not
another prayer of Jonah's, but that of the sailors who reluctantly decide
that the only way to save the ship is to throw Jonah overboard, but
who, fearful of the retribution of Jonah's God, feel they must placate
him:

> Wherefore they cried unto the Lord, and said, We beseech thee, O Lord, we
> beseech thee, let us not perish for this man's life,and lay not upon us inno-
> cent blood: for thou, O Lord, hast done as it pleased thee.
>
> (Jonah 1 : 14)

Once again the difference seems to be one of degree, not of kind. The
first prayer could just about pass as an urgent plea, while the second holds
up the action for a considerable time and is clearly couched in rather
formal terms. But both prayers seem to be torn out of their speakers by
the pressure of circumstances, and they are equally efficacious. Surely we
have to read them both in the same way.

But does that mean that they should both be set out as poetry? What
then of Moses' 'Heal her now, O God, I beseech thee'? We see once
again how questions about the layout of this book lead straight to questions about meaning and function. For is it not the case that what we are
faced with in the more extended prayers and hymns of thanksgiving is
merely an elaboration of something that is there throughout the Bible,
perhaps whenever someone opens his or her mouth? Are we perhaps
simply talking about speech in the Bible? But if so, then it is clear that
speech here differs from that which we find in the traditional novel. The
question is, how different is it, and how does it relate to the central
themes of the Bible?

We should perhaps start by thinking about those extended examples of
formalized discourse which punctuate the Bible: Jacob's blessing, the
Song of the Sea, the song of Deborah, David's lament over Saul and
Jonathan. Earlier scholarly treatments of the Bible have tended to discuss
these as survivals from much older traditions, slipped into the later narrative by editors and redactors. But I want to ask how they *function*
within the narratives in which they are embedded. Clearly, there are two
aspects to any answer. One will deal with how the formal utterance

affects our sense of the whole narrative in which it occurs, and the other with how it affects our sense of the character who utters it.

In his essay on *Don Giovanni* Kierkegaard makes the important point that Mozart is able, through his music, to say things denied to Molière, who has to rely entirely on character and speech.[4] The point would have been instinctively understood by earlier dramatists. The Greek trage-dians were masters of choreography as well as dramaturgy, and their choruses function very much like Mozart's music, adding elements which cannot be included in the 'story' developed by the simple interplay of character. Shakespeare no longer had a chorus to work with, but he found substitutes in his clowns and the songs that form such an integral part of his plays. Clearly, if the Bible works in some of the same ways, then scholars and interpreters, poring over the meaning of the words, have not been in the best position to appreciate this aspect of the book. The songs of Moses and Deborah and the lament of David do in fact function rather like the arias and choruses of Mozart: We are led to the point of utterance, the narrative pauses, and the main character or a chorus sings, recapitulating what has happened and exploring its impli-cations. When they have finished the action picks up again, perhaps at the point where it left off – but we have travelled a long way in the meantime and our perspective is now radically altered.

As with Mozart, the Bible could be said to work by 'numbers'. The Song of the Sea may be a spontaneous outburst, but it is carefully pre-faced by a phrase telling us what the protagonist is now going to do:

> Then sang Moses and the children of Israel this song unto the Lord, and spake, saying, I will sing unto the Lord, for he hath triumphed gloriously: the horse and his rider hath he thrown into the sea.
>
> (Exod. 15:1)

It is the same with David's lament: 'And David lamented with this lamentation over Saul and over Jonathan his son' (2 Sam. 1:17). He laments (*yikonen*) with a lamentation (*hakinah*). The *kinah* is a lament for the dead, so once again the narrative gives us the technical term for what follows.

We are dealing with an artistic effect, but of course we are not just dealing with that. The notion that lament can be both formal and spontaneous is one that is taken for granted by traditional societies. So Beowulf's comrades mourn his passing, and in Malory Arthur mourns that of Lancelot. And so too do the three women in Hector's life, his mother, his wife and his sister-in-law Helen, mourn his passing in the last book of the *Iliad*. For the modern reader Helen's is perhaps the most surprising tribute:

> Hector, far dearest to my heart of all my husband's brethren!...this is now the twentieth year from the time when I went from thence and am gone from

my native land, but never yet heard I evil or despiteful word from thee; nay, if any other spake reproachfully of me in the halls...yet wouldst thou turn them with speech and restrain them by the gentleness of thy spirit and thy gentle words.

(Iliad, tr. Murray, XXIV. 762–72)

Such laments are foreign to the Christian spirit. They belong to oral cultures, where the primary unit is the clan and where death is the ultimate disaster. Those close to Jesus, by contrast, may mourn his passing or be bewildered by the nature of his death, but they respond as individuals, not as a group, and they seem, if anything, to be robbed of all speech by what has occurred. But the ultimate feeling, of course, is not one of silence and bewilderment but of rejoicing at Jesus' resurrection. There is no real place for lament in the Christian scheme of things because the ultimate shape of life is seen as a comedy rather than a tragedy. At the same time, since Christianity is a personal religion, it cannot easily accommodate songs of triumph at the salvation of the clan such as the Hebrew Bible puts into the mouths of Moses and Deborah.

But that is not all. As we will see in later chapters, the change in the very notion of self which the New Testament both urges and demonstrates, and of which we are the heirs, whatever our religious beliefs, makes it very difficult for us to understand how to take such formal yet personal outbursts. We do not know how to relate them to their social context or to their speakers. But we have to learn how to do both if we are to get to grips with a central feature of the Hebrew Bible.

It is clear, first of all, that the narrative could do perfectly well without these formal outbursts. At the same time, all the pieces we have looked at so far could stand up perfectly well by themselves, like the Psalms, or like the Old English *Battle of Maldon* or the ballad of the battle of Bannockburn. Moreover, the very sparseness of the writing, which is such a feature of biblical narrative, makes these passages, when they occur, all the more striking. And it seems to me that their main effect is to make us recognize the importance of utterance in our lives. Singers still have a privileged place in our society because they give voice to some things we feel at a deep level of ourselves but cannot by ourselves bring to the surface. Our response to the songs of Moses and Deborah works, I believe, at that primitive level: we rejoice not at their triumph (though that comes into it) but at their way with words.

This is not primarily a matter of skill. It has to do with the kind of daring and willingness to go naked which we also find in the great tragic heroes. That is why divas and pop stars are held in almost magical awe. David's lament for Saul and Jonathan is rightly famous. But it is not, of course, David's only lament. Indeed, he is *the* great mourner of the Bible, just as tradition makes him *the* great praiser of the Lord:

> And the king was much moved, and went up to the chamber over the gate, and wept: and as he went, thus he said, O my son Absalom, my son, my son Absalom! would God I had died for thee, O Absalom, my son, my son!
>
> (2 Sam. 18:33)

There is nothing formal or 'poetic' about this, but it is of a piece with the lament over Saul and Jonathan. David's grief, which is such a cause of concern to Joab, is what makes the death of Absalom bearable both for him and for us.

But passages like these worry scholars in search of the historical David. To ask 'Did David exist?' seems to be a reasonable sort of question. But if we ask: 'Did he really give vent to the lamentations the Bible puts into his mouth?' we seem to have to answer by talking about poetic licence and the like. This is dangerous ground. For if we try to eliminate all such speeches we find very quickly that we are left with hardly anything at all. If David's lament over Saul and Jonathan must go, then so must his lament over Absalom, and if that goes then so surely must Moses' reply to God's 'Moses, Moses': 'Here am I.' After that we might as well forget the Bible and concentrate solely on the archaeological and historical evidence.

Take away the fact of utterance and you take away a central strand of the book. For what is becoming obvious, surely, is that *all* utterance, from the shortest and most emotional to the longest and most poetically elaborate, is at once personal and formal. It is personal in that it seems to correspond to a need on the part of the speaker, and it is formal in that to speak at all is to adopt the words and forms given by society.

And this brings us back to prayer. As Moshe Greenberg points out,

> scholarly appreciation of the embedded prayers in the Hebrew Scriptures has been bedevilled by disabling preconceptions. The arch-devil is the dichotomizing of prayer into spontaneous free invention on the one hand, and preformulated, prescribed prayers on the other.

Typical of this tendency is Friedrich Heiler's great book, *Prayer*, first published in 1918. True prayer, asserts Heiler, is the 'original, simple prayer of the heart', while 'formal literary prayers are merely [their] weak reflection'.[5] This view would at first sight seem to be reinforced by what we find in the prophets, their persistent critique of prayer which does not come from the heart, as in Amos':

> I hate, I despise your feast days, and I will not smell
>   in [i.e. take delight in] your solemn assemblies.

> Though ye offer me burnt offerings and your meat offerings,
>   I will not accept them: neither will I
>   regard the peace offerings of your fat beasts.

> Take thou away from me the noise of thy songs; for I
> will not hear the melody of thy viols.
>
> But let judgment run down as waters, and righteousness
> as a mighty stream.
>
> (Amos 5 : 21–24)

But is Amos really saying here that the only thing God will tolerate is a religion of the heart, as Heiler argues? Is not the simple contrast between inner and outer, ritual and true feeling, too simplistic? Does it not, in fact, remind us too much of Protestant critiques of Catholicism for us to be confident that it applies to the biblical situation?

The Bible gives us many details about how Temple services were carried out, but there is no mention of how to pray. Greenberg points out that the Talmud gives us a framework for prayer but not the words to be used. He quotes Joseph Heinemann, the foremost authority on the subject:

> When the sages ordained the obligatory fixed prayers, they did not prescribe their exact wording – contrary to what is usually thought and written in popular books on prayer. They prescribed a framework: the number of benedictions comprising each prayer – such as the eighteen of the week-day 'amida, the seven of the sabbath and festivals, and so forth. They also prescribed the topic of each benediction; for example, in a given benediction one must ask for the rebuilding of Jerusalem; in another for the ingathering of the exiles. But they did not, nor did they ever seek to, prescribe the wording of any benediction or any prayer. That was left as a rule to the pray-er – to be exact, to the prayer-leader [a layman].

And Greenberg notes that this is in stark contrast to both Babylonian and Roman practice, where, if the exact wording of a prayer was not followed, the prayer was deemed invalid.[6]

What then is involved? Let us return to Hannah and to her first prayer. She goes to the Temple at Shiloh, bitter at heart because she is barren, and vows a vow, asking the Lord not to forget her:

> And it came to pass, as she continued praying before the Lord, that Eli marked her mouth. Now Hannah, she spake in her heart; only her lips moved, but her voice was not heard: therefore Eli thought she had been drunken. And Eli said unto her, How long wilt thou be drunken? put away thy wine from thee. And Hannah answered and said, No, my lord, I am a woman of a sorrowful spirit: I have drunk neither wine nor strong drink, but have poured out my soul before the Lord.

> (1 Sam. 1 : 12–15)

Hannah's prayer is clearly far removed from anything that could be construed as 'merely external'. Yet her lips move and she forms words. She speaks from the heart, pouring out her soul to the Lord, but she speaks the language of men and women.

Hannah's murmured prayer raises the question: if prayers are not fixed, how does the individual know what to say? Greenberg's answer to this seems wholly convincing. One speaks to God, he suggests, as one speaks to another person. The Bible records many examples of 'prayers' made by one individual to another, from Judah's words to Joseph: 'Oh my lord, let thy servant, I pray thee, speak a word in my lord's ears, and let not thine anger burn against thy servant' (Gen. 44:18), to those of Saul's son Mephibosheth to David: 'my lord the king is as an angel of God: do therefore what is good in thine eyes' (2 Sam. 19:27). Particularly interesting in this regard is David's response to Abigail. She has begun her address to him with: 'Upon me, my lord, upon me let this iniquity be: and let thine handmaid, I pray thee, speak in thine audience, and hear the words of thine handmaid.' David responds with: 'Blessed be the Lord God of Israel, which sent thee this day to meet me: And blessed be thy advice, and blessed be thou, which hast kept me this day from coming to shed blood, and from avenging myself with mine own hand' (1 Sam. 25:24, 32–33). Here his prayer to God and to Abigail takes the same form, confirming our sense that there is no difference between a petition to a person and a petition to God.

When Jeremiah addresses God as 'a righteous judge', and refers to his plea as 'a case at law' ('I have laid my case before you' – Jer. 11:20), or when Isaiah says: 'He is near that justifieth me; who will contend with me?' (Isa. 50:8), the terms they use are those of human law courts. As Sheldon Blank says:

> The terms which are employed in passages which reflect the concept of God as judge do not differ from the terms employed in references to ordinary human courts. Accordingly...the language which a man used when, in prayer, he appealed to God as judge, corresponded to the language of a man defending himself before a human court.[7]

What both Greenberg and Blank are suggesting is that prayer finds its forms in the forms of ordinary language and in the linguistic and social usages of the community to which the one who prays belongs. This is what mediates between inner and outer, a fact long recognized by philosophers and anthropologists, but which theologians and Bible scholars have been reluctant to accept. Thus the Catholic theologian, Hans Urs von Balthasar, can equate prayer quite simply with contemplation, and spend an entire book entitled *Prayer* dealing successively with 'The Act of Contemplation', 'The Object of Contemplation', and 'Polarities in Contemplation'; while the Protestant Friedrich Heiler can talk about prayer as being 'an inner contact of the heart with God'.[8]

But we need to go further than Blank and Greenberg. We need to establish not only the necessity for prayer of such social facts as courts of law and forms of address, but also the relation between language and *need*. Hannah moving her lips is crucial testimony to the fact that prayer, like lament, is an utterance, an *outering*. Hannah's two prayers are of a piece, even if one is very much her own and the other takes the form of a thanksgiving psalm that could appear in the Psalter. In both cases the available forms of language are what help the heart to flow.

One of the most common ways of starting to utter a prayer is the one David uses when replying to Abigail: 'Blessed be the Lord God of Israel ...'. David blesses the Lord? How can that be? Scholars have set about explaining it historically, suggesting that once YHWH was only one god among many and subject to forces greater than himself. But we don't need so far-fetched an explanation, as Greenberg rightly observes.[9] To say 'Blessed be YHWH' is not to call on some higher power to bless the Lord, but to put oneself in a certain posture in relation to the Lord, to move the lips in a certain way, which will allow the heart to be poured out like water. It is a form of speech which asks for nothing and says nothing about the world; but that does not mean that it is an uncommon form of speech. On the contrary, it is the most common form there is, even if it is only with certain modern dramatists like Beckett and Pinter that Western literature has come to acknowledge that fact.

In Beckett's *Not I* words pour in an almost incomprehensible torrent from the mouth which is the only visible part of the only figure on stage who speaks. The condition of the character's speech is that she cannot say 'I', and the implications of this are profoundly ambiguous. On the one hand it is a denial of personal responsibility, a refusal to acknowledge herself, and as such calls forth a gesture of melancholy resignation from the other, silent, figure on the stage, each time she approaches that 'I' and then veers away from it into 'What?...Who?...No!...She!...' On the other hand, her ability to bypass the 'I' allows her to speak, and thus utter what has been bottled up inside her all her life. It is perhaps in a somewhat similar fashion that David comes to terms with his own anger against Nabal as he confronts Abigail, or that Jeremiah, arraigning God (who, in this strange trial, is both defendant and judge) for letting his enemies triumph, is finally led to understand that the error is not the Lord's but his.

We come back then to the contrast drawn by the prophets between the 'pouring out' of the heart and the 'hardening' of the heart. By themselves words are nothing, 'mere' words. But without words there is nothing either. We tend to think of sincerity as the revealing of the heart and hypocrisy as the concealing of it, but it is both much simpler and much more complex than this. Simpler because we are dealing not with something exceptional but with something which is so much a part of our daily lives that we are not even aware of it; more complex because the modern (and Protestant) contrast between inner and outer leaves no place not only for prayer but also for our most mundane daily activities.

We are thus faced with a situation where we have neither the vocabulary nor the images to explain to ourselves something with which we are instinctively familiar.

To pour out means to trust; to trust that language will help me to discover what it is I need to say. To say 'Blessed be' rather than 'I' is to give language its head, not to seek to say only what *I* have already decided *I* am going to say. We may find this odd, but we see it in the remarks of many artists. In the catalogue of a recent exhibition of paintings by Ken Kiff, for example, the artist is quoted as saying: 'I don't know of any paintings that were altered so endlessly. . . . At the end of the period a couple of paintings resulted and I felt yes, I must be that kind of painter.'[10]

Only by making a great many paintings could Kiff discover what kind of a painter he was; only by speaking can one discover what it is one wants to say. To harden one's heart is precisely to substitute an idol of oneself, an image of what one thinks one is and what it is one ought to say, for the person one is, a free being made in God's image. God made man out of dust. Then he gave him language and a wife. By entering language and the community of men I find myself. To speak to God is to acknowledge this, that in speaking I trust that I will find myself. That is why the poems of Herbert, the English poet most deeply imbued with the Psalms, so often exhibit a profound change at the end; for it is the act of making the poem, of uttering it, that leads to change, to an unblocking, and so to a new simplicity, a new clarity, 'something understood'.[11]

Let us return to Jonah. Before his prayer, as I've said, comes that of the sailors. They are not Hebrews, and when the storm gets up each man prays to his own god. However, this seems to do no good, for the storm continues unabated, and when Jonah tells them it is his god who made the winds they seem to decide it would be a good idea to pray to him. So 'they cried unto YHWH' (Jonah 1 : 14). Two verses later we learn that they 'feared YHWH exceedingly' and 'offered a sacrifice unto the Lord' (16). But though the seas are calmed when Jonah is thrown overboard, we leave the sailors at this point and travel with Jonah into the belly of the big fish. It is here that he utters his long prayer, which forms chapter 2 of this four-chapter book, and the form of his prayer has long puzzled commentators. 'I cried by reason of mine affliction unto the Lord, and he heard me; out of the belly of hell [*Sheol*] cried I, and thou heardest my voice. . .' (2 : 2). *Karati*, 'I cried', says Jonah. But why does he speak in the past tense? Is he not crying out now, inside the fish's belly? Commentators have tried to explain this by saying that he spoke the prayer *after* his sojourn in the belly of the fish; or that what we are dealing with here is an example of the so-called 'prophetic perfect', that is, a past tense which really denotes future; or that the prayer is an interpolation.

All these explanations are attempts (as so often in Bible studies) to avoid the oddity of the original. And it is very odd indeed. It exists in the present of narration ('Then Jonah prayed unto the Lord his God out of the fish's belly, And said. . .' – 2 : 1–2), but it tells of something which seems to be past. Yet the past action it tells of is nothing but the present action of praying: 'I cried by reason of mine affliction unto the Lord . . . out of the belly of hell cried I . . .'. It is as if Jonah were looking at himself praying in the fish's belly from some quite other vantage point. But this surely is his way of not saying 'I'; and, as in Beckett's play, the avoidance of responsibility for himself becomes a way of accepting it.

For now, instead of simply running away from God, as he tried to do in chapter 1, he speaks to him, even if in this strange indirect way. And as he speaks of this figure who once spoke, he enters areas he had not ever thought or wished to enter:

> The waters compassed me about, even to the soul: the depth closed me round about, the weeds were wrapped about my head. I went down to the bottoms of the mountains; the earth with her bars was about me for ever.
>
> (Jonah 2 : 5–6)

In verse 2, in a phrase I deliberately left out when quoting the passage above, he says: 'Out of the belly of hell cried I, *and thou heardest my voice.*' God's hearing his voice does not at this point carry much conviction, though it is perhaps the act of saying it that allows him to continue. By verse 6, however, he can return to it a little more confidently: 'the earth with her bars was about me for ever: yet hast thou brought up my life from corruption, O Lord my God.' Now he acknowledges that the Lord is *his* God, and he can go on: 'When my soul fainted within me I remembered the Lord: and my prayer came in unto thee, into thine holy temple' (7). We are still in the past, but now the 'cry' of the opening has become a 'prayer' (*tefilah*).

Jonah is still thinking very much of himself – *I* remembered, *my* prayer – but there is the sense of something unblocking. It leads to the rather odd phrase which follows, seemingly unrelated to what has gone before: 'They that observe lying vanities forsake their own mercy' (8). But in fact the objective tone heralds an important gain. If this reads like one of the duller proverbs, it nevertheless prepares the way for the sudden flurry of futures that follow: 'I will sacrifice unto thee with the voice of thanksgiving; I will pay that that I have vowed.' And so, finally, to a kind of open present, for the first time in the prayer, and, in a sense, for the first time in the narrative: 'Salvation is of the Lord.' (*yeshu'atah* 'salvation', NEB for some reason translates as 'victory', which seems to ruin the passage.) At this point, having finally accepted to open his heart to the Lord, to recognize him as his God, to speak out his praise with no thought of himself, Jonah is freed from his affliction and restored to the dry land: 'And the Lord spake unto the fish, and it vomited out Jonah upon the dry land' (2 : 10).[12]

But we have not finished with Jonah; or rather, the book of Jonah has not finished with us. The final irony is that when Jonah does eventually preach to Nineveh he is so effective that the city repents, whereupon the Lord shows it mercy; Jonah is furious at this, as though his authority as a prophet had been impugned, and he prays again for the Lord to take his life from him, for 'it is better for me to die than to live' (4 : 3). The very same word, *yitpalel*, is used here as in 2 : 1, suggesting that prayer is a neutral term for a particular action rather than a positive term for some sort of sacred contemplation. In the fish's belly Jonah could find no help through his own wits and in despair turned to God, who, as always, was ready to hear. But now Jonah is in no danger. His prayer is petulant, childish. And God answers, as he answered Job, not with a statement, not with a deed, but with a question: 'Doest thou well to be angry?'

Jonah does not reply, and shortly after we get a repetition of this extraordinary scene. Jonah makes himself a booth and sits in its shade, waiting to see what will happen to the city. God makes a gourd grow up overnight to give Jonah more protection, but then destroys it through sun and wind. Jonah is indignant once again, and the book ends, strangely, with the prophet, the Lord's spokesman, silent in the face of God's question:

> Then said the Lord, Thou hast had pity on the gourd, for the which thou hast not laboured, neither madest it grow; which came up in a night, and perished in a night: And should not I spare Nineveh, that great city, wherein are more than sixscore thousand persons that cannot discern between their right hand and their left hand; and also much cattle?
>
> (Jonah 4 : 10–11)

It is as though God himself had a need to utter. Not just to outer himself by creating the world and its creatures (through speech in the first place, of course), but by talking to them once they had been created. And when he does so his forms of speech are not just orders, as they are with tyrants like Pharaoh and Herod, but questions, pleas and exhortations.

As we have seen, the most terrible thing the Psalmist can envisage is to go down to Sheol, because there one cannot extol God. But praise of the Lord, in which, as Psalm 19 says, all of nature takes part, is not qualitatively different from songs of triumph and lamentation, or from such direct human utterances as Moses' 'Here am I' or David's 'Oh my son, my son!' The primary function of language, the Hebrew Bible shows, is not to convey information but to enable us to outer ourselves and thus come fully alive.

There is, however, one final twist that needs to be noted. Psalm 137 has always been recognized as one of the supreme examples of the genre, a wonderful poem of exile and lament (though the last verse has caused problems to those whose notion of a loving God is not quite the same as the Bible's):

> By the rivers of Babylon, there we sat down, yea, we
> wept, when we remembered Zion.
>
> We hanged our harps upon the willows in the midst
> thereof.
>
> For there they that carried us away captive required
> of us a song; and they that wasted us required
> of us mirth, saying, Sing us one of the songs
> of Zion.
>
> How shall we sing the Lord's song in a strange land?
>
> If I forget thee, O Jerusalem, let my right hand
> forget her cunning.
>
> If I do not remember thee, let my tongue cleave to
> the roof of my mouth; if I prefer not Jerusalem
> above my chief joy.
>
> (Ps. 137:1–6)

The most obvious way to take the poem is to imagine it as written after the return from Babylon, and as a reminder of what the professional Temple singers and players experienced there, though we might also take it, like Jonah's prayer, as written in the exile yet as though looking back on it.[13] The singers are asked to perform their songs for the entertainment of their captors, rather as Samson was required to perform in Gaza. But how can they do this? Their songs are not entertainment, they are not 'art'.[14] So it is better to respond with silence, to hang up the harps and refuse to play.

But the irony of this is immense. We have seen in the previous chapter the importance of remembering for Israel. We have seen how for Jonah remembering and praying seem to be almost one. Prayers are frequently couched in the form of a petition that God should not forget the person praying, and when God says that he will remember Israel it means that, in spite of everything, he is prepared to go on playing his part in the covenant relation. Yet here to remember is to refuse to speak, for 'How shall we sing the Lord's song in a strange land?' And the speaker goes on to make a vow: If I forget you, O Jerusalem, let me lose the ability ever again to play the harp and sing the Lord's songs. By singing *here* he will lose the ability to sing *when he returns*. Only by keeping silent can he preserve the precious gift of speech; only by not speaking when to speak would be to speak falsely, can he remember.

For one who holds that the only true prayer is internal there is no problem. But for one who believes that it is man's role on earth to sing the praises of the Lord; that the only way the Lord will help us is if we ask for help; who knows that we are not fully ourselves till we outer ourselves in speech – for such a one the condemnation to silence is like the condemnation to death. Yet in that willing death alone lies the possibility that our daily life will again flourish. As so often in the Bible, it is the moment of paradox which drives the reality of the everyday home to us.

IX

DIALOGUE AND DISTANCE

Without the injunction to remember and to tell, we have seen, there would have been no Bible. Without the recognition of man's need to utter, no matter what, in moments of crisis, of triumph and despair, the Bible would have been quite other than it is. But the bed-rock of speech is of course dialogue. The Bible opens with an utterance dividing the envelope of silence, and this is followed by God making the world out of speech and conferring on Adam the power to name the animals. But naming is not really typical of speech. Speech implies another, and it is in dialogue with man that God reveals how utterly different he is from the other gods of the ancient world. He, the creator of all things, the utterly other, both talks to man and, more important, listens.

It is one of the characteristics of dialogue that it both maintains distance between the two persons engaged in it and bridges that distance. Walter Benjamin, commenting on a poem of Brecht's, and writing not about dialogue but about friendship, puts it beautifully. 'It does not abolish the distance between human beings,' he says, 'but brings that distance to life.'[1] Yet dialogue will only do this if both partners abide by its rules. It is always possible for one of them to refuse to take part, or to try and flout the rules. In fact the best way to approach a study of dialogue in the Bible is to look at one or two examples of such a refusal.

The first occurs almost as soon as the possibilities of dialogue are established by the creation of man. We are told that when Adam had eaten of the tree of knowledge he became self-conscious and wished to cover up his nakedness. When he heard 'the voice of the Lord God walking in the garden in the cool [*ruach*, 'breath'] of the day' (Gen. 3:8), he hid himself. Why? Because speech implies coming face to face with the person with whom one is speaking; Adam hides himself because he cannot face God. When God finds him – and the ensuing dialogue is wonderfully airy, unlocalized, yet direct, so that we do not know if Adam and God are actually facing each other or are talking across a screen of trees and leaves – when God finds him we can imagine that he bowed his face to the ground in shame and could not look God in the eye.

This tells us something important about dialogue: a person can conceal his feelings in a letter, but in actual dialogue his voice is likely to betray him. 'The voice is Jacob's voice, but the hands are the hands of Esau' (Gen. 27:22), says the blind Isaac, as his groping fingers touch the hairy covering Jacob has put on to conceal his true identity. Leah, in Jacob's bed instead of his beloved Rachel, and Tamar in her harlot's guise making sure that Judah's seed is preserved, must, we feel, have kept their words down to a minimum, or they would have been discovered.

But note the ironies of the episode of the blessing of Jacob. Jacob says 'I am Esau' to his blind father, and the old man has no option but to believe him. For if the voice is likely to give one away, words may trick one's interlocutor. The serpent can mislead Eve and Jacob Isaac, and Hushai may persuade Absalom to take the wrong course of action, though in the last two instances it may be that, from God's point of view, the right outcome has been achieved after all.

Jacob's lie leads to his being blessed instead of his brother. And once the blessing is given, even if it is given in error, it seems that it cannot be taken back. That would appear to follow from the fact that while the voice is natural, language is conventional; it is because lies such as Jacob's are possible that it is also possible for there to be promises, convenants, blessings; that is, certain forms of language which are guaranteed not through any inherent virtue but through agreement between the parties.

The blessing is a performative utterance: there is not on the one hand speech and on the other blessing. Note though how the words of blessing grow out of the whole scene:

> And his father Isaac said unto him, Come near now, and kiss me, my son. And he came near, and kissed him: and he smelled the smell of his raiment, and blessed him, and said, See, the smell of my son is as the smell of a field which the Lord hath blessed: Therefore God give thee of the dew of heaven, and the fatness of the earth, and plenty of corn and wine: Let people serve thee, and nations bow down to thee: be lord over thy brethren, and let thy mother's sons bow down to thee: cursed be every one that curseth thee, and blessed be he that blesseth thee. And it came to pass, as soon as Isaac had made an end of blessing Jacob,

that Esau arrived and the trick was discovered:

> And Isaac trembled very exceedingly, and said, Who? where is he that hath taken venison, and brought it me, and I have eaten of all before thou camest, and have blessed him? yea, and he shall be blessed. And when Esau heard the words of his father, he cried with a great and exceeding bitter cry, and said unto his father, Bless me, even me also, O my father. And he said, Thy brother came with subtility [bemirmah, from the same root as arum, the

descriptive epithet for the serpent, a significant echo which AV picks up but not NEB, which has 'treacherously' here], and hath taken away thy blessing.

(Gen. 27 : 26–35)

Once the words have been spoken, the blessing given, it cannot be taken back.

There is an even more terrible example of the irreversibility of words solemnly spoken in the story of Jephtha:

> And Jephtha vowed a vow unto the Lord, and said, If thou shalt without fail deliver the children of Ammon into mine hands, Then it shall be, that whatsoever cometh forth of the doors of my house to meet me, when I return in peace from the children of Ammon, shall surely be the Lord's, and I will offer it up for a burnt offering.
>
> (Judg. 11 : 30–31)

Rabbinic commentary is quick to point out Jephtha's culpability; he is, say the rabbis, one of three men who framed a vow carelessly. As is often the case, the reason they give for their view may strike us as unconvincing, but their instinct is surely right: it could, they say (*Taan* 4a), have been an unclean beast, and thus one unfit for sacrifice, which would have been the first to meet Jephtha, and thus he is rightly punished for his rash oath. However blame is apportioned, though, the facts remain. Jephtha goes out to fight and returns in triumph, to be met by his only daughter, 'with timbrels and with dances', and 'it came to pass, when he saw her, that he rent his clothes, and said, Alas, my daughter! thou hast brought me very low, and thou art one of them that trouble me: for I have opened my mouth unto the Lord, and I cannot go back' (Judg. 11 : 34–35).

Speech takes place in time, and, like time, it cannot be wound back. The Bible does not stop to comment or to apportion blame; it simply shows how things are. And the story of Jephtha of course has parallels in ancient Greek literature, thus alerting us to the fact that some at least of our difficulties with it have to do with its belonging to an ancient culture. John Jones, for example, in his book on Greek tragedy, has pointed out that when Aeschylus makes Agamemnon walk on the red carpet at the turning-point of the *Agamemnon*, our natural tendency today is to take this carpet as a symbol of the king's pride, whereas the correct way to read the scene, argues Jones, is much more literally: such carpets were part of the wealth of the house, and by making the head of that house trample its wealth under foot Clytemnestra was forcing him to undertake a quite literal desecration. Hence his revulsion is absolutely direct and physical and not at all symbolic.[2]

Even when we are reminded of such things, however, it is very hard for us not to feel that somehow, somewhere, there must be more than the literal reading, that something symbolic must be meant. What we cannot grasp is the horror, the religious horror, that literal trampling would arouse, because for us the religious, the familial and the economic are separated one from the other. So we do not even have a sense of mis-reading the scene. And a similar problem exists with the Bible. We must constantly renew the effort not to translate what we read into our own terms, but always try to grasp it in the terms in which it is presented. When we do so we will often find, not an unbridgeable gulf between its world and ours, but rather that it reminds us of things we always knew but have somehow forgotten.

If words are irreversible, there is also no escape from dialogue:

> Now the word of the Lord came unto Jonah the son of Amittai, saying, Arise, go to Nineveh, that great city, and cry against it; for their wickedness is come up before me. But Jonah rose up to flee unto Tarshish from the presence of the Lord....
>
> (Jonah 1 : 1–3)

Rather than talk to God face to face (or mouth to mouth, as the Bible so often and suggestively puts it), Jonah tries to flee. He boards a ship going to Tartessos in Spain, the very limit of the known world. But God will not let him go. It is interesting to note that when the mariners, desperate because of the storm God has raised up and which is about to destroy them, rouse Jonah, he is sleeping in the very bowels of the ship.[3] And the word the Bible uses for his deep sleep is *vayeradam*, the verb con-nected to *tardemah*, the deep sleep which comes upon Adam when Eve is drawn out of his side by God. It seems to be a loss of consciousness, which in the case of Jonah one can only feel to be willed, a reversion, as the story makes clear, to the time before man was called upon to speak, when he could claim he was still unformed, still a part of the earth. Jonah's removal from ship's belly to whale's belly is only a confirmation by God of that state. However, after three days and three nights in the fish's belly, Jonah discovers that this is not where he wants to be. As we saw in the last chapter, he suddenly finds it in himself to give voice; he calls out to God and God responds.

That there is no escape from dialogue is recognized by all those who are called by God: Noah, Abraham, Moses, Samuel, Isaiah, Jeremiah. When God first calls them their response is usually: 'Please, leave me alone. I don't want to speak to you. I'm not worthy. I can't do it. Try someone else.' Nevertheless, they answer, and God strengthens them, telling them he will always be with them:

> And when the Lord saw that he turned aside to see, God called unto him out of the midst of the bush, and said, Moses, Moses. And he said, Here am I. And he said, Draw not nigh hither: put off thy shoes from off thy feet, for the place whereon thou standest is holy ground.... And Moses said unto God,

Who am I, that I should go unto Pharaoh, and that I should bring forth the children of Israel out of Egypt? And he said, Certainly I will be with thee.

(Exod. 3:4–12)

The same elements are found in the calling of Jeremiah:

Then the word of the Lord came unto me, saying, Before I formed thee in the belly I knew thee; and before thou camest forth out of the womb I sanctified thee, and I ordained thee a prophet unto the nations. Then said I, Ah, Lord God! behold, I cannot speak: for I am a child. But the Lord said unto me, Say not, I am a child: for thou shalt go to all that I shall send thee, and whatsoever I command thee thou shalt speak. Be not afraid of their faces: for I am with thee to deliver thee, saith the Lord. Then the Lord put forth his hand, and touched my mouth. And the Lord said unto me, Behold, I have put my words in thy mouth.

(Jer. 1:4–9)

The words in the two instances are almost identical, and they occur again and again whenever dialogue with God begins: 'here am I', *hineni*. Let us pause for a minute now to examine the expression and the drama in which it occurs.

I use the word 'drama' here advisedly. Talk by theologians about the primacy of event in the Bible can make us forget that dialogue too is an event. In the Hebrew Bible the call of God and the answer *hineni* constitute moments of particular dramatic significance. *Hineni* is a performative utterance, as much as 'I promise' and 'I bless'. By saying *hineni* the speaker accepts responsibility for himself and for whatever task God may impose upon him. Adam and Jonah, quite simply, refuse to say *hineni*.

Note how, in the encounter with the burning bush, neither we nor Moses can be sure of the outcome. It seems to happen by chance, and it is certainly unrelated to any particular spot. Moses has come from Egypt to Midian and got married. He drives his father-in-law Jethro's flock out of the settlement 'to the backside of the desert' (*achar hamidbar*), and comes to a mountain. He sees a bush burning but not burnt up, and 'turns aside' even from his pathless desert track to see what this means. It is at this point that God speaks to him. But even after he has said *hineni* we feel that Moses is still restless, that he might still decide to break away: 'Who am I, that I should go unto Pharaoh?' he asks, and then, 'When I come to the children of Israel, who shall I say sent me?' Even when God replies at length to this, saying that Moses must tell them that I AM THAT I AM has sent him, Moses is still unconvinced: 'But, behold, they will not believe me, nor hearken unto my voice.' It is not that Moses, like Jonah, refuses; it is that until an event is accomplished, it is always possible that something other than the expected will happen. Unlike Odysseus or Achilles, Moses does not appear to us with a fixed character; events make him what he is.

It is interesting too to compare this episode with an epiphany described in ancient Greek literature. In *Oedipus at Colonus* the aged Sophocles pays homage to his own little spot of ground, Colonus, outside Athens. To this sacred site comes the old blind Oedipus, led by his daughter, to seek refuge from his enemies. Oedipus' blindness is actually what makes us *see* the place, for as he gropes his way about the stage, helped by Antigone, the fact that he has to feel his way helps transform an empty space into the sacred spot. And at the end, when Oedipus encounters the god who calls for him, and is taken from the earth, Sophocles again denies us the fact of sight, that we may experience the more: the messenger *tells* us how he saw Theseus *hiding his eyes* as he was about to see Oedipus taken up, and that triple remove from the actual encounter brings it home to us in a way no stage machinery could ever have done. The play is at once a celebration of place and of the theatre, and it makes us realize how appropriate it is that the theatre should have been the chief glory of the Greeks, for whom every grove was sacred.

By contrast, the burning bush could be anywhere. What is celebrated is not the place but the encounter, not vision but speech. God speaks and he calls forth speech from Moses. That is enough, even for this key moment in the history of God's relations with men, and with Israel in particular. The Bible of course has its share of holy places, from the cave of Machpelah to Jerusalem; but its emphasis lies elsewhere. By the same token its form is narrative, and when a writer called Ezekiel tried, in the second century BCE, to write a tragedy in the manner of the Greeks, about the events which make up Exodus 1–15, the result was laughable:

MOSES: Aha! What token this from yonder bush,
        some sign beyond belief to mortal men?
        A bush that sudden burns, with raging flame,
        and yet its shoots remain all green and fresh.
        What then! I shall advance and view this sign,
        so great it seems incredible to men.

GOD: Stay, Moses, best of men, do not come near
        till you have loosed the bindings from your feet;
        the place on which you stand is holy ground.[4]

If this sounds like the mechanicals' play in A *Midsummer Night's Dream*, it is only partly the fault of the translator and the author; the main reason is that the material is simply intractable. Dialogue does not equal drama, as many novelists have found out to their grief.

What is striking about the biblical episode is that though it is one of the central encounters between God and man in the whole book, there is nothing elevated about the language and the narrative moves as fast as it always does. Though *hineni* is the common response to the call of God, it is not used uniquely in conversations between God and man, just as we saw that the phrase 'Blessed be' was not unique to encounters between God and man. In the episode of the blessing of Jacob it is significant that Esau says *hineni* to his father, and Isaac says it to Jacob, but the disguised Jacob never uses the phrase. He cannot, of course, because he only obtains the blessing by denying his own self.

The word is particularly obtrusive in Genesis 22:

> And it came to pass after these things, that God did tempt Abraham, and said unto him, Abraham: and he said, *hineni*. . . . And Isaac spake unto Abraham his father, and said, My father: and he said, *hineni*, my son. . . . And the angel of the Lord called unto him out of heaven, and said, Abraham, Abraham: and he said, *hineni*.
>
> (Gen. 22 : 1, 7, 11)

Isaac, the angel and God all use the same form of words, and to each Abraham replies, *hineni*, so that a sense is established of reciprocal trust between Abraham and God, Isaac and Abraham.

An even clearer example of the naturalness of the use of the term is provided by the story of the calling of Samuel. The child Samuel, it will be recalled, ministered to the Lord before Eli, and when he lay down to sleep 'the Lord called Samuel: and he answered, *hineni*. And he ran unto Eli, and said, *hineni*; for thou calledst me. And he said, I called not; lie down again.' This happens three times, and finally Eli understands what is going on: 'Go,' he says to Samuel, 'lie down: and it shall be, if he call thee, that thou shalt say, Speak, Lord; for thy servant heareth.' (1 Sam. 3 : 4–9)

We can now perhaps see why the commandment, you shall make to yourselves no graven images, must be central. 'And the Lord spake unto you out of the midst of the fire,' we read in Deuteronomy; 'ye heard the voice of the words, but saw no similitude; only ye heard a voice' (4 : 12). The commandment follows at once:

> Take ye therefore good heed unto yourselves; for ye saw no manner of similitude on the day that the Lord spake unto you in Horeb out of the midst of the fire: Lest ye corrupt yourselves, and make you a graven image, the similitude of any figure.
>
> (Deut. 4 : 15–16)

The fear of idols is not simply the fear of the gods of the nations in the midst of which Israel finds itself. It springs from the sense Israel has of two totally opposed views of the world. In one view the world is given, the gods control it, and their worship is linked to the worship of nature and the visible world; and just as the gods reside in nature so they reside in idols made from nature, objects in which are magical powers. These objects may be kept in the house, even under the bed or inside one's clothes. Because power resides in the idol, though, if it is stolen or defaced you are in danger, and therefore you have to be perpetually vigilant. For Israel, on the other hand, God is not a possession or an object of any kind. He is a person with whom one can talk. The fear of him is not the magical fear of an object which possesses occult power, but stems from the realization that to be called by God means having to respond, and that this is never an easy or a painless thing. On the other hand, wherever you are, in the desert or at sea, he will always be ready to listen and reply.

Such a reply will never, in the nature of things, be final. Dialogue takes place in time. Promises and covenants, as we have seen, are only an extension of dialogue. They too depend on the acceptance of the future as open. The meaning of Israel's destiny, like that of each individual, is not something that is given once and for all, or something which we can examine like a diagram; it is something that grows and changes and develops, just as the meaning of any exchange of words between two people resides not in any single word or sentence but rather in the whole encounter. And even that encounter is only one of many and takes its meaning from those which precede and follow it. Had Moses not been told the stories of God's appearance to the Patriarchs he would not have been so ready to respond to him, and had we not been living with this God from the beginning of Creation, so to speak, we would not have known what to make of him when he speaks to Abraham.

Dialogue, however, can be frustrating. Men hunger for certainties which speech will always deny. The Bible recognizes this hunger and its dangers, and so it shows us both the primacy of dialogue and the way men try to avoid it. But to avoid it is to fall into idolatry. There is no third way. In the episode of the Tower of Babel we see how men try to bypass dialogue and its uncertainties and to reach up to heaven not through words but through the erection of a giant tower which, they feel, will close for ever the gap which exists between heaven and earth. As a result of this they are dispersed over the earth and their language is fragmented into mutually incomprehensible tongues. Dante, following midrashic tradition, tells us that the giant Nimrod was the builder of the tower,[5] and his punishment in Hell consists in his being cut off entirely from the speech of men (*Inferno* xxxi). When Dante puts a question to him he can only gabble incoherently, leading Virgil to rebuke him: 'Stupid soul, keep to your horn and with that vent yourself when rage or other passion takes you.' Then he turns to Dante the pilgrim and says:

> He is his own accuser: this is Nimrod, through whose ill thought one language only is not used in the world. Let us leave him alone and not speak in vain, for every language is to him as his is to others, which is known to none.

> (*Inferno*, tr. C. S. Singleton, xxxi. 70–80)

To speak, to enter into dialogue, implies the acceptance of distance and limitation. It depends on a voluntary giving up of a part of the self.

Dante rightly places Nimrod deep in the pit of Hell, for Hell is the place where those who will not renounce the self reside. What Nimrod tries to do, Dante suggests, is speak a language of pure subjectivity. He refuses to abide by the rules of speech which we all have to observe if we are to say anything at all. And this attempt at total freedom naturally results in total bondage, the bondage to one's private whims and fancies, whereas the acceptance of language and its limitations leads us back both to the world and to ourselves. Thus any true dialogue will have to accept what God accepted from the start: that we will not be bound by any image of ourselves but will trust dialogue to reveal to us our own potential.

There is of course one other place in the Bible where men try to bypass the process of dialogue and to become like God instead of being content to speak to him. That is the episode of the eating from the forbidden tree. Meir Sternberg has made the point that in other ancient cultures what separates gods and men is the fact of immortality, whereas in the Bible it is knowledge.[6] What he fails to bring out is that even God does not possess knowledge as a kind of lump, that though he may indeed know the hearts of men he does not know where what he has created will lead him: it is not a problem only for Moses and Jeremiah, that they are free to refuse.

The temptation offered by the serpent is simple: eat and you will not need to talk to God any more, for you will *be* a God and know all. Instead of recognizing that we must go by way of dialogue, that we cannot ingest knowledge, Adam and Eve listen to the words of another and accept them, even when those words urge them to do something which will bring about the end of words. We can relish the irony of it. Adam, already a product of splitting when he emerged from the *adamah*, and split again when he and Eve were separated, is now, as a result of that further split, attempting to return to a primal wholeness, to a state in which the perpetual splitting, to which dialogue bears witness, will no longer take place. Does the snake know the truth? Does he know that God does not know in the way Adam imagines? Who can tell? As readers we follow the exchanges, and can now finally understand the full irony of Adam's shamed attempt to hide himself from God when God calls out to him in the cool of the day: he who had tried to overcome speech has forfeited speech; when God calls out he can only hide.

Every event that takes place in the Hebrew Bible seems to have a meaning, but this does not imply that the meaning can be spelt out. We sense that the binding of Isaac is meaningful, but our way of asserting it is not to dissect it but to *repeat* it. Events, as I suggested in an earlier chapter, are not so much interpreted as lovingly recalled and retold. Questions are certainly raised, but there is no great urgency to answer them. That Sarah conceived after the age at which such things are possible, that Joseph survived and brought his brothers and father down to Egypt, that God made it possible for Moses to lead the descendants of Jacob back out of Egypt – that is what is important. Why and how these things happened is much less so. Events in the narrative portions of the Hebrew Bible happen in the way they do because the world in which they occur goes easy, so to speak, on interpretation. We invoke such events, remember them in wonder, question them. But a question is never meant to throw up an answer, only another question.

With the writing prophets, however, we see a new will at work. Meaning becomes of vital importance; how things are interpreted becomes crucial. It is as if the weight of dialogue had become too great for the nation of Israel. It splits into two: those who will not listen to the word of God, and those who denounce the others for not listening.

We do not know where Isaiah was the day God called him. We know only that, unlike Moses, who only saw a bush burning as he went about his task of looking after Jethro's flock, and then heard a voice calling him, Isaiah had quite an elaborate vision, apparently in the Temple. He tells us that he 'saw...the Lord sitting upon a throne, high and lifted up', and describes his throne, his train, the six seraphim who surround him, the smoke filling the sanctuary, and the voice, so powerful that the very door posts move, saying: 'Whom shall I send, and who will go for us?' (Isa. 6:1–8)

Unlike Moses, Isaiah answers at once: 'Here am I. Send me.' But send him to do what? Moses had to deliver the people from bondage to Egyptian taskmasters; Isaiah is only asked to speak: 'Go,' says the Lord, 'and tell this people.' But what is he to tell them? At the time the small northern states of Aram and Israel were preparing to attack Judah, depose the king and establish a puppet ruler. Various strategies were being mooted for dealing with the situation: capitulation was one, and alliance with the much greater power of Assyria was another. The removal of the king, however, would mean the disappearance of the line of David from the throne in Jerusalem. Isaiah, it seems, was to press the king and the people not to panic, to inform them that soon the threat from Aram and Israel would evaporate and they would be swallowed up by Assyria; but he was also to warn the people that if they did not trust in the Lord Assyria would in turn devour them:

> Then said the Lord unto Isaiah, Go forth now to meet Ahaz, thou, and Shear-jashub thy son.... And say unto him, Take heed, and be quiet; fear not, neither be fainthearted for the two tails of these smoking firebrands....
> (Isa. 7:3–4)

At this point, rather oddly, the Lord speaks directly to Ahaz, but not as he spoke to Abraham or Moses. He tells him to 'ask thee a sign of the Lord thy God' (7:11). Ahaz is not a bad man, but, like most of us, he would rather not take risks, at the same time as he wants to appear to be doing the right and noble thing. So he says: 'I will not ask, neither will I tempt the Lord' (12). But Isaiah sees through him. If he will not ask for a sign, a sign will be given to him whether he likes it or not:

> And he said, Hear ye now, O house of David; . . . the Lord himself shall give you a sign; Behold, a virgin shall conceive, and bear a son, and shall call his name Immanuel.
>
> (Isa. 7:13–14)

Moses too had asked God for a sign, and had been shown the miracle of the staff that turned into a snake and the hand that became leprous. But the signs in Isaiah are much harder to decipher. Names seem suddenly to mean a great deal. First we had Isaiah's own son, called 'A Remnant Will Return' (she'ar yashuv) and now we learn of another child, called 'God Is With Us' ('imanu el). What are we to make of it? What does Ahaz in fact make of it?

Very little, it seems, for the Lord's next instructions to Isaiah are to make his message much more explicit. He is to take a tablet and write upon it 'Maher-shalal-hash-baz' ('The spoil speedeth, the prey hasteth' – 8:1). He is to have this recorded by two faithful witnesses, and then to seal it up so that no one may later accuse him of falsifying the deed after the event. But it is the next sequence of events which is really surprising:

> And I went unto the prophetess; and she conceived, and bare a son. Then said the Lord to me, Call his name Maher-shalal-hash-baz. For before the child shall have knowledge to cry, My father, and my mother, the riches of Damascus and the spoil of Samaria shall be taken away before the king of Assyria.
>
> (Isa. 8:3–4)

It is as though the written and sealed message is not enough, just as the merely uttered message about Immanuel had not been enough. Isaiah's own child will be given the name that implies the imminent destruction of the two nations, so that when he grows up he may be a living witness to the correctness of his father's prophecy, and, perhaps, a living witness to Ahaz's folly in ignoring it. 'Bind up the testimony,' he commands, and 'seal the law among my disciples',

> And I will wait upon the Lord, that hideth his face from the house of Jacob, and I will look for him. Behold, I and the children whom the Lord hath given me are for signs and for wonders in Israel from the Lord of hosts, which dwelleth in mount Zion.
>
> (Isa. 8:16–18)

And he warns them: in times of danger you will be tempted to seek out 'familiar spirits' and 'wizards that peep, and that mutter' (8:19). But that is only to act like Ahaz refusing to ask anything at all. Rather, let the people hear the message that he brings.

But 'hear' is of course a metaphor here. For the message is enshrined in the boy and his name. Isaiah and his sons stand before the king and the people as living witnesses of God's message.

It is as if words can no longer bear the burden of what they are being asked to do. They have become the 'peeping' and 'muttering' of familiar spirits. On the other hand, for the prophets the words God speaks seem more powerful and more terrible than ordinary words. They are a roaring like that of a lion, says Amos, and Jeremiah confesses that 'his word was in mine heart as a burning fire shut up in my bones, and I was weary with forbearing, and I could not stay' (Jer. 20:9). It is no wonder that such words cannot simply be passed on to men, that they have somehow to be supplemented by that which is other than words, that which will guarantee the validity of words.

The prophetic books are full of visions and actions whose function is to supplement words, to speak, as it were, louder than words. First of all there is the simple emblematic or allegorical vision:

> The Lord shewed me, and, behold, two baskets of figs were set before the temple of the Lord.... One basket had very good figs, even like the figs that are first ripe: and the other basket had very naughty [ra'ot, 'bad'] figs, which could not be eaten, they were so bad. Then said the Lord unto me, What seest thou, Jeremiah? And I said, Figs; the good figs, very good; and the evil, very evil, that cannot be eaten, they are so evil. Again the word of the Lord came unto me, saying, Thus saith the Lord, the God of Israel; Like these good figs, so will I acknowledge them that are carried away captive of Judah.... And as the evil figs, which cannot be eaten, they are so evil; surely thus saith the Lord, So will I give Zedekiah the king of Judah, and his princes, and the residue of Jerusalem, that remain in this land, and them that dwell in the land of Egypt: and I will deliver them to be removed into all the kingdoms of the earth for their hurt, to be a reproach and a proverb, a taunt and a curse, in all places whither I shall drive them.
>
> (Jer. 24:1–9)

A little more complex is the incident described in chapter 19. God orders Jeremiah to take an earthen pot and to go with the priests and elders to a certain spot, and there exhort them and tell them that God will destroy Jerusalem because the people have forsaken him. Having done so, he must break the pot in front of them: 'And [thou] shalt say unto them, Thus saith the Lord of hosts; Even so will I break this people and this city, as one breaketh a potter's vessel, that cannot be made whole again' (19:11). Here, though we still have the visual equivalent of an action , the prophet himself is involved and the vision is no longer static but being acted out before the people.

It is only a short step from this to God's command to Isaiah:

Go and loose the sackcloth from off thy loins, and put off thy shoe from thy foot. And he did so, walking naked and barefoot. And the Lord said, Like as my servant Isaiah hath walked naked and barefoot three years for a sign and wonder upon Egypt and upon Ethiopia; so shall the king of Assyria lead away the Egyptians prisoners, and the Ethiopians captives, young and old , naked and barefoot, even with their buttocks uncovered, to the shame of Egypt.

(Isa. 20:2−4)

This is disturbing because it is no longer simply emblematic. Since Isaiah has to act like this for three years it suggests that he somehow takes the suffering and shame of Egypt upon himself, and that if he did not do so it would not be visible.

Some of the same feeling adheres to the extraordinary episodes described in Jeremiah 27–28:

In the beginning of the reign of Johoiakim the son of Josiah king of Judah came this word unto Jeremiah from the Lord, saying, Thus saith the Lord to me; Make thee bonds and yokes, and put them upon thy neck.... And it shall come to pass, that the nation and kingdom which will not serve the same Nebuchadnezzar the king of Babylon, and that will not put their neck under the yoke of the king of Babylon, that nation will I punish, saith the Lord....

(Jer. 27:1–8)

However, the false prophet Hananiah will have none of this. He takes the yoke from the neck of Jeremiah and breaks it: 'And Hananiah spake in the presence of all the people, saying, Thus saith the Lord; Even so will I break the yoke of Nebuchadnezzar king of Babylon from the neck of all nations...' (28:11). The Lord, however, urges on Jeremiah: 'Go and tell Hananiah, saying, Thus saith the Lord; Thou hast broken the yokes of wood; but thou shalt make for them yokes of iron' (13). Language is now quite secondary. Not only must every statement be accompanied by a visual image, but the argument itself is reduced to a curious ritualized dumb-show.

Isaiah naming his son 'The Spoil Speedeth, The Prey Hasteth', walking barefoot for three years, Jeremiah yoking himself like a beast of burden – we are dealing here with something more than symbols or emblems. There is a drive towards total identification of the individual with the nation, towards showing God's message at work in the physical world, even to the point of taking a whole group's sins and pains into one's own body. It is perhaps most evident in Ezekiel. The Lord tells him:

Lie thou also upon thy left side, and lay the iniquity of the house of Israel upon it: according to the number of the days that thou shalt lie upon it thou shalt bear their iniquity.... And when thou hast accomplished them, lie again on thy right side.... And, behold, I will lay bands upon thee, and

thou shalt not turn thee from one side to another, till thou hast ended the
days of thy siege.

(Ezek. 4 : 4–8)

Such behaviour is not just supplementary to language; it swamps
language completely. One senses in all these prophets a terrible longing
for escape from the limited, contingency-bound use of words, to some
absolute state where all will be visible and unambiguous. This is so
important that they are willing to sacrifice themselves in order to show
upon their very bodies the meaning of the events that are occurring
around them and which the people refuse to acknowledge. Hosea takes a
whore to wife as a signal of Israel's whoredoms, and calls his children 'No
Mercy' and 'Not My People'. Even more striking is the passage in Ezekiel
which tells of the death of the prophet's wife:

Also the word of the Lord came unto me, saying, Son of man, behold, I take
away from thee the desire of thine eyes with a stroke: yet neither shalt thou
mourn nor weep, neither shall thy tears run down. Forbear to cry, make no
mourning for the dead, bind the tire of thine head upon thee, and put on thy
shoes upon thy feet, and cover not thy lips, and eat not the bread of men. So
I spake unto the people in the morning: and at even my wife died; and I did in
the morning as I was commanded. And the people said unto me, Wilt thou
not tell us what these things are to us, that thou doest so? Then I answered
them, The word of the Lord came unto me, saying, Speak unto the house of
Israel, Thus saith the Lord God; Behold, I will profane my sanctuary, the
excellency of your strength, the desire of your eyes, and that which your soul
pitieth; and your sons and your daughters whom ye have left shall fall by the
sword. And ye shall do as I have done: ye shall not cover your lips, nor eat
the bread of men . . . ye shall not mourn nor weep; but ye shall pine away for
your iniquities. . . . Thus Ezekiel is unto you a sign: according to all that he
hath done shall ye do: and when this cometh, ye shall know that I am the
Lord God.

(Ezek. 24 : 15–24)

This is terrible. Even the loss of his wife becomes a sign of something
else, visible evidence of the unity of all things, of the way the future is
already forming in the present.

We have already had occasion to discuss the intrication of the future
in the present when looking at the episode of Joseph and his dreams.
When Joseph dreamed that his father and brothers were bowing down
to him, he had a vision of the future. What we discovered in that case,
though, was that the narrative 'placed' the dream, revealed its motivation and true meaning. Joseph was right, his father and brothers *did*
come and bow down to him, but he was not as right as he imagined.
For it was to Judah that Jacob would say in blessing him: 'thy hand shall
be in the neck of thine enemies; thy father's children shall bow down

before thee' (Gen. 49:8). And so it came to pass when David finally acceded to the throne. But that was hidden from Joseph, and only much later revealed to us. Nevertheless, as it is presented in the Bible it emerges as the context in which we are to evaluate Joseph's dream.

At the other end of the Bible another dreamer appears, another Hebrew at a foreign court: Daniel. Like Joseph he is an interpreter of dreams; like Joseph's his life is in danger; like Joseph he reaches a position of great authority at a foreign court, defeating the local wise men at their very own speciality. But there is a difference. Daniel does not appear in a continuous narrative but in a short one which bears his name, and this time the narrative and the dream are one. That is, the narrative does not qualify the visions of Daniel, for the narrative is, to a large extent, made up of those visions. 'And now will I shew thee the truth', he says, and he proceeds to describe how it will be in future times, how 'there shall stand up yet three kings in Persia' (Dan. 11:2), and how they will be overthrown, how 'at that time shall Michael stand up' (12:1) and 'many of them that sleep in the dust of the earth shall awake, some to everlasting life, and some to shame and everlasting contempt' (12:2). As for the 'I' who sees and tells these things, he is told to wait in patience for the end, 'for thou shalt rest, and stand in thy lot at the end of the days' (12:13). With that the book ends.

Michael Fishbane, trying to grasp the nature of the shift from prophecy to apocalyptic, says: 'Spoken prophecies have become envisaged omens to be decoded, and the prophet has become a wise man graced with special divine understanding.'[7] This is well put. But perhaps Fishbane does not recognize clearly enough the very oddity of the prophetic stance we have been examining. Listening and speaking are no longer enough for the prophets. God and man can no longer speak in the tones and using the expressions of everyday conversation. It is as though the voice had to carry across a great distance now, and if this is partly because the audience blocks its ears, it is also because God no longer seems able to speak simply and directly. Things no longer happen, they always *mean*. But what? That is the problem: different men read the signs in different ways, and if certain men wish to persuade others of the rightness of their view they will have to use very special means. Language, at such times, seems thin and inadequate, while the distance that separates those engaged in dialogue becomes something intolerable, to be bridged at any cost. The writers of apocalyptic claim special skills, bend over the evidence, then rise to tell us what it means; but the prophets, desperate for the people to see and understand, act out that meaning on their own bodies.

The world of the Hebrew scriptures can hardly be described as a peaceful and serene one. Wars, plagues, murders and rapes abound. And yet, compared with that of the NT, it is one of normality and ordinariness. For the aberrations are set against an implicit norm, and, as we have seen, even when that norm is under the greatest strain, the underlying rhythm is always present, even if only as a faint echo. By contrast the NT presents us with a world in crisis. Crowds rush about, hysterics and epileptics abound – we are closer to the world of Dostoevsky than to that of Abraham, a world of startling peripeties and terrifying heights and depths. People talk, but not to each other. They talk to ask questions, to conceal and deny. Only fleetingly, in Jesus' parables, does the world of harvests and meals, with its ordinary simple rhythms, come to the fore. Most of the time Jesus speaks in strange, incomprehensible ways, not answering questions directly but following his own line of thought. Yet his speech is potent: he need only say 'Come forth', or 'Arise', and the sick are cured, the dead rise up.

The episode of the Gadarene swine is a good example of how the attitude to language changes in the NT. The man who comes out to meet Jesus as he emerges from the ship which has carried him safely over the water is typical of those who confront Jesus in the course of his ministry, 'a man with an unclean spirit, Who had his dwelling among the tombs' (Mark 5 : 2–3). He is so afflicted that 'no man could bind him, no, not with chains' (3). He keeps away from his fellow men, hiding among the tombs and in the mountains, crying and gashing himself with stones. When he sees Jesus he comes to him as do all those who want to be healed, but instead of begging for help he calls out: 'What have I to do with thee, Jesus, thou Son of the most high God? I adjure thee by God, that thou torment me not' (7). It seems that Jesus' mere presence is a torment greater than any of the fetters with which men have tried to bind him, yet it is also a torment he desires, for only by undergoing it will he finally be free of his demons.

Jesus has no difficulty in reading the situation. He speaks at once not to the man but directly to the tormenting spirit inside him, and a most mysterious dialogue ensues. He asks the spirit its name, whereupon it answers: 'My name is Legion: for we are many' (9). And this multiple spirit then begs Jesus first to send him/them away 'out of the country', and then, perhaps seeing that Jesus does not respond to this, begs that he send him/them into the herd of swine feeding near by. Jesus complies at once, and the herd, now itself possessed, rushes headlong over the cliff.

This powerful episode is a prime example of Jesus' ability to cure what no one else can. It inspired Dostoevsky to write one of his greatest works and it still retains, as these NT stories so often do, a mythic, resonant quality. But it is worth examining a little more carefully the nature of this myth and the attitude to dialogue and language in general displayed by the episode.

We know today that a man afflicted with epilepsy or schizophrenia is not himself, that he feels himself to be possessed by outside forces. We know too that a central feature of addiction is both to want and not to want to be cured. Jesus responds instinctively to all this. He pays no attention to anything except the essential, and, by asking the spirit its name, forces it to reveal itself. Once it has done so it is at his mercy and he proceeds to deal with it in such a way as to free the man and destroy the spirit. When we last see the man he is 'sitting, and clothed, and in his right mind' (15), and the miracle of his sudden transformation appears to frighten the villagers more than his former frenzy.

But what, we may ask, is 'his right mind' (*sōphronounta*)? We talk quite naturally today about 'pulling ourselves together', 'finding ourselves', 'knowing who we really are', and so on. The Markan narrative reinforces that predisposition: the multiple voices tearing at the man are dispelled and he is able once more to speak in his own voice, to be one, himself. At the same time he who had been an outcast is restored to society. The encounter between the man and Jesus is thus a paradigm of Jesus' encounter with the whole of mankind. For the Gospels tell us that where before there was separation and confusion there will now be clarity and unity; where men were once lost to themselves they will now be restored to themselves and to society.

This is a powerful vision. But the Hebrew scriptures present us with a very different sense of self and language. The NT story shows us a man filled with voices, with demons; Jesus expels these and the man is once more 'himself', and quiet. But Isaac and Jacob are not thought of as vessels filled with spirits. They exist in time and they do what they do for varied and sometimes contradictory reasons. When Isaac asks Jacob, 'Who are you?' he cannot, like Jesus, be sure of the true answer. 'I am Esau', says Jacob, and though his voice gives him away, his covering of skin fools the blind old man, and when the truth is discovered it is too late, the blessing has already been given. The NT, on the other hand, does not know the words 'too late'. Its thrust is always towards a future which will bring final clarification.

But do we not feel, each of us, that we are filled with many different voices? Are we sure that this is a sickness and that it is right that these voices should be reduced to one, the voice of our 'right mind'? Is there not, as we saw in the last chapter, always the need to utter, to praise and lament and not say 'I'?

The episode of the Gadarene swine cannot, however, be turned simply into an example of that supreme banality, the reintegration of the self into society, in the manner beloved of certain orthodox Freudians. For beyond the immediate dialogue another kind of discourse is going on. Read aright the episode has many of the qualities of the symbolic actions we saw the Hebrew prophets undertaking. It prefigures the ultimate tricking of the Jews, who are allowed to do what they want to Jesus precisely in order that his mission of replacing them with a new Chosen People may be accomplished. Anthony Hecht hints at this in a moving poem, called, simply, 'Pig':

> In the manger of course were cows and the Child Himself
>   Was like unto a lamb
> Who should come in the fullness of time on an ass's back
>   Into Jerusalem
>
> And all things be redeemed – the suckling babe
>   Lie safe in the serpent's home
> And the lion eat straw like the ox and roar its love
>   To Mark and to Jerome
>
> And God's Peaceable Kingdom return among them all
>   Save one full of offense
> Into which the thousand fiends of a human soul
>   Were cast and driven hence
>
> And the one thus cured gone up into the hills
>   To worship and to pray:
> O swine that takest away our sins
>   That takest away.[8]

In other words, what about the swine? And is Legion drowned for good, or will he/they only reappear elsewhere if dealt with in this way?

In the Hebrew scriptures the prophets had been the interpreters of tradition: as God once led our fathers forth out of Egyptian bondage, so will he one day lead us out of Babylon; as once he defeated the dragon of the sea, so will he one day defeat Assyria and Egypt. In the New Testament Jesus too is an interpreter, but he does not talk about the great events of the day, he talks *about himself*: 'But as the days of Noe were, so shall also the coming of the Son of man be' (Matt. 24 : 37). And, again in Matthew:

> Then certain of the scribes and of the Pharisees answered, saying, Master, we would see a sign from thee. But he answered and said unto them, An evil and adulterous generation seeketh after a sign; and there shall no sign be given to it, but the sign of the prophet Jonas: for as Jonas was three days and three nights in the whale's belly; so shall the Son of man be three days and three nights in the heart of the earth.
>
> (Matt. 12 : 38–40)

Moses showed the people signs; Isaiah, Jeremiah and Ezekiel presented *themselves* to the people as signs. But they were signs of something else. Jesus presents something else *as a sign of himself*.

I think we may not have seen quite how extraordinary this is, how it alters the very nature of signs. The prophets sensed the inadequacy of ordinary dialogue, so they went and acted out on their own bodies, or in the names they gave their children, the significance of what was about to happen. But Jesus merely asserts that certain things will be acted out upon him.

Jesus is concerned with one and only one story, and everything is done to lead his listeners to concentrate on that story. In interpreting the events of the Hebrew scriptures, the sacred books of himself and of most of his interlocutors, he selects a specific range of meanings and then acts out a drama which will set the seal on his interpretation and cut out for ever all other possible ways of seeing God's relations with man. He does this carefully and apparently consciously, and, because the final seal is nothing less than his own death, the conviction carried by this particular interpretation is enormous. It is no longer a matter, as with Daniel, of studying the signs and predicting the future; it is no longer a matter, as with the prophets, of stepping forward and deliberately acting out certain symbolic actions before his audience; Jesus has simply to live the life and die the death that will come to him, and that life and that death will allow the world to find its voice.

To understand what is involved, it may be helpful to look at a story by Borges. It is called 'The Theme of the Traitor and the Hero'. The action takes place in Ireland. The narrator, Ryan, is the great-grandson of Fergus Kilpatrick, a heroic leader assassinated in his prime on the eve of a victorious rising against the English. Ryan is fascinated by the circumstances of his ancestor's death. Like Lincoln, Kilpatrick was assassinated in a theatre; other aspects of his murder have affinities with the killing of Julius Caesar in Shakespeare's play. All this makes Ryan at first suppose that there exists 'a secret form of time, a pattern of repeated lines'. But somehow the parallels, not just with other historical murders but even with fictional ones, are too numerous. Ryan grows suspicious. He investigates further.

Eventually he discovers the facts: Kilpatrick was not a hero but a traitor; his fellow conspirators found this out just in time and condemned him to death. But in order to further their cause they contrived matters so that Kilpatrick's guilt would never be known, and it would look as though he had been shot by the English and died a hero and a martyr to the cause. The new leader, James Nolan, had planned it all:

> Nolan, urged on by time, was not able to invent all the circumstances of the. . .execution; he had to plagiarize another dramatist, the English enemy, William Shakespeare. He repeated scenes from *Macbeth*, from *Julius Caesar*. The public and secret enactment comprised various days. The condemned man entered Dublin, discussed, acted, prayed, reproved, uttered words of pathos, and each of these gestures, to be reflected in his glory, had been pre-established by Nolan. . .Kilpatrick was killed in a theatre, but the entire city

was a theatre as well, and the actors were legion, and the drama crowned by his death extended over many days and many nights.[9]

Jesus is both Nolan and Kilpatrick. We feel that all the other characters in the Gospels are actors in a play the action of which Jesus (and, of course, the reader) grasps, but of which the other characters are at best only vaguely aware and at worst totally ignorant. But Jesus does more than simply 'grasp' what is going on. He lives out his life so that, as the Gospels tell us, 'it might be fulfilled', the 'it' here being the secret pattern of history, at last made manifest. 'Thinkest thou', he says when he is captured, 'that I cannot now pray to my Father, and he shall presently give me more than twelve legions of angels? But how then shall the scriptures be fulfilled, that thus it must be?' (Matt. 26:53–54)

The climax of the play occurs on the cross. We expect a person's last words to be uniquely his own, but here a truly amazing thing happens. Jesus speaks not his own words, 'from the heart', but those of Psalm 22: 'My God, my God, why hast thou forsaken me?' The effect is astonishing. Jesus seems in that moment to give up not just his life but something perhaps even more precious, the right to speak what he feels. But at this moment too the whole vast story which began with the creation of the world is turned inside-out: instead of Jesus being reduced to a cipher by his self-denial, all that has gone before (including, of course, Psalm 22) is turned into an expression of his being. Jesus, at this moment, has appended his signature to the book, so to speak. It is now *his* book. By his death he has given it a meaning, a centre, an end and a beginning. John's Gospel only makes this explicit as it rewrites Genesis 1:1:

> In the beginning was the Word, and the Word was with God, and the Word was God. The same was in the beginning with God. All things were made by him; and without him was not any thing made that was made. In him was life; and the life was the light of men. And the light shineth in darkness; and the darkness comprehended it not.
>
> (John 1:1–5)

There are many centres to the Hebrew Bible: Abraham and his journey from Haran; Moses and the exodus from Egypt; Sinai; Jerusalem; Babylon and exile. There are also many meanings, some of which seem to contradict others: the David of Chronicles, for example, is very different from the David of 1 and 2 Samuel. But that is as it should be. What this book keeps drumming home to us is that we cannot stand back and decide what things mean, any more than the characters themselves can. To imagine we can do so is to fall into deeper error, to commit the folly of Adam or of the builders of the Tower of Babel. It is to try and abolish dialogue.

With the prophets, as we saw, there is a new desperation, a new determination to find meaning, to make it manifest. In the Gospels meaning is spelt out, the author appends his signature to his book. And this exclusivity of meaning will be taken further in the later books of the NT, until the book of Revelation merely adds the final full stop.

And yet. And yet. For one thing, there are four Gospels, not one. This already acts as a brake on the centralization of meaning, the establishing of one single and absolute meaning. For another, in contrast to the apocryphal gospels, the canonical Gospels, and especially that of Mark, leave us with a strong sense of precisely that distance, that primacy of dialogue, which we saw to be so integral a part of the historical books of the Hebrew scriptures. Where this occurs most powerfully is, ironically, in one of the very few places in the entire book where God remains silent before a genuine appeal:

> And he went forward a little, and fell on the ground, and prayed that, if it were possible, the hour might pass from him. And he said, Abba, Father, all things are possible unto thee; take away this cup from me: nevertheless not what I will, but what thou wilt. And he cometh, and findeth them sleeping, and saith unto Peter, Simon, sleepest thou? couldest not thou watch one hour?
>
> (Mark 14 : 35–37)

God's silence presses in upon one as one reads this, asserting his presence as a partner in the dialogue. For a moment distance is re-established.

Four

CONFIGURATIONS OF CHARACTER

*Frederick, however, held to a theory
that a random collision of the natal
genes had determined in him a bent for
acting only substantial parts in plays
by Strindberg, Ibsen, Marlowe and Chekhov
(but not Shakespeare); and so far as that
went he was right, everything being
drably right in the sphere of hypotheses,
nothing being measurably or redeemably
wrong.*

MURIEL SPARK, *The Public Image*

χ

DAVID AND TEARS

When it is clear that David has become a rebel leader and will not be cajoled into returning to the court, Saul gives his daughter Michal, David's wife, to a certain Phalti, son of Laish (1 Sam. 25:44). We hear nothing more of this man, who had not previously been mentioned, until, after the death of Saul and Jonathan, Abner, the captain of Saul's army, makes peace overtures to David, now king in Hebron. David is prepared to Iisten, but only on condition that Abner bring him Michal, 'which I espoused to me for an hundred foreskins of the Philistines' (2 Sam. 3:14). Clearly more is at stake here than the return of a beloved wife. Michal stands for Saul's succession, and both Ishbosheth, Saul's sole surviving son, now clinging to the kingship of Israel, and David himself know it. And, since David has the power (and the support of so cunning a politician as Abner, who can smell shifts in the balance of power almost before they occur), there is little Ishbosheth can do about it:

> And Ishbosheth sent, and took her from her husband, even from Phaltiel the son of Laish, And her husband went with her along weeping behind her to Bahurim. Than said Abner unto him, Go, return. And he returned.
>
> (2 Sam. 3:15–16)

We never hear of Phalti again. We do not even know if he is really called Phalti or Phaltiel. He is a mere pawn in the game being played out between Saul and David and David and Saul's descendants; or, from a different perspective, only one tiny cog in the long chain of history which God is unfolding, the history of his relations with Israel and with mankind. It would have been perfectly easy for the narrator to say: 'And David took again his wife Michal, daughter of Saul, which Saul had given to Phalti'; or even to leave Phalti out altogether: 'And David took again his wife Michal, daughter of Saul.'[1] But no. In less than ten words the Bible gives us a living, sentient being, enmeshed in his own life and troubles, a person who lives on for us, once we have read those words, as much as does David himself.

We grope for ways of expressing how this comes about, why this silent
figure 'comes alive', as thousands of others do in this book, in ways that
even the most fully described characters of Thucydides and Livy do not.

Of course this 'coming alive' is profoundly related to the central
themes of the book, as both Auerbach and Alter have sensed. Alter, who
devotes some excellent pages to this issue, contrasts biblical with
Homeric character, pointing out that no biblical character could ever
have an epithet attached to him, as Homer's do, since what is important
in the Bible is the possibility of change. Thus no 'wily Jacob' or 'sagacious
Moses', but characters defined by their actions and their relations to
others.[2]

Alter does not make the mistake of picking for comparison a weak
passage from Homer and a strong one from the Bible. For his main
comparison he selects one of the greatest scenes in ancient literature, the
meeting between Achilles and the aged Priam in the last book of the
Iliad, and David's response to the illness and then death of his first child
by Bathsheba. In Homer, says Alter,

> Part of the power of the scene comes from the fact that the connection
> between these two figures, weeping together as each separately recalls his own
> lost ones, is so lucidly revealed through the narrator's simultaneous overview
> of the external scene and the inner experience of both characters.

In the Bible, on the other hand, nothing prepares us for David's actions
and his words (David, I would say, is as unprepared as we are for his
reactions):

> Then said his servants unto him, What thing is this that thou hast done?
> thou didst fast and weep for the child, while it was alive; but when the child
> was dead, thou didst rise and eat bread. And he said, While the child was yet
> alive, I fasted and wept: for I said, Who can tell whether God will be gracious
> to me, that the child may live? But now he is dead, wherefore should I fast?
> can I bring him back again?
>
> (2 Sam. 12:21–23)

In Homer, suggests Alter, both Achilles and Priam act 'according to
character'; in the Bible David's character is discovered in action. 'The
narrative art of the Bible', Alter goes on, 'is more than an aesthetic
enterprise', and the kind of consciousness expressed in the depiction of
character 'was of course expressed ideologically in the legislative and
prophetic impulses of the Bible, but in biblical narrative it was also
realized through the bold and subtle articulation of an innovative literary
form.'[3]

Other recent critics have also tried to understand why biblical
characters seem so 'lifelike'. Meir Sternberg has talked about the contrast
between the partial knowledge of the characters themselves and the full

knowledge of God; and Frank Kermode has argued that it is precisely the absence of information about characters like Judas or the mysterious boy in the loin cloth in the Garden of Gethsemane which forces the reader to bring them to life.[4]

There is some truth in all these formulations, but none of them, it seems to me, fully accounts for the phenomenon of Phalti. I feel that our sense of character in the Bible is directly related to our sense of God and the world as being *other*, always more than and different from what any character or reader can grasp imaginatively. That otherness is of course also a central theme of the legislative and prophetic portions of the book, but it is at the very moment when the individual clashes with it that we as readers are stirred in a remote and normally inaccessible part of ourselves.

One way in which this clash manifests itself is so obvious that it can easily be overlooked: there are so many characters here, so many generations of men, that any single life and death acquires quite a different aspect from that which it has in even the longest book. The second way is the one I want to focus on now. It is manifested when words give out and we are left only with silence or with tears. Words are our way of making sense of things, and tears are forced from us at those moments when we can no longer make sense of the world, they are the acknowledgement that, however powerful we may be, however intelligent, power and intelligence have to give way before life itself. It is at such moments that the natural reticence of biblical narration comes into its own, and that the figure bereft of words moves from being a casual acquaintance to being a part of ourselves, impossible to dislodge. Let us keep Phalti in mind as we explore the ways in which the Bible brings alive for us the two figures to which it devotes most space, David and Jesus:

> And Ishbosheth sent, and took her from her husband, even from Phaltiel the son of Laish. And her husband went with her along weeping behind her to Bahurim. Then said Abner unto him, Go, return. And he returned

I argued earlier that in the story of Joseph we have a fairy-tale beginning followed by a 'realistic' second part, though we needed to look rather closely at the text in order to see that this was indeed the case, and that Joseph's whole life was not a perfect fairy-tale. Nevertheless, what we saw there was that a fairy-tale consists of the projection into the world of the individual's idea of what he would like for himself, his dream of centrality and omnipotence. The Bible, I suggested, takes pleasure in allowing such dreams their full force, but then sets them against reality – the dreams of others and the facts of life, such as failure and death.

This pattern is to be found in the depiction of nearly every biblical character from Adam to Jesus. Adam's is the archetypal fairy-tale, followed by the archetypal intrusion of reality. When God tells Adam that there is no going back, that once he has eaten the fruit he must accept the laws of a new reality, he can only feebly say: 'The woman. . .gave me of the tree, and I did eat' (Gen. 3 : 12). We have seen Aaron attempting to excuse himself in similar fashion and we will see Saul doing the same thing. Jacob, like David, never denies responsibility for what he has done, but in his life too the pattern is at work. In his early life he is the successful trickster, gaining his own ends with surprising ease. But then he comes up against another trickster, Laban, and he who had defrauded an elder brother of the blessing is himself tricked into marriage with an elder sister; he who had manipulated time, turning the second-born into the first-born, is made to learn what seven years of labour mean when another seven are added to his initial contract with Laban. Moses' life too begins as fairy-tale, with the baby floating in the river and protected by the king's daughter, but it ends with his not being allowed to enter the Promised Land – not, as Kafka acutely observed, because of any sin, but because he is a man. And to be a man, Kafka implies, is to be born into a world which is other than our dreams and desires.[5]

I also suggested earlier that we misread Joseph's 'story' if we take it by itself. It needs to be read in the context of the 'story' of the sons of Jacob, and even in the larger one of God's relations with Israel and with mankind. And the same is true of David. It is important, if we are to understand him, that we read his 'story' in relation to that of both Saul and Absalom.

Saul himself, of course, cannot be understood apart from the last chapters of Judges, with their sinister refrain: 'In those days there was no king in Israel: every man did that which was right in his own eyes.' (This connection is obscured by the Christian Bible, which interpolates the book of Ruth between Judges and Samuel.) Samuel appears at the start of 1 Samuel as a saviour, like Gideon and Samson, taking over from the sons of Eli, who, we are told, 'were sons of Belial; they knew not the Lord' (1 Sam. 2:12). However, it appears that the continuity of hereditary rule, which plays such an important part in holding together the destinies of Egypt and Babylon, is not valid for Israel. Genealogy is important, as we have seen, but because the ruler is no God but on the contrary has always to be subservient to God, a single leader cannot engender a line of leaders. Thus when Samuel makes his own sons judges, we learn that they too 'walked not in his ways, but turned aside after lucre, and took bribes, and perverted judgment' (1 Sam. 8:3).

At this point the people ask for a king. God explains to them that kings are no good, that they will only enslave the people (thus, he implies, turning the clock back to the time the Israelites were slaves in Egypt). However, the people are adamant. Just as when Moses vanished up the mountain they cried out to Aaron to make them 'gods' to lead them to safety, and recalled how in Egypt they at least had food and shelter and the comfort of an ordered life, so now they persist in their request for a king like other nations. Reluctantly the Lord accedes to their request.

It is here that the fairy-tale which is Saul's early life begins. Though he insists that he is an insignificant member of an insignificant family, the choice falls upon him. And after all, as the narrator tells us, he is a fine figure of a man, a head taller than other men, and of noble bearing. He is duly anointed by Samuel and then publicly acclaimed; the spirit of the Lord descends upon him, and he swiftly delivers the people from the Philistine yoke.

Very soon, however, doubts begin to creep in as to his ability to act as king. Just as Aaron and the people, confused by Moses' prolonged absence, did something other than what the Lord had commanded, so Saul's first error is to disobey the instructions of Samuel and make a burnt offering in the hope of warding off the enemy. At that moment Samuel appears, like God walking in the Garden of Eden in the cool of the evening:

> And Samuel said, What hast thou done? And Saul said, Because I saw that the people were scattered from me, and that thou camest not within the days appointed, and that the Philistines gathered themselves together at Michmash; Therefore said I, The Philistines will come down now upon me to Gilgal, and I have not made supplication unto the Lord: I forced myself therefore, and offered a burnt offering. And Samuel said to Saul, Thou hast done foolishly: thou hast not kept the commandment of the Lord thy God, which he commanded thee: for now would the Lord have established thy kingdom upon Israel for ever. But now thy kingdom shall not continue: the Lord hath sought him a man after his own heart. . ., because thou hast not kept that which the Lord commanded thee.
>
> (1 Sam. 13 : 11–14)

Saul has no answer to this and Samuel goes his way. It may be that the suddenness and enormity of what has happened simply cannot be taken in by Saul. But though the reader too is baffled, half wondering why God chose this man in the first place if he is going to reject him so soon, he also enters into a new relationship with Saul. Instead of the giant of noble appearance, chosen by the Lord, able to do anything, he suddenly has become a man like us, uncertain, confused, liable to make mistakes, and, what is more, mistakes which seem trivial at the time but which turn out to be irrevocable.

As we have seen happening so often in the Bible, the narrative advances by means of repetition with variation. A long and complex episode follows which reveals further aspects of Saul's weakness. First he makes a rash vow, proclaiming that any man who eats food before the evening will be cursed. This is the kind of arbitrary show of will which cost Jephtha so dear, and though in this case the consequences are not so terrible, they only demonstrate once again what little genuine authority and clarity of mind Saul possesses. Jonathan, his son, is out of the camp on a punitive expedition against the Philistines when the curse is announced, and so does not hear it. Consequently he transgresses, and when Saul learns of this he is adamant: 'thou shalt surely die, Jonathan' (1 Sam. 14:44). But the people are outraged at this and soon Saul, recognizing the strength of their feelings, submits and spares his son. The narrative does not comment on the anomaly of a father relenting when about to sacrifice his son not out of pity or through God's command, but because he is afraid of an insurrection, but it does not need to. And one simple phrase reveals that Samuel's prophecy in 13:11–14 was not idle: 'And Saul asked counsel of God, Shall I go down after the Philistines? wilt thou deliver them into the hand of Israel? But he answered him not that day.' (14:37) Because Saul did not trust God in the first place God has now withdrawn from him. As in Dante, so often in the Bible, punishment is only the externalization of an existing state of affairs.

Saul's final error is merely a further repetition of the first one. He is told by Samuel to destroy Agag the king and all the Amalekites, leaving nothing alive. Once more he takes it on himself to reinterpret the order, and spares the king, his sheep and his cattle. God speaks to Samuel:

> It repenteth me that I have set up Saul to be king: for he is turned back from following me, and hath not performed my commandments. And it grieved Samuel; and he cried unto the Lord all night.
>
> (1 Sam. 15:11)

However, by the next morning he is ready to deliver his message. Once again the conversation between him and Saul reminds us of that between God and Adam in the Garden. Samuel asks him what is the meaning of the bleating of sheep and lowing of oxen which he hears. Saul explains that he has spared these to sacrifice to the Lord, 'and the rest we have utterly destroyed', he adds defensively. Soon, however, like Adam passing the blame on to Eve, and Aaron on to the people at the time of the making of the Calf, Saul insists that it was the people who took from the spoil 'of the things which should have been utterly destroyed', in order to offer up sacrifice. Samuel is not impressed: 'Hath the Lord as great delight in burnt offerings and sacrifices, as in obeying the voice of the Lord?' (15:22)

At this point Saul caves in, though still subtly suggesting that it is the fault of the people: 'I have sinned: for I have transgressed the commandment of the Lord, and thy words: because I feared the people, and obeyed their voice' (1 Sam. 15:24). Having partially confessed his sin he pleads with Samuel: 'Now therefore, I pray thee, pardon my sin, and turn again with me, that I may worship the Lord' (25). But, just as Isaac could not take back his blessing once it had been given, nor Jephtha his oath, so here: 'And Samuel said unto Saul, I will not return with thee: for thou hast rejected the word of the Lord, and the Lord hath rejected thee from being king over Israel' (26).

Once again Samuel turns away. There is nothing more to be said. But Saul cannot accept this. He grabs hold of Samuel's mantle to detain him and it tears in two in his hands. This is a moment of particular eeriness and horror for the way in which the ordinary and the supernatural are bound up together, and for the way in which it demonstrates that actions we do without thinking, on the spur of the moment, can suddenly take on momentous significance: 'And Samuel said unto him, The Lord hath rent the kingdom of Israel from thee this day, and hath given it to a neighbour of thine, that is better than thou' (1 Sam. 15 : 28). We have seen how fond the prophets are of symbolic actions. What is awesome here is that it is not Samuel who instigates the action but Saul himself, and we sense that it is an index of his indecisiveness, his need for reassurance, his inability to do things cleanly and swiftly. A moment before there still seemed to be something to argue about; once the mantle has been torn we can no longer doubt that things will fall out as Samuel prophesies, no matter what Saul now does.

Yet Saul, being human, still hopes, and will go on hoping to the end, that all is not lost. And the narrator does not tell us that he is wrong. He simply lets us discover this through the events which ensue. Once again Saul begs Samuel: 'honour me now, I pray thee, before the elders of my people, and before Israel, and turn again with me, that I may worship the Lord thy God' (1 Sam. 15 : 30). Is Saul begging for forgiveness, or only asking that God shield him from shame? We will never know, and perhaps Saul himself does not know. The narrator simply says: 'And Samuel turned again after Saul; and Saul bowed down to the Lord' (31). (This is weakened in the AV by the insertion of the causal 'So' in place of the first 'And', a decision followed by NEB but eschewed by JB— which, however, inexplicably leaves the conjunction out altogether, thus giving the passage a staccato, Hemingway-like quality which is quite alien to the Hebrew.)

But it is all too late, though Saul does not know it, or refuses to accept it, for we are now told that 'Samuel came no more to see Saul until the day of his death', a mysterious phrase which will only grow more mysterious when we learn that Samuel has died before Saul, and which only fully makes sense when we reach the episode of the woman of Endor. The narrative, however, has not yet finished with its little shocks: 'nevertheless', we read, 'Samuel mourned for Saul.' 'And', it goes on, as though refusing to pause over individual human feelings, 'the Lord repented that he had made Saul king over Israel' (1 Sam. 15 : 35). The expression, *va'aonai nicham ki himlikh et Shaul 'al Yisrael*, is immediately reminiscent of the expression used in Genesis when the Lord sees what a mess men have made of the world: 'And it repented the Lord that he had made man on the earth, and it grieved him at his heart' (*vayinachem adonai ki 'assa et ha'adam ba'aretz wayit'atzev el' libo*) (Gen. 6:6). In both cases what God particularly resents is the refusal of his creatures even to acknowledge that they have done wrong. That refusal, we will see, is, in the case of Saul, brought out into the open by the contrast with David.

As is so often the case in Genesis, we now have a wholly new start after the failure of one attempt. Saul has failed him and so God will appoint a wholly new king. This new king's early exploits are also going to be tinged with a fairy-tale colouring, and nothing makes us certain that this time the experiment will work. Indeed, with the experience of Judges behind us we must surely imagine that things will, if anything, turn out worse than before. As always with this book there is no way of standing outside the narrative and judging it from a position of superiority. We have to interpret events only in the light of those events, and by comparing them with others, and how we assess David's career will depend on the perspective we adopt: that of the two books of Samuel; that of Chronicles; or that of the New Testament.

David is not even the seventh son, but the eighth, an afterthought. He is out looking after his father's sheep when Samuel arrives at the house. But though the old prophet is not at his best, mistaking the striking first son for the one God means to choose, God soon puts him right. And of course, though humble, David is 'ruddy, and withal of a beautiful countenance, and goodly to look to'. At Saul's court he immediately becomes a favourite, playing the harp to soothe the melancholy king, who 'loved him greatly'. There follows a different version of his arrival at court, but with an equally fairy-tale feel to it: the defeat of the giant Philistine, Goliath, by the little lad with nothing but a sling, in order not only to save his people but also to win the hand of the king's daughter, and having to overcome the sarcasm of his elder brothers on the way.

Once David is established at court the narrative takes on a new colouring. Usually in the Bible the parataxis of the syntax is matched by narrative parataxis, as we have seen: Abraham dies and Isaac is left; a Judge or a king dies, and another succeeds him. Even when two lives overlap they are not intertwined but laid alongside each other, as with Judah and Tamar and Joseph. But at this point the narrator decides to keep the two lives going together, Saul's and David's, and he further intertwines them by having both Saul's children, his daughter and his son, love David. This may be the only time in the Bible that we hear of a woman loving a man ('And Michal Saul's daughter loved David' : 1 Sam. 18:20). Thus if we have moved away from pure fairy-tale we are still firmly in the world of romance: Michal and Jonathan love David; he triumphs over his enemies; Saul turns against him with irrational hatred. When he becomes a guerrilla leader in the wilderness, driven out by Saul's murderous intentions, there is no question but that he will triumph. And yet, as we shall see, it is only a matter of time before, for David too, the tide turns; and when that happens neither his luck nor his looks will help him.

Fairy-tale and romance do not know the meaning of time, or of other places, other lives: they function in a timeless present in which the hero is the centre of the universe. Here, however, echoes of earlier events abound. When Michal helps David fool her father we remember Rachel and Laban; when David slaughters a huge number of Philistines to gain the bride he desires, we remember Samson. Our sense of similarity and difference gives us a perspective which is denied the hero. And other aspects of the narrative reinforce this feeling. When we are told that Saul 'became David's enemy continually' (*kol hayamim*, 'all the days': 1 Sam. 18:29), that 'continually' helps muddy the pure waters of romance. Most of all it is Saul's presence and the narrator's care that we should see him as he sees himself, as well as how David sees him, which helps to convey the sense that we are in new territory here. As Saul is driven by his evil spirit he turns into a sort of Macbeth (even going so far as to remind Jonathan that as long as David is alive he, Jonathan, as Saul's descendant, will never be able to rest easy); but the story never turns into tragedy. It refuses climax, preferring instead to convey the sense of the centre of power gradually shifting from Saul to David.

Two important and connected aspects of David's character emerge in the course of these episodes. The first is an unwillingness to lay the blame on others, as we have seen Saul doing. The second is his concern for his men. When Saul kills some of his supporters he feels profoundly guilty: 'I knew it that day, when Doeg the Edomite was there, that he would surely tell Saul: I have occasioned the death of all the persons of thy father's house' (1 Sam. 22:22). Interestingly, the Chronicler places at the start of his version of David's career an episode which in Samuel comes near the end. David's refusing to drink himself, out of solidarity with his thirsty troops (1 Chr. 11:15–19), as though the Chronicler recognized that this was a central aspect of David's character.

Saul chases after David and follows him to his hide-out in En-gedi. He stops in a cave to relieve himself and David creeps in after him and cuts off a piece of his robe as proof of how easy it would have been to kill him (are we to recall the tearing of Samuel's robe?). Now we have entered a world which is neither that of fairy-tale nor of romance, nor even that of the struggle for dynastic succession. Something much more mysterious is going on, and the sign of this is: tears. David calls out after Saul as he is leaving the cave, and bows himself to the earth. He tells him what he has done, yet insists that 'mine hand shall not be upon thee'. And insists too on his own lowliness: 'After whom . . . dost thou pursue? after a dead dog, after a flea' (1 Sam. 24 : 14). 'And it came to pass, when David had made an end of speaking these words unto Saul, that Saul said, Is this thy voice, my son David? And Saul lifted up his voice, and wept' (16).

Saul weeps, as Phalti will weep, and as we all weep, because he is the meeting-point of two contradictory elements, neither of which will give way to the other or be subsumed by reason: his desires for himself and the reality of the world. And what happens as we read the phrase 'and wept' (*vayevkh*) is that we too enter this space of incompatibles, a space where Saul wishes David were dead and wishes that he didn't wish that; where he recalls God's words to him and his first sight of Samuel, come to anoint him; where he knows how it will all end and refuses to believe that it will end like that. No amount of description of inner feelings, no amount of soliloquy on his part, would ever be able to convey all that, yet as we read we have no difficulty in understanding it all. The Bible here is not 'dark', it is not 'fraught with background', as both Kierkegaard and Auerbach have argued. It just works in a style which is different from that of the classic novel. It is a style better suited to its purpose, which is to deal not with that which can be understood but with that which must be accepted.[6]

There is nothing sentimental about Saul's tears. He has reached a moment of crisis. But the Hebrew Bible knows that even the most profound crisis passes, that it is in man's nature to try and cope as best he can. And if David is politic, then so, in his way, is Saul. Having wept and acknowledged his error ('Thou art more righteous than I: for thou hast rewarded me good, whereas I have rewarded thee evil' – 1 Sam. 24 : 17),[7] he accepts that David will indeed be king, but begs him to spare his descendants. David agrees and each goes his way. Despite the sense of crisis and climax, nothing tangible has been changed by the episode, only our feeling of the tide beginning to run strongly in David's favour.

The narrative though does seem to gather momentum after this. Samuel dies and at once we are plunged into the episode of Nabal, the coarse bully, and his gentle wife Abigail. This is the first time we see clearly how life plays into David's hands. For shortly after her meeting with David, Abigail's husband dies (of a sort of apoplexy, it seems, at hearing what his wife has done), and David sends for her and she becomes his wife. There follows a parallel episode to the one at En-gedi. Again David could have killed Saul but refrains, and again he retreats to a safe distance and points this out to the demented king. 'Is this thy voice, my son David?' (1 Sam. 26 : 17) asks Saul in amazement. David acknowledges that it is and repeats that he is nothing compared with the king.

Then come two verses, spanning the end of chapter 26 and the start of 27, which bring out marvellously well the way in which style and meaning work together in this book:

> Then Saul said to David, Blessed be thou, my son David: thou shalt both do great things, and also shalt still prevail. So David went on his way, and Saul returned to his place. And David said in his heart, I shall now perish one day by the hand of Saul: there is nothing better for me than that I should speedily escape into the land of the Philistines.
>
> (1 Sam. 26:25–27:1)

I don't think Saul is meant to be seen here as a scheming liar. Nor does anything he says appear to explain David's sudden crucial decision. On the contrary, he blesses him and says he, David, will prevail. Nothing then could have prepared us for David's decision, yet once it is taken we sense its rightness. It may be that a great deal happens in his mind between the end of Saul's speech and his own soliloquy. But the point is that there will always be a gap between thought and action. Decisions are never wholly dependent on prior reasoning, they are acts of trust in the future. All we can say is that David is good at taking decisions – and will go on being good at it to the end of his life – while Saul is not. But we must also note that if decisions are indeed never linked by direct causality to thought, then narrative will always escape the web theology seeks to cast over it. Or perhaps one should say that it is in moments like these that we see at work a theology of narrative.

David, then, throws in his lot with the Philistines, with all the paradoxes engendered by that Coriolanus-type action. But where we might expect the narrative to stay with him, since he is now obviously the chosen one of God, the narrator has other ideas. The next chapter tells us how Saul banished all witches and soothsayers from Israel on Samuel's death. Fearing the Philistines, who are advancing to meet him at Mount Gilboa, he calls on the Lord, but again 'the Lord answered him not, neither by dreams, nor by Urim, nor by prophets' (1 Sam. 28:6). In this intolerable silence he now decides to consult a witch, again revealing his confusion of mind and refusal to face the facts.

Where David is always clear about the boundaries between life and death, Saul has tended to be muddled, and it is fitting that his last action should be a visit to the woman of Endor. The scene is rich and complex. The woman, perhaps recognizing him, reminds him that King Saul had banished witches from the land. The king promises that no harm will befall her, and asks her to raise the ghost of Samuel. She complies, but, as might have been expected, Samuel's ghost, which now appears, merely repeats what the living Samuel had said: God has left you and gone over to your enemy; because you did not obey him he has torn the kingdom from you: 'tomorrow shalt thou and thy sons be with me' (1 Sam. 28:19). With these chilling words the ghost vanishes.

Like Nabal before him, who fell down dead when he heard what his wife Abigail had done, as though the power of the truth had to be denied even at the cost of life or consciousness, Saul falls to the ground in a faint. But now a minor theme, which has been present throughout, emerges into perhaps surprising prominence. This is the theme of bread as sustenance, of food as the prime necessity of life. In chapter 21 we had seen David taking the shewbread from the altar of Ahimelech when he and his men were on the point of starvation; in chapter 25 we had seen Nabal refusing food to David's men and Abigail averting disaster by bringing David the food he required of her own accord. Now we find the Witch of Endor demonstrating to Saul that we cannot live by grand gestures alone, and that while the mind may momentarily deny reality, the body will soon remind one of it.

It is one of those remarkable biblical episodes which are not strictly necessary as far as the story is concerned, but which colour our response to the whole and guide our reading of more overtly 'significant' episodes in ways we hardly realize:

> And the woman came unto Saul, and saw that he was sore troubled, and said unto him, Behold, thine handmaid hath obeyed thy voice, and I have put my life in my hand, and have hearkened unto thy words which thou spakest unto me. Now therefore, I pray thee, hearken thou also unto the voice of thine handmaid, and let me set a morsel of bread before thee; and eat, that thou mayest have strength, when thou goest on thy way. But he refused, and said, I will not eat. But his servants, together with the woman, compelled him; and he hearkened unto their voice. So he arose from the earth, and sat upon the bed. And the woman had a fat calf in the house; and she hasted, and killed it, and took flour, and kneaded it, and did bake unleavened bread thereof: And she brought it before Saul, and before his servants; and they did eat. Then they rose up, and went away that night.
>
> (1 Sam. 28:21–25)

It is typical of Saul that he should first refuse, just as it is typical of David that he should be prepared to take bread even from the altar if that means saving his men from starvation. But it is also typical of these narratives that Saul should eventually be prevailed upon to eat, and strangely moving how the witch turns into a hostess and the meal into a muted celebration of the basic elements of life.

Yet when Saul leaves Endor he goes out to his death on Mount Gilboa. It is the second time that events outside his control have played into David's hands. The first was the convenient death of Abigail's husband. Now, having sworn to Saul that he would never lay a hand on him or his house, David is spared any awkward choices by the Philistine decision not to employ him in the decisive battle against Saul, and by the death of both Saul and Jonathan at other hands than his own. When a man enters David's camp and announces that he has killed the king, David has him promptly put to death, and then delivers his great lament over the king and his son. It would be wrong to ask here whether David is playing to the gallery or is genuinely moved. As we saw in an earlier chapter, our notion of real feelings as opposed to 'pretended' ones is not shared by the Hebrew Bible, and neither is the notion that joy and sorrow cannot co-exist but that one must be 'true' and the other 'feigned'. All we can say here is that Saul and Jonathan have died in battle; that David delivers a magnificent lament over them; and that he then sets about consolidating his position, first by having himself crowned in Hebron and then by insisting on the return of Michal.

Events at this stage are still playing into David's hands. Joab, his chief commander, kills Abner, Saul's captain, who had come over to David's side, in revenge for the murder of Joab's brother. Without our realizing it, though, a new theme is emerging, and from now on the fate of Joab and his remaining brother Abishai will be linked to that of David.[8] For the moment though David rebukes him, tears his clothes, and refuses to eat till sunset. This show of ritual mourning pleases the people. With un-erring instinct David goes on doing the right thing both for himself and for Israel. He seizes Jerusalem, destroys the Philistines, and brings the ark there. Nathan takes the place of Samuel and through him the Lord tells David that he will be with his house for ever. This is of course in marked contrast to Saul, to whom such a promise was never made, and carries echoes of the covenant with Noah. However, there is a warning. Though God won't abandon David's 'house', if any member of it 'commit iniquity, I will chasten him with the rod of men, and with the stripes of the children of men: But my mercy shall not depart away from him, as I took it from Saul.' (2 Sam. 7 : 14–15) Armed with this assurance David proceeds to destroy the Philistines, and can afford to invite Mephi-bosheth, Jonathan's lame son, to eat at his table.

But, as so often happens in this book, before we quite realize it, what was hope has become despair, what was freedom has become its opposite. Suddenly we are in the midst of a crisis from which even David will not be able to escape unaffected:

> And it came to pass, after the year was expired, at the time when kings go forth to battle, that David sent Joab, and his servants with him, and all Israel; and they destroyed the children of Ammon, and besieged Rabbah. But [MT: *va*, 'and'] David tarried still at Jerusalem.
>
> (2 Sam. 11 : 1)

We don't know why David stayed behind and we don't even, at this point, see anything wrong with that. The MT lays down the facts non-committally in contrast to the AV, which pushes interpretation at us by translating *va* as 'but'. However, the combination of absent army and idle king is to prove disastrous. As the king walks on his roof one evening he sees a beautiful woman bathing in a neighbouring house. 'And David sent messengers, and took her; and she came in unto him, and he lay with her; for she was purified from her uncleanness: and she returned unto her house' (11 : 4). We are still not sure how to take this. It could be that we will hear nothing more of Bathsheba. Or it could be that, like Abigail, for whom David also sent in peremptory fashion, she will become his wife. Unfortunately the woman is no widow, like Abigail when David sent for her, but 'the wife of Uriah the Hittite'. Moreover, 'the woman conceived, and sent and told David, and said, I am with child' (5). Now we understand why we were told early on that she was clean: the father can only be David.

The situation is totally new. If the truth comes out both the adulteress and David will be stoned to death. And he is not only a man of strong desires; he also needs the respect and admiration of his subjects. David decides to recall Uriah from the front and hopes that, once he has slept with his wife, he will not realize that the child is not his. But Uriah won't play David's game, whether because he knows what has happened and is determined not to be David's stooge, or, as he himself says, because it would be wrong to go home and enjoy the comforts of home life while his comrades are enduring the hardships of the front. As Meir Sternberg has shown, we can read the episode either way; the text will not tell us which is 'the truth'.[9]

The world and David's desires are fast parting company. To cover his adultery David is now driven by Uriah's obstinacy to plan his murder. He sends Uriah himself back to the front with a letter to Joab, instructing him to make sure Uriah is killed in battle. Joab does just what David asks. The secret seems to have been covered up, though of course David is now to a certain extent in Joab's hands. The narrative, however, moves serenely on:

> when the wife of Uriah heard that Uriah her husband was dead, she mourned for her husband. And when the mourning was past, David sent and fetched her to his house, and she became his wife, and bare him a son.
>
> (2 Sam. 11 : 26–27)

However, as we have seen with Adam, and then with Judah, ugly deeds cannot stay hidden. Even if you succeed in hiding what you have done from men you cannot hide it from God: 'the thing that David had done displeased the Lord. And the Lord sent Nathan unto David' (2 Sam. 11 : 27–12 : 1). Because David has killed Uriah the Hittite with the sword, 'the sword shall never depart from thine house', and, because he tried to keep hidden the evil he had done another man through his wife, 'I will take thy wives before thine eyes, and give them unto thy neighbour, and he shall lie with thy wives in the sight of this sun. For thou didst it secretly: but I will do this thing before all Israel, and before the sun.' (12:10–12) However, unlike Adam, Aaron and Saul, David does not try to bluster or excuse himself: 'And David said unto Nathan, I have sinned against the Lord. And Nathan said unto David, The Lord also hath put away thy sin; thou shalt not die.' (13) It is the child, though, who will die.

It might seem grossly unfair to us that Saul, who merely held back from carrying out God's cruel command to destroy Agag utterly, should have his kingship removed for that reason, while David, an adulterer, a murderer and a liar, should be allowed to escape with both his life and his throne. The first point to be made about this is that there is always a gap in the Bible between what we might expect and what is, a gap which at times seems deliberately created in order to force us out of any easy moral conclusions we might make. The second is that in some ways the re-tribution which overtakes a person is only the outward expression of what that person himself experiences: because Saul doubts God, he loses him; because David trusts God, God remains with him. Impulsive in his sins and crimes as well as in his trust, David at once acknowledges his misdeeds and is at once personally absolved. God cannot, however, alter the consequences of what David has done, and these will continue to dog him for the rest of his life. Like Adam, who was free till he ate the fruit, David was free till he sent for Bathsheba. Once that threshold has been crossed each enters the world of real suffering, the world of con-flicting loyalties and self-division. We could say that they enter the real world.

The child dies, and we have already seen David's response: he fasts and mourns while there is still a chance of recovery, but once the child is dead he gets up and asserts the reality of the situation: 'I shall go to him, but he shall not return to me' (2 Sam. 12:23). And, as if with this acknowledgement a partial healing at least had become possible,

> And David comforted Bathsheba his wife [note that at the end of the pre-vious chapter she was still 'the wife of Uriah'], and went in unto her, and lay with her: and she bare a son, and he called his name Solomon: and the Lord loved him.
>
> (2 Sam. 12:24)

When we try to look back at the tangled skein leading to Solomon's birth we are indeed confronted with darkness: had David not stayed at home when his men were fighting the enemy; had he not seen Bathsheba; had he not desired her and called for her; had she not come; had she not conceived; had Uriah not refused to play David's game; had he not been killed at David's orders – Solomon would not have been born. To grasp this, it seems to me, is to grasp the ironic ambiguities of a saving history. But that is badly put. We cannot 'grasp' it; we can only assent to it: read it and read on.

No sooner has Nathan's prophecy about the sword not departing from the house of David been uttered than it starts to come true. David's son, Amnon, like his father, is seized with the sudden desire for a woman and will not rest till he has satisfied it. The woman in question, however, is his half-sister, Tamar. He rapes her and sends her packing. But he can no more escape retribution than his father. Tamar's brother, Absalom, David's favourite son, bides his time and then kills Amnon and his brothers. David, helpless in the face of all this – and it is hard to remember that just a few chapters earlier he was the all-powerful king, in absolute control – tears his clothes in ritual mourning and rolls on the ground in agony. Absalom flees, but 'David mourned for his son every day' (2 Sam. 13:37). We are, in effect, seeing a distorted replay of the David – Saul – Jonathan relationship, but compressed into just two characters. Like David then, Absalom is the younger claimant to the throne, exiled because of the reigning king's anger; like David then, loved by Jonathan, Absalom is loved by one very close to the king – here the king himself. But, unlike David, he is vain and impulsive as well as handsome and lovable; unlike David then, he now makes a bid for the throne, setting up his standard in Hebron and rallying the men of Israel to him.

As Absalom advances on Jerusalem David flees:

> And David went up by the ascent of mount Olivet, and wept as he went up, and had his head covered, and he went barefoot: and all the people that was with him covered every man his head, and they went up, weeping as they went up.
>
> (2 Sam. 15:30)

When Phalti had followed his wife weeping nobody had had any time for him, and he was rudely ordered back. Now it is David who walks weeping, and the tears are again an index of contradictory emotions: it is no longer that he and his beloved son are separated geographically; it is that the beloved son has actively and openly turned against his father. The world is no longer showing itself kind to David.

Yet even here neither his natural piety nor his political acumen desert David. He begins by sending back one of his henchmen, Hushai, with orders to infiltrate Absalom's council and report back what he hears. David also sends the ark back to Jerusalem, thus (in stark contrast to the Danites in the book of Judges) putting himself entirely in God's hands, without any attempt to keep by him any substitute for the Lord. Then, when one of Saul's men, Shimei, meets and curses him, and Joab wishes to kill Shimei, David rebukes Joab, saying that perhaps he deserves such a curse.

Absalom enters Jerusalem and the rest of Nathan's prophecy comes true, for, in full view of everyone, he 'goes in unto' his father's concubines, who have been left behind, thus publicly proclaiming his right to the throne and all that had belonged to David, as well as 'bringing to light' David's secret meeting with Bathsheba. Yet God has not deserted David. When Absalom seeks advice about how he is to proceed against his father, the sound counsel of Ahithophel is rejected in favour of the bad but skilfully presented counsel of David's agent, Hushai. Without fuss Ahithophel accepts defeat, returns home, and hangs himself.

For some time though we have had the sense that David is no longer in proper control. Joab has been moving further and further into a position of power, and we sense that when David puts him in charge of the army which is to fight Absalom, and orders him to make sure he spares his son, Joab will pay no attention but only do what he considers best for himself. We have moved a long way from Mount Gilboa, when David's inactivity paid off and his enemies were killed without his having to stain his hands (though among those enemies, even then, was his beloved Jonathan). Now it is Absalom's turn to die, as he is caught by his beautiful hair in a tree and, as he hangs there helpless, is stabbed to death by Joab. 'Absalom gloried in his hair,' comments the Mishnah laconically, 'therefore he was hanged by his hair.'[10]

At this point, however, the narrator brilliantly slows down the action. A single messenger had arrived with the news of Saul's death, and was promptly put to death. Now two runners are seen coming from the battlefield:

> And the watchman said, Me thinketh the running of the foremost is like the running of Ahimaaz the son of Zadok. And the king said, He is a good man, and cometh with good tidings. And Ahimaaz called, and said unto the king, All is well. And he fell down to the earth upon his face before the king, and said, Blessed be the Lord thy God, which hath delivered up the men that lifted up their hand against my lord the king. And the king said, Is the young man Absalom safe? And Ahimaaz answered, When Joab sent the king's servant, and me thy servant, I saw a great tumult, but I knew not what it was. And the king said unto him, Turn aside, and stand here. And he turned aside, and stood still. And, behold, Cushi came; and Cushi said, Tidings, my lord the king: for the Lord hath avenged thee this day of all them that rose up against thee. And the king said unto Cushi, Is the young man Absalom safe? And Cushi answered, The enemies of my lord the king, and all that rise against thee to do thee hurt, be as that young man is. And the king was much moved, and went up to the chamber over the gate, and wept: and as he went, thus he said, O my son Absalom, my son, my son Absalom! would God I had died for thee, O Absalom, my son, my son!
>
> (2 Sam. 18:27–33)

We are not told anything about what David looked like or where he was waiting for the news, because we don't need it. Compared with Homer everything moves very fast, and yet the narrator manages to convey the sense of the terrible length of time that passes before David receives any hard information. And even then that information, for us as for David, is couched in the elaborate language of courtly flattery, so that it has to be unpacked before the stark truth can shine through: Absalom is dead. We cannot tell if the messenger knows the effect that the news he brings will have on David. Perhaps he really thinks it is good news he is bringing. As in a sense it is. David has squashed the rebellion and is once more secure as king. But from his repeated question: 'Is the young man Absalom safe?' we know that his throne means nothing to him now. The narrator does not need to try and describe his thoughts and feelings: they are so complex that no description could ever do them justice, and so simple that only a few words uttered by him will convey them to us. He has triumphed, but also lost. Any further actions in his life will be done listlessly, almost automatically. He did not die for his crime against Uriah; instead Bathsheba's first son died. Now Absalom has died we feel that David has in a sense gone too. The great commander, who thought first of his men and then of himself, has no room now for any other thought than that of his loss, even though his public mourning, as Joab is quick to point out to him, is an insult to the men who fought for him.

Yet David has one more surprise in store for us. He is old now, and cannot keep the cold from his limbs, even with the help of the beautiful young virgin, Abishag. Around him everyone schemes: Adonijah, who sees himself as a second Absalom; Joab; Bathsheba and Nathan on behalf of Solomon. David, making one final decision, installs Solomon as king and has him publicly anointed. Then he prepares for the end and calls Solomon to his death-bed. 'I go the way of all the earth,' he tells him, clear-sighted as always in the face of death. He urges him to walk always in God's way, and then turns to a few pieces of unfinished business. Joab must be removed: 'let not his hoar head go down to the grave in peace' (1 Kgs. 2:6). Barzilai and his sons must be rewarded, 'for so they came to me when I fled because of Absalom thy brother' (2:7). But as for Shimei, who cursed David on his way out of Jerusalem and whom David promised not to touch, 'hold him not guiltless: for thou art a wise man, and knowest what thou oughtest to do unto him; but his hoar head bring thou down to the grave with blood' (2:9). Having tied up these few loose ends, David can now die at peace: 'So David slept with his fathers, and was buried in the city of David' (2:10).

We have come a long way from the lad with the sling and the harp. True, he dies in his bed, in ripe old age, like the Patriarchs, and unlike Saul and Absalom. Perhaps that is only right, for he was in his lifetime at once more humble and more honest than either of them. But who, after all, are we, to say what is right and what is wrong? If his life took the course it did, then that is the course his life took. It has no meaning apart from its twists and turns, its mixture of good and bad, strength and weakness, temptations resisted and temptations succumbed to. The narrator does not try to sum up and neither does David. But it is precisely that refusal which makes him live for us. We cannot 'make sense' of him; we can only repeat his story. The feeling of reality conveyed by a text has, it would seem, nothing to do with 'realism', with the accumulation of accurate detail about clothes and appearance. Does it even have anything to do with provable facts? David lives for us much more immediately, much more fully, than figures far better attested to by history: Caesar, Napoleon, Hitler. And he does so because we are made to sense at so many moments the way in which life always runs ahead of meaning, in which, as Franz Rosenzweig said in another context, 'we only know it when – we *do*'.[11]

XI

JESUS: NARRATIVE AND INCARNATION

It has become a commonplace of Gospel criticism that we must not read these works as biographies. The scholars point out that the Greek word translated as 'gospel', *evangelion*, means 'glad tidings', usually 'glad tidings orally communicated' (and the fee for those tidings paid to him who brought them). It is significant that the early Church does not think of four gospels, but of *the* gospel, 'according to' (*kata*) Mark, Matthew, Luke and John. In other words there is a single message of good, relayed in four different ways.[1] However, if we ask *how* the four evangelists communicated their glad tidings, the answer has to be: through a narrative about the life and death of Jesus Christ. And this, surely, is what we mean by biography. An entry in a biographical dictionary need contain only dates and salient particulars, but a biography is a narrative of the life and death of the subject, and we say a biographer has succeeded if we feel he has brought his subject to life. In the same way the evangelists must have felt that they had succeeded to the extent that they managed to bring Jesus to life.

Of course there is a special problem connected with the Gospels. Christianity, after all, depends on our acceptance of the fact that Jesus really did live and suffer and die and rise again, while the appreciation of Keats's poetry, for example, does not depend on our accepting what biographers tell us about him. Nor is this all. Dr Johnson and Keats merely lived their lives, leaving it to their biographers, with perhaps a nudge here and there in the case of Johnson, to make sense of those lives. But Jesus' life consisted in large part in trying to persuade all those with whom he came in contact that he was indeed the Son of God, and that his appearance before them heralded a decisive turning-point in the history of the world. The evangelists' attempts at persuasion thus precisely mirror Jesus' own; or perhaps one should say that Jesus' attempts at persuasion as recounted in the narratives precisely mirror the evangelists' attempts to convey to us the good news by means of these narratives.

Chapter 8 of John's Gospel brings this out clearly. It begins with the episode of the woman taken in adultery (8:3–11). Jesus comes down from the Mount of Olives to the Temple, where he sits and teaches. An adulterous woman is brought before him and he is asked by her accusers: 'Moses in the law commanded us, that such should be stoned: but what sayest thou?' As so often in his career, Jesus does not reply to this in any expected fashion. Instead he writes in the dust, as though he had not heard the question, and then turns on the accusers with a challenge of his own: 'He that is without sin among you, let him first cast a stone at her.' At this they slink away, until Jesus is left alone with the woman.

Though the episode is usually remembered by itself, it is merely the prelude to this rich and complex chapter.[2] Jesus tells the woman *he* does not condemn her: 'go, and sin no more' (8 : 11). He then comes out with one of his riddling sayings: 'I am the light of the world: he that followeth me shall not walk in darkness, but shall have the light of life.' This time, however, the Pharisees are less easily put off. (It is typical of the Gospel narratives that we are uncertain if this is the same group of Pharisees or if we have moved to a different time and venue. The transition is only marked by *palin oun*, 'again therefore Jesus spoke to them, saying...' [12].) They reply: 'Thou bearest record of thyself; thy record is not true.' In other words, you say so, but we deny it.

How will Jesus persuade them? He begins rather lamely: 'Though I bear record of myself, yet my record is true: for I know whence I come, and whither I go; but ye cannot tell whence I come, and whither I go' (8 : 14). It is not enough simply to go on asserting something if your opponent denies it. If you cannot prove it you at least need to try and persuade. Since the Pharisees are trying to find out by what authority Jesus can say to the woman, 'Go, and sin no more', it is not enough merely to say: You deny my authority but I know I have it. Jesus seems to realize as much and changes tack. You judge according to the flesh, he says, but I judge no man. Nor do I rely merely on my own testimony, 'for I am not alone, but I and the Father that sent me.' The reason for this abrupt addition is made plain in what follows: 'It is also written in your law, that the testimony of two men is true. I am one that bear witness of myself, and the Father that sent me beareth witness of me.' (16–18) Quite logically, however, the Pharisees reply: 'Where is thy Father?' In other words, produce this second witness and we shall see. To which Jesus can only reply with bluster: 'Ye neither know me, nor my Father: if ye had known me, ye should have known my Father also.'

Clearly a stalemate has been reached. Unless a new element is introduced both parties will only be able to reiterate their claims. Jesus tries with: 'Whither I go, ye cannot come' (8 : 21). They, evidently puzzled, wonder if he means he is going to commit suicide. But no: 'Ye are from beneath; I am from above: ye are of this world; I am not of this world.' At this point they decide to ask him outright: 'Who art thou?' Jesus is ready for this, as God was when Moses asked a similar sort of question. But where God remained enigmatic (*ehyeh asher ehyeh*, Exod. 3:14), Jesus tries to explain: 'Even the same that I said unto you from the beginning . . . he that sent me is true; and I speak to the world those things which I have heard of him' (John 8:25–26).

At this point the evangelist is moved to explain: 'They understood not that he spake to them of the Father' (8:27). This seems to be like the narrator stepping in to tell us that 'the thing that David had done displeased the Lord' (2 Sam. 11:27). However, there is a difference. We are dealing here with an argument, not a narrative, and the evangelist's aside will only be understood and accepted by us if we have already understood and accepted what Jesus himself is saying. It does not advance matters, as does the narrator's remark in Samuel.

Jesus, though, now makes an effort to do so. He launches into a longer speech, telling his questioners that 'When ye have lifted up the Son of man, then shall ye know that I am he' (John 8:28). In other words, I cannot persuade you *now*, but coming events will prove my point. If you obey my word you will be my disciples, and you will know the truth, 'and the truth shall make you free.' In other words, take the plunge and you will then see that I am right. But this puzzles them more than ever. What can Jesus mean by saying that the truth will make them free? 'We be Abraham's seed, and were never in bondage to any man: how sayest thou, Ye shall be made free?'

This seems a promising line to follow, and Jesus starts to argue that whoever commits a sin is in bondage to that sin, and that 'if ye were Abraham's children, ye would do the works of Abraham. But now ye seek to kill me, a man that hath told you the truth, which I have heard of God: this did not Abraham.' (8:39–40) But is this argument any better than the earlier ones? The Pharisees do not try to point out its weaknesses, but merely deny the charge: 'We be not born of fornication; we have our Father, even God.' But Jesus persists: 'If God were your Father, ye would love me: for I proceeded forth and came from God; neither came I of myself, but he sent me.'

Then, perhaps sensing that he is merely repeating himself, he changes tack again:

> Why do ye not understand my speech? even because ye cannot hear my word. Ye are of your father the devil, and the lusts of your father ye will do. He was a murderer from the beginning, and abode not in the truth.
>
> (John 8:43–44)

This, however, is too much, even for his long-suffering interlocutors: 'Say we not well that thou art a Samaritan, and hast a devil?' 'I have not a devil,' answers Jesus. 'I seek not mine own glory: there is one that seeketh and judgeth. Verily, verily, I say unto you, If a man keep my saying, he shall never see death.' (50–51)

The Pharisees, however, have had enough:

> Now we know that thou hast a devil. Abraham is dead, and the prophets; and
> thou sayest, If a man keep my saying, he shall never taste of death. Art thou
> greater than our father Abraham, which is dead? and the prophets are dead.
> (John 8 : 52–53)

However, this only pushes Jesus in a new direction. Having repeated that
it is *their* God who is *his* father, and who honours him, he presses on:
'Your father Abraham rejoiced to see my day: and he saw it, and was
glad.' 'Thou art not yet fifty years old,' they reply commonsensically, 'and
hast thou seen Abraham?' This is just what Jesus needs: 'Verily, verily, I
say unto you, Before Abraham was, I am' (58).

If he expected acquiescence, however, he is disappointed. The response of the Pharisees is indeed to give up the debate, but not in order
to grant Jesus the victory: 'Then they took up stones to cast at him: but
Jesus hid himself, and went out of the temple' (8 : 59). It is a tribute to
the evangelist's sense of form that the long, meandering, inconclusive
chapter should end with Jesus in the place of the adulterous woman.

What the chapter demonstrates is that argument alone will not advance the cause of either Jesus or John. But the temptation to prove the
truth of their claims is a powerful one, and, as the Gospel nears its end,
John cannot resist it. We see him striving, as Jesus strove, to authenticate his story, and we see that, as with Jesus, his only recourse is to fall
back on personal testimony: What I tell you is true because I was witness
to it. Unfortunately such assertions remain nothing but words, and the
rule of the game seems to be that the more an author asserts the truth of
what he is saying the less likely we are to believe him.

This can be demonstrated by looking at the last few moments of
the gospel. John's account of the crucifixion ends, frighteningly and
movingly:

> Then came the soldiers, and brake the legs of the first, and of the other which
> was crucified with him. But when they came to Jesus, and saw that he was
> dead already, they brake not his legs: But one of the soldiers with a spear
> pierced his side, and forthwith came there out blood and water.
> (John 19 : 32–34)

Yet John ruins it by adding: 'And he that saw it bare record, and his
record is true: and he knoweth that he saith true, that ye might believe'
(35). And this recourse to personal testimony, with the corollary that
the first person himself needs to be authenticated, grows more and more
insistent as the gospel draws to its close: 'Therefore that disciple whom
Jesus loved saith unto Peter, It is the Lord' (21 : 7). Who is this disciple?
None other than the author of the narrative we have been reading?[3]
But if he is the author, the implied argument goes, then all the more

reason to believe what he says:

> Then Peter, turning about, seeth the disciple whom Jesus loved following; which also leaned on his breast at supper, and said, Lord, which is he that betrayeth thee? Peter seeing him saith to Jesus, Lord, and what shall this man do? Jesus saith unto him, If I will that he tarry till I come, what is that to thee? follow thou me.... This is the disciple which testifieth of these things, and wrote these things: and we know that his testimony is true.
>
> (John 21 : 20–24)

The insistence on the truth of what the narrator tells is only one sign of anxiety in the Gospels. There are others. Matthew, for example, opens strikingly enough with the genealogy of Jesus, which leads us straight from the OT into the present. But once it is over the tone changes. In his anxiety to persuade us Matthew loses no opportunity to tell us that everything that happens in his account happens 'that it might be fulfilled which was spoken of the Lord by the prophet' (1 : 22). Thus the angel comes to Mary 'that it might be fulfilled'; the firstborn are slaughtered and 'Then was fulfilled that which was spoken by Jeremy the prophet, saying, In Rama was there a voice heard, lamentation, and weeping, and great mourning, Rachel weeping for her children, and would not be comforted, because they are not' (2 : 17–18); Joseph goes to Nazareth 'that it might be fulfilled which was spoken by the prophets, He shall be called a Nazarene' (2 : 23); when Jesus starts to preach, and leaves Galilee for Capernaum, we are told that this was so 'That it might be fulfilled which was spoken by Esaias the prophet, saying... The people which sat in darkness saw great light' (4 : 14–16); when Jesus heals the sick this is so 'That it might be fulfilled which was spoken by Esaias the prophet, saying, Himself took our infirmities, and bare our sicknesses' (8 : 17).

It is not that the connections between prophecy and fulfilment some-times seem to be rather loose; it is that in his anxiety to drive home the reasons for Jesus' life and actions Matthew throws away his strongest card. By making fulfilment appear to be purely mechanical he seems to deny Jesus his power of choice and so, ultimately, his humanity. This comes out clearly in the great scene which Matthew describes so graph-ically, when, in the Garden of Gethsemane, one of Jesus' followers takes out his sword to defend him:

> Then said Jesus unto him, Put up again thy sword into his place: for all they that take the sword shall perish with the sword. Thinkest thou that I cannot now pray to my Father, and he shall presently give me more than twelve legions of angels? But how then shall the scriptures be fulfilled, that thus it must be?
>
> (Matt. 26 : 52–54)

Matthew subverts Jesus' real message here by his manner of telling. For if Jesus' weakness, his humanity, is only a front, only there to bring about the fulfilment of prophecy, then it is no different, in essence, from the deployment of twelve legions of angels. We can no more identify with Jesus, respond to his plight, in the one case than in the other.

One has only to compare Matthew with Mark to see what is gained by *not* stressing fulfilment of prior prophecies apart from Jesus' own conscious awareness of such a link. Since Mark says nothing about Jesus' childhood, but plunges us straight into his life at the time of his baptism by John, we immediately get the impression of a wilful, sentient human being. And this is essential if we are to experience the force of the Passion. What emerges from Mark's Gospel is the sense of Jesus' continuous and often anguished decisions as he sets about forging a context in which his nature will indeed be revealed:

> And they laid their hands on him, and took him. And one of them that stood by drew a sword, and smote a servant of the high priest, and cut off his ear. And Jesus answered and said unto them, Are ye come out, as against a thief, with swords and with staves to take me? I was daily with you in the temple teaching, and ye took me not: but the scriptures must be fulfilled. And they all forsook him, and fled.
>
> (Mark 14:46–50)

By multiplying the examples of fulfilment, and by having them occur mainly when Jesus is too young to take any decisions himself, Matthew gives a purely magical quality to Jesus' life; Mark, by contrast, starting with Jesus as an adult, and here having him assert fulfilment himself, conveys a drama in which the protagonist achieves what he does in large part by virtue of his own belief in his actions and in fulfilment. As in the OT, we are left to decide at the end of the scene in the Garden whether 'they all forsook him, and fled' is the result of his words or has some other cause. The scene remains with us, puzzling and powerful, full of mystery and imbued with the personality of Jesus.

All the evangelists except Mark betray, at one time or another, so great an urgency to persuade that their rhetoric backfires. One way in which this manifests itself is in their multiplication of witnesses. On his way to Jerusalem for the last time, for example, Jesus stops at Jericho. Mark tells us:

> as he went out of Jericho with his disciples and a great number of people, blind Bartimaeus, the son of Timaeus, sat by the highway side begging. And when he heard that it was Jesus of Nazareth, he began to cry out, and say, Jesus, thou Son of David, have mercy on me.
>
> (Mark 10:46–47)

This is an important moment, because it is the first objective testimony we have that Jesus is indeed the Messiah, Son of David. The fact that it is a blind man, and a beggar as well, who utters the words, reinforces our sense of its truth.

Matthew, however, chooses to tell the story like this:

> And as they departed from Jericho, a great multitude followed him. And, behold, two blind men sitting by the way side, when they heard that Jesus passed by, cried out, saying, Have mercy on us, O Lord, thou Son of David.
> (Matt. 20 : 29–30)

Why should two witnesses be better than one? It is easy to see why Matthew thought they were, but he was mistaken. For we are not dealing here with a court of law but with narrative, and in narrative, if one character is going to be disbelieved, a hundred will do no better. For not believing a literary witness means feeling that words are being put into his mouth by the author, and the multiplication of witnesses will only reinforce our sense of the author behind the scenes, manipulating things. Contrast, moreover, the vague 'two blind men sitting by the way side' in Matthew, with 'blind Bartimaeus' in Mark (though telling us that *bar* or 'son of' Timaeus is the son of Timaeus suggests a story passed down orally rather than witnessed). We do not know the man, but the way he is presented in Mark makes us immediately accept him.

But we should beware of thinking that simply naming someone makes him come alive. In Mark 14 : 46–47, as we have just read: 'And they laid their hand on him, and took him. And one of them that stood by drew a sword, and smote a servant of the high priest, and cut off his ear.' In John this becomes: 'Then Simon Peter having a sword drew it, and smote the high priest's servant, and cut off his right ear. The servant's name was Malchus' (*ēn de onoma tōi doulōi Malchos* – John 18 : 10). The servant's name is added awkwardly; it feels as though it were put in precisely to make the man appear more real. By contrast Mark's naming of Bartimaeus seems simply to be a reference to someone we all know. It has the unforced authority of the OT genealogies.

I am not saying that Mark is telling the truth and Matthew and John are not. I am only saying that the way the narrative works in each case is different, that Mark *feels* true and the others contrived, literary. Indeed, Luke's version of the blind beggar episode is as convincing as Mark's, though the man is not named:

> And it came to pass, that as he was come nigh unto Jericho, a certain blind man sat by the way side begging: And hearing the multitude pass by, he asked what it meant. And they told him, that Jesus of Nazareth passeth by. And he cried, saying, Jesus, thou Son of David, have mercy on me.
> (Luke 18 : 35–38)

Our sense of this scene as having really occurred stems from one simple fact: Mark and Matthew had: 'And when he heard...when they heard. . .'. Luke makes us enter into the blind man's world: 'And hearing the multitude pass by, he asked what it meant. And they told him. . .'. It is the same set of events in each case, but our response differs radically from gospel to gospel.

Elsewhere, though, Luke succumbs to Matthew's desire for the multiplication of witnesses. Here is Mark telling how the three Marys came to the tomb after Jesus' burial:

> And very early in the morning the first day of the week, they came unto the sepulchre at the rising of the sun. And they said among themselves, Who shall roll us away the stone from the door of the sepulchre? And when they looked, they saw that the stone was rolled away: for it was very great. And entering into the sepulchre, they saw a young man sitting on the right side, clothed in a long white garment; and they were affrighted. And he saith unto them, Be not affrighted: Ye seek Jesus of Nazareth, which was crucified: he is risen; he is not here: behold the place where they laid him.
>
> (Mark 16:2–6)

Matthew tries to inject wonder and awe into the scene, but the result, as with his rather similar depiction of the Transfiguration, only serves to arouse our suspicion:

> In the end of the sabbath, as it began to dawn toward the first day of the week, came Mary Magdalene and the other Mary to see the sepulchre. And, behold, there was a great earthquake: for the angel of the Lord descended from heaven, and came and rolled back the stone from the door, and sat upon it. His countenance was like lightning, and his raiment white as snow: And for fear of him the keepers did shake, and became as dead men. And the angel answered and said unto the women, Fear not ye: for I know that ye seek Jesus, which was crucified. He is not here: for he is risen, as he said.
>
> (Matt. 28:1–6)

Luke will have nothing to do with such science-fiction, yet still feels that a single angel is not enough:

> Now upon the first day of the week, very early in the morning, they came unto the sepulchre, bringing the spices which they had prepared, and certain others with them. And they found the stone rolled away from the sepulchre. And they entered in, and found not the body of the Lord Jesus. And it came to pass, as they were much perplexed thereabout, behold, two men stood by them in shining garments: And as they were afraid, and bowed down their faces to the earth, they said unto them, Why seek ye the living among the dead? He is not here, but is risen: remember how he spake unto you when he was yet in Galilee.
>
> (Luke 24:1–6)

What these examples once again demonstrate is that the more we sense an author's desire to authenticate his narrative, the less likely we

are to assent to it, while the less conscious he seems to be of the effect he
is making, the greater will be that effect. Mark describes the incident as
though it were the most ordinary thing in the world: 'And entering into
the sepulchre, they saw a young man sitting on the right side, clothed in
a long white garment; and they were affrighted'. The conjunction joining
the last clause to what has gone before functions precisely as it does in
the great OT narratives: two elements are joined together, but just how
they relate to each other is left to us to decide. The women see the young
man *and* they are frightened. Why? Just because it is all so ordinary? The
conjoining of the two facts, both irrefutable, the young man and the
women's fear, forces us to enter the scene ourselves, to feel the terror
engendered by the events that are occurring, and so to project ourselves
back to the mystery of the missing body.

By contrast Matthew's 'And for fear of him the keepers did shake, and
became as dead men' alienates us with its detail. Matthew seems not to
have any real intuitive grasp of how the women feel and so has to whip
up emotion artificially; the second limb of his sentence adds nothing to
the first, only confirms us in our response. Luke, as always, is scrupulous
about detail, telling us about the spices the women brought with them,
for instance. This is not off-putting because it clearly has no designs upon
us. Like Mark he is intent only on what he sees in his imagination or
memory. On the other hand, when he gets to the two men in shining
garments he seems too concerned to signal to us that these are angels.
Thus he misses Mark's powerful effect of dislocation, for in Luke's version
the fear of the women is purely perfunctory and could almost have been
omitted.

What we find, then, in varying degrees, in Matthew, John and Luke, is
the need to authenticate, to justify, in order to confirm authority. Not
just the authority of Jesus, but also that of the narrator. However, we
need to put all this in perspective if we are to understand why the Church
in its wisdom decided that all four of these gospels should form part of the
canon. And the best way to do this is to look at other versions of the life
of Jesus, other gospels, which were rejected by the Church.[4] Only by
examining these will we be able to assess the temptations facing the
writers of the canonical gospels, and to see how finely, for the most part,
they resisted them; and to see too that, if Mark's Gospel is the one that
comes nearest in style and feeling to the great narratives of the Hebrew
scriptures, all four gospel narratives seem nevertheless to belong to the
same book as Genesis and 1 and 2 Samuel.

As soon as we open M. R. James's splendid edition of the non-
canonical material, *The Apocryphal New Testament*, we find ourselves in
a totally different world. Here, for example, is part of the description of

the Flight into Egypt from the Gospel of Pseudo-Matthew:

> They came to a cave and wished to rest there. Mary dismounted and sat with Jesus in her lap. There were three boys with Joseph and a girl with Mary. Suddenly a number of dragons came out of the cave, and all cried out in fear. Jesus got down from his mother's lap and stood before the dragons, which worshipped him. Thus was fulfilled the word, 'Praise the Lord out of the earth, ye dragons and all deeps'. . . . On the third day Mary saw a palm and wished to rest under it. When she was seated there she saw fruit on it, and said to Joseph that she should like to have some. Joseph said he was surprised she should say that because the tree was so high: he himself was thinking more about water, of which they had very little left. Jesus sitting in Mary's lap with a joyful countenance bade the palm give his mother of its fruit. The tree bent as low as her feet and she gathered what she would. He bade it rise again, and give them of the water concealed below its roots. A spring came forth and all rejoiced and drank of it.
>
> (James, 74–5)[5]

This belongs firmly to the world of fairy-tale and romance, though, as the first part shows, it is also concerned to link Jesus' actions with OT prophecy. Its central principle is that the laws of nature are suspended, or rather are completely subservient to the hero, who has only to wish for something in order to get it. At the same time this becomes a licence for the narrator, who can allow his fancy to roam free and unconstrained by any need for verisimilitude. The trouble with this of course is that it can easily degenerate into the completely arbitrary and so quickly lead to boredom. The best fairy stories are those which find ways of creating fresh constraints to take the place of the natural ones. But it remains a problem which the genre recognizes, as we can see by the number of tales which survive about the three wishes granted a foolish person and the mess that person makes of the opportunities granted him or her, or by the tale of King Midas and his golden touch.

The authors of the apocryphal gospels try to use this freedom in their elaboration of Jesus' life and death. In the process they uncover the paradox that underlies any narrative concerning the incarnation of a god. Thus in the Greek Gospel of Thomas we read:

> This little child Jesus when he was five years old was playing at the ford of a brook: and he gathered together the waters that flowed there into pools, and made them straightway clean, and commanded them by his word alone. And having made soft clay, he fashioned thereof twelve sparrows. And it was the sabbath when he did these things. . . . And there were also many other little children playing with him. And a certain Jew when he saw what Jesus did, playing upon the sabbath day, departed straightway and told his father Joseph: Lo, thy child is at the brook, and he hath taken clay and fashioned twelve little birds, and hath polluted the sabbath day. And Joseph came to

the place and saw: and cried out to him, saying: Wherefore doest thou these things on the sabbath, which it is not lawful to do? But Jesus clapped his hands together and cried out to the sparrows and said to them: Go! and the sparrows took their flight and went away chirping.... After that again he went through the village, and a child ran and dashed against his shoulder. And Jesus was provoked and said unto him: Thou shalt not finish thy course. And immediately he fell down and died.

(James, 49–50)

In the Gospels Jesus blasts a fig tree, but that is in order to make a symbolic point. Here there is no point in Jesus' killing of the child except the petulance of a supernatural being. At the start here he is presented as engaged on a second creation, and this is mingled with the Gospel theme of the breaking of the sabbath laws. But in the Gospels there is no secondary creation, only a bringing of the dead to life, and the breaking of the sabbath laws has a good humanitarian reason behind it (and one, incidentally, recognized by the Pharisees and going back, as Jesus points out, to David's stealing the shewbread to feed his men).[6]

Faced with writing of this kind, we can see that what is striking about the canonical Gospels is not, as eighteenth-and nineteenth-century theologians tended to think, the fact that miracles occur in them, but rather the fact that so very few miracles occur. These, moreover, are never designed merely to demonstrate that Jesus can do just what he wants, but always serve the larger concerns of Jesus' teaching. One more example from the apocryphal gospels (again, that of Thomas) will make this quite clear:

Now his father was a carpenter and made at that time ploughs and yokes. And there was required of him a bed by a certain rich man, that he should make it for him. And whereas one beam, that which is called the shifting one, was too short, and Joseph knew not what to do, the young child Jesus said to his father Joseph: Lay down the two pieces of wood and make them even at the end next unto thee. And Joseph did as the young child said unto him. And Jesus stood at the other end and took hold upon the shorter beam and stretched it and made it equal with the other. And his father Joseph saw it and marvelled: and he embraced the young child and kissed him, saying: Happy am I for that God hath given me this young child.

(James, 52–3)

By contrast the Gospel miracles always have to do with people. The loaves and fish are multiplied that all may share a communal meal; the sick are healed that they may realize the potential for healing which exists in the world and in themselves.

Even when natural forces are subverted in the Gospels the effect is quite different from that of the apocryphal gospels. I gave some examples earlier of the need felt by the Gospel writers to impress the reader with the awesomeness of what they are describing, or to persuade him by doubling the number of witnesses; a glance at the apocryphal gospels will show how very restrained they are in this. The apocryphal gospels tell us in detail how the Virgin looked, what she wore, and how well she did at school. In a fragment of a gospel 'According to the Hebrews' we read: 'He said unto him: Go, sell all that thou ownest, and distribute it unto the poor, and come, follow me. But the rich man began to scratch his head, and it pleased him not.' (James, 6) If we are to believe current narrative theory, which is often no more than post-Romantic prejudice dressed up in scientific garb, it is precisely the surprising detail which helps establish the reality of a scene. But does the description of the rich man scratching his head really help convince us of the reality of this scene? Are not the effects of narrative altogether subtler than that, depending more on what, borrowing from the world of social intercourse, we might call tone and tact?

The author of the above lacks the tact to see that the intrusion of even the tiniest realistic detail into a scene where ultimate choices are at issue is out of place. Matthew tells us nothing about the rich man, makes no effort to 'bring him to life', but he remains in our mind for ever once we have read this passage:

> And, behold, one came and said unto him, Good Master, what good thing shall I do, that I may have eternal life?. . .Jesus said unto him, If thou wilt be perfect, go and sell that thou hast, and give to the poor, and thou shalt have treasure in heaven: and come and follow me. But when the young man heard that saying, he went away sorrowful: for he had great possessions.
> (Matt. 19:16–22; cf. Mark 10:17–22)

Frank Kermode has plausibly suggested that the development of the figure of Judas in the Gospels is purely midrashic, that he is a function of the narrative, which needs an Opponent for Jesus. First of all 'Betrayal becomes Judas', and from there it is but a short step to Matthew's version of events, which (drawing on Ahithophel's suicide in 2 Sam. 17:13) recounts how Judas went and hanged himself.[7] The underlying implication seems to be that if this can happen to the figure of Judas it is likely to have happened with all the other characters in the Gospels, not excluding Jesus himself.

As so often, beneath Kermode's urbane and detached tone there lies a radical challenge. I will take up that challenge in a later chapter; but meanwhile a glance at what the apocryphal gospels do with the figure of Judas should make us at least question whether Kermode's unstated but ever-present opposition between 'the facts' and 'fictional elaboration' is quite the best way of approaching the Bible. Here, for example, is an episode from the Greek Acts of Pilate:

> And departing to his house to make a halter of rope to hang himself, he found his wife sitting and roasting a cock on a fire of coals or in a pan before eating

it: and saith to her; Rise up, wife, and provide me a rope, for I would hang myself, as I deserve. But his wife said to him: Why sayest thou such things? And Judas saith to her: Know of a truth that I have wickedly betrayed my master Jesus to the evil-doers for Pilate to put him to death: but he will rise again on the third day, and woe unto us! And his wife said to him: Say not nor think not so: for as well as this cock that is roasting on the fire of coals can crow, just so well shall Jesus rise again, as thou sayest. And immediately at her word that cock spread his wings and crowed thrice. Then was Judas yet more convinced, and straightway made the halter of rope and hanged himself.

(James, 116)

Is this simply a little more detailed than the Gospels? A little more magical? Or is there a qualitative difference? And if so, in what does it reside? And what are its implications? We are not yet quite ready to answer such questions, and it must anyway not be imagined that the answer will have to do with one version being 'true' and the other 'false'. For it is the nature of narrative falsity and truth that we are attempting to understand.

The authors of the apocryphal gospels are determined to impress. Of that there can be no doubt. We read that at the Transfiguration great rays emanated from Jesus' eyes and terrified the viewers, while at the Crucifixion a lintel of immense size fell off the Temple and was shattered. Yet what is moving and awesome in the canonical Gospels is precisely that so few of the trappings of mystery surround the most mysterious episodes. At the Transfiguration Jesus is simply dressed in white and simply talks to Moses and Elijah. What is impressive is that neither he nor the evangelist is trying to impress. At the Crucifixion only the veil of the Temple is rent. But, after all, even the tiniest deviation from the laws of nature is as much of a miracle as the greatest, and that God should talk to Abraham or make the bush burn for Moses is as much to be wondered at as that he should split open mountains and roll back the earth. More so, even, for it testifies to a constant theme of the Bible, the naturalness of God's interventions in the affairs of men.

This brings us to the final difference between the apocryphal gospels and the canonical ones, a difference which was at the heart of the firm distinction drawn by the Church between the two. It has to do with modes of narration and modes of reading, but at the same time it has to do with the nature of the Incarnation.

Not all the apocryphal gospels are technically Gnostic, but they all have strong Gnostic tendencies.[8] Indeed, we could say that the fairy-tale or romance genre is itself a Gnostic genre, since it depends on our accepting a world divided into light and darkness, good and bad, spirit and matter. Here, for example, is M. R. James's paraphrase of a passage from the Book of the Resurrection of Christ by Bartholomew the Apostle:

> Christ is on the cross, but his side has been pierced, and he is dead. A man in the crowd named Ananias, of Bethlehem, rushes to the cross and embraces and salutes the body breast to breast, hand to hand, and denounces the Jews. A voice comes from the body of Jesus and blesses Ananias, promising him incorruption, and the name of 'the firstfruits of the immortal fruit'. The priests decide to stone Ananias: he utters words of exultation. The stoning produces no effect. They cast him into a furnace, where he remains till Jesus has risen. At last they pierce him with a spear. The Saviour takes his soul to heaven, and blesses him.
>
> (James, 182)

The theme of the triumph over death is developed in detail a little later, in a strange combination of Gnostic fantasy and ancient Near Eastern myth:

> Joseph of Arimathaea buried the body of Jesus. Death came into Amente [the underworld], asking who the new arrival was, for he detected a disturbance. He came to the tomb of Jesus with his six sons in the form of serpents. Jesus lay there (it was the second day...) with his face and head covered with napkins. Death addressed his son the Pestilence, and described the commotion which had taken place in his domain. Then he spoke to the body of Jesus and asked: 'Who art thou?' Jesus removed the napkin that was on his face and looked in the face of Death and laughed at him. Death and his sons fled.
>
> (James, 182)

The Jesus who is presented here does not suffer, and for very good reason: he is always in command, can do what he likes and only *appears* to inhabit a body which is like that of other men. At the same time the message he comes to deliver has to be kept secret. Jesus is the master of esoteric doctrine and can discourse about the mysteries of the letter *aleph* like any master of cabbala. Better, of course, since he is the maker of the universe and has the key to all its secrets. And it is these secrets which the gospels will pass on to the few who are prepared to receive them. The principle is enunciated in the Gospel of Bartholomew:

> And again Bartholomew saith unto him: Lord, is it lawful for me to reveal these mysteries unto every man? Jesus saith unto him: Bartholomew, my beloved, as many as are faithful, and are able to keep them unto themselves, to them mayest thou entrust these things. For some there are that be worthy of them, but there are also other some unto whom it is not fit to entrust them: for they are vain (swaggerers), drunkards, proud, unmerciful, partakers in idolatry, authors of fornication, slanderers, teachers of foolishness, and doing all works that are of the devil, and therefore are they not worthy that these should be entrusted to them.
>
> (James, 179–80)

As is usually the case with such arguments, the notion of a secret entrusted to the chosen few is allied to a Manichaean view of human character: the few who are privileged to know the secret must be good, pure and true. It is likely too that they will have to be ascetic, for only those who subdue the body will be able to understand the word of the spirit and come to the truth. It is very different in the Gospels. No secret is being proclaimed there, but rather the life and words and actions of a man who is also the son of God. What Jesus offers is not wisdom, *gnōsis*, *sophia*, but a new life. And anybody can partake of this new life, provided he is humble enough and ready to acknowledge Jesus.

Even when we encounter what looks superficially like the Gnostic argument, it turns out that something very different is being presented:

> And he said unto them, Unto you it is given to know the mystery of the kingdom of God: but unto them that are without, all these things are done in parables: That seeing they may see, and not perceive; and hearing they may hear, and not understand; lest at any time they should be converted, and their sins should be forgiven them.
>
> (Mark 4:11–12)

The passage has long puzzled commentators. Recently Frank Kermode has compared it to the equivalent passage in Matthew and shown how Matthew waters down the distinction between insiders and outsiders which is so clear-cut in Mark.[9] But Jesus' notion of insiders is not connected with *gnōsis*, morality or asceticism, but with the completely amoral notion of election. As Schweitzer noted long ago, there seem to be two different strands running through the Gospels. The first is a radical ethics, the teaching that to be saved we must give up earthly possessions, we must be kind to our neighbours, we must not harbour envy or desire what is not ours, we must not confuse the letter and the spirit of the law. The second is an apocalyptic predestinarianism, the sense that the hairs on each man's head are numbered and there is nothing we can do about it.[10] It is this latter strand that is expressed in the passage in Mark, and not any notion of a secret to which we may gain access either by taking part in certain secret rituals or by leading an ascetic life.

This may seem shocking to us, but it is there in the Gospels, and it makes of them something very different from the Gnostic documents and apocryphal gospels which have come down to us. Indeed, it is one of the things that gives the Jesus of the Gospels his peculiar power and lifts him above his disciples with their calculus mentality. Just as we found it shocking that Jacob should steal his brother's birthright, and just as David's servants were shocked at his behaviour during the illness and then death of Bathsheba's child, so the disciples are shocked when Jesus allows the woman at Bethany to waste her precious ointment by pouring it on his head. But Jesus answers them, rather as David rebuked Joab for his criticism of Shimei: 'Why trouble ye the woman? for she hath wrought a good work upon me. For ye have the poor always with you; but me ye have not always.' (Matt. 26:10–11; cf. John 12:7–8) We as readers are as shocked as the disciples at this announcement of the eruption of another kind of time into this world. The apocryphal gospels, by contrast, never shock, however violent their imagery, because, once we have granted them their premises they are only too predictable.

Jesus, particularly in Mark's Gospel, appears as a force, a whirlwind which drives all before it and compels all who cross his path to reconsider their lives from the root up. He has access, not so much to a secret of wisdom as to a source of power. This power is inseparable from his physical presence and his mode of speech, and the canonical Gospels never let us forget that his is in the first place a physical presence. But how, we may ask, do they manage to do this, given that they too, after all, only have words at their disposal?

We saw at the start how difficult it was for Jesus to persuade either the Pharisees or the reader of his authority. And we saw too the traps into which the evangelists tended to fall whenever they attempted to prove their assertions about Jesus. However, for the most part they instinctively sense that this is not the way to go about their task. Rather, like the narrator of Genesis and 1 and 2 Samuel, they withdraw and let the actions and words of Jesus speak for themselves. Nevertheless there is no doubt that we are far more acutely conscious of Jesus' physical presence in the Gospels than we are of Adam's or Abraham's or even David's. Let us see how this is achieved.

The larger pattern of Jesus' life is one which should by now be very familiar to us: a fairy-tale start turns into something quite different as a world which knows nothing of fairy-tales or the wishes of men impinges upon it. The difference between Jesus on the one hand and Adam, Jacob, Saul and David on the other, is that the world in which Jesus lives and acts does indeed turn out, ultimately, to have a fairy-tale pattern, to conform to the wishes of the protagonist. But this makes the task of the narrators harder rather than easier. For they will only succeed in making us grasp the nature of the second, deeper pattern if they can convince us of the genuineness of the first. If all is fairy-tale as in the apocryphal gospels, then Incarnation and Resurrection are without meaning; but if all is the harsh reality of the world then they are also without meaning.

Of course to talk about difficult tasks is misleading. We have seen that when the evangelists feel they must try hard they tend to fail, and they succeed when they appear to take it for granted that what they are telling is merely what happened; when, in other words, the Incarnation is seen not as a problem but a datum. Given that fact all the rest follows. But as we read those narratives we can see how that given fact is brought home to us.

Crowds constantly press in upon Jesus. This makes us aware of his body as, like ours, needing space. At times he escapes the crush by fleeing to the desert or the lake. But most often he just accepts it. When the man sick of the palsy is lowered through the roof to bring him before Jesus because there is such a dense crowd round the house that he cannot be got through the door (Mark 2 : 2–5), the ingenuity and effort this requires make us aware of Jesus' bodily presence in a way no amount of argument could ever succeed in doing. When the woman touches Jesus and is healed, he suddenly feels 'that virtue had gone out of him' (Mark 5 : 30; cf. Luke 8 : 46), and we sense the physical cost of this healing activity. Then too he is always in movement. No OT figure, not even Jacob, is so restless, so continuously on the move. And we do not need a map of Palestine open before us to recognize what this entails, we only need to have used our legs ourselves.

But it is not only his feet which are in motion. It is also his mind. Scholarly attempts to break down the individual chapters into so many pericopes destroy the sense the ordinary reader gets of the sheer tempo and variety of Jesus' debates and arguments. Take chapter 9 of Luke. It begins with Jesus calling his disciples to him and then sending them out to preach and heal the sick. They depart and go 'through the towns, preaching the gospel, and healing every where' (9 : 6). Then we switch to Herod and his questions to his followers about Jesus: Who is he? John the Baptist come back from the dead? Elijah? The miracle of the loaves and fishes follows, and then Jesus is again alone with his disciples and asks them to tell him who they think he is. Peter answers that he is 'The Christ of God' (20). Jesus prophesies his own death, and this is followed by the Transfiguration, where he is seen talking to Moses and Elijah. Then comes the cure of a possessed youth, and a rebuke to the disciples for not having the faith to cure him. Jesus again tells them about his end. They wish to call down fire from heaven to consume those who will not take Jesus in, but he rebukes them: 'Ye know not what manner of spirit ye are of. For the Son of man is not come to destroy men's lives, but to save them' (55–56). A man appears and asks to be allowed to follow Jesus. First though he has to go and bury his father. 'Let the dead bury their dead' (60), Jesus says to him; and to another: don't look back; follow me. So the chapter ends.

Again, in chapter 13 of Luke we begin with a discourse on repentance, followed by the parable of the fig tree, the healing of the woman 'which had a spirit of infirmity eighteen years, and was bowed together, and could in no wise lift up herself' (13 : 11 – it is not only *Jesus'* physical presence which is brought home to us by these narratives), the parable of the mustard seed, the parable of the master who shut the door and refused to let those outside come in, another encounter with the Pharisees, and the chapter ends with Jesus' lament on Jerusalem, modelled on the OT prophetic laments over sinful cities.

The cumulative effect is very different from the effect of each single episode. Reading on from one encounter to the next we become aware much more of Jesus the person, acting, speaking, moving, healing, than of what he says. It may even be that, as with a Zen master, it is the sudden switch from one topic to another that is the real point of Luke 13. To try and sort out what is 'authentic' and what added by the evangelist or some later redactor is to shut oneself off from the impact of these chapters, from the whirlwind that sweeps through them.

The fact that Jesus' favourite form of instruction is the parable adds a further layer of density. For if these are stories told by Jesus it is also true that they have the same sort of realism as the Gospels themselves. They do not tell us about magic and wonders, as do the apocryphal gospels, but about fathers and sons, masters and servants, poor men and rich. A few, it is true, are purely schematic, but the great ones, like the Gospels themselves, require not decipherment, but a response such as one would accord to *Hamlet* or *Lear*.

Let us look at what happens when we read a parable like that of the Prodigal Son. It may indeed be the case, as scholars have argued, that a certain tradition of reading it in purely ethical terms has caused us to overlook its allegorical and eschatological thrust.[11] It may well be that the elder son is meant to stand for the Jews, the younger for the Christian Church. But what will first strike the reader is how well the parable conforms to the ethos of the rest of Luke's Gospel. His narrative everywhere strives to reconcile conflicting positions rather than, like Mark, to drive a wedge between them. Here he is not simply showing the elder son as cursed and the younger as blessed, but attempting to bring out the self-destructiveness of envy:

> And he said unto him, Son, thou art ever with me, and all that I have is thine. It was meet that we should make merry, and be glad; for this thy brother was dead, and is alive again; and was lost, and is found.
>
> (Luke 15:31–32)

We may start to read this with the firm notion that the elder son 'stands for' this or that, but once we enter the narrative we have to abandon our preconceptions and surrender ourselves to it. This means that we have to experience what the father and *both* sons are going through. Though the elder son gets no chance to reply (perhaps *because*, as with the end of the book of Jonah, he gets no chance to reply), we are left with a sense of him struggling to come to terms with what has just happened. And whether we want to or not we too enter his struggle.

John Drury is absolutely right to see echoes of Joseph and his brothers here, and just as we saw that the problem with Judah was to come to terms with the fact that parental love is never distributed fairly, so it is here. The story makes something happen inside us; we are forced to shift our ground, to acknowledge feelings we too have had but perhaps never admitted, even to ourselves. The parable works like this upon us because it does not try to deny these feelings but rather to bring them out into the open and turn them into something positive rather than destructive and self-destructive. It is, like all the greatest narratives, easy to read while teaching a hard lesson.

Bernard Harrison has generalized from this insight to good effect:

> The parabolic narrative is...set askew to these underlying structures of social practices and their corresponding systems of concepts, so that the mind can find no resting-place in the story; cannot find, in terms of the underlying scheme of practices and associated concepts, a clear point and structure in the story.

That is, where our parable is concerned, 'the father's behaviour makes nonsense of common considerations of fairness and justice in the management of family affairs'. The parables, Harrison argues, force the mind to reach beyond accepted social and ethical structures 'to something which transcends these structures and constitutes a kind of judgement upon them'. Yet if we try to discover a general scheme from which to operate, try, that is, to generalize the ethical lessons of the parables, by saying, for example, that the dignity of the person has to come before any considerations of fairness, we find ourselves once more in a manifestly false position.

For suppose I wish to make this idea of 'the dignity of the person' into the basis of my relationships with other people: what exactly, in practical terms, am I to do?

> Am I, for example [Harrison continues], with my strength of character, my moral vision and my remarkable powers of love transcending all common-place moral relationships, to take charge of my weaker fellow men in the manner of Dostoevsky's Grand Inquisitor? Or more prosaically should I, if I have servants, treat them 'as one of the family', taking an interest in their lives, helping them in trouble and so on?

The parables give no help. And of course we all know how spiritual guidance can become spiritual tyranny and helping those in inferior social positions a hypocritical paternalism. So how can we know the difference? In other words, what is it the parables are teaching, and how are they doing it? Harrison's answer is to invoke the later Wittgenstein:

> Wittgenstein says that we show that we have understood the principle of a series by continuing the series. What we have in the parables...is precisely a

series of narratives bound to one another by a single principle. . . . How can we show our understanding but by continuing, in other narratives or in our own lives, the series of which we have been given, as it were, the first few integers?[12]

In other words we cannot stand back as uninvolved spectators and simply work out the allegorical or ethical implications. Reading narratives of this kind means learning how to continue the series (or discovering that we do not know how to continue it). This is something every reader of the Bible grasps immediately and intuitively, but errors tend to creep in when we try to conceptualize our intuitions. There is, moreover, so much anxiety attached to the reading of religious documents that the natural processes of reading are interfered with by external notions of what it is one should be looking for far more than with other writings.

The parables bring us back to the question of authority. Kierkegaard, trying to rescue Christianity from a vague Romantic ethics, argued that it is not so much *what* is said in the New Testament that is important as the authority of the speaker. If I said you were to love your neighbour you could ignore me, is the form of his argument, but because it is Jesus who says it we have to obey.[13] One can sympathize with Kierkegaard's project while disagreeing with this kind of argument. As we saw in our discussion of John 8, there is no way that Jesus or the evangelist can prove his authority to the sceptic. What the parables show us is that authority resides in the mode of telling. We read, or listen, because we have come to trust the teller. And, reading or listening, we are then constrained to carry on the series.

Luke himself recognizes the paradoxes of the problem of authority. In chapter 16 he tells the story of the beggar Lazarus and the rich man Dives. The beggar dies and is carried into Abraham's bosom, while the rich man is cast into the torments of Hell, from which he cries out, begging Abraham to have mercy on him. Abraham is adamant: 'between us and you there is a great gulf fixed' (16:26). However, Dives will not be put off. I have five brothers still living, he says, let Lazarus go to them and tell them just how things are after death, so as to save them from a fate similar to mine. Abraham replies that they have Moses and the prophets as guides (i.e. the Hebrew scriptures minus the miscellaneous last section), so 'let them hear them'. But Dives answers: 'Nay, father Abraham: but if one went unto them from the dead, they will repent. And he said unto him, If they hear not Moses and the prophets, neither will they be persuaded though one rose from the dead.' (30–31) This, we are meant to understand, is how the Jews will receive Jesus. But is it not also how many of us will receive this narrative? How then to persuade us?

The way is clearly not to describe as many miracles as possible performed by Jesus, as the apocryphal gospels do, for that leaves us precisely where we began. It is to do what Jesus himself does in his parables: to force us to enter the world of the narrative. This is what the evangelists do, by and large. And they do this, as we have seen, not because of any excess of detail but by forcing apparent contradictions upon us and yet giving us the confidence that this and no other way was how it was. To a large extent they accept the limits of story-telling and the limits of comprehension, and merely point us towards what took place without trying to explain it or prove it. But, just because Jesus, unlike Adam and David, is himself free to do what he wants, he too needs to establish boundaries, limits within which to operate so as to persuade us and his disciples of his fleshly reality. Naturally the most pure limit of all is death, for, as Kafka sensed, he who cannot die cannot be said to have lived, and for him who has never lived death is impossible.[14]

We have, in the course of the Gospels, come to take it for granted that Jesus is someone essentially like ourselves: someone who can be kind but also gets angry; who has inexhaustible reserves of self-confidence yet can suddenly lose heart; someone who, like Joseph, knows he is right, and yet, like Joseph in the pit, can suddenly fear for his life. There are two moments in particular where Jesus' sense of failure and despair becomes, paradoxically, the index both of his own success and that of the evangelists. The first is the moment in the Garden of Gethsemane, when he 'began to be sore amazed, and to be very heavy' (Mark 14:33; cf. Matt. 26:36–46, Luke 22:39–46). The second is on the cross, when Jesus, rather than discoursing at length about his power, as he does in the apocryphal gospels, calls out in agony to God, asking why he has forsaken him, and then cries 'with a loud voice, and gave up the ghost' (Mark 15:37; cf. Matt. 27:50; Luke 23:46, John 19:30) Neither of these moments is conceivable in the apocryphal gospels. External reality and internal desire clash here, as they so often do in the Hebrew Bible, and it is the dreams and desires that have to give way. At such moments, as with Phalti and David, we experience what it means to be a human being in this world of ours. Sensing how alone they are in their sorrow which no words can convey, we find we are at one with them.

For the evangelists the narrative cannot end there. And if a sorrow beyond words in the face of death is what confers reality on Jesus, then won't his freedom from death once again rob him of that reality? The evangelists adopt different strategies for dealing with this, each designed to avoid the trap into which the apocryphal gospels fall, of returning us to the world of fairy-tale from which the Passion had freed us. We have seen how John loses his nerve at this point and tries to assert the truth of his narrative by insisting that he himself saw it happen and that he, the beloved desciple, cannot but be telling the truth. Mark and Luke, however, far from losing their nerve, rise to the challenge.

Mark had begun his gospel with Jesus' sudden appearance in the desert and his baptism by John. He ends, if anything, even more abruptly: the women go to the tomb, find there the young man dressed in white, and are seized with fear:

> And he saith unto them, Be not affrighted: Ye seek Jesus of Nazareth, which was crucified: he is risen; he is not here: behold the place where they laid him. But go your way, tell his disciples and Peter that he goeth before you into Galilee: there shall ye see him, as he said unto you. And they went out quickly, and fled from the sepulchre; for they trembled and were amazed: neither said they any thing to any man; for they were afraid.
>
> (Mark 16:6–8)

As with David's 'I shall go to him, but he shall not return to me' (2 Sam. 12:23), we come face to face here with a mystery that can only be accepted, as the narrator withdraws, leaving us alone with the speaker. We listen with the women, and our response is dramatized within the narrative: the women flee in terror. A lesser writer, one with a thesis to propound, would have had the women rejoice at the news; Mark seems merely to tell us how it was: the most joyful tidings are also the most frightening.

The best early MSS of Mark stop at this point, but our modern Bibles include twelve more verses, which tell of Jesus' reappearance and end the book on a more openly comforting note. This doesn't feel like Mark at all, but on the other hand there are problems about ending at 16:8. The Greek *ephobounto gar* ('they were afraid for') would, if correct, be the only known instance of a Greek sentence ending with a preposition. Mark is so original a writer, so strikingly daring, that it is not absolutely impossible that he would have ended his entire gospel with an apparently impossible grammatical construction. On the other hand those with an instinctive sense of what is possible in Greek would rule out such an ending.[15] My own feeling is that we do not have to choose. We can think of verses 9–20 as being rather like the final chapter of Job, which differs sharply in style and intensity from what has gone before (though there, it is true, it merely returns to the style of the opening chapter). What is important is that our sense of the possibility of resurrection is given imaginative impetus not by the narration of the exploits of the risen Christ but by the empty tomb and the women's terrible fear.

Luke's solution is so different from Mark's that we could not possibly have imagined two such different versions unless we had actually encountered them. Yet each is consistent with the rest of the gospel. Mark is abrupt and violent, Luke gentle and rich in detail, drawing out episodes until he has fully exploited all their possibilities. Just as he begins not in the desert and not even with Jesus' birth, but long before that, with the parents of the Baptist, so he ends not with an empty tomb or Jesus' simple reappearance, but with an entirely new bit of narrative.

His final chapter begins, as Mark's does, with the empty tomb and the women being told that Jesus is risen. But at once we switch to two of the disciples on the way to Emmaus, and the stranger who joins them on the way. The reader is made privy to the fact that this is Jesus, but the two disciples remain ignorant of that fact until the moment he vanishes:

> And it came to pass, as he sat at meat with them, he took bread, and blessed it, and brake, and gave to them. And their eyes were opened, and they knew him; and he vanished out of their sight.
>
> (Luke 24 : 30–31)

They return at once and tell the others: 'The Lord is risen indeed.' 'And,' says the narrator, 'they told what things were done in the way, and how he was known of them in breaking of bread.' But as they are speaking, Jesus appears amongst them. This is the difficult moment for the narrator. How will Luke, with nothing but words at his disposal, persuade us that Jesus is not spirit but flesh?

First of all, of course, through all that has gone before. If we have learned to trust him over the preceding 23 chapters we will be likely to trust him here. Secondly, by actually facing the issue rather than ignoring it, like the apocryphal gospels:

> And they told what things were done in the way, and how he was known of them in breaking of bread. And as they thus spake, Jesus himself stood in the midst of them, and saith unto them, Peace be unto you. But they were terrified and affrighted [*ptoēthentes de kai emphoboi genomenoi*], and supposed that they had seen as spirit.
>
> (Luke 24 : 35–37)

At this point the evangelist can let Jesus speak for himself:

> And he said unto them, Why are ye troubled? and why do thoughts arise in your hearts? Behold my hands and my feet, that it is I myself: handle me, and see; for a spirit hath not flesh and bones, as ye see me have. And when he had thus spoken, he shewed them his hands and his feet. And while they yet believed not for joy, and wondered, he said unto them, Have ye here any meat? Any they gave him a piece of a broiled fish, and of an honeycomb. And he took it, and did eat before them.
>
> (38–43)

Jesus does not stop at 'handle me, and see', which would have been obviously aimed at proving (to both them and the reader) that he had risen again from the dead in bodily form. He proves it in the best possible way, unwittingly, by demonstrating his hunger. At this point Luke could have written: 'And they gave him meat and he did eat before them', or he could, in the style of the apocryphal gospels, have given us the details of a three-course meal eaten by Jesus. But no: 'And they gave him a piece of a broiled fish, and of an honeycomb. And he took it, and did eat before them.' Some MSS leave out the honeycomb, and these are followed by the NEB, which consequently gives us: 'They offered him a piece of fish they had cooked, which he took and ate before their eyes.' The effect, however, is not very different in the two instances. Jesus points to his wounds, but he does not wait for the disciples to be persuaded; he is hungry (after his long sleep?) and interrupts their speculations with the simple human request: 'Have ye here any meat?' Whereupon they give him of their simple fare. We recall the encounter of Saul and the Witch of Endor, and how that scene ended:

> But he refused, and said, I will not eat. But his servants, together with the woman, compelled him; and he hearkened unto their voice. So he arose from the earth, and sat upon the bed.
>
> (1 Sam. 28:23)

Saul sitting on the bed, Jesus asking for food and then eating the piece of a broiled fish – it is hard to see how anything else could have been so effective in conveying to us the sense of the bodily presence of the two men.

This climactic scene in Luke shows us how we have been reading the Bible throughout: not as a set of secrets to be deciphered but as accounts of lives to which we listen and respond. This might seem obvious, and Christians have always been aware, at least theoretically, that it is this which constitutes the difference between their religion and those mystery cults with which it otherwise has so much in common. This, they have said, is what Incarnation means. But though that has been the theoretical response, in practice those who have taken it upon themselves to discuss the Gospels, particularly since the eighteenth century, have tended to take a rather different line. They have wished to get *behind the words* to some truth supposedly hidden there which will authenticate their beliefs: either the truth of the spade, which would reveal the Jesus of history; or an existential truth, which would shatter the narrative and change their lives once and for all. They have somehow shied away from reading these narratives in the simple and natural way in which they ask to be read, that is, as we read or listen to all narratives which engage our interest but about which we are not asked to hold particular views.

When matters are put so starkly the usual response is to admit the errors of the extreme positions and to insist that we must indeed take these narratives first of all 'on faith'. The trouble is that 'faith' here seems to be something quite distinct from anything else in our affective lives. It becomes a question of believing 'against the odds'. But that is the position of the positivist who still wants to cling to religious truth but cannot see how to integrate it with the rest of his intellectual experience. Frank Kermode's *The Genesis of Secrecy*, though ostensibly written by one who wishes to stand outside theological controversies, brings this out clearly. And it does so because Kermode realizes that what we are really talking about is modes of reading. He feels that as we read the Gospels we sense ourselves to be perpetually shut out, denied access to some secret. As a result, he feels, we can either go on reiterating our sorrow at this state of affairs or we can invent stories which we know, alas, to be the result of purely private imaginings about what it is like within the Kingdom.

But that is not how we normally read narrative nor how the Gospels ask to be read. We assent to narratives, as we do to people, to the degree that we grow to feel we can trust them. In biblical narrative, as we have seen, it is moments of ordinariness, as when someone realizes he is hungry and takes sustenance from others, which establish the grounds of our trust; and it is the moments of vulnerability, the moments when the protagonist can no longer find words to make sense of his life, and is reduced to tears or cries of despair, which make us experience his body in our own, *as* our own. At those moments the narratives cease to exist as narratives and we are torn by what Proust called 'the mark of authenticity'.

XII

ST. PAUL AND SUBJECTIVITY

Saul's story is first told us by the narrator of Acts:

And Saul, yet breathing out threatenings and slaughter against the disciples of the Lord, went unto the high priest, And desired of him letters to Damascus to the synagogues, that if he found any of this way, whether they were men or women, he might bring them bound unto Jerusalem. And as he journeyed, he came near Damascus: and suddenly there shined round about him a light from heaven: And he fell to the earth, and heard a voice saying unto him, Saul, Saul, why persecutest thou me? And he said, Who art thou, Lord? And the Lord said, I am Jesus whom thou persecutest: it is hard for thee to kick against the pricks [*sklēron soi pros kentra laktizein* – omitted in many MSS and therefore by the NEB translators]. And he trembling and astonished said, Lord, what wilt thou have me to do? And the Lord said unto him, Arise, and go into the city, and it shall be told thee what thou must do. And the men which journeyed with him stood speechless, hearing a voice, but seeing no man. And Saul arose from the earth; and when his eyes were opened, he saw no man: but they led him by the hand, and brought him into Damascus. And he was three days without sight, and neither did eat nor drink.

(Acts 9 : 1–9)

This story, with a few minor variations, of which the most striking is the effect on the bystanders, is repeated twice more in the course of the 28 chapters of Acts. Both these later retellings are by Saul himself. The first time is when, having been apprehended in the Temple, he begs leave of his captors to speak to the people. It is worth quoting the passage in full precisely because the most significant thing about it is its iteration:

And when he had given him licence, Paul stood on the stairs, and beckoned with the hand unto the people. And when there was made a great silence, he spake unto them in the Hebrew tongue, saying, Men, brethren, and fathers, hear ye my defence which I make now unto you. . . . I am verily a man which am a Jew, born in Tarsus, a city in Cilicia, yet brought up in this city at the feet of Gamaliel, and taught according to the perfect manner of the law of the fathers, and was zealous toward God, as ye all are this day. And I persecuted this way unto the death, binding and delivering into prisons both men and women. As also the high priest doth bear me witness, and all the estate of the elders: from whom also I received letters unto the brethren, and went to Damascus, to bring them which were there bound unto Jerusalem, for to be punished. And it came to pass, that, as I made my journey, and was come nigh unto Damascus about noon, suddenly there shone from heaven a great light round about me. And I fell unto the ground, and heard a voice saying unto me, Saul, Saul, why persecutest thou me? And I answered, Who art thou, Lord? And he said unto me, I am Jesus of Nazareth, whom thou persecutest. And they that were with me saw indeed the light, and were afraid; but they heard not the voice of him that spake to me. And I said, What shall I do, Lord? And the Lord said unto me, Arise, and go into Damascus; and there it shall be told thee of all things which are appointed for thee to do. And when I could not see for the glory of that light, being led by the hand of them that were with me, I came into Damascus.

(Acts 21 : 40–22 : 11)

In Damascus a certain Ananias comes to him and tells him that

The God of our fathers hath chosen thee, that thou shouldest know his will, and see that Just One, and shouldest hear the voice of his mouth. For thou shalt be his witness [*hoti esei martus autōi*] unto all men of what thou hast seen and heard. And now why tarriest thou? arise, and be baptized, and wash away thy sins, calling on the name of the Lord.

(22 : 14–16)

As a result of this he returns to Jerusalem, prays to the Lord, and hears his voice urging him on. But Saul cannot forget what he has done:

And I said, Lord, they know that I imprisoned and beat in every synagogue them that believed on thee: And when the blood of thy martyr Stephen was shed, I also was standing by, and consenting unto his death, and kept the raiment of them that slew him. And he said unto me, Depart: for I will send thee far hence unto the Gentiles.

(22 : 19–21)

The core narrative here is nearly identical with the one recounted earlier by the narrator, but there are some interesting additional details. We learn here of Saul's childhood and studies; we note how baptism is mentioned as though it were merely the confirmation of a prior conversion; and we find him expostulating with God rather like Moses and the prophets when they are called and yet insist on their inadequacy – though with the added twist here that Saul is not simply saying he is inadequate to the task, but the very last person to be sent since only a short while before he was one of the Christians' chief persecutors.

Most of this is repeated by Saul once again in chapter 26, when he is brought before the governor, Agrippa, and asked to speak in his own defence. There too he begins by stating that he was brought up as a

Jew, and even that 'after the most straitest sect of our religion I lived a Pharisee' (26:5), and he repeats how

> many of the saints did I shut up in prison, having received authority from the chief priests; and when they were put to death, I gave my voice against them. . .and being exceedingly mad against them, I persecuted them even unto strange cities.
>
> (Acts 26:10–11)

He tells how he went to Damascus and on the way, at midday, saw a bright light shining about him, and how all who were with him fell down before it, and he heard the voice speaking and saying: 'Saul, Saul, why persecutest thou me? it is hard for thee to kick against the pricks'; how he asked who was speaking and was told, 'I am Jesus whom thou persecutest'; and how Jesus told him to rise up and do his bidding:

> for I have appeared unto thee for this purpose, to make thee a minister and a witness [*hupēretēn kai martura ōn* – the word *hupēretēn* originally meant 'one who rows on a ship', and thus a servant, and thus eventually one who ministers in the Mithraic cult] both of these things which thou hast seen, and of those things in the which I will appear unto thee; Delivering thee from the people, and from the Gentiles, unto whom now I send thee, To open their eyes, and to turn them from darkness to light, and from the power of Satan unto God, that they may receive forgiveness of sins, and inheritance among them which are sanctified by faith that is in me.
>
> (26:16–18)

Though they are the most complete accounts, they are not the only times Saul, or Paul as he now calls himself, returns to the moment on the Damascus road and to his sudden conversion from a persecutor of the Christians to the witness of Jesus. It seems indeed that he cannot keep away from the subject. To the Galatians he says:

> For ye have heard of my conversation in time past in the Jews' religion, how that beyond measure I persecuted the church of God, and wasted it. . . . But when it pleased God. . .To reveal his Son in me, that I might preach him among the heathen; immediately I conferred not with flesh and blood.
>
> (Gal. 1:13–16)

He reminds the Ephesians how God made himself known to him (Eph. 3:1–4), and the Philippians how he persecuted the church (Phil. 3:6); to Timothy he says how he thanks Jesus for 'putting me into the ministry [*themenos eis diakonian*]; Who was before a blasphemer, and a persecutor, and injurious: but I obtained mercy, because I did it ignorantly in unbelief' (1 Tim. 1:12–13); to the Corinthians he confesses:

> I am the least of the apostles, that am not meet to be called an apostle, because I persecuted the church of God. But by the grace of God I am what I am: and his grace which was bestowed upon me was not in vain.
>
> (1 Cor. 15:9–10)

Scholarship has tended to concern itself with the truth or otherwise of Paul's claims: Had he really studied with Gamaliel? What precisely was his status within the administration when he persecuted the Christians? What exactly happened on the road to Damascus and afterwards in the city? What was his relation to the Jerusalem church? Was he even, as he claimed, a Jew?[1] I am concerned here, not with whether what Paul said was true (as with the Hebrew scriptures, clues are so scanty that scholars tend to use them to fit in with a position they have already taken up), but with what Acts and Paul's own letters reveal to us: his continuous and eloquent self-projection.

Of course there is a perfectly sound reason for this. He has been called as a witness not, like the evangelists, to Jesus' life and death and resurrection, but to his saving power. It is therefore natural that he should use the circumstances of his own life to persuade others, for if he was saved there is no reason why they should not be: 'Brethren, I beseech you, be as I am; for I am as ye are' (Gal. 4:12). And since this is the case, then men must be brought to see its truth in every way possible. Wake up! is his constant message. Do not sleep as I slept, but awake to the truth as I eventually did: 'The night is far spent, the day is at hand: let us therefore cast off the works of darkness, and let us put on the armour of light' (Rom. 13:12).

His call is a rousing one, and it has not ceased to stir the hearts of Christians through the ages. Not only that: he is also a master of rhetoric. So great a master that we may, dazzled by his performance, fail to see that there was nothing inevitable about his way of conveying the Christian message. Even in Acts we find many examples of appeals to conversion which make no play with Pauline dramatizations of the self. The story of the Ethiopian eunuch, a man 'of great authority' (8:27–39), is a case in point. He is riding to Jerusalem in his chariot, reading the book of Isaiah. Philip approaches him and asks him if he understands what he is reading. How can I, says the man, 'except some man should guide me?'. He points to the verse he has been reading: 'He was led as a sheep to the slaughter; and like a lamb dumb before his shearer...' (quoting Isaiah 53:7–8 from LXX). Who does this refer to? asks the eunuch, and when Philip has explained that it is Jesus, and 'preached unto him Jesus', the man is persuaded and asks to be baptized. Here, as in the Epistle to the Hebrews, which I will be looking at in the next chapter, it is the evidence of Scripture which persuades, not anything Philip says about himself.

Even more striking in its contrast to the Pauline mode is the speech made by Stephen earlier in the previous chapter of Acts. Like Paul Stephen has been haled up before the authorities and asked to give an account of himself and his actions. This is *his* defence:

Men, brethren, and fathers, hearken; The God of glory appeared unto our father Abraham, when he was in Mesopotamia, before he dwelt in Charran, And said unto him, Get thee out of thy country, and from thy kindred, and come into the land which I shall shew thee. Then came he out of the land.... And God...gave him the covenant of circumcision: and so Abraham begat Isaac, and circumcised him the eighth day; and Isaac begat Jacob; and Jacob begat the twelve patriarchs. And the patriarchs, moved with envy, sold Joseph into Egypt: but God was with him....

(Acts 7:2–9)

He goes on to tell how the people multiplied in Egypt, how a king rose in Egypt who did not know Joseph, how he persecuted the Jews, how Moses was called; he tells of the exodus, the years of wandering in the desert, the building of the tabernacle, which was brought into the Promised Land by Jesus/Joshua; how David found favour before God and Solomon built the Lord a house: 'Howbeit the most High dwelleth not in temples made with hands; as saith the prophet' (7:48).

And so he comes to the peroration, drawing a parallel between those in ancient times who did not walk in God's way and were castigated by the prophets, and the present generation:

Ye stiffnecked and uncircumcised in heart and ears, ye do always resist the Holy Ghost: as your fathers did, so do ye. Which of the prophets have not your fathers persecuted? and they have slain them which shewed before of the coming of the Just One; of whom ye have been now the betrayers and murderers: Who have received the law by the disposition of angels, and have not kept it.

(Acts 7:51–53)

At this the crowd is incensed and rushes upon him. As they do so he cries out: 'Behold, I see the heavens opened, and the Son of man standing on the right hand of God.' And, as he dies: 'Lord, lay not this sin to their charge.' (56–60)

Stephen is the first Christian martyr, and his death is of course very reminiscent of that of Jesus. But he is not a witness (*martyr*) in the way Paul is. He says nothing about himself, and in fact his speech here is not very different from the many recapitulations of saving history in the Hebrew scriptures. Compare, for example, Joshua's final speech:

And Joshua said unto all the people, Thus saith the Lord God of Israel, Your fathers dwelt on the other side of the flood in old time, even Terah, the father of Abraham.... And I took your father Abraham from the other side of the flood, and led him throughout all the land of Canaan, and multiplied his seed, and gave him Isaac. And I gave unto Issac Jacob and Esau.... I brought your fathers out of Egypt.... Then Balak...arose and warred against Israel.... And ye went over Jordan, and came unto Jericho.... I have

given you a land for which ye did not labour.... Now therefore fear the
Lord, and serve him in sincerity and in truth.

(Josh. 24:2–14)

Both Stephen and Joshua seek to persuade by reminding the people of
how God acted for them in the past, and end by making a plea for the
maintaining of the right relation to God in the present. Stephen combines Joshua's objective account with a rousing climax derived from the
prophets, but that is not entirely missing from Joshua's speech either.

The contrast with what we have seen of St. Paul is striking. Even
when he sets himself to do what Joshua and Stephen did, as happens
when he preaches at Antioch, the emphasis is very different. He spends
six verses on OT episodes of God's saving history, and then devotes
thirteen verses to the life and death of Jesus. And his peroration is quite
different from anything that had come before in the Bible:

Be it known unto you therefore, men and brethren, that through this man is
preached unto you the forgiveness of sins: and by him all that believe are
justified from all things, from which ye could not be justified by the law of
Moses.

(Acts 13:38–39)

What is new here is the whole message. Jesus is no longer just the last in
a long line of prophets persecuted by the very people who should be
listening to him; they are no longer simply breakers of a law with which
they have been entrusted. No. 'Through this man is preached unto you
forgiveness of sins', and all who believe are 'justified from all things',
which merely keeping the commandments of Moses would not do for
them. There is thus a mystical component, in that somehow, through
faith in Jesus, we are forgiven all our sins; and a historical component, in
that what Paul is preaching is a radical break with Jewish 'law'.

It would be absurd to ask which came first for Paul, the message or the
impulse towards personal witness, for each clearly reinforces the other.
We can only fully understand the latter if we understand at least the
broad outlines of the former. I say broad outlines because the doctrine
that Paul preaches in his letters has of course been the subject of discussion and debate almost from the moment he began to preach, and no
two commentators have ever agreed exactly on what it is he is saying.
This is not simply a matter of scholarship, of understanding the meaning
certain words and phrases would have had for him, but rather of recognizing that St. Paul, like St. Augustine, was not so much elaborating a
system as reacting polemically to specific situations. It is also a matter of
human response: as with the Hebrew prophets, the Pauline 'message'
changes for us as we change and can never be exhausted. Nevertheless, it

is fundamentally quite simple – and that indeed is the reason for much of its persuasive power.

Paul's vision on the road to Damascus gave him an image of man and an image of history which interlock. Man was made in God's image, but the Fall shattered that image and doomed man to sin and darkness. Thus in our natural state we are embedded in sin and cannot get free of it, no matter how hard we try, by our own efforts. This state is symbolized by the Law of the Jews, and it is from this that Jesus has come to save us. He gave himself willingly to death and rose again so that we might, by believing in him, rise with him from bondage to sin and death. However diligently we carry out the Law it cannot save us. Only faith in Jesus can do that. The wages of sin is death, but the gift of God, if we will only accept it, is eternal life.

This entails, naturally, a completely new understanding of history as Scripture presents it. Jesus is the Second Adam, undoing the fault of the First. Abraham himself was a man of faith before he was a man of the Law, since he had faith in God before he was physically circumcised. His two sons, Isaac, born of the freewoman Sarah, and Ishmael, born of the bondwoman Hagar, represent those born 'by promise', that is, the Christians, and those born 'after the flesh', that is, the Jews (Gal. 4 : 23). Those who have renounced the Law and decided to follow only Jesus are none other than that remnant who alone, according to Isaiah and Hosea, would be saved (Rom. 9 : 25–27).

Thus Paul, whose own life was transformed in a moment on the road to Damascus, develops a strong set of oppositions which between them account for everything: Law / Grace, Works / Faith, Old Man / New Man, Jew / Christian, blindness / sight. For him everything depends on our sudden ability to see and, seeing, to recognize our previous blindness. That is why he keeps returning to his own experience and to the paradoxical moment when he was himself struck blind by a great light and saw for the first time; and that is why there is no place in his thought for any gradual change, and little interest in the sacraments except as images of transformation:

> But before faith came, we were kept under the law, shut up unto the faith which should afterwards be revealed. Wherefore the law was our schoolmaster to bring us unto Christ, that we might be justified by faith. But after that faith is come, we are no longer under a schoolmaster. For ye are all the children of God by faith in Christ Jesus. For as many of you as have been baptized into Christ have put on Christ.
>
> (Gal. 3 : 23–27)

It is important to grasp how different is the image of man and sin put before us in Paul's letters from that presented in the Hebrew scriptures. They start with the notion that man is good so long as he walks in God's

way. As I argued in chapter III, Genesis 2–3 makes no mention of a Fall,
and the story of the Garden of Eden plays a relatively unimportant role.
If you sin, then, like David, you may repent, or, like Ahab, you may not.
Even if you do you may, like Jonah, sin again. Sin is not a single, all-
embracing concept or state; there are specific sins a man may commit,
but he is not in a condition of *sinfulness*. As Hyam Maccoby puts it:

> For the Jew only outrageously wilful behaviour can jeopardize his condition of
> being 'saved' – and thus the expression 'saved' is not even part of the Jewish
> religious vocabulary. For Paul, however, the human condition is itself desper-
> ate, and the only issue is salvation.[2]

When someone's eyes are opened in the Hebrew Bible it is not so that
they may suddenly understand the falsity of their whole past life but only
the immediate error under which they have been labouring:

> Then the Lord opened the eyes of Balaam, and he saw the angel of the Lord
> standing in the way, and his sword drawn in his hand: and he bowed down his
> head, and fell flat on his face. And the angel of the Lord said unto him,
> Wherefore hast thou smitten thine ass these three times? . . . surely now also I
> had slain thee, and saved her alive. And Balaam said unto the angel of the
> Lord, I have sinned; for I knew not that thou stoodest in the way against me:
> now therefore, if it displease thee, I will get me back again. And the angel of
> the Lord said unto Balaam, Go with the men.
>
> (Num. 22 : 31–35)

In the Hebrew Bible, and in Judaism till the present day, the term for
repentance is *teshuvah*, a turning. You have gone astray in this way or
that and now you recognize and admit this and turn back to the right
way. The great series of feasts connected with the new year culminates in
the Day of Atonement, when, having repented fully, you are forgiven
and so can start afresh with the slate wiped clean. But for Paul the
important act is not repentance but awakening, an act of faith which
totally transforms life, and which can happen at any time and in any
place. The psychological and theological power of this notion and of
Paul's exposition of it are not in doubt, and twenty centuries of
Christianity have shown its ability to remain perpetually relevant. It is,
however, worth seeing what are its implications for the concept of the
individual.

What is important for Paul is not the taking part in a ritual but the act
of conversion. Thus it is not surprising that he systematically takes the
ancient Jewish rituals and transforms them into inward events: circumcision must be of the heart, the outward deed is meaningless; the
unleavened bread of Passover, which, for the Jews, was a sign and a
reminder that their ancestors did not have time to make leavened bread
as they escaped from Pharaoh, is used to make a complex point about the
inner self:

> Know ye not that a little leaven leaveneth the whole lump? Purge out
> therefore the old leaven, that ye may be a new lump, as ye are unleavened.
> For even Christ our passover is sacrificed for us: Therefore let us keep the
> feast, not with old leaven, neither with the leaven of malice and wickedness;
> but with the unleavened bread of sincerity and truth.
>
> (1 Cor. 5:6–8)

Indeed, the very history of the Jewish people, and events in that history
such as Moses' drawing water from the rock, are allegorized and internalized: 'they drank of that spiritual Rock that followed them: and that
Rock was Christ' (1 Cor. 10:4).

Now if all externals are meaningless, part of the Old Law, the domain
of the Devil, and if history itself is allegorized and internalized, if
everything that happened takes on a purely spiritual meaning, then it
becomes vitally important to give to spiritual meanings some sort of
objective status or the whole is in danger of simply disappearing. That is
why Paul is so concerned to tell his story and why the stages of that story
are so crucial: not only to explain it to others, but to keep it always before
his own eyes, to make sure it really exists. He needs to keep projecting an
image of what he was and what happened to him just because it all
happened internally and in an instant. This is the reason why there is
such an amazing proliferation of autobiography in the epistles. This is
why he not only tells his listeners that he was once blind, and evil, and
now can see, and is good, but also tells them about his sufferings in the
furtherance of the work of Christ: how he was scourged and pursued and
imprisoned; how the boats he travelled on were buffeted by storms and he
and his fellow travellers shipwrecked; how, since his conversion, he has
toiled and travelled and spoken and written. This is why he constantly
describes himself as being in physical danger, fending off this threat or
that. This explains his fondness for dwelling on his imprisonment, for
that is a proof of his new faith. And this explains too his fondness for
another image of encasement: his wearing of the armour of Christ's
troops. Finally it suggests the particular emotional charge of his references to exile and return: you were aliens, he tells his audience, and now
you have found a fatherland in Christ; you were wanderers and now you
have come home. When you have cut yourself off from your family and
from the culture and beliefs of your birth such a vision of oneness in
Christ is indeed sweet.

At the same time, since all that has happened has happened within
the individual, there is a new insistence on morality as the external
guarantor of that inner change. Put aside fornication, uncleanness,
covetousness, filthiness, foolish talking and jesting, he tells the Ephesians (5:3–5); if you live 'after the flesh' you will die, he tells the
Romans, 'but if ye through the Spirit do mortify the deeds of the body, ye
shall live' (8:13). This is what Nietzsche particularly objected to, the

idea of a bargain being struck in which the reward for the mortification of the flesh will be knowledge and eternal life. But for our purposes what is important is not whether or not Paul was right, or whether what he preached was good or bad for man, but the reasons why his preaching took the form it did.

The answer seems clear: basing everything as he does on a single moment of conversion, and making of this a purely inward event, he is desperate for outward evidence of election, yet has from the beginning ruled out any reliance on 'works'. So what must somehow be in evidence is not good works but good*ness*, and since that is invisible and intangible, it must constantly be buttressed by the assertion of inner worth. Otherwise the thought remains that perhaps we are still lost in darkness, still struggling in the toils of sin:

> For they that are after the flesh do mind the things of the flesh; but they that are after the Spirit the things of the Spirit. For to be carnally minded is death; but to be spiritually minded is life and peace. Because the carnal mind is enmity against God: for it is not subject to the law of God, neither indeed can be. So then they that are in the flesh cannot please God. But ye are not in the flesh, but in the Spirit, if so be that the Spirit of God dwell in you. Now if any man have not the Spirit of Christ, he is none of his.
>
> (Rom. 8:5–9)

How to tell though whether the Spirit does or does not dwell in you? The whole of this chapter of Romans keeps returning compulsively to the theme: 'For we are saved by hope: but hope that is seen is not hope: for what a man seeth, why doth he yet hope for?' (24). We know how things should be, and yet

> whom he did foreknow, he also did predestinate to be conformed to the image of his Son, that he might be the firstborn among many brethren. Moreover whom he did predestinate, them he also called: and whom he called, them he also justified: and whom he justified, them he also glorified. What shall we then say to these things? If God be for us, who can be against us?
>
> (Rom. 8:29–31)

We can now see clearly why Saul of Tarsus dramatized for his listeners what had happened to him and how he became Paul the Apostle. And we can also see that in this he was, after all, only doing what Bernard Harrison, following Wittgenstein, has suggested all readers do: he was completing or continuing a series, and the series he chose to continue was that which concerned the Prodigal Son. Gone, however, is the elder brother, gone is the father's admonition to that brother, gone therefore is the familial tension which, we saw in the last chapter, made the parable an echo of the story of Joseph and his brothers. Instead what is developed is the story of the sinner who repents and is welcomed back, who leaves off wallowing in the dirt with pigs and returns home to be feasted by a loving father.

To compensate for the loss of the elder brother (though of course he is still vestigially there in St. Paul's comments on the Jews and their Law) there are new complexities. But these are all internal. What St. Paul is interested in is the state of mind of the Son before his return. 'Sin, taking occasion by the commandment,' he writes to the Romans, 'wrought in me all manner of concupiscence' (7 : 8). Sin is a cunning deceiver, taking advantage of a man's weakness to sneak in under his guard, thus making of the inner self a battlefield of opposing forces:

> For we know that the law is spiritual: but I am carnal, sold under sin. For that which I do I allow not: for what I would, that do I not; but what I hate, that do I. If then I do that which I would not, I consent unto the law that it is good. Now then it is no more I that do it, but sin that dwelleth in me. For I know that in me (that is, in my flesh,) dwelleth no good thing: for to will is present with me; but how to perform that which is good I find not. For the good that I would I do not: but the evil which I would not, that I do. . . . I see another law in my members, warring against the law of my mind, and bringing me into captivity to the law of sin which is in my members. O wretched man that I am! who shall deliver me from the body of this death?
> (Rom. 7 : 14–24)

When David saw Bathsheba bathing he was tempted and fell. He did everything to hide his deed, but when Nathan confronted him with the truth he could only accept it and beg God for forgiveness. With St. Paul we have entered a different realm. This struggle within the self between warring factions is something with which literature has made us so familiar that it is hard for us to realize that it is not the only way to think about the self. The word Edgar Allan Poe used to describe it is 'perversity', and Dostoevsky, who explored the ramifications of perversity more fully than anyone else, made the explicit point in his *Notes from Underground* that it was a concept unknown to Plato or to the philosophical tradition descended from him, and implied that only a Christian vision of man could make sense of it. What he did not ask was whether any vision of man other than the Pauline had need for such a term.[3]

That of course is not a question to which there is any single or simple answer. I raise it here merely to point to the link between Paul's theology and his self-dramatization. For it is clear that it is precisely the notion of warring factions within the self which leads to the need for autobiography. Dostoevsky's Underground Man finds in writing the only balm to his troubled spirit, and we can see, in chapter 8 of Romans, how Paul's struggle with his inner demons seems almost to cry out for verbal articulation. I deliberately quoted a fairly lengthy portion of the chapter in order to catch the flavour of a mind moving compulsively round and

round the same set of issues, unable to find any resolution to the problems it finds itself saddled with.

That there is a link between perversity and autobiography, and, at a
deeper level, between the Pauline vision of man and the impulse towards
self-projection, is made manifest by what is generally regarded as the first
proper autobiography, St. Augustine's *Confessions*. The *Confessions*
would not have been possible without St. Paul. It is not only that when
the decisive moment comes Augustine picks up and opens Paul's epistles
and finds himself reading Romans 13 : 13–14:

> Not in revelling and drunkenness, not in lust and wantonness, not in quarrels
> and rivalries. Rather, arm yourselves with the Lord Jesus Christ; spend no
> more thought on nature and nature's appetites.

'I had no wish to read more,' Augustine says,

> and no need to do so. For in an instant, as I came to the end of the sentence,
> it was as though the light of confidence flooded into my heart and all the
> darkness of doubt was dispelled.

> (*Conf.* VIII. 12)[4]

It is that, as one can see from this passage, the image of the Prodigal Son
as acted out by St. Paul is the controlling image of the entire book.

It is true that Augustine begins, as Paul does not, with his birth, and
spends much time on his childhood. But that is only a fleshing out of
the Pauline drama. No man is free from sin, not even as a baby, and
Augustine wants us to see what this subjection to sin implies. And as
with Paul, one suspects too that he wants to explain not just to others but
to himself. This makes his descriptions, like Paul's, wonderfully dramatic: 'I was tossed and spilled, floundering in the broiling sea of my
fornication' (II. 2). In the story of the theft of the pears he gives us the
very archetype of perversity: 'Perhaps we ate some of them, but our real
pleasure consisted in doing something that was forbidden' (II. 4). 'The
evil in me was foul,' he goes on, 'but I loved it. I loved my own perdition
and my own faults.' The identification with the Prodigal Son is not slow
in coming: 'I was wandering far from you,' he confesses to God, 'and I
was not even allowed to eat the husks on which I fed the swine' (III. 6).
The sensuousness which is always a component of perversity is never far
away: 'These were the stages of my pitiful fall into the depths of hell, as I
struggled and strained for lack of the truth.' 'For nearly nine years were
yet to come during which I wallowed deep in the mire and the darkness
of delusion. Often I tried to lift myself, only to plunge the deeper.' (III.
11)

As Augustine approaches the moment of conversion the divisions
within himself grow deeper. Though he seizes 'eagerly upon the venerable writings inspired by your Holy Spirit, especially those of the Apostle

Paul' (VII. 21), yet 'my heart had still to be rid of the leaven which remained over'. (VIII. 1 – Note how naturally he, like Paul, allegorizes the Jewish ritual, though whether he is conscious of quoting Paul or not it is difficult to determine.) All the time, though, he knows that

> You too, merciful Father, rejoice more over one sinner who repents than over ninety-nine souls that are justified and have no need of repentance.... The joy of Mass in your Church moves us to tears when we hear the gospel which tells us how the younger son died and returned to life, and how he was lost and found again.
>
> (*Conf.* VIII. 3)

The Prodigal Son merges effortlessly into the image of the Apostle Paul:

> He too, the least of the apostles, chose to change his name from Saul to Paul to mark the great victory when Sergius Paulus, the proconsul, his pride laid low by the apostle's bold words, submitted to the gentle yoke of Christ and became a subject of the Great King. For the firmer our enemy the devil holds a man in his power, and the greater the number of others whom he holds captive through this man, the greater the victory when he is won back.
>
> (*Conf.* VIII. 4)

But still Augustine feels like a man trying to wake up and unable to do so. Should he or should he not take the plunge? He goes out into his garden and his very body seems torn in two as he describes his fevered movements and how he felt himself to be twisting and turning as if on a chain. And then, suddenly, it is all over. The child starts to sing near by, and the refrain floats across to him: 'Take it and read, take it and read' (*tolle lege, tolle lege*) (VIII. 12). So he picks up the book, opens it, reads, and all is resolved. The *Confessions* goes on for another hundred or so pages, as he explores the mysteries of the inner life, of memory and time, but the book is to all intents and purposes over: he has reached the point from which it can be written.

Its influence was, of course, immense, and constant. But, like that of the Pauline epistles, it found more echoes in the hearts of Protestants than it ever really did in those of medieval men and women.[5] The place of Romans and Galatians in the Protestant tradition from Luther to Barth needs no comment. What is interesting to us here is how the importance of St. Paul is bound up with the Protestant impulse towards spiritual autobiography. The central document in that tradition is Bunyan's *Grace Abounding*, and the full title of that book, which was to be so popular in the centuries to come, announces that it is another version of the Prodigal Son filtered through St. Paul and St. Augustine: 'Grace Abounding to the Chief of Sinners, or the brief relation of the exceeding Mercy of God in Christ to his poor servant John Bunyan'. As we might expect by now, the book tells of Bunyan's lowly birth, his wicked child-

hood, his gradual awakening to religion as the result of reading books of
devotion, his strong temptations to sin, and his final call.

It was published in 1666, but already the conventions of what Patricia
Caldwell has called 'the Puritan conversion narrative' were well established: 'sin, preparation, and assurance; conviction, compunction, and
submission; fear, sorrow and faith'. Towards the end of her book
Caldwell makes a telling point:

> When the eighteenth century looked back upon the Puritans' idiosyncrasies,
> it was struck – sometimes with amusement and sometimes with anxiety – by
> the saints' apparent propensity for reporting the exact order of events in their
> conversions. So peculiar did this habit seem that Joseph Addison could vastly
> entertain the readers of *The Spectator* by recording a fictitious interview
> between an Oxford student and a Puritan minister who, brushing aside the
> youth's training in the classical languages, was interested only in 'whether he
> was of the Number of the Elect; what was the Occasion of his Conversion;
> upon what Day of the Month, and the Hour of the Day it happened; how it
> was carried on, and when compleated'.[6]

What Caldwell fails to see is exactly why it was so important to record
the precise order of events in this way. The reason, it seems to me, is the
same as that which first led St. Paul to explore with such minuteness the
workings of perversity in himself and to return so frequently to the narrative of his conversion: when everything vital happens *inside* a person it
is only by giving public expression to it that we can convince ourselves
that it did indeed occur; and when what is of crucial importance in our
lives takes place in an instant it is vitally important to find a way of
spreading it out and fixing the stages that led up to it in such a way as to
give it objective status.

Conversion, in other words, both confers upon us the right to narrative
structure and necessitates such a structure. The link between Puritanism
and the rise of the novel has long been accepted. But it is important to
see that the real connection lies in the need for a narrative in the first
person on the part of the Protestant convert. Conversion is the end
moment which provides both a beginning and a pattern which links that
beginning with the present. To this day the novel naturally gravitates
towards a first-person narrative in which the hero, lost at first, eventually
finds himself. And it is so difficult to disentangle critically from memoir,
confession and autobiography precisely because that 'finding', being private and internal, calls out to be fixed in writing. The impulse of the
novelist and his hero thus mirror each other, and each attempts to
legitimate the other.[7]

I say each attempts to legitimate the other because the final seal of
legitimacy can never in fact be given. This is concealed in Puritan auto-

biography and the early novel, but it emerges into the light of day in that further twist given to the Pauline tradition by German Romanticism and its aftermath. When Hegel and Kierkegaard after him divided Western culture into Ancient and Modern, and placed the beginnings of the Modern in the New Testament, they grasped something which has been obscured by the way in which theological speculation has split off from the philosophical and the aesthetic. There is no better place to go if we are to understand what is at issue than to Kierkegaard's essay on 'The Ancient Tragical Motif as Reflected in the Modern', in *Either/Or*.

Kierkegaard begins with the observation that Greek tragedy consists of lyric and chorus as well as dialogue, and he points out that if dialogue is the exchange between two individuals, then those two other forms of expression are precisely what cannot be included in character, 'the more which will not be absorbed in individuality'. And the reason why it is there in ancient Greek but not in modern drama is that in Greek culture, 'even if the individual moved freely, he still rested in the substantial categories of state, family, and destiny'. Modern man, on the other hand, is alone, and takes all his decisions for himself. Thus tragedy is alien to him, for by throwing 'his whole life upon his shoulders, as being the result of his own acts', one transforms an aesthetic guilt into an ethical one. The tragic hero merely becomes bad, and badness and goodness are not subjects of aesthetic interest. Hence 'the whole tendency of our age toward the comic'.[8]

This is extremely suggestive, and goes some way, I believe, towards explaining the weaknesses of plays by those modern dramatists, such as Ibsen and Arthur Miller, who have gone on trying to write tragedy as though nothing had changed between us and the Greeks. But I have not brought in Kierkegaard's essay in order to make points about modern tragedy. It is the step Kierkegaard takes next which is important for my argument. There is, he says, a truly modern kind of tragedy, which has not been explored by playwrights. The reason for this is that in a sense it cannot be written down, it does not belong to the realm of the aesthetic at all. This is a totally inward kind of tragedy, and its paradigm is Christ, who lived a life of absolute obedience without any outward evidence that he was doing so. Though Kierkegaard refers to Christ, his view of Jesus' 'tragedy' clearly owes more to Pauline notions of Faith versus Law than it does to anything in the Gospels, where, after all, external signs abound.

To demonstrate the difference Kierkegaard – or rather, his narrator, for *Either/Or* is a veritable set of Chinese boxes of editors, manuscripts, narrators and the rest – takes Sophocles' *Antigone* and contrasts its central figure with an invented 'modern' Antigone. The classical Antigone nurses a sorrow which is public and external to her. It will not go away, but the fact that it is public and external means that its burden on her is not all-engulfing: 'In the Greek tragedy Antigone is not at all concerned about her father's unhappy destiny.' She 'lives as carefree as any other young Grecian maiden', but this not because of thoughtlessness or because the individual in such cases does not worry about his relationship to the family. On the contrary:

> Life-relationships are once and for all assigned to them, like the heaven under which they live. If this is dark and cloudy, it is also unchangeable. This furnishes the keynote of the Greek soul, and this is sorrow, not pain. In Antigone the tragic guilt concentrates itself about one definite point, that she had buried her brother in defiance of the king's prohibition. If this is seen as an isolated fact, as a collision between sisterly affection and piety and an arbitrary human prohibition, then *Antigone* would cease to be a Greek tragedy, it would be an entirely modern tragic subject. That which in the Greek sense affords the tragic interest is that Oedipus' sorrowful destiny re-echoes in the brother's unhappy death, in the sister's collision with a simple human prohibition; it is, so to say, the after effects, the tragic destiny of Oedipus ramifying in every branch of his family. This is the totality which makes the sorrow of the spectator so infinitely deep. It is not an individual who goes down, it is a small world, it is the objective sorrow, which, released, now advances in its own terrible consistency, like a force of nature, and Antigone's unhappy fate, an echo of her father's, is an intensified sorrow.[9]

This is beautifully expressed. Kierkegaard makes us see how difficult it is for us to understand the ancient, family-orientated concept of character and destiny, and how crude and banal are our attempts to understand this ancient drama in purely ethical terms.

But he does all this in order to make us understand a deeper form of modern tragedy, which is not ethical but religious (though he will not use the term until he comes to write *Fear and Trembling*, his study of Abraham and the sacrifice of Isaac; it will not escape his reader, though, how similar his modern Antigone is to his Abraham). Here we have to imagine an Oedipus who has killed his father and married his mother and begotten children upon her, but who has not been found out and punished for it. Oedipus is now dead. Antigone suspects the truth, but she is not sure. Anxiety thus weighs on every moment of her life. She is caught in its toils. She can tell no one her suspicions, for to do so would in a sense be a betrayal of her father. She cannot even tell the man she loves and who is in love with her, and yet how can she give herself to him and hold back so central a part of herself?

Here is how Kierkegaard imagines it, clearly drawing, as he does in his exploration of Abraham, upon his sense of the dreadful secret his own father has imposed on him and how he has had to give up his fiancée, Regina, because he has found that he can neither tell her about this nor keep so large a part of himself from her:

> Antigone is mortally in love...and he who is the object of her affections knows that she loves him. My Antigone is no ordinary woman, and con-

sequently her dowry is unusual – it is her pain. She cannot belong to a man without this dowry.... To conceal it from such an observer would be impossible, to wish to conceal it would be a betrayal of her love; but can she marry him with it? Dare she confide it to any human being, even to the beloved?...With every assurance of his love, he increases her pain, with every sigh he sinks the dart of sorrow deeper and deeper into her heart .... The beloved must constantly strive to wrest her secret from her, and yet this means her certain death. By whose hand, then, does she fall? By the hand of the living or the dead? In a certain sense, the dead...; in another sense, by the hand of the living, in so far as her unhappy love makes that memory kill her.[10]

Thus there is no beginning and no end to the modern Antigone's sorrow. It cannot be spoken and will only disappear with her death.

But am I not contradicting myself? I have been saying that what characterizes both St. Paul and St. Augustine is the need to talk in order to fix the flux of inner turmoil and objectify the crucial act of conversion, and I have suggested that there is a direct line of descent from them to the modern Antigone; yet Antigone, as Kierkegaard describes her, is characterized by the fact that she cannot speak her sorrow. But the contradiction is more apparent than real. For Antigone's silence and the talk of Paul and Augustine are mirror images of each other. Talk which seeks to legitimize and objectify the purely internal is only another version of that silence which cannot free itself of its burden of guilt. Antigone cannot talk to others, to An Other, but she does not cease to talk to herself, to go round and round the labyrinth of her anguish. And, as I have suggested, Kierkegaard's Antigone is only a projection of himself, the guilt-ridden son of his father who gives up the woman he loves because he feels that God has called him – and yet, unlike Moses and Isaiah, can never be sure that it is indeed God and not the Devil.

Yet Kierkegaard has in effect gone a step beyond St. Augustine. He does not simply act out his version of the Prodigal Son (and it is appropriate that the modern version of the parable, like Mann's modern version of the Faust story, should locate the final temptation not in sensuous indulgence but in ethical goodness, in marriage and family life). He dramatizes within the pages of Either/Or what such acting out would entail. Within the multiple ironies of his book the story of the Prodigal Son becomes simply one of the dreams of the aesthetic, to be derided by the happily-married Judge of the second part; but it also becomes one of the many little bombs planted under the pompous pronouncements of the Judge himself.

Modern literature has followed Kierkegaard in this respect. The modern novel has developed by asking questions about the very foundations of traditional autobiography and the traditional novel. It has either, as in Dostoevsky's *Notes from Underground*, Proust's *À la recherche*, the works of Kafka and novels like Louis René des Forêts's *Le Bavard* (The Chatterbox), made it clear that the conventions of the classical novel are conventions and nothing more, and that once we start talking to ourselves our speech rightly has no end; or it has, in the case of writers like Marguerite Duras and Muriel Spark, turned its back on the probing of the inner life and accepted that the true springs of life are best tapped through dialogue and action.

This last response, not surprisingly perhaps, takes us right back behind St. Paul to the style and method of OT narrative. For, as we have seen so often in earlier chapters, this is a style which eschews description of people or places or inner feelings, yet manages to say a good deal about the way human beings behave in their relations both to others and to their own deepest aspirations. Let us therefore, for one last time, compare St. Paul and the Hebrew scriptures, not in order to establish that the treatment of character is more true to life in the one than in the other, but only to draw up a balance sheet of losses and gains.

No character in the Hebrew Bible looks back over his or her life from a vantage point from which he or she can say with certainty: till now I have been blind, but now I can see. He may, like Adam and Aaron and Saul, attempt to justify a particular transgression. He may, like David, try to cover up a sin, and then, when he realizes that God at least has seen what he has done, admit his fault and repent. When his eyes are opened, as in the case of Balaam, this is not to be taken as a metaphor but quite literally: God opens Balaam's eyes and he sees the angel.

Nor does any character in the Hebrew Bible struggle with conflicting desires. Moses and Jeremiah are, it is true, at first reluctant to assume the burdens of prophecy. Saul, it is true, seems uncertain what to do throughout his career, but he is implicitly criticized for this, and his uncertainty is anyway very different from St. Paul's description of the self as torn between wishing to do good but clinging to evil none the less. Sometimes, as with Jonah, God forces the character into a position where he has to acknowledge his error and cry out for mercy, but there is nothing to guarantee that even such heartfelt pleas will betoken a permanent change of heart. As soon as Jonah is safe on dry land he starts to complain again and to accuse God of not playing fair. The book of Jonah ends, characteristically, not with Jonah's words but with God's.

With Jesus a new element enters the situation. We see a man making his own destiny, conscious all the time of the shape and meaning of his life. Abraham and David did not live like that. They had no need to shape things, only to use their wits and walk, if possible, in God's way, leaving the shaping to him. Yet Jesus, as we have seen, lives for us most at precisely those moments when he seems to feel that he is not wholly in charge, that there is another who knows more than he does. With Paul, however, as he is presented to us in Acts and in his epistles, we have left the ancient Hebrew attitude to character for good. Paul looks back at his own life and it makes perfect sense to him. He *knows*, and he is determined to pass that knowledge on to others. Rejecting the simple fact of tribal descent in favour of a spiritual kinship, rejecting the rituals of the Jews as no longer relevant, he casts himself alone upon the mercy of a God who cannot be known through any outward manifestation. With this step Paul opens up a whole new world of inwardness, a world he himself explores and describes with passionate detail, and which will always have room for fresh explorers, such as Augustine, Pascal and Rousseau. Yet the cost of this is high. Giving up this world of confusion, uncertainty and limited horizons for the apparently surer world of the spirit, he condemns himself to the sustaining of his vision by nothing other than the sheer power of his imagination and the constant reiteration of the drama of his conversion.

If Kierkegaard's analysis is right, then the men of the Hebrew Bible have more in common with Sophocles' Antigone than with his modern Antigone. For them too 'life-relationships are once and for all assigned. . ., like the heaven under which they live. If this is dark and cloudy, it is also unchangeable.' And that gives them, like Sophocles' Antigone, a carefree quality. With St. Paul that quality has gone, and for good reason. Perpetual vigilance is required now, perpetual self-questioning and self-examination. Talk therefore of autobiography emerging from 'the Judaeo-Christian tradition'[11] is wide of the mark. Both autobiography and the classic novel emerge in almost direct opposition to the Hebrew scriptures, though directly out of St. Paul. And if this is so then we can perhaps begin to understand why it was so difficult, in the earlier chapters of this study, to find even the terms with which to talk about narrative and character in the Hebrew Bible – for the very terms we use today are an inheritance from St. Paul.[12]

Five

READING AND INTERPRETATION

As if giving grounds did not come to an end sometime. But the end is not an ungrounded presupposition: it is an ungrounded way of acting.

LUDWIG WITTGENSTEIN

XIII

THE EPISTLE TO THE HEBREWS
AND THE MEANING OF HISTORY

'Understandest thou what thou readest?' Philip asks the Ethiopian eunuch when he comes upon him reading the book of Isaiah. 'How can I,' the other answers, 'except some man should guide me?' So Philip gets into the carriage with him, looks at the place he has reached, and explains to him that 'He was led as a sheep to the slaughter; and like a lamb dumb before his shearer' is a reference to none other than Jesus. When the man has listened for a while to Philip expounding the text and telling him about Jesus, he says: 'See, here is water; what doth hinder me to be baptized?' And Philip says: 'If thou believest with all thine heart, thou mayest. And he answered and said, I believe that Jesus Christ is the Son of God.' So he orders the chariot to stop, gets out, and Philip baptizes him. (Acts 8:27–38)

What does Philip say to the Ethiopian to persuade him? The Epistle to the Hebrews is the most profound and sustained exploration in the Bible of the relation of Jesus to the Old Testament, and it suggests to us just what Philip might have said. If we are to understand how the NT sees itself in relation to the Hebrew scriptures we cannot do better than turn to that epistle.

Before doing so, however, we need to try and understand a little more about the mechanism of conversion, what it is that would make someone merely reading a text feel that through the expounding of that text everything, not only about the past but also about the present, had suddenly fallen into place. And it so happens that the Bible also provides us with an example of the process at work – not, this time, with men like the Ethiopian, who have had nothing previously to do with Jesus, but with those who have followed him and yet, after his death, are still puzzled as to exactly what his life and teachings may mean for them.

The passage is one we have glanced at, but which we now need to look at in more detail. I will therefore quote it in full. It comes from the last chapter of Luke's Gospel:

And, behold, two of them went that same day to a village called Emmaus,
which was from Jerusalem about threescore furlongs. And they talked
together of all these things which had happened. And it came to pass, that,
while they communed together and reasoned, Jesus himself drew near, and
went with them. But their eyes were holden that they should not know him.
And he said unto them, What manner of communications are these that ye
have one to another, as ye walk, and are sad? And one of them, whose name
was Cleopas, answering said unto him, Art thou only a stranger in Jerusalem,
and hast not known the things which are come to pass there in these days?
And he said unto them, What things? And they said unto him, Concerning
Jesus of Nazareth, which was a prophet mighty in deed and word before God
and all the people: And how the chief priests and our rulers delivered him to
be condemned to death, and have crucified him. But we trusted that it had
been he which should have redeemed Israel: and beside all this, to day is the
third day since these things were done. Yea, and certain women also of our
company made us astonished, which were early at the sepulchre; And when
they found not his body, they came, saying, that they had also seen a vision
of angels, which said that he was alive. And certain of them which were with
us went to the sepulchre, and found it even so as the women had said: but
him they saw not. Then he said unto them, O fools, and slow of heart to
believe all that the prophets have spoken: Ought not Christ to have suffered
these things, and to enter into his glory? And beginning at Moses and all the
prophets, he expounded unto them in all the scriptures the things concerning
himself. And they drew nigh unto the village, whither they went: and he
made as though he would have gone further. But they constrained him,
saying, Abide with us: for it is toward evening, and the day is far spent. And
he went in to tarry with them. And it came to pass, as he sat at meat with
them, he took bread, and blessed it, and brake, and gave to them. And their
eyes were opened, and they knew him; and he vanished out of their sight.
And they said one to another, Did not our heart burn within us, while he
talked with us by the way, and while he opened to us the scriptures? And they
rose up the same hour, and returned to Jerusalem, and found the eleven
gathered together, and them that were with them, Saying, The Lord is risen
indeed, and hath appeared to Simon. And they told what things were done
in the way, and how he was known of them in breaking of bread.

(Luke 24 : 13–35)

This could be a parable about interpretation. The two men walk
towards Emmaus, deeply troubled by the events of the past few days.
They are so concerned with trying to understand what *has happened* that
they pay no attention to what *is happening*: the risen Jesus walks beside
them, but 'their eyes were holden' (*hoi de ophthalmoi autōn ekratounto*)
We learn then how they see the events which have just come to pass:
Jesus, a mighty prophet, has been put to death by the authorities. And
yet 'we trusted that it had been he which should have redeemed Israel'.
(The JB translates *elpizomen* by 'our hope had been' and *lutrousthai* by
'set free', instead of by the AV's more loaded 'trusted' and 'redeemed'.)

We are left to infer the effect of the events on their expectations, for the narrative, typically, does not elaborate. The men simply go on to say that the tomb has been found empty and that though the women who first went there had a vision of angels who told them that Jesus was alive, the men who followed merely 'saw him not'. At this point the stranger addresses them, calling them fools and 'slow of heart' to believe what has long since been written. To back this claim he reminds them of what Scripture has said about the coming of Christ and what would happen to him.

The narrative does not tell us how the men react to this; not because it is deliberately elliptical but because the men themselves presumably do not know. Like all men everywhere their reactions are probably so mixed that they cannot sort them out and feel no need to do so. Moreover, they do not have much time, they are walking, are presumably tired, have a lot on their minds – they are, in fact, in precisely the sort of situation in which information comes to us in life unless we happen to be acquiring it from a book or a lecture. When they arrive at the village the stranger wants to press on, but they persuade him, because it is late, to enter with them. At table he blesses the bread, breaks it, and gives it to them. At this point their eyes are opened and they suddenly grasp the identity of their companion, whereupon he vanishes. However, they can now understand in retrospect what they experienced on the way: 'Did not our heart burn within us, while he talked with us by the way, and while he opened [*diēnoigen* – JB 'explained'] to us the scriptures?' Something which they would have forgotten because it fitted into no pattern is given meaning by another, apparently unrelated event, the blessing and breaking of the bread.

Once the flash of illumination has occurred, all locks together and every element immediately reinforces every other: the crucifixion, the empty tomb, the words of the angels to the women, the words of Scripture, the stranger at their table, the blessing and breaking of the bread. And so they rise and return at once, late though it is, to Jerusalem, to report to the other disciples what they have learned. And, with wonderful honesty, they relate what happened on the way and how it was only subsequently that they recognized Jesus. Then, in immediate confirmation of the truth of what they say – and which we knew all along, since the narrative had told us from the start that the stranger was none other than Jesus – he stands in their midst, shows his wounds, eats the piece of fish they offer him, and explains that 'all things must be fulfilled, which were written in the law of Moses, and in the prophets, and in the psalms, concerning me'. So 'opened he their understanding, that they might understand the scriptures', saying to them, 'Thus it is written, and thus it behoved Christ to suffer, and to rise from the dead the third day.' (Luke 24:36–47)

We thus have four distinct stages: the confused events leading up to Jesus' death; the disappearance of the body; the giving of information which is not understood, even though the two disciples are presumably familiar with Scripture; and final illumination through a specific action which casts retrospective light over all that has gone before. No one of the pieces by itself would make sense, yet if one takes away any single element – the death, the empty tomb, the Scriptures, the living presence and action – the whole collapses. Taken together they have the incontrovertible ring of truth: the events give meaning to Scripture and Scripture in turn confers meaning upon the events.

In one sense the remaining portions of the NT only develop and repeat this climactic scene of Luke's Gospel. Different aspects of it form the focus of John's Gospel, the Acts of the Apostles, the epistles of Paul, the Catholic epistles, and Revelation. But it is in the Epistle to the Hebrews that the argument is most fully developed. As Graham Hughes, one of the most astute modern students of that Epistle, has observed:

> The writer of Hebrews is the theologian who, more diligently and successfully than any other of the New Testament writers, has worked at what we now describe as hermeneutics. The question which has preoccupied him more deeply than any other...has been that of saying how we may conceive of the Word of God...as being subject to historical processes and yet remaining, recognizably, God's Word.

This is excellently put, though, as I hope to show, the project raises more problems than Hughes is willing to concede.[1]

The argument of the Epistle to the Hebrews could be summarized thus: God, in times past, spoke to us in shadows and enigmas, but the sacrifice of Jesus, his Son, has now made his meaning plain. The men of the Old Covenant were, like us, pilgrims, moving towards their goal and final resting place. However, while they never reached it, we know the goal and are in a position to reach it. That is why a letter like this is needed, to comfort and encourage those who might, through fear or laziness or both, be falling back, losing faith, refusing to see the obvious truth. Like the disciples on the road to Emmaus, the people addressed in the letter have all the evidence before them and have even at moments understood, yet their eyes still have a tendency to be 'holden'.

How, then, to open those eyes once and for all? St. Paul did it by asking his listeners and readers to look inside themselves. The author of the Epistle to the Hebrews asks them to look at the Scriptures. We, like the men on the road to Emmaus, know the Scriptures. And we know too of the life and death of Jesus. Can we be persuaded to see things in the way he would like us to see them?

He begins by drawing a contrast between Jesus and the angels.

Through scriptural proof drawn from Psalms, Samuel and Deuteronomy, he demonstrates Jesus' superiority to the angels: Jesus is the Son, the inheritor of everything and the one through whom God made everything; he is the radiant light of God's glory and the perfect copy of nature, and now that he has destroyed sin he has gone to take his place at God's right hand in heaven, 'Being made so much better than the angels, as he hath by inheritance obtained a more excellent name than they' (Heb. 1:4). Pay careful attention, he exhorts, lest you drift away. Jesus was a son, like us, and his death redeems us, 'Forasmuch then as the children are partakers of flesh and blood...For verily he took not on him the nature of angels; but he took on him the seed of Abraham', thus becoming 'a merciful and faithful high priest in things pertaining to God' (2:14–17).

Scholars have argued that the author of the epistle was concerned to combat a current Judaic belief in the power of angels and the temptation to confuse Jesus with the angels. But we should also, I think, in the light of the letter's inclusiveness, see this as part of the author's strategy of systematically going through the Scriptures and setting Jesus against them. Just as the first few chapters of Genesis tell of the Creation and then of the sons of God mingling with the daughters of men and the production of the race of giants, before we move on to Abraham and the story of his descendants, so here the author will start with the angels before he moves on to Abraham and then Moses. At the same time he introduces what will in effect be one of the central themes of the letter: the relation of Jesus to the High Priest of the Temple.

Having adumbrated the central tenet of the Incarnation by stressing that the Son 'took not on him the nature of angels; but he took on him the seed of Abraham' (2:16), the author now develops a contrast between Jesus and Moses. Moses was a faithful servant to God, but Jesus is faithful not as a servant but as the son and master of the house of the faithful; 'whose house are we,' he reminds his listeners, 'if we hold fast the confidence and the rejoicing of the hope firm unto the end' (3:6). The argument here is not factual, as it was with the angels, but metaphorical and imaginative, the contrast between servant and son in a household merely allowing the author to lead his listeners to an understanding of the special nature of Jesus' role and of our own link to him. But the mention of Moses leads naturally to thoughts of the Promised Land and to the fact that Moses and his generation failed to enter it because they lacked faith: 'For unto us was the gospel preached, as well as unto them: but the word preached did not profit them, not being mixed with faith in them that heard it' (4:2). Under Joshua the Hebrews did reach their goal, but in a deeper sense they did not. Playing on the fact that 'Jesus' and 'Joshua' are the same name, the author goes on:

For if Jesus [JB and NEB: Joshua] had given them rest, then would he not afterward have spoken of another day. There remaineth therefore a rest to the people of God. For he that is entered into his rest, he also hath ceased from his own works, as God did from his. Let us labour therefore to enter into that rest, lest any man fall after the same example of unbelief.

(Heb. 4:8–11)

Yet there is no reason why we should, 'Seeing then that we have a great high priest, that is passed into the heavens, Jesus the Son of God' (4:14).

With the reiteration of the high-priest theme the author moves into his next set of comparisons and contrasts. Every high priest, he points out, is taken from among men and appointed to act as mediator, making offerings for himself as well as for the people. Yet the High Priest is chosen by God, as Aaron was. Christ, however, is more than Aaron. You recall, the author goes on, how Melchizedek came out to meet Abraham, and Abraham gave him tithes. This king of righteousness (*melek tzedek*) this king of peace (*salem/shalom*), was no ordinary mortal. He was, we are told, 'for ever', and the fact that he is given no ancestors or descendants confirms his immortality. Jesus is a high priest 'after the order of Melchisedec' (6:20). He is of a different order from the High Priests of the Temple, for they succeed each other, but Jesus is for ever; they offer sacrifices repeatedly, but he sacrificed himself once and for all; they offer animals, but he offers himself (7:1–8:5).

Now the author can develop his argument: 'if that first covenant had been faultless, then should no place have been sought for the second' (8:7). This is driven home by a quotation from Jeremiah:

Behold, the days come, saith the Lord, when I will make a new covenant with the house of Israel and with the house of Judah: Not according to the covenant that I made with their fathers in the day when I took them by the hand to lead them out of the land of Egypt; because they continued not in my covenant. . . . I will put my laws into their mind, and write them in their hearts: and I will be to them a God, and they shall be to me a people.

(Heb. 8:8–10; Jer. 31:31–33)

This in turn leads to an elaboration of the contrast between Old and New Covenants, the Old Law and the New, and to the reassertion that whereas the High Priests sacrificed continually, Jesus sacrificed himself once and for all. In a dazzling passage the author plays with these ideas:

Having therefore, brethren, boldness to enter into the holiest by the blood of Jesus, By a new and living way, which he hath consecrated for us, through the veil, that is to say, his flesh; And having an high priest over the house of God; Let us drew near with a true heart in full assurance of faith, having our hearts sprinkled from an evil conscience, and our bodies washed with pure water. Let us hold fast the profession of our faith without wavering; (for he is faithful that promised).

(Heb. 10:19–23)

With the reiteration of the word 'faith' the way is opened to the climactic chapter of the book: 'Now faith is the substance of things hoped for, the evidence of things not seen' (11:1), it begins, and then develops into a mighty roll-call of the OT champions of the faith: Abel, Enoch, Noah, Abraham, Sarah: 'These all died in faith, not having received the promises, but having seen them afar off, and were persuaded of them, and embraced them, and confessed that they were strangers and pilgrims on the earth' (13). The list continues: Abraham again, Isaac, Jacob, Joseph, Moses, Rahab, Gideon, Barak, Samson, Jephtha, David, Samuel, the prophets. Hardly a single major OT figure is omitted, and to these are joined all the recent martyrs who died for their faith in Christ. The effect is rather like a condensed recapitulation of all that has gone before in a piece of music. 'Wherefore', concludes the author,

> seeing we also are compassed about with so great a cloud of witnesses, let us lay aside every weight, and the sin which doth so easily beset us, and let us run with patience the race that is set before us, Looking unto Jesus the author and finisher of our faith.

(Heb. 12:1–2)

The epistle is drawing to its close. There is a final reminder to the recipients not to be like Esau, who sold his birthright for a mess of potage and, when he later wanted to obtain the blessing, was rejected even though he begged with tears for his father to change his mind; and a final comparison of the revelation to Moses on Sinai with the revelation from the new Sion, the 'city of the living God, the heavenly Jerusalem', into which the recipients have arrived (12:18–22). 'See', the author warns them, 'that ye refuse not him that speaketh' (25). With that reiteration of the central theme of a God who speaks and must be listened to, the epistle moves into its final exhortation and prayers.

As we have got to know more about the background to the NT we have learned what fierce intellectual struggles were taking place among the different Jewish sects to gain control of the interpretation of Scripture.[2] Pharisees, Sadducees, Essenes and Christians were all firmly convinced and bent on convincing others of the rightness of their views. After all, on the interpretation of Scripture depended not merely happiness in this life but the possibility of eternal joy or torment. We can see this clearly in the closing lines of the Second Epistle of Peter:

> But the day of the Lord will come as a thief in the night; in the which the heavens shall pass away with a great noise, and the elements shall melt with

fervent heat, the earth also and the works that are therein shall be burned up. Seeing then that all these things shall be dissolved, what manner of persons ought ye to be in all holy conversation and godliness...?...Wherefore, beloved, ...account that the longsuffering of our Lord is salvation; even as our beloved brother Paul also according to the wisdom given unto him hath written unto you; As also in all his epistles, speaking in them of these things; in which are some things hard to be understood, which they that are unlearned and unstable wrest, as they do also the other scriptures, unto their own destruction.

(2 Pet. 3:10–16)

It is in Hebrews, however, that we find the most powerful and inclusive attempt to read the Hebrew scriptures from a particular point of view. No one, reading that epistle, is ever likely to be able to read what comes before it in the Bible in quite the same way again. Not only does it mirror many present-day scholarly and theological concerns, as theologians such as Moule and Hughes have argued;[3] it also mirrors for us what is involved in the reading and interpretation of any text. Yet for the simple reader of the Bible, as opposed to the first-century Christian or the twentieth-century theologian, it raises problems which neither its author nor his apologists seem to recognize.

Hughes argues persuasively that Hebrews is profoundly Christian in its desire to see the coming of Christ in the context of salvation history and in its effort to justify its arguments by an appeal to truth 'out there'. 'The greatest part of [the author's] exegetical work is built around the eminently sound principle of hearing what the scriptures have to say about themselves,' he insists. It is not a Gnostic or a Neoplatonic document, he says, because it is concerned with real events in real history. If someone were to prove one day, for example, that Jesus was not descended from Judah but from Levi, then we would have to face the fact that one whole strand of the author's argument had been destroyed, for he asserts that Jesus is different *in kind* from the Levitical priesthood, since, like Melchizedek, he does not belong to any priestly tribe. 'Though history does not "prove" faith's claims,' Hughes continues, 'it nevertheless both provides the opportunity for faith and, certainly, informs the content of faith. That is why this particular fact is seized upon so triumphantly by the writer.' Similarly, the Epistle's whole argument would be affected if its view of Jesus' inner sufferings were ever proved factually wrong. 'That', says Hughes, 'is what it means, in part, to have a theology of incarnation.'[4]

In discussing the use of biblical quotations he dismisses the strictures of scholars on the Christianizing of non-Messianic texts, pointing out for example that though neither Genesis 22 nor Psalm 8 has ever been claimed to be directly Messianic, the Epistle to the Hebrews' use of them in 6:14 and 2:6–8 shows that 'the object of the author's concern is the possibility of despair. . .; he counters the possibility by directing his readers' attention to the accomplished eschatology of Jesus' exaltation.' In other words

> this prophetic Word of God (1:1) is now allowed to function in a new way in the light of the more recent event of God's Address through his exaltation of Jesus. . . . It is no more the concern of the writer to force an identification of Jesus with the 'son of man' than it was to identify the content of the Christians' promise with that given to Abraham.

The necessary first element is the OT passage, with its crucial phrases, 'a little lower than the angels', 'thou. . .hast crowned him with glory and honour', and 'thou hast put all things under his feet' (Ps. 8:5–6); but 'these are to become the vehicles for the new *logos*, and without them it could not have come into existence.'[5]

Seeing the NT in the Old in this way should not be too difficult for readers of modern literature. After Eliot and Borges we are perhaps more aware than nineteenth-century scholars that what comes after has the power of altering our apprehension of what came before. Knowing Kafka's work, for example, we do not simply read Kafka into older authors, but actually *uncover* him there. Before, we had eyes but could not see; now our eyes have been opened. So we do not need to be believing Christians today to understand that the binding of Isaac or Virgil's Fourth Eclogue can carry a Christian message, as the Middle Ages believed.[6]

And yet I remain worried both by Hughes's arguments and by those of the epistle itself. The travellers on the road to Emmaus listened to what the stranger had to say and, later, when they recognized Jesus in their midst, understood why they had burned as they listened; though if Jesus had not made himself known to them they would probably have forgotten the entire incident. The reader of the Bible who has not broken bread with Jesus must, I think, remain unpersuaded.

This is a difficult and delicate area. I phrased the above remarks with deliberate ambiguity, for I am not sure if what I mean is 'the reader who has not had the privilege of dining with Jesus at Emmaus' or 'the reader who is not a Christian'. The only way to probe the issue is to look in a little more detail at the way the author of Hebrews deploys his quotation from Jeremiah and his references to Melchizedek and Abraham, on which much of his argument turns. Once we have examined them we can see if indeed, as Hughes says, the work is built 'around the eminently sound principle of hearing what the scriptures have to say about themselves'.

Jeremiah 31:31–33, quoted earlier, seems to say quite unequivocally that the Lord will in days to come make a new covenant with Israel, an internal one this time, engraved on the hearts of his people, and not

merely an external one, sealed by such things as circumcision. The
author of Hebrews uses this quotation to develop his theme that those
days have now come and that the new covenant has been sealed by Jesus'
sacrifice. But is this indeed the point of the passage in Jeremiah? The
context is the promised restoration of Israel after the carnage which
accompanied its overthrow. 'Again I will build thee, and thou shalt be
built, O virgin of Israel,' says the prophet (Jer. 31:4), and then goes on
to describe in detail how the vines will once more flourish and the people
will come forth to sing and dance:

> Behold, I will bring them from the north country, and gather them from the
> coasts of the earth, and with them the blind and the lame, the woman with
> child and her that travaileth with child together: a great company shall
> return thither.
>
> (Jer. 31:8)

He digresses for a moment to criticize Israel for backsliding, but quickly
returns to his promise:

> As yet they shall use this speech in the land of Judah and in the cities thereof,
> when I shall bring again their captivity.... Behold, the days come, saith the
> Lord, that I will sow the house of Israel and the house of Judah with the seed
> of man, and with the seed of beast. And it shall come to pass, that like as I
> I have watched over them, to pluck up, and to break down, and to throw
> down, and to destroy, and to afflict; so will I watch over them, to build, and
> to plant, saith the Lord.
>
> (31:23–28)

It is at this point that the passage quoted by the author of Hebrews comes
in. It is followed by another hymn of praise, and the chapter ends:

> Behold, the days come, saith the Lord, that the city shall be built to the Lord
> from the tower of Hananeel unto the gate of the corner.... And the whole
> valley of the dead bodies, and of the ashes, and all the fields unto the brook of
> Kidron, unto the corner of the horse gate toward the east, shall be holy unto
> the Lord; it shall not be plucked up, nor thrown down any more for ever.
>
> (31:38–40)

With a Psalm or a self-contained narrative such as Genesis 22 it is
perhaps possible to extend the meaning, because meaning is not
circumscribed in the first place; with prophecy it is a little different.
Jeremiah's words apply specifically to the restoration of Israel after
devastation. Restoration here is not abstract, it is not a description of the
inner workings of the self; it involves rather such things as vineyards,
animals, towers and gates. The law may be inscribed in the hearts of
men, but here a real Jerusalem and real fields and farms are being referred
to. It is not simply that the author of Hebrews has given the passage a
meaning which the original did not have, but that by so doing he has

obscured the meaning it did have. The concreteness of God's dealings with Israel, his concern not with an abstract entity but with animals and trees and buildings, has completely vanished from Hebrews. It is not that an old meaning has been subsumed into a new one but that a new meaning has blotted out the old.

Let us turn to a rather different kind of scriptural passage, the episode recounted in Genesis 14:17–20 and touched on in Psalm 110:4. This concerns the meeting between Abraham and Melchizedek. In Genesis this occurs at the end of a description of how Abraham was (rather surprisingly) caught up in the military and political events of the Middle East. He joins an alliance against another grouping of chiefs in the region, and, when he returns triumphant from his wars against them, is met first by the king of Sodom and his confederates. Then

> Melchizedek king of Salem brought forth bread and wine: and he was the priest of the most high God. And he blessed him, and said, Blessed be Abram of the most high God, possessor of heaven and earth: And blessed be the most high God, which hath delivered thine enemies into thy hand. And he gave him tithes of all.
>
> (Gen. 14:18–20)

In chapter 7 of Hebrews the author, having in his usual manner slipped the name of Melchizedek into the argument a little earlier and then returned to it at the end of the previous chapter, proceeds thus:

> For this Melchisedec, king of Salem, priest of the most high God, who met Abraham returning from the slaughter of the kings, and blessed him; To whom also Abraham gave a tenth part of all; first being by interpretation King of righteousness, and after that also King of Salem, which is, King of peace; Without father, without mother, without descent, having neither beginning of days, nor end of life; but made like unto the Son of God; abideth a priest continually.
>
> (Heb. 7:1–3)

Consider, he goes on, how great such a man was, 'unto whom even the patriarch Abraham gave the tenth of the spoils' (4). The priests of the tribe of Levi, who take tithes from the people, are descended from Abraham, but 'he whose descent is not counted from them received tithes of Abraham, and blessed him that had the promises. And without all contradiction the less is blessed of the better.' (6–7) Here, he goes on, it is mortal men who receive tithes, but there the receiver was immortal; and Levi, who was, so to speak, already there in Abraham's loins, paid tithes at that moment to the immortal high priest of Salem.

Thus we can see that the priests of Levi are by no means perfect; but Jesus, who sprang from the tribe of Judah, is perfect and immortal, like Melchizedek, 'for that after the similitude of Melchisedec there ariseth another priest, Who is made, not after the law of a carnal commandment, but after the power of an endless life. For he testifieth, Thou art a priest for ever after the order of Melchisedec.' (7 : 15 – 17) So the chapter rises to its climax: 'For the law maketh men high priests which have infirmity; but the word of the oath, which was since the law, maketh the Son, who is consecrated for evermore' (28).

This key passage has been the subject of much scholarly debate.[7] It does not, however, seem to matter very much whether the author of Hebrews was using Genesis 14 or Psalm 110 or both. Nor does it seem to affect our reading of Hebrews to know that the rabbis had developed a mode of arguing 'from absence', which would lead to the belief that since nothing is said here of Melchizedek's birth or death he must be immortal and must always have existed. We might indeed ask why, if Levi is already there in Abraham's loins, Judah is not there as well; but that, after all, is an extra little twist, not perhaps central to the author's argument.

However, there are other aspects of the passage and its interpretation which might worry the attentive reader of Genesis. At 14 : 20 the AV has: 'And he gave him tithes of all.' This is a precise translation of the Hebrew, *Vayiten lo ma'aser mikol*. The JB and NEB try to sort out the pronouns: 'And Abram gave him a tithe of everything' (JB); 'Abram gave him a tithe of all the booty' (NEB). This is clearly how the author of Hebrews understands the passage, since he too says 'to whom also Abraham gave...'. Indeed, the modern translations no doubt clarify the ambiguity of the pronouns in this way precisely because of the passage in Hebrews. (The LXX for its part faithfully retains the ambiguity: *kai edōken autōi dekatēn apo pantōn*.) But to the reader of Genesis the sense is surely just the opposite. Melchizedek brings out food and drink for the exhausted but triumphant Abraham, blesses him and his god, and gives him one-tenth of all he has. The context requires this; any other reading goes against the plain meaning of the passage.

It is not enough to say that already in Hebrew midrash Melchizedek is linked to David and set over against the line of the Aaronite priesthood, and that Rashi too read 'he' as Abraham.[8] Two wrongs do not make a right. Moreover, a great deal depends, for the author of Hebrews, on our reading the episode his way and not the natural way. But we can only do this, it seems to me, as a kind of metaphysical conceit; and that is clearly wrong since the author of Hebrews is no Donne or Marvell; he is in deadly earnest. Unfortunately, the more earnest he is the more foolproof his argument should be. That, as Hughes rightly says, is what it means to have a theology of incarnation.

All this might, even so, not be too serious. We might feel that these are small blemishes, the product of an overzealous attempt to persuade, or simply of the fact that no man can rise above the modes of interpretation current at the time he is writing. But it is, I think, part of a deeper problem, a problem more visible perhaps to the reader of the Bible as a whole than to the scholar or theologian. The best way to approach the issue is by way of chapter 11, the great and justly famous roll-call of the OT heroes of the faith:

> Now faith is the substance of things hoped for, the evidence of things not seen.... By faith Abel offered unto God a more excellent sacrifice than Cain, by which he obtained witness that he was righteous.... By faith Enoch was translated that he should not see death.... By faith Noah, being warned of God of things not seen as yet, moved with fear, prepared an ark to the saving of his house.... By faith Abraham, when he was called to go out into a place which he should after receive for an inheritance, obeyed; and he went out, not knowing whither he went.... Through faith also Sara herself received strength to conceive seed, and was delivered of a child when she was past age, because she judged him faithful who had promised.... By faith Abraham, when he was tried, offered up Isaac...Accounting that God was able to raise him up, even from the dead.... By faith Isaac...By faith Jacob...By faith Joseph...By faith Moses...refused to be called the son of Pharaoh's daughter; Choosing rather to suffer affliction with the people of God, than to enjoy the pleasures of sin for a season; Esteeming the reproach of Christ greater riches than the treasures in Egypt.... By faith the walls of Jericho...By faith the harlot Rahab...And what shall I more say? for the time would fail me to tell of Gedeon, and of Barak, and of Samson, and of Jephthae; of David also, and Samuel, and of the prophets: Who through faith subdued kingdoms, wrought righteousness,...turned to flight the armies of the aliens. Women received their dead raised to life again: and others were tortured, not accepting deliverance; that they might obtain a better resurrection....And these all, having obtained a good report through faith, received not the promise: God having provided some better thing for us, that they without us should not be made perfect.
>
> (Heb. 11 : 1–40)

This is a powerful and rousing call, but it must leave readers of the OT a little uneasy. As we read this chapter we inevitably ask ourselves whether it corresponds to our own memory of the text. Is this all there is to say about these people? We remember Sarah laughing when God tells Abraham in her hearing that she will bear a son, a scene important enough to be commemorated in the very name of the child, Yitzhak; we remember the early life of Moses; we remember the enormously complex and ambiguous relation of David to God – and we wonder: can all this be summed up under the single rubric of faith? And it is not enough to answer that faith was the most important element in their lives and that the author of Hebrews was clearly not going to recount the entire Hebrew scriptures. It is not enough precisely because the effect of Sarah's laugh, of David's passion for Bathsheba, is to deny us the possibility of summing up their lives or their relations to God in terms of any single concept. These stories of the Hebrew Bible seem almost designed to leave us with a baffling but fruitful ambiguity: they are clearly meaningful, not a mere chronicle of events: and yet meaning, in a strange way, inheres *in* them rather than being anything we can extract *from* them. Jacob is not necessarily better or more faithful than Esau, Judah is hardly above reproach, David sins as much as or more than Saul. Yet they and not the others are the chosen ones. How can that be? we ask, and that seems to be the very question these stories again and again want us to ask. Hebrews 11, by providing an interpretation, removes the question.

It is a fact of interpretation that once something is presented to us in one way it becomes very difficult to see it in any other way. Gombrich has demonstrated this often enough in relation to vision, but Wallace Stevens provides a more helpful example here. For when he placed his jar in Tennessee

> It made the slovenly wilderness
> Surround that hill.
>
> The wilderness rose up to it,
> And sprawled around, no longer wild.[9]

And just as the jar 'takes dominion everywhere', so does the notion of faith in this passage. Yet for readers of the Bible who have lived through the agony of Abraham on his way to Moriah or of David pleading with God to spare his son, such an interpretation can only seem a travesty. It turns these episodes into clear black and white, like those of Christian martyrdom with which the catalogue so movingly ends. And it finally confirms us in our feeling that if the author of Hebrews does see Jesus in terms of the OT past, his sense of that past is remarkably thin.

I take the term 'thin' from Mary Douglas, whose *Natural Symbols*, though actually a critique of Protestant internalization of ritual and its anthropological significance, is directly relevant to this discussion. 'We arise from the purging of old rituals', she writes,

> simpler and poorer, as was intended, ritually beggared, but with other losses. There is a loss of articulation in the depth of past time. The new sect goes back as far as the primitive church, as far as the first Pentecost, or as far as the Flood, but the historical continuity is traced by a thin line. Only a narrow range of historical experience is recognized as antecedent to the present state.[10]

Christian theologians have always stressed that what distinguishes Judaism and Christianity from other religions is their concern with history. It has become almost obligatory for those writing on the New Testament to pay homage to this notion. But too often the theory is taken for a fact. Even so sensitive a reader as Amos Wilder can write:

'Those expressions of Christian hope are most vital which relate themselves most fully to the biblical past', but then support this claim only by saying that Paul appeals to David, Moses, Abraham and Adam. Similarly Graham Hughes, at the end of his book, asks what the differences are between the OT and the NT, and replies that the OT writings 'manifest and address themselves to a situation which is predominantly one of expectation'.[11] This assertion hardly fits Genesis or Judges or Samuel. In fact he is clearly thinking only of the prophets (though it could be argued that it is not even true of the bulk of their writings). In both cases we feel that the authors' sense of the Hebrew scriptures is, in Mary Douglas's word, thin. And it is a thinness which is particularly striking because what is most characteristic of the Hebrew Bible, as we have seen, is precisely its density, the fact that it seems always to escape reduction to a single or simple meaning.

Of course this criticism should not be levelled only at the author of Hebrews or only at modern Christian scholars. We find it in rabbinic interpretations of the Hebrew scriptures, with their almost manic need to explain everything. We find it in portions of the Hebrew Bible itself. Chronicles, for example, is, like Hebrews, a retelling of stories we already know from other parts of the Bible. Like Hebrews it cuts a swath through these stories in the interests of a single argument. And, as with Hebrews, the strategy is likely to backfire with readers who are already familiar with the other versions. For example, when we read in the opening chapter of 1 Chronicles: 'Adam, Sheth, Enosh, Kenan, Mahaleel, Jered, Henoch, Methuselah, Lamech, Noah, Shem, Ham, and Japheth', we can see what the author is up to: he wants to give us a clear sense of the line from Adam to Abraham without distractions. But the effect is to make us ask at once: what of Cain and Abel? What of the Flood? Omission brings the omitted material back even more vividly; it suddenly grows precious when we realize how easily it might never have come down to us. And the same is true of Hebrews.

There is, however, a difference. The argument of Hebrews is part of the central argument of the NT, whereas in the Hebrew scriptures passages of different and even contradictory material are simply left side by side. We are not asked to choose, to resolve contradictions. Individual books of the OT may be single, thin strands, but they all go to make up a very thick rope.

As in the cases analysed by Mary Douglas, the thinness of the line of history in Hebrews reflects a persistent contrast between inner and outer, New Covenant and Old. We have already seen the author in chapter 8 using selective quotation from Jeremiah to establish the contrast between the Old Covenant, with its merely external rituals, and the New, graven on the heart of each man. In the two following chapters he develops this theme in a way which shows his familiarity with Hebrew Temple ritual, or at least his fascination with it:

> the first covenant had also ordinances of divine service, and a worldly
> sanctuary. For there was a tabernacle made; the first, wherein was the
> candlestick, and the table, and the shewbread; which is called the sanctuary.
> And after the second veil, the tabernacle which is called the Holiest of all.
>
> (Heb. 9 : 1–3)

The priests went into the first sanctuary, but into the second only the
High Priest ever entered, and that only once each year:

> But Christ being come an high priest of good things to come, by a greater and
> more perfect tabernacle, not made with hands, that is to say, not of this
> building; Neither by the blood of goats and calves, but by his own blood he
> entered in once into the holy place, having obtained eternal redemption for
> us. For if the blood of bulls and of goats, and the ashes of an heifer sprinkling
> the unclean, sanctifieth to the purifying of the flesh: How much more shall
> the blood of Christ, who through the eternal Spirit offered himself without
> spot to God, purge your conscience from dead works to serve the living God?
>
> (9 : 11–14)

This annihilation through transformation of the old priestly ritual is of
course part of something larger, something we have already touched on
when looking at St. Paul. This is the view of the OT as having to do with
mere externals and revealing confusion and imperfection, while Christ
reveals to us the inner man and brings clarity and perfection, an end to
doubt and the fulfilment of what had been promised:

> For the law having a shadow of good things to come, and not the very image
> of the things, can never with those sacrifices which they offered year by year
> continually make the comers thereunto perfect. . . . For it is not possible that
> the blood of bulls and of goats should take away sins. . . . But this man, after
> he had offered one sacrifice for sins for ever, sat down on the right hand of
> God. . . . For by one offering he hath perfected for ever them that are
> sanctified.
>
> (Heb. 10 : 1–14)

The conclusion is clear:

> Having therefore, brethren, boldness to enter into the holiest by the blood of
> Jesus, By a new and living way, which he hath consecrated for us, through
> the veil, that is to say, his flesh; And having an high priest over the house of
> God; Let us draw near with a true heart in full assurance of faith, having our
> hearts sprinkled from an evil conscience, and our bodies washed with pure
> water.
>
> (10 : 19–22)

This contrast between the old Jewish ritual and the new Christian
one; between the sacrifice of animals, the complex topography of the
Temple, the High Priest and the rest, and the mystic sacrifice of Christ,

causes modern commentators no difficulty, it seems. Thus Moule remarks that Jesus 'was satisfied with nothing but the absolute sincerity and spirituality of which the Temple was meant, but too often failed, to be the medium'. And Hughes comments: '[The author of Hebrews] has actually replaced the sacrificial ritual with the infinitely more profound concept of the sacrifice of the will.'[12] But was the Temple meant primarily to be the medium of 'absolute sincerity and spirituality'? And why is the concept of the sacrifice of the will 'infinitely more profound'? Much of the work of anthropologists in the past half-century, as well as that of historians of the early Church such as Peter Brown and Richard Southern, has been directed towards making us see that such distinctions hold good only for those who already accept nineteenth-century liberal and Protestant assumptions.[13] Moule and Hughes, so sophisticated elsewhere, are, in their view of ritual, still subscribing to the long-discredited views of nineteenth-century anthropologists.

There is no better discussion of the assumptions that lie behind those attitudes and the distortions they impose than the opening chapters of Mary Douglas's *Natural Symbols*. 'Ritual is become a bad word signifying empty conformity,' she points out. Ritual, 'defined as a routinized act diverted from its normal function, subtly becomes a despised form of communication.' 'The ritualist,' she goes on,

> becomes one who performs external gestures which imply commitment to a particular set of values, but he is inwardly withdrawn, dried out and uncommitted. This is a distractingly partisan use of the term. For it derives from the assumptions of the anti-ritualists in the long history of religious revivalism.

Moreover, 'to use the word ritual to mean empty symbols of conformity, leaving us with no word to stand for symbols of genuine conformity, is seriously disabling to the sociology of religion.'[14] And, she might have added, to the study of ancient literature, of which the Bible is a prime example.

What is so interesting about the Bible, though, is that it contains between its covers both old and alien ways of thought *and* hints of precisely those attitudes of mind we associate with Protestantism and nineteenth-century liberal thought. Of course the mystic ritual alluded to in Hebrews 10 cannot be interpreted as a simple contrast between inner and outer, spiritual and fleshly, as Moule and Hughes tend to see it. The author's vision is more mysterious and richer than that. Nevertheless it is possible to see here, as in St. Paul, the emergence of a tone and a vocabulary which makes the kind of reading I have criticized above seem entirely plausible. Even the Gospels which, as we have seen, retain so much of the quality of the narratives of the OT, mark, by their insistence on the fact that the Kingdom of God is not of this world, a fundamental shift in the way we are to conceive of human nature and culture. And there are good reasons for this. From the start Christianity was a religion not of a people but of individuals, not of a locality but of all places and times. It was natural therefore that despite its attempt to retain much of the vocabulary of the Hebrew culture from which it sprang, it would be forced to drain that vocabulary of its original meaning.

Anyone who has followed the argument of this book through will have no difficulty in seeing this transformation at work. He will note that the Law invoked by St. Paul and the author of Hebrews seems to resemble Roman law much more than that Law or Torah in which God asked Abraham and his descendants to 'walk', and which was an entire way of life rather than an externally imposed code of restrictions. He will note that the word *berit*, for example, means 'treaty' and is so used for treaties between kings, between individuals, and between man and God, so that to use the word 'covenant' for the latter is already to separate the two domains – is already, in other words, a small and unobtrusive but decisive step on the road to the splitting of inner and outer which occurs in the NT and culminates perhaps in Descartes.[15] He will see that the OT figures invoked in Hebrews and the Catholic epistles have been transformed from historical characters, living out their often confused and contradictory lives in the stream of time, into moral exemplars. Be patient, James exhorts his readers, remember the patience of Job. Obey your husbands, Peter counsels the women in his congregation, 'even as Sara obeyed Abraham, calling him lord' (1 Peter 3:6). Love one another, says John, do not be like Cain (1 John 3:11–12). 'Even as Sodom and Gomorrha, and the cities about them in like manner,' says Jude, 'giving themselves over to fornication, and going after strange flesh, are set forth for an example, suffering the vengeance of eternal fire' (Jude 7).

One can of course find many of the themes and arguments of the NT in Jewish apocalyptic.[16] Nevertheless, coming where it does in the Bible, the NT has a peculiar potency. For a struggle is taking place within the pages of this book, a struggle over meaning. Once you claim, as Jesus does to the disciples on the way to Emmaus, that in one person (himself) all that was written is fulfilled, you perform a major act of colonization. Those elements which do not fit disappear into the darkness, and only those which do seem to fit remain. As with Gombrich's diagrams, one cannot see both pictures at once, no matter how fast one's eyes move between them.

What is confusing is that for the Hebrew Bible as well as for the NT, history is meaningful. The difference is that the NT claims to know what that meaning is, whereas for the most part the Hebrew Bible merely claims that there *is* a meaning. Its insistent message, as we have seen, is:

Remember! Remember how the Lord delivered you from Egypt; remember how the Lord made a treaty with Abraham; remember how an angel wrestled with Jacob. By contrast the insistent message of the NT is: See, know, understand! For, as John says, 'the darkness is past, and the true light now shineth' (1 John 2:8). The very variety of the Hebrew texts, their frequent contradictoriness, keeps them in fruitful dialogue: Lamentations with the Song of Songs, Job with Genesis, Chronicles with Genesis–Kings. The NT, on the other hand, is single-minded: everything makes sense, it is all part of a single story, and those who refuse to see this can only be accused of wilful blindness.

We gain a strong sense of this from all the NT writings. But it is in Hebrews that we really see the power of such notions as perfection and fulfilment as hermeneutical tools. Once we ask of an OT event, 'What does it mean?', once we say, 'This is the fulfilment of that', it is very difficult to regain our sense of the plenitude and even contradictoriness of what went before. But, as Nietzsche tried to show in relation to Homer and Plato, and as later scholars such as Eric Havelock have made clear, the will to truth and clarity is itself in need of justification.[17] By the same token it is necessary to find ways of letting the *Iliad* or Genesis speak in the face of the interpretative tyranny of a Plato, a Jesus, a Paul, or a document such as the Epistle to the Hebrews. It is not enough to point out that *figura* operates in the Bible: we have to ask what are the gains and losses involved in reading the Hebrew scriptures figuratively.[18] It is not enough to say that because the Bible is full of patterns we must read it ahistorically, as a set of such patterns.[19] It is not enough, because what is at issue in much of the Bible is precisely the nature of patterning, of God's design for the world.

The Epistle to the Hebrews forces us to ask such questions. Is clarity better than unclarity? Fulfilment than non-fulfilment? And what does 'better' mean in this case? By giving such a convincing and powerful reading of the OT, Hebrews forces readers who have responded to the earlier stories and events to ask themselves: Is *this* what they were about? What were they *really* about? And what does 'really' mean here?

Perhaps we do not need to choose. But we should at least recognize the price of Truth.

THE MAN IN THE FIELD

It is time to draw the threads of my argument together. I propose to do so, for reasons which will become obvious as I proceed, not by making any large theoretical statements but by focusing closely on one example, already touched on in chapter I, but deliberately left in suspense there. The passage concerns the man who meets Joseph when he has been sent out by his father to look for his brothers:

> And his brethren went to feed their father's flock in Shechem. And Israel said unto Joseph, Do not thy brethren feed the flock in Shechem? come, and I will send thee unto them. And he said to him, Here am I. And he said to him, Go, I pray thee, see whether it be well with thy brethren, and well with the flocks; and bring me word again. So he sent him out of the vale of Hebron, and he came to Shechem. And a certain man found him, and, behold, he was wandering in the field: and the man asked him, saying, What seekest thou? And he said, I seek my brethren: tell me, I pray thee, where they feed their flocks. And the man said, They are departed hence; for I heard them say, Let us go to Dothan. And Joseph went after his brethren, and found them in Dothan. And when they saw him afar off, even before he came near unto them, they conspired against him to slay him.
>
> (Gen. 37:12–18)

The passage is not one that immediately springs to mind when one recalls chapter 37, and it is easy to see why. It is obviously transitional: the narrator wants to get Joseph from the safety of his father and home and into the clutches of his brothers. But why, if that was all he wanted, introduce the complication of the man in the field? Why not simply say: 'So he sent him out of the vale of Hebron, and he came to Dothan. And when his brothers saw him afar off they conspired against him'?

The man in the field seems to cause embarrassment to modern commentators. The *Cambridge Bible Commentary* is silent on the subject. Von Rad, in the OT Library, is cautious:

> The way Joseph finally found his brothers after initial aimless wandering is told with strange minuteness, for in the continuation of the narrative it is

quite a secondary matter. Perhaps the narrator wishes to show the dangers which beset Joseph from the beginning on this way. Dothan, known as an ancient Canaanite city in the Egyptian sources of the second millennium, is identical with modern Tell Dotha north of Samaria.[1]

Note the 'perhaps' with which he launches on his interpretation, and the moral/realistic explanation which follows: 'Perhaps the narrator wishes to show the dangers which beset Joseph from the beginning on this way.' And note too the evident relief with which he turns to 'facts'. The trouble is that the man in the field does not seem particularly threatening, is in fact quite helpful. This presumably explains von Rad's hesitation in putting forward his hypothesis. What he is really saying is: I have no idea why the man is there or why the story unfolds 'with strange minuteness'; the only explanation I can suggest is that it is meant to show the dangers which beset Joseph from the moment he leaves the family home, but that isn't really very convincing. So let me turn to something I can tell you about, the name and location of Dothan.

This is a not untypical piece of commentary. And at least von Rad responds to the manner of the telling, even if he is baffled as to why the story should be told like that. Speiser, in the Anchor Bible *Genesis*, does even less well. He only provides a note telling us that Dothan is 'modern Tell Dothan, about a day's journey north of Shechem', making no attempt to account for the man in the field. In his general note to the chapter he tackles the problem of authorship. He believes that we are dealing here not with one author but two. Fastening with relish on the oddities connected with Joseph's apparently first being sold to the Ishmaelites and then drawn up from the well by the Midianites, he calls the chapter 'a parade example of the problems involved in documentary detection of this kind, as well as the benefits which may lie in store'. However, he is convinced that 'J's hand is apparent in the first part of the chapter, and E's toward the end; but the middle portion is chaotic at first glance'.[2] Here too we may note the evident relief with which Speiser moves away from tricky questions of narrative interpretation and on to the 'facts' – though it soon becomes evident that the documentary hypothesis he deploys with such confidence and relish does not get him very far: the middle portion is 'chaotic at first glance', but we are never told what it is like at second glance.

By contrast with the modern commentators, the ancient Jewish commentators have no problems with this passage: the man is none other than the angel Gabriel:

Joseph reached Shechem, where he expected to find his brethren.... Not finding his brethren and the herd in Shechem, Joseph continued his journey in the direction of the next pasturing place, not far from Shechem, but he lost his way in the wilderness. Gabriel in human shape, appeared before him, and asked him, saying, 'What seekest thou?' And he answered: 'I seek my brethren.' Whereto the angel replied, 'Thy brethren have given up the Divine qualities of love and mercy. Through a prophetic revelation they learned that the Hivites were preparing to make war upon them, and therefore they departed hence to go to Dothan. And they had to leave this place for other reasons, too. I heard, while I was still standing behind the curtain that veils the Divine throne, that this day the Egyptian bondage would begin, and thou wouldst be the first to be subjected to it.' Then Gabriel led Joseph to Dothan. When his brethren saw him afar off, they conspired against him, to slay him. . . .

This is an amalgamation of different midrashes as presented by Louis Ginsberg in his *The Legends of the Jews*,[3] but it accurately reflects the tone of all of them. Some commentators, it is true, hold that the 'man' is simply a man and no angel, but they are in a minority, and even they subscribe to the main point, which is that the 'man' was sent by Divine Providence. That is the nub of the matter. Where modern commentators, if they venture an opinion, hold like von Rad that the narrator introduces the man to show the dangers besetting Joseph from the start, the Jewish exegetes are in no doubt at all that what we are witnessing here is Divine Providence at work. That the figure is the angel Gabriel is attested by the reference to him in Daniel 9:21 as 'the man Gabriel'. But whoever he is, he is sent by God to further God's plans, and this fits in with the rabbis' consistently held basic premise that the Bible is written by God and reflects his concern for mankind.

This being so, no part of the Bible, as we saw in the first chapter, is without significance. Thus in Genesis 37:13 Jacob is called 'Israel' to alert us to his role as the spiritual architect of the destiny of his descendants. Thus it is Shechem where the brothers go to pasture their flocks, either because this was the place where family unity was forged when Simeon and Levi banded together to avenge the dishonour to their sister Dinah, or on the contrary because Shechem had already been and was to be in the future a place of ill omen for Abraham's descendants. It was here that Dinah was dishonoured, here that the Ten Tribes of Israel rebelled against the House of David, here that Jeroboam was installed as king. Thus Joseph answers his father with the phrase *hineni*, 'here am I', to show his humility and readiness to do his father's bidding although he is well aware of his brothers' hatred of him. Some commentators even suggest that Joseph knows already what he is being asked to do, and what will ensue, but submits to the wish of his father and the will of God. Thus we are told that 'he sent him from the depth (*'emek*) of Hebron' (14) when it is known that Hebron was in fact a mountain (Num. 13:22, Josh. 14:12), to signify that Jacob's decision is in fulfilment of the profound design which had been confided to Abraham (who was buried in Hebron) at the Covenant Between the Parts (Gen. 15). There

Abraham had been informed that his descendants would for four hundred years be aliens in a strange land, where they would be subjugated and enslaved; here we see the beginning of that period of servitude which would persist till the exodus from Egypt. As the *Zohar* observes, that Jacob should send his favourite son into danger against his every instinct, illustrates the Hand of Providence as the Prime Mover.[4]

So it is that, starting from the assumption that the Bible is written by God and that therefore not only every episode but every word and every letter has a meaning, the rabbis are able to account for the most minute details of any biblical text. The explanation naturally has to entail the notion that we, like the angel, are standing behind the Divine Throne and are privy to God's plans. It entails too the idea that Joseph, like Jesus in the Christian story, is the willing (though perhaps unconscious) victim, sacrificed in order to bring about the fulfilment of God's plan.[5] And it is clearly because most modern scholars are unwilling, at least where the OT is concerned, to accept such a view of Scripture and God's Providence, that they cannot account for the man in the field.

We are thus left with three clear alternatives. We can say that this is how it happened and there's an end to it. The trouble, though, is that a good deal more must have happened than the narratives tell us – so why was this episode included? We can say that the man is there in order to show us how dangerous Joseph's trip was – but if that was indeed the narrator's intention he could surely have made a better job of it. Or we can say that the man is a part of the workings of Divine Providence – but our unease with that stems from an unwillingness to accept the rabbis' initial premise about the way the text is encoded.

What then are we to do? Frank Kermode has tried to suggest some answers when dealing with the rather similar NT episode of the boy with the loin cloth in the Garden of Gethsemane. The incident, which is only recounted in Mark, occurs immediately after the arrest of Jesus, when all his followers 'forsook him, and fled': 'And there followed him a certain young man, having a linen cloth cast about his naked body; and the young men laid hold on him: And he left the linen cloth, and fled from them naked.' (Mark 14 : 51–52) Who is this boy and what is he doing there?

Kermode suggests six possible answers: (a) he is the result of a scribal error; (b) he is Mark himself, 'signing' his gospel, *à la* Hitchcock; (c) he is there to give an 'effect of verisimilitude'; (d) he is the tip of a repressed story; (e) he is there for figural reasons; (f) we must accept that we will never know. Kermode dismisses (a) and (f) as too defeatist. That we prefer enigmas to muddles is the constant theme of his book, and here he asks rhetorically: 'Why...does it require a more strenuous effort to believe that a narrative lacks coherence than to believe that somehow, if we could only find out, it doesn't?'[6] For somewhat similar reasons he is unsympathetic to (b), partly because it has not met with favour among scholars, but more because it is the kind of answer which cannot be proved or disproved, and which does little to help us understand the Markan narrative. This leaves him with three possibilities: that the episode is there to heighten the realism of the whole; that it is there because there was once a much fuller narrative which has for some reason been suppressed – though, our two verses suggest, not entirely satis-factorily; and that it is there to show the NT as fulfilling the OT.

It is the second and third explanations which really fascinate Kermode. The second has been developed by Morton Smith, who argues that buried beneath Mark's Gospel is a secret libertine Gnostic gospel, a knowledge of which reveals that the 'baptism' of the Gospels is a euphemism for a secret homosexual initiation rite. Hence, in Kermode's paraphrase,

> the young man in Mark's account of the arrest is on his way to be baptized; that is why he is naked under his *sindōn*, a garment appropriate to symbolic as well as to real burial, and appropriate also to symbolic resurrection, both to be enacted in the ceremony. The baptism would take place in a lonely garden, under cover of night. We know that Jesus set guards (on this theory, to prevent interruption), and we know that the guards fell asleep. He was then surprised with the naked youth.[7]

Morton Smith's theory has never won general acceptance and I find it unconvincing. But it is not Kermode's purpose to convince. He merely wants to show that such a theory is *a possibility*, that it is a fact about our response to enigmatic texts that we should want to explain them in this kind of way.

He is more drawn, I suspect, towards the view of the boy as an exemplification of *figura*. This is the view developed by Austin Farrer, whose argument about the boy rests on two OT passages. One is Genesis 39:12: 'And she [Potiphar's wife] caught him [Joseph] by his garment, saying, Lie with me: and he left his garment in her hand, and fled, and got him out.' The other is Amos 2:16: 'And he that is courageous among the mighty shall flee away naked in that day, saith the Lord.' Farrer suggests that these two texts determined the shape and elements of the scene before us. However, the view was received with disfavour by the clerical establishment and was later rejected by Farrer himself as giving the impression (which indeed it does) that the whole of Mark's Gospel was a fabrication, constructed in order to demonstrate the figural links of the events of Jesus' life with events in the OT. However, as in the previous instance, Kermode is concerned not with the truth or otherwise of the hypotheses he raises, but simply with their form. If you want explanation, he seems to say, then this is a plausible type of explanation and one, moreover, which has a long and venerable tradition.

However, what he really wants to stress is that we prefer enigma to muddle. 'We are in love with the idea of fulfilment,' he says, 'and our interpretations show it. In this we resemble the writers of the New Testament and their immediate successors, who were...in love with fulfilment.' He notes the endless repetition of *plērōma* (fulfilment) and related words in the NT, and concludes: 'We are all fulfilment men, *pleromatists*; we all seek the centre that will allow the senses to rest, at any rate for one interpreter, at any rate for one moment.'[8]

To demonstrate the way our minds work when faced with a text, Kermode compares the boy with the *sindōn* to the Man in the Macintosh in *Ulysses*. This seems to me a red herring. Joyce is clearly playing with the reader in a way an oral and anonymous narrative never does. He shows the steps whereby a word misheard becomes a false newspaper report and finally a full-fledged character in a novel. That is, he teases the reader by demonstrating to him how easy it is for a novelist to create a character out of thin air. Behind this episode, as behind the whole of *Ulysses*, lies the double-edged modernist refusal to play the game of the classical novelist by pretending that what has come out of his head is true. It is double-edged because on the one hand it is refreshing and liberating to have the novelist acknowledge that he is in charge only of words and not of history; yet that knowledge is a kind of poison which leads the artist either towards melancholy and silence or towards manic verbalism. Nabokov catches the doubleness beautifully when he has his imprisoned *alter ego*, Humbert Humbert, lament: 'Oh my Lolita, I have only words to play with!' But the Bible does not betray any of these symptoms, any more than the *Odyssey* does. Odysseus may fool Polyphemus by saying his name is Nobody, but as far as Homer, his audience and the present-day reader are concerned, Odysseus is not a word and not Nobody but someone who comes very close to being killed and eaten by the Cyclops. And the same is true of characters in the Bible.

If fulfilment is central to the NT, this is clearly not true of the OT. But if Genesis 37:12-17 is similar to Mark 14:51-52, that leaves us with a problem. In its simplest form it would be this: are we reading the OT in a NT way, the Jewish scriptures in a Christian way, if we look for meaning and fulfilment there? Or should we perhaps read Mark in an OT way, not in terms of *plērōma* but in some other terms?

To engage with these questions it may be helpful at this point to turn to one final commentator on the Genesis passage, one who has thought as deeply about it as any of those we have looked at so far, but who has the added advantage of being a maker of narratives himself: Thomas Mann.

In *Joseph and His Brothers* Mann has quite a lot to say about the man in the field. Indeed, a whole chapter is devoted to the encounter.[9] He first appears, like a typical Thomas Mann character, filtered to us through Joseph's own consciousness:

He saw him quite clearly. This was not yet a man in the full meaning of the word, being only a few years older than Joseph; but taller, really tall; wearing a sleeveless linen tunic drawn loosely through a girdle, thus freeing the knees, and a little mantle flung back over the shoulder. His head, resting upon a somewhat thick neck, seemed small by comparison; his brown hair made an oblique wave that partly covered the forehead down to the eyebrows. His nose was large, straight, and firmly modelled, the space between it and the small red mouth very narrow, but the depression beneath so soft yet so pronounced that the chin jutted out like a full round fruit. He turned his head rather affectedly on his shoulder and looked across it at Joseph. His eyes were not unlovely, but half-shut, with weary, half-dazed expression, as of one politely forbearing to yawn. His arms were round, but white and rather weak. He wore sandals and carried a stick which he had obviously cut for a staff.

(Mann, 360)

As in the Bible, Joseph asks him where his brothers are, and the man replies that they are not there. Do you know them then? asks Joseph. A little, answers the stranger. 'As much as is needful'. And in turn he asks why Joseph is looking for them:

'Because my father sent me to them, to greet them and to see whether things go well with them.'
'Indeed! Then thou art a messenger. Even as I. I often make journeys on foot with my staff. But also I am a guide.'
'A guide?'
'Yes, truly. I guide travellers and open the ways for them; that is my business and therefore I spoke to thee as I saw that thou wast seeking as thou wentest.'

(Mann, 360)

One does not need to be familiar with Mann's method to guess that this is none other than Hermes Psychopomp, the guide of souls and thus patron deity of interpreters, with his sandals and staff.

But Mann's mythopoeic imagination loves amalgamation and metamorphosis, and before the scene is over the character has changed. He grows surly and aggressive; he insists that he will lead Joseph to his brothers in Dothan but criticizes Joseph's ass: 'Its pasterns are too weak.' When Joseph gently reproves him he becomes insolent and says it would be better for Joseph not to contradict him. He seems to dislike Joseph calling his father Israel, and when Joseph asks him in turn: 'Who then sendeth thee?', replies: 'Thou mayest understand that many messengers go to and fro between the great lords east and south through this land.' Suddenly he fires at Joseph: 'Dost thou love mankind?' and, when Joseph replies: 'We usually smile at each other, mankind and I', launches into a long diatribe, saying that that's because Joseph is himself so beautiful and well-favoured:

'Thou wouldst do better to show them a gloomy mien and say: "What would you with your smiling? These hairs will fall out, alas, and these now white teeth as well; these eyes are only a jelly of blood and water; they will dissolve away and this whole hollow charm of the flesh will shrivel and shamefully decay."'

(Mann, 363)

The man then is not only Hermes, but also Satan, sent by God to go to and fro in the world on God's business; and, as such, he is conceived by Mann as a Gnostic or Manichaean figure, an idealist who turns appalled from the flesh because it is corrupt. He is persuasive too, but in the smiling unselfconscious Joseph he appears to have met his match: what you want then, Joseph tells him, is not men but the image of Adonis, that idol annually bewailed by the women, who does not die because he was never alive.

We know how fond Mann is of figures like this. As soon as they appear on the scene, whether in *Death in Venice* or in *Dr. Faustus*, his style quickens, the work seems to take off. Characteristically they change before the hero's eyes, as though the very notion of essence was one Mann was glad to be free of, and characteristically they tempt by telling the hero what a part of him already believes. It does not surprise us then to come on the man again, sitting by the well when Reuben, not knowing that Joseph has already been taken by the Midianites, comes back alone to free him:

Someone sat there beside the well, and it was uncovered. The two halves of the lid lay one on top of the other on the flags, and the figure sat on them in a short mantle, leaning on his staff, and looked at Reuben sleepily, saying not a word.

Big Reuben's legs felt shaky from his stumbling. He was so dazed that for a moment he thought he saw Joseph before him, Joseph who had died and now, a spirit, sat beside his tomb.

(Mann, 412)

Reuben, after his initial shock at seeing someone there, manages to ask the man who he is and what he is doing. As with Joseph, the stranger equivocates, or at least makes no satisfactory answer. 'Who hath rolled away the stone from the well?' Reuben persists. 'Was it thou, perchance?' Again the man's answer is incomprehensible. But now Reuben decides that if the stranger will not go away he will have to go about his business with the man there. But the other tells him: 'The grave is empty.' Reuben peers in to see and indeed it is so. He calls out in agony, but only the man replies: 'Comest here to talk into an empty hole? What unreason! Here is no boy, far and wide. If one was once there, then the place did not hold him.' In anguish Reuben turns to him and begs for help: 'Tell me, help me, who hath rolled away the stone and where has Joseph gone?'

'Seest thou?' said the stranger. 'Thou camest to the well-house, thou wast incensed at my presence and vexed because I sat upon the stone; but now thou comest to me for comfort and advice. And thou dost quite rightly; perhaps it is thou on whose account I am set here near the grave, that I should sink one or other seed-corn in thy understanding and it might germinate there. The boy is no longer here, that thou seest. His dwelling standeth open, it has not held him, thou wilt see him no more. But someone there must be to cherish the seed of expectation, and since it was thou who camest to save the brother, thou shalt be the one.'

(Mann, 415)

But Reuben cannot understand this: 'What shall I await, if Joseph is gone, stolen and dead?' I don't know what you understand by dead, the other replies, 'but yet I may remind thee of the grain of corn when it lieth in the grave, and ask thee how thou thinkest of it in reference to life and death....For it is so that the corn falling into the earth and dying bringeth forth much fruit.' Still Reuben will not understand. Is he dead or alive then? he asks. Manifestly he is dead, the other answers, and yet who can say?

'I saw a youth descend into the grave in garland and festal garment, and above him they slaughtered a beast of the flock, whose blood they let run down, that it ran all over him and he received it with all his limbs and senses. So when he ascended again he was divine and had won life – at least for some time to come; for he had to go again into the grave, for the life of mankind cometh to an end several times, and each time cometh the grave and the rebirth, and many times must he be, until at length he finally is.'

(Mann, 416)

But Reuben can only grasp at fragments of the other's discourse: 'Ah, the wreath and the festal garment,' he moans, 'they lie torn and the boy is gone naked into the grave.'

We are not yet finished with the ubiquitous stranger. He appears one last time, reverting to his initial role as Hermes Psychopomp, when, uninvited, he offers to guide the Midianite caravan to which Joseph is now attached across the desert into Egypt. He and Joseph converse again, and he tells him his precious ass is safe and sound and of his encounter with Reuben. But as they approach the borders of Egypt and prepare to face the guards at the fort of Thel the man vanishes once again, this time for good.

It is easy to see what Mann has done. Picking up hints in the Church Fathers, he has cast Joseph as a type of Christ: he is three days in the well, then rises miraculously; he lies for three years in Pharaoh's prison, then rises to fame and honour in Egypt; Jacob, hearing of his beloved son's death, describes him as a shorn lamb; Egypt is continually described as the Underworld; later the vista opens out: Moses will lead the exiled people out of this land of the dead as Jesus will lead out the dead at the

Second Coming; Joshua will lead them across the Jordan in which Jesus will be baptized, and so on. Mann's brilliance, here as in *Dr. Faustus*, lies in the way in which he moves between the realism of the novel and the freedom of myth. There is a perfectly good 'realistic' explanation for everything that happens to Joseph, and yet, against his will and even that of the narrator, it seems, the mythic pattern emerges. And in the end the role of the man in the field can only be explained if one accepts the mythic premise – although a lingering doubt remains, as Mann indeed wants it to, that perhaps...perhaps...

At the same time, as the extended quotations I have just given should make clear, Mann wishes to say something about the relation of Jesus/Joseph to other mythic configurations. Joseph, torn by beasts but coming alive again, dying a second time in Pharaoh's prison and rising again, is a figure of the risen vegetation deity of the ancient Near East, that Tammuz for whom the women annually lament. And yet he is not, as he himself says, a wooden figure with blood painted on, but a man of flesh and blood who exists in time. The argument with the man in the field is about precisely this: Joseph in effect argues that he is both man and seed, that in a certain perspective man's life too has to be seen in this mythic way. The matter gets complicated, since the man at times appears to argue against this and at times for it; but it seems that, at least while he embodies the Devil, he is consumed with hatred for the ever-smiling youth whose destiny will be to prove his whole conception of mankind false and perverted. He does not mind myth and ritual so long as they are merely myth and ritual, but finds himself forced to help in the process whereby myth and human life are miraculously made one.

What was Mann up to in this novel? The dates are important. *Joseph and his Brothers* was the major novel Mann worked on between *The Magic Mountain* (1924) and *Dr. Faustus* (1947). It came out in several parts between 1934 and 1945, in a period, that is, of both political and artistic crisis for Mann. It was the book which, he said, helped him to bear his exile from his beloved Germany and the horrors of the rise of Nazism, the Second World War and the extermination of the Jews. But it was also the book in which he explored most fully the direction his own art had taken, from the early stories to *The Magic Mountain*, a direction which had led him away from the great nineteenth-century realist tradition he so admired in Tolstoy and towards the combination of realism and myth whose roots, it seemed to him, went back to Goethe. Put very simply, the problem facing him was this: if a novel is no more than an anecdote fleshed out and given the trappings of history, then what justification is there for it? In *Dr. Faustus* he would explore the tragic dimensions of this question; in *Joseph*, leaning on Scripture and myth, he explored the possibility of writing a narrative which would be other than anecodote, which, though not 'realistic', would nevertheless be true to human experience, to the experience both of individuals and of whole communities, perhaps of 'mankind' itself.

But this conflict between novel and myth, when the artist no longer has faith in the novel form, is in effect the same conflict we have touched on in connection with the man in the field, between the arbitrary and the meaningful, between seeing the man as the product of the narrator's skill, as he tries to suggest that Joseph is in danger from the start of his trip, and as the manifestation of the working of Divine Providence. In order to see how Mann tries to resolve this contradiction we need to look at his treatment of the climax of the whole story of Joseph and his brothers.

As the book draws towards its close Joseph becomes more expansive on the subject of his life and destiny. 'In fact,' he tells his servant Mai, 'this whole story is written down already in God's book' (Mann, 1056). And a little later, as they wait for the brothers and Benjamin to arrive: 'It has turned out as it ought to, they have come. The third day from today they should be here – with the little one.... This God-story of ours made a pause for a while.... But time does not stand still....One must steadfastly trust himself to time and trouble about it hardly at all...for it continues to ripen and brings everything in its train.' (1089) Finally, in a scene rich in ironies, he sits at table with Benjamin, unknown as yet to his brothers, and tells Benjamin about his lost brother Joseph, pretending to be able to see what happened to him in a sort of vision, and more or less repeating the words of the man in the field to Reuben:

> Certainly the grave is serious enough, a deep dark pit; but its power to hold fast is not so great after all. Its nature is to be empty, you must know that – empty is the hollow when it awaits the prey, and if you come when it has taken it in, lo, it is empty again – the stone is rolled away. I do not say it is worth no weeping, the grave; one must even wail shrilly in its honour, for it is there, a fact, a profoundly melancholy dispensation throughout the world; and part of the story of the feast in all its hours. I would go so far as to say that out of reverence for the grave one should not betray one's knowledge of its inherent emptiness and impotence. That would be treating a serious matter far too lightly. So shall we weep and wail, aloud and shrilly; but privately we may tell ourselves that there is no descent whatever upon which a rising does not follow.
>
> (Mann, 1100)

We are here close not just to the heart of the Gospels, but of *The Winter's Tale* as well, and Mann would surely not have been displeased to have applied to his novel Northrop Frye's marvellous words about Shakespeare's comedies demonstrating 'the archetypal function of literature in visualizing the world of desire, not as an escape from "reality", but as the genuine form of the world that human life tries to imitate'.[10] In both *The Winter's Tale* and *Joseph and His Brothers* there is no question of time standing still, and both recognize the truth of Eliot's words: 'Only through time time is conquered'. Hermione is brought back from the dead, but she has not remained the young woman who died in Act II. And Judah explains to the astonished Jacob:

> You must consider that not death gives him back to you, but life. Death, if that were thinkable, would give him back to you as he was; but since it is life at whose hand you receive him back, he is no more the faun of other days but a royal stag of four points.
>
> (Mann, 1137)

Thus Mann solves the problem of fiction by his adoption of myth. He frees himself from the burden of creating the merely anecdotal and arbitrary by sinking himself into the biblical story and discovering there the archetypal patterns of life and history. What happens to Joseph happened to Isaac and will happen to Jesus; it will happen again and again, yet each time it will happen for the first time. Out of death will come life as surely as the seasons renew themselves, and out of time will come the fruits of time.

And yet I cannot help feeling that Mann's solution does not command our full assent. We feel it to be a moving and beautiful solution, but it lacks, for me at any rate, the stamp of authenticity. One way of approaching the problem is to ask why it does not feel quite consonant with the Genesis story.

As I suggested in chapter IV, to see the story of Joseph in the context of history is to see it rather differently from the way Joseph himself sees it. For unlike *The Winter's Tale*, the story of Joseph and his brothers is embedded in a continuum. Before Jacob and Joseph history stretches back to Abraham and beyond; ahead of him it stretches forward to Moses, Joshua, Jesus and ourselves. In the Bible, as we have seen in the course of this study, the personal and the historical make sense only when seen together. Mann is not unaware of this. As the family of Jacob gathers in Egypt we glimpse Tamar, now Judah's wife, striding past, a son on either side of her, and bowing haughtily to Joseph: 'For to herself she was saying: "I am in the line of descent and you are not, no matter how much you glitter" (Mann, 1157). And she is right, of course, for hers is the true line of descent, through David to the Messiah.

Again, it would be wrong to suggest that Mann minimizes or ignores the fact of death. In his book, as in Genesis, the closing scenes are taken up with Jacob's death. He calls Joseph to him as he lies on hs death-bed and asks him to swear that he will not bury him in Egypt but will take his bones back to Canaan and bury him there next to Abraham, Sarah, Isaac and Rebecca, and next to his own wife Leah too, in the cave of Machpelah in Hebron. Then, seeing a shadow cross Joseph's face, he imagines that he knows the reason, and goes on to talk of Joseph's mother, his beloved wife Rachel:

> There is a grave by the way, only a little piece towards Ephrath, which now
> they call Bethlehem, where I put to her last sleep that which was dearest to
> me on God's earth. Will I not lie by her side..., set apart, by the way? No,
> my son, I will not. I loved her, I loved her too dearly; but things do not go
> according to feeling and the luxurious softness of the heart but according to
> their importance and according to duty. It is not suitable that I lie by the
> way, rather with his fathers will Jacob lie and by Leah his first wife, from
> whom came the heir.

(Mann, 1177)

As in the Hebrew Bible there is no getting away from the fact of death.
Jacob is taking leave of his beloved son for the last time, and in the
moment of death he renounces the dictates of his own heart and accepts
the will of God.

Yet even here there is something that should give us pause. Though
Mann's Jacob does all that the biblical Jacob did, his words are greatly
in excess of those of his biblical counterpart. It might be argued that
this is not only natural, in a book at least twenty times the length of its
prototype, but that that is the whole point of it; to repeat Genesis would
be pointless: what is needed is precisely to give voice to its hidden
assumptions.

But is that possible? And does Mann indeed do that? Let us leave aside
the very unbiblical, indeed the rather Virgilian conflict between duty and
desire: 'I loved her, I loved her too dearly; but things do not go according
to feeling and the luxurious softness of the heart, but according to their
importance and according to duty.' That is only an aspect of a deeper
divergence. For note how the call of duty is artfully bound up with
accepting one's mortality, and yet how, by referring to Rachel's burial
place as Bethlehem, after the insistent references to Joseph as a type of
Christ, Mann slips in, for the reader, if not for Joseph and Jacob, the hint
of a triumph over death which changes the scene abruptly from the
realistic to the mythical, in a way typical of the entire novel.

At the same time it suggests that Mann and his readers know more
than the protagonists. Yet there have been hints that some at least of
the characters are privy to this kind of knowledge. 'This God-story of
ours', Joseph says to his servant, and, at the very end, to his brothers,
'You have missed the meaning of the whole story we are in' (Mann,
1207). The biblical Joseph never speaks like this, and, as we have seen,
the Bible story casts grave doubts on any such reading. When we
experience Joseph's story in the context of the whole we see that he is far
from knowing what the story is, in which he finds himself. And in the
well, as we have seen, he cries out in despair, as Jesus does on the cross.

But have I not been saying that Mann is aware of the ironies of
history, that by not ignoring Tamar and her story he is being absolutely

faithful to the Bible? Again, there are subtle but decisive differences between the biblical presentation of Tamar and Mann's. In Genesis we read:

> And it was told Tamar, saying, Behold thy father in law goeth up to Timnath to shear his sheep. And she put her widow's garments off from her, and covered her with a vail, and wrapped herself, and sat in an open place, which is by the way to Timnath; for she saw that Shelah was grown, and she was not given unto him to wife.
>
> (Gen. 38:13–14)

The impression we get from these lines is that Tamar does what she does not because she *knows* she is part of the story, but because she feels obscurely that she has to do what is right: beget children, and beget them from the family of Judah. She no more knows that her line will be that of David than does Ruth when she lies beside Boaz. In Mann on the other hand, she bows haughtily to Joseph because she says to herself: 'I am in the line of descent and you are not, no matter how much you glitter.' The difference is absolutely crucial. Not only does it make the knowers, Joseph and Tamar, seem unbearably smug, but it falsifies the whole relation of the contingent to the necessary.

One could almost say that the Bible is so written as to tease us about precisely this relation. David, as we have seen, becomes both adulterer and murderer and yet his actions lead to the birth of Solomon. But is that birth itself to be seen as miraculous bounty or as necessary retribution? We are simply asked to recognize the mysterious connections between cause and effect, to recognize how little *we* can understand them. This does not mean that all is random. There seems to be a pattern, but what that pattern is will always escape us.

There is in fact one whole biblical book written as an exploration of just this problem: Job. For the issue in Job is not only the meaning of suffering but also the meaning of meaning. Job says there is no meaning any more, while the comforters insist that there is and that they know what it is. At the climax of the book God speaks and asserts (a) that of course there is meaning, and (b) that it cannot be known by man but must be *accepted*.

This is sometimes seen as an intolerable assertion of God's absolute and arbitrary power. And of course if one holds that God should both exist and create a world that makes sense to us, it is intolerable. But those who argue in this way fail to see where such an argument will lead them. Muriel Spark, it seems to me, is much truer to the OT than is Mann. In her novel, *The Only Problem*, she intuitively grasps what is really at issue in Job and in the rest of the OT. Harvey, the hero of her book, who has been trying to write an essay on the book of Job, has the last word. 'What will you do now that you've finished *Job?*' asks his erstwhile brother-in-law, Edward. 'Live another hundred and forty years. I'll have three daughters, Clara, Jemima, and Eye-Paint', answers Harvey.[11] Muriel Spark has understood that the end of Job, like the beginning, is not a mere frame. It is the assertion of the fact that meaning will never be able to catch up with life:

> So the Lord blessed the latter end of Job more than his beginning: for he had fourteen thousand sheep, and six thousand camels, and a thousand yoke of oxen, and a thousand she asses. He had also seven sons and three daughters. And he called the name of the first, Jemima; and the name of the second, Kezia; and the name of the third, Keren-happuch ['box of eye-paint']. . . . After this lived Job an hundred and forty years, and saw his sons, and his sons' sons, even four generations. So Job died, being old and full of days.
>
> (Job 42 : 12–17)

The book of Job is about the impossibility of man's ever understanding the causal links (the story), and yet his need to trust that God does indeed uphold the world, that there is a story there of which we are a part. It shows that man must neither simply accept that there is a story nor refuse to believe that there is one, but that it is his duty constantly to question God (and himself) about it. In Kierkegaard's wonderful phrase, it keeps 'the wound of the negative open'.[12]

This suggests that what might be at issue here, in my contrast of the biblical narrative and Mann's, is related to the quarrel between Kierkegaard and Hegel. Kierkegaard's *Concluding Unscientific Postscript* is the fullest expression of his attack on Hegel, though it colours everything he wrote and we have already seen it surface in his essay on tragedy in *Either/Or*. Hegel, says Kierkegaard, presents us with history seen in terms of its ends, as a story which we, from our privileged vantage-point, can decipher. But, says Kierkegaard, that leaves out of account precisely what it means to live in the world. It leaves out of account the choices men always have to make without any knowledge of ends, and it leaves out of account the directions not taken, relegating to darkness those who have made the wrong choices or the choices not condoned by history. Ultimately, it leaves out the fact that we each of us have one life and one death, which is ours and no one else's.

It has been suggested that Kierkegaard misunderstood Hegel, that the two are in fact closer than he imagined.[13] It may be that what Kierkegaard was criticizing was not Hegel but the smug Hegelianism of the Church of his day. That is not an issue that need concern us.

Fear and Trembling is Kierkegaard's fullest attempt to explore his position. Its main theme is simple, though not easy to grasp, since it questions many of the assumptions that govern our affective lives. Agamemnon (or any tragic hero), says Kierkegaard, is someone I can understand. He has to choose between two ethical codes: should he sacrifice his daughter so that the fleet which he commands and for which he is responsible may sail, or should he save his daughter and sacrifice the fleet? Abraham, on the other hand, Kierkegaard says, I cannot understand. For his choice is not between two ethical codes but between a fatherly instinct which it seems natural to follow and a command which makes no sense (since God has told him explicitly that he will be blessed in his seed and has given him Isaac by a miracle in his and Sarah's extreme old age). Thus, insists Kierkegaard, I know only one thing: that I do not know Abraham.

In the course of his book Kierkegaard in effect tries out a number of midrashes on Genesis 22, but only in order to show that their very plurality leaves us as far as ever from any understanding of Abraham. As with his version of *Antigone*, which I considered in chapter XII, one of the things that gives his account its edge is his evident sense that in the story of Abraham and Isaac is reflected the story of his own relations with Regina. But it would be wrong to dismiss his analysis for this reason. His personal anguish helps him articulate his feelings about the profound errors of both the philosophy and the Church of his day: both, he insists, fail to grasp the meaning of the Christian dispensation, and in their complacency fail to understand what it means to live.

In setting Genesis 22 against tragedy, Kierkegaard is in effect raising questions about how we understand our condition and how we express that understanding. The simple point is that Isaac's story is not a drama or even a short story. It is part of a continuum. Abraham and Isaac 'walk together' (the phrase is twice repeated), and chapter 22 is only one chapter among the fifty that make up Genesis. As Harold Fisch puts it: 'Such a mode of imagining explodes the very structure of mythical time, indeed all fables of circularity.'[14]

Fisch has clearly seen what is at issue here. In a brilliant chapter of his book, *A Remembered Future*, he argues that 'the crucifixion and resurrection of Jesus...is itself a kind of midrash on the *akedah*' or binding of Isaac. But the traditional Christian version, he suggests, gives us a model which we find it easier to accept; in Kermode's terms, it presents us with closure, and closure is deeply satisfying. Thus the author of the Epistle to the Hebrews, though he appears to be speaking about Abraham and Isaac, is in fact speaking about the Christian God and Jesus:

> By faith Abraham, when he was tested, offered up Isaac: and he who had received the promises was ready to offer up his only son. Of whom it was said, Through Isaac shall thy seed be called: Accounting that God was able to raise him even from the dead, and from the dead he did, in a sense, receive him back.

(Heb. 11 : 17–19)

As Fisch remarks: 'The *akedah*, rounded out in this fashion, does not require a complete break with pagan forms of myth-making: we can still remain rolled around in earth's diurnal course with rocks and stones and trees. And that rolling around is what men need constantly to be assured of.'[15]

In the terms of our discussion, what Fisch – and Kierkegaard – is saying, is that there can be no accommodation between Genesis 22 and myth, that the central theme of the *akedah* is precisely the refusal of the consolations of myth. The complication comes from the fact that for Fisch this suggests a total disjunction between Judaism and Christianity, while for Kierkegaard what it suggests is a total disjunction between true Christianity and the Christian Hegelianism which he saw as the dominant religion of his time. As for Mann, he seems to suggest that, seen from the correct perspective, the *akedah*, the Gospel story, *and* the myths of the ancient Near East are all one, and all true. Have we then been multiplying distinctions only to end up with the view that all are really variants of the one?

I don't think so. And what can help us here is the memory of that refrain about going down to the grave 'old and full of days' which punctuates Genesis and which we saw concluding Job. And the memory too of the function of children in the Hebrew scriptures. They arrive not in order that a story may be *fulfilled*, but because children are precisely the expression of that trust in what is other than oneself, what one cannot ever imagine or understand. They are that 'leap' of which Kierkegaard talked so much, but a leap drained of its existential connotations of crisis and its mythical connotations of resurrection.

The story of Tamar and Judah illustrates this to perfection. Judah, fearful for his youngest son, has to learn that in life we must let go. We cannot protect our children for ever, just as we cannot protect ourselves by imagining our future lives. That would be to deny our children (and ourselves) their future life. We have to trust that our children will find their feet, and by so trusting we ensure that they do. The children of Job are his (and God's) silent retort to the comforters who think the world is consonant with their imagining of it or else simply that God knows best.

I said 'silent retort' and I was thinking of Kierkegaard's remarks about Abraham and silence:

> Abraham keeps silent – but he *cannot* speak. Therein lies the distress and anguish. For if I when I speak am unable to make myself intelligible, then I am not speaking – even though I were to talk uninterruptedly day and night. Such is the case with Abraham. . . . The relief of speech is that it translates me into the universal.[16]

Kierkegaard half sensed that by speech he here meant discursive speech. That is why he tried so hard to escape from philosophical discourse into narrative. But he was trained as a philosopher and he felt he had something to say – even if what he had to say was that the truly important thing cannot be said. He was thus caught in a double bind, for the more he said this the less he was saying it. Curiously, in *Either/Or* he allowed the debate to turn on marriage and the begetting of children, but he did not see that the equivalent of children for the solitary man, the single man, as he called him, was – narrative. For to trust in narrative, as the author of Job realized, is to make the same act as to trust in children: it is to give up the impossible desire for understanding.[17]

This then, finally, is what distinguishes the biblical narrative from that of Thomas Mann. Mann cannot allow a figure to appear in his work who seems merely arbitrary. Rightly he senses the weakness of the traditional novel with its subjection to the twin tyrants of realism and morality. But by turning each character into a creature of myth, by having him always *return*, he tries to escape from the anecdotal into the true, yet succeeds only in turning truth into the image of our desires. Everything falls into place in his book, but when that happens the essential features of the biblical narrative disappear. But how could it be otherwise, once he had decided not to write but to rewrite?

If my analysis is correct, then the alternatives have been wrongly posed. It is not a matter of either anecdote or myth, either chaos or enigma, either a figure introduced by the author to make a moral and psycho-logical point or by God to show the workings of his Providence. If I am right, then both Genesis 37 : 12–18 and Mark 14 : 51–52 bring us face to face with characters who can be neither interpreted nor deconstructed. They are emblems of the limits of comprehension. What is important about them is precisely that they *are*, not that they *mean*. All our attempts to do more with them than the biblical text itself does will end in either distortion or failure. They are emblems, ultimately, of the story-teller's trust in story-telling, and of our trust in him, which means his trust and ours in the world. And that trust is not blind but has been built up by the establishment of a rhythm to which we have responded from the very beginning.

So we come back at last to Kermode's 'effects of verisimilitude', *effet du réel*. As the term implies, this is a writer's device. He puts something there to give the impression of reality, in other words, to pretend that something is real when he knows it is not. I am arguing, on the other hand, that in both biblical instances we have to accept the figures as given. Maybe they were put there for quite arbitrary reasons, but as we read we do not think of them as being 'put there' at all. To go against our intuitive response to the narratives by retrospectively asking who put them there and why is not an act of clear-sightedness but of simple misreading.

But if this is so, then, as I hinted earlier, Mark's narrative may be much closer to that of Genesis than to that of St. Paul or the Epistle to the Hebrews. It is not directed towards fulfilment, and we are pleromatists only in so far as we are bad readers.

Literary critics and theoreticians, since the war, have been fascinated by biblical commentary. First it was Christian commentary, and in particular the Christian idea of *figura*. Recently they have switched their attention to Hebrew midrash.[18] No doubt there is much to be learnt from both traditions. But if theories of reading are going to be based on our experience of reading rather than dictating to that experience, then theoreticians might do well to turn their eyes from commentary and focus rather on the liturgical tradition of synagogue and church. For in both the *reading* comes before the sermon or explication. In both what is vital is that the story be read aloud. Commentary is secondary.

The man in the field and the young man in the *sindōn* stand for the primacy of narrative over interpretation. How they came to be there will never be known. That they are there cannot be gainsaid. To interpret them away, to provide explanations as to why they are there, is to do away with the whole Joseph story, the whole Passion narrative, and, in the wake of this, with the whole of Genesis, the whole of Mark, the whole Bible – and, in the end, with the whole of literature.

Six

THE BOOK OF GOD

In this way poems are on the move:
they are aiming to get somewhere.

Paul Celan

XV

RESPONDING TO THE BIBLE

'If thou wouldest abound in grace,' wrote the Puritan John Preston in 1630,

> study the Scriptures, much attend to them, much meditate in them day and night, labour still to get some new spark of knowledge, some new light out of them, and thou shalt find this, that grace will follow, as it is the Apostle's exhortation to *Timothy*, saith he, *Give attendance to reading, and to learning, so shalt thou save thyself, and shalt be able also to save others.* The meaning is, the way to get that grace that will save a man, is to give much attendance to reading and to learning. . . . Thus he is begotten to GOD, and made a new man, a new creature.[1]

Such an attitude to the Bible remains the dominant one, at least in English-speaking countries, to the present day. Naturally, in the centuries that have elapsed since Preston wrote, fewer and fewer people have felt either that they could rise to such an appeal or that they even wanted to; nevertheless, the impression has remained that this is what reading the Bible implies.

As I hope this book has demonstrated, such a notion is historically conditioned and springs from extended meditation on one small part of the Bible, the Pauline epistles. That other ways of responding to Scripture exist can be seen by the passage in Exodus, for example, which explains what the Israelites are to make of the story of the escape from Egypt which has just been recounted:

> And it shall come to pass, when your children shall say unto you, What mean ye by this service? That ye shall say, It is the sacrifice of the Lord's passover, who passed over the houses of the children of Israel in Egypt, when he smote the Egyptians, and delivered our houses.
>
> (Exod. 12 : 26–27)

Here the injunction is not to study the Scriptures in order to find grace and be made a new man, but to tell a story in order to remind those who were not present of what once happened.

Of course it is not a question of contrasting Puritanism with Judaism.

Our concern is with responses to the Bible, and the rabbis, no less than the Puritans, seem to have been unwilling to respond to the text as it stands. The Creation account of Talmudic Judaism, for example, differs markedly from that of the Bible:

> In the beginning, two thousand years before the heaven and the earth, seven things were created: the Torah, written with black fire on white fire, and lying in the lap of God; the Divine Throne, erected in the heaven...; Paradise on the right side of God, Hell on the left side; the Celestial Sanctuary directly in front of God, having a jewel on its altar graven with the Name of the Messiah, and a Voice that cries aloud, 'Return, children of men.'[2]

This is magnificent, but it is not the Bible, which says nothing of Hell or of a Messiah at the beginning. Even more striking is the way the Talmud needs to tame the text by asserting that it existed, whole and complete, before even the universe began. By contrast, as we have seen, the Bible presents us with the origin of all things as coterminous with the beginning of the book which tells of that origin.

We have seen how difficult it is to read books as they demand to be read, how much we need to rid them of their ambiguity, how much we need to master narrative by explaining why it is as it is. We have seen that any attempt to go behind the narrative surface of the Bible quickly leads to the dismissal of all that is unique *to* the Bible. On the other hand, it cannot be denied that modern scholars like Barr and Kugel are right to be worried by the assimilation of the Bible to 'literature'. They are right because the Bible is not 'literature'; but what distinguishes it from 'literature' is not quite what they have in mind. Barr argues that it is not literature because it is a collection of documents and not a whole, and about real not invented people; Kugel argues that it is not literature because it consists of laws, prophecies, wisdom sayings and many other genres that we do not normally classify as literature. I, on the other hand, have tried to argue that it is not 'literature' because it has no time for 'literature'. *Lekh lekha*, up and begone, God says to Abraham, and Christ says to the man who would follow him but wishes first to say goodbye to his family: 'No man, having put his hand to the plough, and looking back, is fit for the kingdom of God' (Luke 9:62).

Yet does any writing worth its salt have time for 'literature'? Listen to Paul Celan, meditating on what he is about: 'Perhaps,' he says,

> perhaps – I am only speculating – perhaps poetry, like art, moves with the oblivious self into the uncanny and strange to free itself. Though where? in which place? how? as what? This would mean art is the distance poetry must cover, no less and no more.

And his translator, Rosemary Waldrop, elaborates:

He [Celan] always finds himself face to face with the incomprehensible, inaccessible, the 'language of the stone'. And his only recourse is talking. This cannot be 'literature'. Literature belongs to those who are at home in the world.[3]

If art is a commodity, an aesthetic product designed to add piquancy to the lives of those who can afford it, then it is not surprising that Kafka and Proust and Beckett all deny that they are artists. Neither purveyors of entertainment nor priests of any sacred cult, they see their writing as the only way to satisfy a desperate need, the need to speak meaningfully of what is meaningful. And they, like Celan, have found a response in the hearts of their readers, because it is a need we all have, and which they can help us to realize.

But does this mean that the Bible is to be linked to those modern writers who are not 'at home in the world', and contrasted with the rest of the world's sacred texts and the bulk of its literature? That is indeed an argument that has been put forward, with varying degrees of emphasis, by a number of recent critics and scholars. Herbert Schneidau, in a book I have already had occasion to refer to, has contrasted the Bible with the epics of the ancient Near East, and argued that it must be seen as a rebellion against a pagan world view which is locked into an eternal cyclic movement and whose natural mode of expression is epic verse. The Bible, on the other hand, favours prose narrative, which is an instrument of exploration rather than the confirmation of pre-existing truths: 'Its very raggedness and incoherence forces the beholder into an extra effort of imagination, giving the work a quality of dramatic vividness.'[4] Harold Bloom has argued that the narratives ascribed to the Yahwist ('Y' or 'J', as he is known to scholars) are quite unique and cannot be assimilated to any known literary form: 'J was no theologian and yet not a maker of saga or epic, and again not a historian, and not even a story-teller as such. We have no description of J that will fit, just as we have no idea of God that will contain [J's] irrepressible Yahweh.'[5] In a much more subtle and nuanced version of this type of argument Meir Sternberg has sought to demonstrate that 'in the flexibility of form and operation [the Bible] not only anticipates but often surpasses the achievements of modernism. . . . The old forms are revitalized and their constraints stretched to accommodate a new poetics.'[6]

All these are really elaborations (though often also qualifications) of what Erich Auerbach said forty years ago, when he contrasted the Bible's mode of narration with that of Homer:

The Bible's claim to truth is not only far more urgent than Homer's, it is tyrannical – it excludes all other claims. The world of the Scripture stories is not satisfied with claiming to be a historically true reality – it insists that it is the only real world. . . . The Scripture stories do not, like Homer's, court our favour, they do not flatter us that they may please us and enchant us – they seek to subject us, and if we refuse to be subjected we are rebels. . . . Far from seeking, like Homer, merely to make us forget our own reality for a few hours, it seeks to overcome our reality: we are to fit our own life into its world, feel ourselves to be elements in its structure of universal history.[7]

As with the remarks of Schneidau and Bloom, it is difficult to tell how far Auerbach is merely trying to express what is unique to this text, and how far he is trying to find words to make us grasp that we simply cannot treat the Bible as a 'text', even a unique one. But that of course has also been the problem faced by a Proust, a Kafka, a Beckett or a Celan: for them satisfaction can only come if they can produce something which is other than literature, something essentially truer and more necessary than literature could ever be. Yet as soon as they have done it, it turns into literature once more. That is why it is always necessary to start again.

Auerbach's subtle remarks seem inexhaustible. Yet they, like those of the other three critics, do seem to raise a number of problems at the very moment that they settle others. It is striking, for instance, that all four seem, implicitly or explicitly, to find a Bible within the Bible. Thus Bloom is only concerned with the Yahwist, and the other three deal almost exclusively with the prose narratives of the Bible. And even here there is selection. Sternberg, for example, insists that he is concerned only with the anonymous narratives, and that Ezra and Nehemiah, like Luke, being written in the first person, do not belong within the field of a truly biblical poetics. Thus some essential qualities of the Bible are illuminated, but at the cost of relegating to outer darkness whatever does not seem to fit in with the critic's view of what the Bible essentially is.

At the same time, the very act of drawing distinctions, while helping to illuminate one member of the contrasted pair, all too often does so at the expense of the other. Is Schneidau, for example, fair to the other cultures of the ancient Near East? Even critics in broad agreement with him seem to feel that his contrasts are too absolute.[8] Is Auerbach fair to Homer? Any reader who has responded to the *Iliad* is bound to ask if it is true that Homer seeks to 'court our favour', to 'flatter us', and 'merely to make us forget our own reality for a few hours'. Surely, he will want to say, Homer too, like the Bible, is keeping memory alive for the audience which hears him, is asking the audience to assent to the world as he depicts it. Indeed, as Eric Havelock has shown, it is precisely because Homer was felt to be so authoritative, so 'tyrannical', to use the striking term Auerbach applies to the Bible, that Plato was concerned to destroy what he saw as his dangerous influence on the young democracy of Athens.[9]

Surely too, we could say, the Bible's similarities to Homer and to Greek tragedy are as important as its similarities to Kafka and Celan. There is, for example, that light-heartedness which Kierkegaard so perceptively noted in Sophocles' *Antigone,* and which we have found in Genesis and Samuel. This springs, as we have seen, from the fact that the characters are rooted in family, race and history in ways which are difficult for us to appreciate today. Character is not the ultimate reference, and though each man has to bear the responsibility for what he has done, this is seen as a sin which can be confessed and expiated, not as a fault of character from which the only escape is a total transformation of the self.

Yet as we look back at these ancient writings we can also see that not long after their appearance they were called into question or openly challenged. Already in the Prophets and in Euripides what happens to a person is felt to be more directly related to what he is and less a conjunction of character and fate. With St. Paul and Plato we find a radically new view of character being put forward as an explicit challenge to the old one. Each man now bears total responsibility for his destiny and both Plato and St. Paul offer a clear route of escape from the meshes of family and fate. The difference between the Greek experience and the Judaeo-Christian one is that the Prophets and St. Paul have much more ambivalent feelings towards the older traditions, because they sense themselves to be a part of them while at the same time wishing to question and subvert them. Moreover, the Bible's mode of parataxis and repetition allows even the most antagonistic views to be placed side by side within a larger whole, whereas it is plain that both Euripides and Plato wish quite simply to substitute their own views for those of their predecessors. This attitude of simultaneous innovation and repetition, which we saw to be present in the Bible from the very first phrase, may perhaps give us a clue as to how to focus on the uniqueness of the Bible while being more accommodating to its variety than the critics we have just cited.

In chapter I I suggested that one way of thinking about the Bible was to see it as more like the Centre Pompidou than like St. Paul's Cathedral. A recent interview with the engineer of the Centre Pompidou, Peter Rice, may help to articulate a little more fully the notion of tradition I have just touched on.

'For Rice,' writes his interviewer, Colin Davies, 'what is important, and moving about this achievement, is that it was the result of collective rather than individual endeavour.' Davies is not, however, talking about the Bible, but about Gothic cathedrals. 'He views the typical inconsistency of an English Gothic structure as an essential rather than an incidental characteristic,' Davies goes on, and then quotes Rice himself:

Take the buttresses at Salisbury, for example. They all perform the same structural function, and yet they are all quite different. The great buildings of Classical antiquity, or of the Renaissance, might be utterly consistent, but they lack the human quality of English Gothic – what the French call *traces des mains*.[10]

The Gothic cathedrals were built over a long period, two or three centuries in some cases, by different master masons, with different bands of workmen. Often the new mason had his own ideas about how to build or even what to build, yet the amazing thing is how we can sense the uniqueness of each cathedral. Chartres, Bourges, Salisbury and Winchester are all different, and all immediately recognizable. This is not only the result of the differences in their original plans, but also of the specific geological and geographical environment of each one. This has affected the initial plans – French cathedrals are lighter and airier than English ones largely because they were built on rock and the English on marshland – but the building has in its turn been affected by the surrounding landscape and climate. We are in effect in the presence not of 'a masterpiece' but of living and therefore infinitely supple traditions.[11]

In the same way the biblical scribes worked within a living tradition, constantly transforming yet always remaining true to the spirit of the whole.[12] Thus the *traces des mains* which are so evident in the Bible should not be seen, as biblical scholarship has always tended to see them, as providing clues to when and where the different elements were written, but rather as a characteristic aspect of its unique being.

Michael Fishbane's recent book, *Biblical Interpretation in Ancient Israel*, though it is ostensibly about the interpretation of the Bible within the Bible, is in fact the fullest account we have of the workings of this living tradition. What Fishbane demonstrates in awesome detail is how a work written over a period of a thousand years by many different hands working in many local traditions, may nevertheless remain itself, and distinctive. He shows how the prophets, for example, subtly transformed the import of many of the laws and stories in the Torah, giving them a more spiritual, ethical and nationalistic flavour than they had; how Chronicles transformed Genesis and Samuel; how later editors and redactors, such as those who placed superscriptions over some of the Psalms ('A Psalm of David, when he fled from Absalom his son', 'Maschil of David; A Prayer when he was in the cave'), attempted to pull the disparate material together. But he also brings out the piecemeal and unsystematic nature of the process. Only a few of the Psalms, for example, are related by their superscriptions to the biblical narratives, while in Isaiah 56 and Ezekiel 44, for example, we find diametrically opposed views attributed to God concerning the place of strangers in the Temple.

One of Fishbane's conclusions is that the Torah was the result of compromise between diverse local traditions. But this surely holds good for the Hebrew Bible as a whole, and even, surprising as it may seem, for the Christian Bible as a whole. For though there were many voices which protested at the inclusion of the Hebrew Bible within the Christian one, they lost the day, and though, as we have seen, St. Paul and the author of the Epistle to the Hebrews had no doubt that their versions of the past were the right ones, their views did not lead to a wholesale rewriting or censorship, but merely added two more voices to the large choir already assembled.

This was only partly the result of compromise. Fishbane does not draw any clear distinctions between rewritings which were deliberately subversive of what had gone before, such as Deutero-Isaiah's 'rewriting' of Genesis 1, and those which were concerned to show the link between past and present, such as the portrayal of Joshua as a second Moses or of Moses as a second Abraham. Perhaps it is impossible to draw such distinctions absolutely; but the notion of a multiplicity of voices was clearly encouraged by the Bible's characteristic way of advancing by repetition and variation. 'Already, only one-sixth of the way into it, we find it has become its own history, its own archaeology.' This is Howard Nemerov commenting on Proust, but his words could apply equally well to the Bible. As we saw in chapter III, almost before it has begun the Bible is already referring back to itself. What Nemerov goes on to say admirably sums up this aspect of the Bible:

> The novel has already become its own memory, and ours as well. . . . As the world of the book gradually expands from the room in Combray to take in Paris and the great world of society, it does so particularly by the echoing, resonant, returning method, whereby people and their doings are considered from a good many points of view; and by these intermittances and returns Proust is imperceptibly building in our own minds the idea of his world as always enlarging yet always self-contained.[13]

Given such a form, which seems able to incorporate new elements into itself with ease, why do we balk when Fishbane concludes that since the Bible was interpretation from the beginning, there is really no sharp break between it and later rabbinic commentary? What was it that made us uneasy with Michael Wadsworth's attempts to use Pseudo-Philo to round out the stories in Judges? Or with James Barr's suggestion that had John's Gospel not been included in the canon we would have found perfectly good reasons for its exclusion? Why, in other words, do we feel that between Pseudo-Philo and Genesis, between the Protevangelium of James and the Gospels, there is some clear yet invisible boundary?

As with all such questions, it is easy to sense the boundary when it is crossed, but less easy to define it. Partly it is a question of anachronism.

When Pseudo-Philo says that Abraham was cast into a fiery furnace by Nimrod because he would not worship idols, this seems to fit neither what we are told about Nimrod nor what we are told about Abraham. The horror of idols, on the other hand, emerges as a powerful theme in later portions of the Bible. Again, when the Talmud comments on one of the greatest moments in the Bible, God's words to Moses: 'And I will take away mine hand, and thou shalt see my back parts [*et acharai*, what is behind me]: but my face shall not be seen' (Exod. 33:23), by explaining that God 'showed [Moses] the Tephillin-knot which is placed behind the head' (*Ber.* 7a; *Men.* 35b), we feel that we are being given the wrong sort of explanation because, whether in actual fact God was in the habit of going round with the tephillin tied to his brow or not, nothing in the narrative so far has led us to infer this, and indeed nothing in the entire Bible ever does so. Moreover, by introducing this explanation the mysterious phrase is immediately robbed of its power and resonance.[14] In the pseudo-gospels too, as we have seen, we are often presented with incongruous bits of information, such as details of Mary's scholarly aptitude or Jesus' skills as a youthful carpenter.

Yet could it not be argued that Chronicles and the Gospel of John, for example, are already pretty close in feel to later midrash and pseudo-gospel? After all, as Fishbane shows, Chronicles alters the emphasis of earlier narratives quite consistently in order to stress the value of Torah study, something which, for obvious reasons, was very far from the concerns of the earlier authors. And John's Gospel has passages which are quite as mystical as many of the pseudo-gospels.

There are two reasons, I think, why this argument will not hold up. The first is that, for all their great variety, the majority of the biblical books do incorporate some or all of the elements I have attempted to isolate: rhythm, speech and character. One has only to read a page of Jubilees or Pseudo-Philo, of the Protevangelium of James or the Gospel of Thomas (or of *Paradise Lost* or *Joseph and His Brothers*) to sense the difference. Their relation to the Bible is a little like that of Viollet-le-duc to the Gothic cathedrals: many of the features may be the same but the spirit which animates them is different; we no longer have the feeling of being within a living tradition, but rather of their authors looking back to that tradition as to an ideal.

The second reason why the argument will not hold up is that once Chronicles and John *have* been incorporated into the book they inevitably engage in dialogue with the other portions. By contrast, Pseudo-Philo and the Protevangelium of James, like *Paradise Lost* and *Joseph and His Brothers*, seem to be telling us that this and only this was how it was; the very fact that they are single makes them seem more assertive and intransigent at the same time as they seem to recognize that their exclusion robs them of authority.

It shocks us, I think, that simply by being excluded or included in a canon certain books are transformed. This is because we still think of all books as being 'created', like Romantic poems and nineteenth-century novels. But the making of objects, even artistic or verbal objects, consists as much of putting together already existing objects as of creating the whole afresh. We do not need to read Lévi-Strauss on *bricolage* to appreciate this, only to remember our own childhoods and how some of our favourite toys were not the expensive items given to us but those we or our parents managed to make out of all sorts of odds and ends. Moreover, it was *use* which conferred value on a particular toy.

If the different strands of which Genesis is made take on a new meaning by being brought together in one book, why should Genesis and Chronicles not take on a new meaning when the two are brought together? Just as verse 2 of Genesis 1 is laid alongside verse 1 and alters its significance, so chapter 38 is laid alongside chapters 37 and 39, and so Chronicles is laid alongside Genesis. There is no attempt to make them one, just as there is no attempt to resolve apparent contradictions within Genesis; the Bible is content to let the reader or listener decide for himself.[15] At the same time we see, in the Prophets, in Chronicles, in the New Testament, a growing urge to forge a single meaning out of the manifold elements of the tradition; yet this urge itself is not allowed to take over, but remains simply another element in the living whole.

We are not dealing here with a kind of liberal pluralism, but with something much more interesting and profound. Let us take, for example, Genesis, Ecclesiastes and Job. In Genesis, as we have seen, we remain inside the continuum of history, and even Joseph, whose dreams seem to come true, is unable to see what history has in store for his descendants. In Ecclesiastes, by contrast, human life is seen *sub specie aeternitatis*. We stand above human strivings and ambitions, and, from this vantage-point, they all seem like so much empty wind. Were Joseph to look down from such a position he would not merely be disappointed at the extinction of his line and the triumph of that of Judah, he would laugh – because he would see that, from an eternal perspective, even Judah's triumph was short-lived. In Job the question seems to turn on which of these two views of human life is the real one. After the comforters and Job have argued at length about 'the meaning' of life and human suffering, God speaks to Job out of the whirlwind. But far from giving us, as we might have expected, a version of Ecclesiastes, what God gives us is something else again. It is itself a personal point of view, but, being God's, it is far more intense than any merely human point of view could ever be. It is also unique, of course, in that it is the point of view of the one who made the entire universe, Job included. It seems as though we are being told that the conventional notion of a Godlike perspective is just as misleading as the conventional notion of personal experience.

The philosopher Thomas Nagel, talking not about the Bible but about some traditional problems in philosophy, catches, it seems to me, the true implications of this dialogue between the parts, when he writes:

> The power of the impulse to transcend oneself and one's species is so great, and its rewards so substantial, that it is not likely to be seriously baffled by the admission that objectivity has its limits. . . . The task of accepting the polarity [of subjective and objective] without allowing either of its terms to swallow the other should be a creative one. It is the aim of eventual unification that I think is misplaced, both in our thoughts about how to live and in our conception of what there is. The coexistence of conflicting points of view, varying in detachment from the contingent self, is not just a practically necessary illusion but an irreducible fact of life.[16]

If 'the coexistence of conflicting points of view, varying in detachment from the contingent self' is produced in the Bible by the inclusion within it of Genesis and Ecclesiastes and Job, it is also, as we have seen, a theme within the narratives. Man's private vision (every man doing what is right in his own eyes) is corrected not by being placed within a universal perspective but by coming up against its own limits. When that happens, language gives out; but the giving out of language is itself a theme within this book. At such moments we arrive at a kind of knowledge of what it is like to be a Phalti or a David or a Jesus,[17] but also at what it is like to be a human being.

But such knowledge is provided not only by the coexistence of two different visions, or by the dramatization of the points at which language gives way to tears. It is also provided by the very style of the book. 'And to Michal the daughter of Saul there was not to her a child until the day of her death' (2 Sam. 6:23). 'And the Lord had respect unto Abel and to his offering: And [not 'but' as the AV has it] unto Cain and to his offering he had not respect' (Gen. 4:4–5). What is the relation between Michal's taunts to David and her barrenness? Between God's grace to Abel and his actions? The Bible does not say. It merely tells us that this is how it was, and leaves us to wrestle with meaning, significance, causality.

There is then a unity to this book, which runs all the way from the ubiquitous use of the particle *wa*, 'and', to the inclusion within it of disparate and sometimes conflicting material. It is the unity of disjunction, at the same time as it is an assertion of conjunction. How and why the parts hold together is not, primarily, a subject for scholars delving into the history of manuscript traditions, but for the reader, from the first sentence to the last. The disjunctions, in other words, are not dark patches in our understanding which are waiting for the light of scholarship to shine upon them, or even for the blinding flash of a once-and-for-all understanding. They are the very fabric of this book. That is why we feel so let down when we find scholars attempting to explain the role of history in the Bible by observing that 'history is the means whereby culture renders account to itself of the past', or theologians and critics attempting to explain the role of narrative by telling us that 'there is no getting away from the need to tell stories in order to explain ourselves as well as to describe the world'.[18] For these are generalizations that apply in a rough sort of way to all cultures and all human beings, but the peculiarity of the Bible is that it keeps calling into question our ability to make sense of our past, and of stories to explain ourselves or describe the world. There is, it is true, a strong tendency in Christianity, already evident in the New Testament, to search for the single story that will give shape to the world; but that tendency exists in tension with the sense, present in the Gospels as well as in much of the Hebrew Bible, that if there is such a story it is not one we will ever be able to know or tell.

Perhaps, instead of thinking about the Bible as a book to be deciphered, or a story to be told, we should think of it as a person. We do not decipher people, we encounter them. And the closer we are to a person the more certain we will be that we cannot tell his story. Yet we also know that we will never be likely to confuse that person with anyone else, even a close relative. The notion of an invisible boundary round a book, which I referred to earlier, was perhaps too visual and too static. What I was really talking about was perhaps more what Walter Benjamin called an aura, that distinct quality of uniqueness which, though indefinable, is felt by all of us when we encounter a particular person or natural object. Looked at in this way, the Bible can be seen to be unique not because it is uniquely authoritative but because it is itself and not something else. Jubilees and Ecclesiasticus may be its brothers, the Koran, *Paradise Lost* and *Joseph and His Brothers* its cousins, once or twice removed, and so may the works of Homer and Sophocles, Kafka, Celan and Proust. They share certain gestures and expressions, but no one who had once got to know them would ever mistake one for the other.

If this is right then understanding the Bible will mean reading the Bible. Such reading will never be able to attain a universal perspective or come to an end. The New Testament at times calls for such a perspective, holds out a prospect of an end, but then so, in their different ways, do Isaiah and Daniel. The tension between our need for such a perspective and our awareness of the folly of imagining we can ever attain it is one more aspect of this book's aura.

For one last time then let us turn to it, not as to an object, but as to a person. In other words, let us read it.

At the end of chapter I I suggested that the story of Jacob wrestling

with the angel was a better model of reading than Saul consulting the
Witch of Endor. But I perhaps laid too much emphasis then on the
moment of existential encounter. We do not expect a revelation every
time we meet a friend. So let us look at the story once more, and this
time take it through to its conclusion:

> And Jacob was left alone; and there wrestled a man with him until the
> breaking of the day. And when he saw that he prevailed not against him, he
> touched the hollow of his thigh; and the hollow of Jacob's thigh was out of
> joint, as he wrestled with him. And he said, Let me go, for the day breaketh.
> And he said, I will not let thee go, except thou bless me. And he said unto
> him, What is thy name? And he said, Jacob. And he said, Thy name shall be
> called no more Jacob, but Israel: for as a prince hast thou power with God and
> with men, and hast prevailed. And Jacob asked him, and said, Tell me, I pray
> thee, thy name. And he said, Wherefore is it that thou dost ask after my
> name? And he blessed him there. And Jacob called the name of the place
> Peniel: for I have seen God face to face, and my life is preserved. And as he
> passed over Penuel the sun rose upon him, and he halted upon his thigh.
>
> (Gen. 32 : 24–31)

The episode is not seen as the climax of Jacob's life, only as one more
episode within a rich and varied life. He emerges alive from the encounter, but with a new name. And the place too receives a name. It is
not a sacred place, like Delphi or Colonus, but only becomes meaningful as the scene of the encounter, the place where Jacob saw God (*El*)
face to face (*panim el panim*).

From the moment that Jacob was left alone at the ford Jabbok we have
lived inside him. As he wrestles in the dark, so do we; as he asks his
desperate questions and calls for the blessing, so do we. But then see
what the narrative does: 'And as he passed over Penuel the sun rose upon
him, and he halted upon his thigh.' Without warning we have been
moved to a place high above him, looking down on him as, small and
defenceless, he limps forward to meet his brother in the light of the
newly risen sun. Perhaps though we are still inside him, and what has
happened is that he too, seeing his shadow in the light of the morning
sun, senses suddenly how he must look to those who might see him from
above. Yet this small limping figure is the man who a moment before had
seen God face to face, a moment commemorated in the name of the
place, which is now, only one verse later, so casually mentioned: 'And as
he passed over Penuel. . .' (The Hebrew has a different word order –
'And there rose upon him the sun as he passed over Penuel' – but the
effect here lies in the sudden transition between the sentences, not in
the order of the words; though no doubt these do affect our response to the
scene to a certain extent.)

The important thing is the shift in perspective, the shock of letting go
as we abruptly part company with Jacob. And then at once there is the

pleasure of balancing the two elements which make up that last sentence: the rising sun and the limping man. He is now both more and less than he was before the encounter: more because he has wrestled with the angel and got himself a new name, a name which signifies that 'as a prince hast thou power with God and with men, and hast prevailed', and less because of the limp which is the result of that struggle. Yet he is still the same man, Jacob, and still, naturally, the centre of his world; but we see him now within the larger world, created, like him, by God.

After the urgency and effort of the previous verses this last verse is strangely quiet. It strives for nothing. It is certainly not 'literature'. But, whatever it is, it is a form of words which, coming where it does, brings us more fully to life, and makes us want to let others share in the experience.

NOTES
BIBLIOGRAPHY
INDEX OF NAMES
INDEX OF BIBLICAL PASSAGES

NOTES

Works cited below in condensed form, or abbreviated after their first occurrence, are listed with full particulars in the Bibliography at p. 326.

Chapter I

1 Wittgenstein comes back to this point again and again in the *Philosophical Investigations* (1963). See, e.g., para. 129.

2 Northrop Frye, *Anatomy of Criticism* (1957; repr. 1971), 25.

3 See, e.g., Umberto Cassuto, *The Documentary Hypothesis* (1961), ch. 1.

4 *The Mishnah*, ed. H. Danby (1933), 781 (*Yadaim* 3, 5). Danby refers the reader to a footnote on p. 626 which is worth quoting for the insight it gives into the context of such debates: 'The reason given for this rabbinical rule', he says, 'is that it used to be the custom to store the Heave-offering with the scrolls, and the mice among the Heave-offering produce destroyed the scrolls; therefore it was ruled that the scrolls suffered "second-degree uncleanness"; similarly the hands which touched the scrolls were deemed to suffer the same "second-grade uncleanness"'.

5 Josephus, *Against Apion*, in *Works*, vol, I (Loeb edn., 1926), 179–81.

6 Swift, *Tale of a Tub* (ed. 1958), 191.

7 James Barr, *Holy Scripture* (1983), 57.

8 Josephus, *Works*, I. 179.

9 Barr, *Holy Scripture*, 45.

10 See for example James Sanders, *Torah and Canon* (1972), and H. von Campenhausen, *The Formation of the Christian Bible* (1972).

11 See Erich Auerbach's classic essay,

'Figura', in *Scenes from the Drama of European Literature* (1959); Jean Daniélou, *From Shadows to Reality* (1960); and, for Frye, esp. *Anatomy of Criticism*, and *The Great Code* (1982).

12 For an assessment of the Reformation not based on the usual Protestant assumptions, see John Bossy, *Christianity and the West* (1985), and my *The World and Book* (1971), chs. 2–4.

13 A slightly different view of the process, but one which agrees with the broad outlines of my argument, is to be found in Hans W. Frei, *The Eclipse of Biblical Narrative* (1974). But see the acute criticism of Frei by Meir Sternberg in *The Poetics of Biblical Narrative* (1985), 81–2.

14 Paul Ricoeur, *Essays on Biblical Interpretation* (1980).

15 Gerhard von Rad, *Old Testament Theology* (1962), esp. I. 105–15.

16 Other scholars, as concerned with historical truth as is von Rad, but more aware of the pernicious effect such attitudes may have on our understanding of the Bible, have begun to question this, one of the bastions on which German biblical scholarship rests. Umberto Cassuto (see n. 3 above), for example, as well as pointing out many places where the theory either results in confusion or is hopelessly contradictory, has shown how discoveries about the composite nature of the biblical

text have, since the eighteenth century, run surprisingly parallel to similar 'discoveries' in the field of Homeric scholarship. Does this not suggest, he wonders, that what we are dealing with here is not a set of facts about the ancient world but rather about the mentality of German Protestant scholars from 1700 to 1900? Cassuto does not indict the documentary hypothesis primarily for being wrong on this or that count, but for its self-fulfilling methodology. For a different attempt to bring us back to a sense of the Bible as it was conceived before modern scholarship got to work on it, see Brevard Childs, *Introduction to the Old Testament as Scripture* (1979).

17 G. von Rad, *Genesis* (1961), 150.

18 For insights into Genesis 10–12 I am indebted to Michael Wadsworth, 'Making and Interpreting Scripture', in *Ways of Reading the Bible*, ed. Wadsworth (1981), 11–12; and to the essay by Lou H. Silberman, 'Listening to the Text', *Journal of Biblical Literature*, CII, no. 1 (1983), 3–26. On the word *hotzetikha* and its implications see J. Weingreen, '*Hotzetikha* in Genesis 15 : 7', in *Words and Meanings*, ed. P. R. Ackroyd and B. Lindars (1968), and the doubts expressed by Michael Fishbane in *Biblical Interpretation in Ancient Israel* (1985), 376 and nn. 144, 145.

19 Robert Alter, *The Art of Biblical Narrative* (1981), 19–20.

20 On Homer, see the article by Oliver Taplin, 'Homer Comes Home', *New York Review of Books*, XXXIII, no. 4 (1986), 39–42. Bernard Harrison comments interestingly on the effect of the seventeenth-century intellectual revolution on hermeneutics in 'Parable and Transcendence', in *Ways of Reading the Bible* (n. 18), 190–212.

21 M. Fishbane's *Biblical Interpretation* gives numerous examples of attempts at 'correction' in the Bible.

22 All three examples are taken from the commentary to *The Soncino Chumash*, ed. A. Cohen (1983).

23 M. Wadsworth, in *Ways of Reading the Bible* (n. 18), 15, 14.

24 M. Sternberg draws attention to the Masoretic Text reading at 1 Sam. 13 : 1: 'Saul was one year old when he began to reign.' (The AV quietly corrects this to 'Saul reigned one year.') Sternberg's point is that in another kind of book – where kings would from their birth be filled with the spirit of the Lord, for example, and the power to rule – such a sentence would be perfectly acceptable. But, given the nature of the biblical narrative, it can only be a corruption. Thus 'it makes more sense to infer a scribal error than a reality-model within which the incongruity will fall into "literary" pattern.' (*Poetics of Biblical Narrative*, 14.)

25 T. S. Eliot, 'Religion and Literature', in *Essays Ancient and Modern* (1936), 96; C. S. Lewis, *Reflections on the Psalms* (1968), 2–3.

26 J. L. Kugel, *The Idea of Biblical Poetry* (1981), 304. Kugel has developed his critique in an essay, 'On the Bible and Literary Criticism', *Prooftexts* I (1981), 217–36, and in an exchange with Adele Berlin, 'On the Bible as Literature', in *Prooftexts* II (1982), 323–32.

27 James Barr: 'Reading the Bible as Literature', *Bulletin of the John Rylands Library*, LVI (1973–4), 13; *Holy Scripture*, 160.

28 Lewis, *Reflections on the Psalms*, 3; Eliot, *Essays Ancient and Modern*, 95.

29 Barr, 'Reading the Bible as Literature' (n. 27), 13, 15.

30 See especially Erich Heller, 'The Hazard of Modern Poetry', appended to *The Disinherited Mind* (1961 edn.).

31 Wittgenstein, *Philosophical Investigations*, para. 129.

32 Ibid., para. 132.

Chapter II

1 I am of course talking here primarily about those brought up in English-speaking countries. But my remarks may awaken echoes in those brought up in other cultures.

2 Samuel Beckett, *Proust and Three Dialogues with Georges Duthuit* (1965), Foreword. The book first came out in

1931. In 1954 Gallimard finally brought out a revised 3-vol. edition of *À la recherche* in their Pléiade imprint, and this has been further revised in their 4-vol. 1988 edition.

3 Marcel Proust, *Contre Sainte-Beuve* (ed. 1954), 237–9, in my own translation. I have discussed the implications of the whole episode at greater length in 'The Balzac of M. Barthes and the Balzac of M. de Guermantes', in *Reconstructing Literature*, ed. L. Lerner (1983), 81–105, from which these paragraphs are taken.

4 Stephen Prickett, *Words and the Word* (1986), ch. 1.

5 Edward Ullendorf, 'Thought Categories in the Hebrew Bible', in *Studies in Rationalism, Judaism and Universalism*, ed. R. Loewe (1966), 257–87.

6 Erich Auerbach, *Mimesis* (1953), chs. 1 and 2.

7 For some pertinent comments on French editions of the Bible, in the same spirit as the preceding paragraphs, see Henri Meschonnic: *Pour la poétique*, vol. II (1980), 425–54, and *Jona et le signifiant errant* (1981), 29–76.

8 J. F. A. Sawyer, *From Moses to Patmos* (1977), has some useful comments on the subject, but since he goes on to concentrate on the shape of the Christian Bible only, he does not fully bring out the implications of the contrast with the Hebrew scriptures. The whole issue is further complicated by the fact that the LXX is a sort of half-way house between the Jewish and the Christian arrangements. However, the MSS of the Greek Bible vary enormously among themselves, and none antedates Christianity. We will probably never know why and how the changes occurred in the LXX. What is important for our purposes, however, is the stark dissimilarity between the Masoretic Text and all Christian Bibles in their organization of the material.

9 Frye, *Great Code*, xiii.

10 The Hebrew should probably be translated as: 'the voice of one crying: in the wilderness prepare ye the way of the Lord'. Mark's version appears to be an example of the kind of unwitting mistranslation I was talking about in ch. I.

11 Frye, *Great Code*, xiii.

12 This is the suggestion of Nahum Sarna in the article on 'The Bible: Canon, Text and Tradition', *Encyclopedia Judaica* (1971), II. cols. 815–32.

13 Here and in following chapters, Talmud references are to *The Babylonian Talmud* in the Soncino Press edn. (1948).

14 See Umberto Cassuto, 'The Sequence and Arrangement of the Biblical Sections', *Biblical and Oriental Studies I* (1973).

15 On the figure of Elijah in later Hebrew thought and culture, see Aharon Wiener, *The Prophet Elijah in the Development of Judaism* (1978).

16 Sid Z. Leiman, *The Canonization of Hebrew Scripture* (1976), 104–20, disputes the interpretation that 'books that defile the hands' (cf. ch. I, n. 4) means 'canonical books'. Instead, he argues, it refers to *inspired* canonical books – there were canonical books which did not appear to 'defile the hands'. However, since by 'inspired canonical books' he seems to mean 'Scripture', the difference may only be a matter of terminology. That the rabbis distinguished between a category of books which defiled and the rest is what is important for our purposes.

17 Isaiah is far more positive about Cyrus: 'the Lord...saith of Cyrus, He is my shepherd, and shall perform all my pleasure: even saying to Jerusalem, Thou shalt be built; and to the temple, Thy foundation shall be laid. Thus saith the Lord to his anointed, to Cyrus, whose right hand I have holden, to subdue nations before him...' (44: 24–45: 1). Yet the Hebrew Bible chooses to end with the words of the Chronicler, not of Isaiah.

18 Sarna, in *Encyclopedia Judaica*, II. cols. 827–8; Leiman, *Canonization of Hebrew Scripture*, 162, n. 258.

19 Sanders, *Torah and Canon*, 48.

20 See C. H. Roberts, 'Books in the Graeco-Roman World and the New Testament', in *Cambridge History of*

the Bible, ed. P. R. Ackroyd and C. F.
Evans, vol. I (1970), 48–66; Saul
Lieberman, 'Jewish and Christian Cod-
ices', *Hellenism and Jewish Palestine*
(1950), 203–8; and Frank Kermode,
The Genesis of Secrecy (1979), 88–9.
However, one should perhaps not make
too much of this claim, since no early
codices containing the entire Christian
Bible have been found. Often they
consist of one or two books of the
Torah or of the four Gospels.

21 See my 'Perec's Homage to Joyce (and
Tradition)', *Yearbook of English Studies*, ed. Rawson (1985), 179–200.
Tsvetan Todorov makes much the same
point in *The Poetics of Prose* (1977),
53–65: ancient narratives are studied
by scholars whose notions of art belong
firmly to the nineteenth century, and
are naturally found wanting; had these
scholars been a bit more responsive to
the art of their own time they might
have been better equipped to deal with
the art of the past.

Chapter III

1 E. A. Speiser, *Genesis* (1964), 3.
2 Von Rad, *Genesis*, 44.
3 Speiser, *Genesis*, 12.
4 *Near Eastern Religious Texts Relating
to the Old Testament*, ed. W. Beyerlin
(1978), 82. I have chosen this rendering, by Hartmut Schmokel, in preference to the most easily available
translation, in J. B. Pritchard's *Ancient
Near Eastern Texts Relating to the Old
Testament* (1969), as the latter is by
Speiser himself, and the reader might
feel it was thus open to suspicion.
5 Speiser, *Genesis*, 12.
6 Von Rad, *Genesis*, 46.
7 Ibid., 47.
8 *Pentateuch*, ed. S. R. Hirsch (1958–
62), I. 1.
9 Von Rad, *Genesis*, 47.
10 Andrew Martin, *The Knowledge of
Ignorance* (1985), 3, 4. This brief,
dense, thought-provoking book develops, in its first two chapters, devoted
to Genesis 1–3, some of the same
themes as my own argument. (The

philological point he is making here depends on André Caquot, 'Brèves re-
marques éxégetiques sur Genèse 1 : 1–
2', in *In Principio* [1973], 9–21.)
11 Speiser, *Genesis*, 12.
12 I have developed this theme in the first
chapter of *The World and the Book*. On
iteration in Proust, see Gérard Genette,
Figures III (1972).
13 L. Wittgenstein, *Culture and Value*
(1980), 80.
14 In recent years scholars have grown
more cautious about these distinctions,
and have tried to do justice to what
they see as the historical dimension of
ancient Near Eastern cultures. See ch.
VII, n. 3, below.
15 These are the concluding lines of the
poem, as given in the Supplement to
Ancient Near Eastern Texts, ed. J. B.
Pritchard, 503. On the Bible's use of
the material of ancient Near Eastern
myths see Frank Moore Cross, *Canaanite Myth and Hebrew Epic* (1973),
and the writings of Umberto Cassuto.
16 Quoted in *Bereshis*, Artscroll Tanach
Series (1980), I. 31.
17 See, for example, Alter, *Biblical Narrative*, 27–32, and Joel Rosenberg,
King and Kin (1986), 1–68. Cassuto,
though not looking at the text from a
literary point of view, nevertheless
strongly rejects the fragmentation imposed on chapters 1–3 by critical scholarship – see *A Commentary on the
Book of Genesis* (1964), I. 7–177.
18 For a clear non-technical account of
the Centre Pompidou, see Brian Appleyard, *Richard Rogers* (1986).
19 I owe this insight to Jonathan Magonet.
20 Herbert Schneidau, *Sacred Discontent*
(1977).
21 Fishbane, *Biblical Interpretation*, 372.
22 Jonathan Magonet, 'Abraham and
God', *Judaism*, XXXIII, no 1 (1984),
160–70, points out the connection
between chapters 12 and 22 of Genesis,
and stresses the importance of the
double *lekh lekha*.
23 Speiser, *Genesis*, 88.
24 On the thematic role of genealogy, see
ch. VII below. On the way the narrative teases us with the notion that it

might be Lot who will inherit, see Lou Silberman's article, 'Listening to the Text' (ch. I, n. 18), 18–24.

[25] Contrast the ancient Egyptian attitude to the god's name in 'The God and His Unknown Name of Power', *Ancient Near Eastern Texts*, ed. Pritchard, 12–14. The editor of the Egyptian section, John A. Wilson, comments: 'To the ancient, the name was an element of personality and of power. It might be so charged with divine potency that it could not be pronounced. Or the god might retain a name hidden for himself alone, maintaining an element of power over all other gods and men.' The supreme god Re, he continues, 'had many names, one of which was hidden and was thus a source of supremacy. The goddess Isis plotted to learn this name and thus to secure power for herself. For this purpose she employed the venom of a snake against Re.' (p. 12)

Chapter IV

[1] G. Scholem, 'Martin Buber's Conception of Judaism', *On Jews and Judaism in Crisis* (1976), 126–71. See also his 'Revelation and Tradition as Religious Categories in Judaism', *The Messianic Idea in Judaism* (1971), 282–303.

[2] Auden has some acute things to say about the assumptions which lie behind detective stories. See 'The Guilty Vicarage', *The Dyer's Hand* (1963), 146–58.

[3] Von Rad, *Old Testament Theology*, I. 172.

[4] Errol McGuire, 'The Joseph Story: A Tale of Son and Father', in *Images of Man and God*, ed. B. Long (1981), 11.

[5] Alter, *Biblical Narrative*, 174–5.

[6] Von Rad, *Genesis*, 348.

[7] James Ackerman, in his article, 'Joseph, Judah and Jacob', in *Literary Interpretations of Biblical Narratives*, vol. II, ed. K. R. R. Gros Louis (1982), 85–113, has some interesting comments on the phrase *ba'al hachalamot*, and, indeed, on the whole Joseph episode, though our conclusions differ.

[8] Lou Silberman's 1983 essay, 'Listening to the Text' (ch. I, n. 18), is one of the few I have come across which note the irony of Judah's eventual triumph. In ch. XIV I discuss Thomas Mann's response to this issue.

[9] Marthe Robert, *Origins of the Novel* (1980). No English phrase can convey the multiple effects of the French title of this work: *Roman des origines et origines du roman*.

[10] Wallace Stevens, *Opus Posthumous* (1957), 96–7.

[11] See the remarks quoted from Rosenberg and Alter in ch. I above. For Proust's methods see Alison Winton, *Proust's Additions* (1977).

[12] I owe this insight to Jonathan Magonet.

[13] Alter, *Biblical Narrative*, 4–5.

[14] See Edmund Leach: *Genesis as Myth* (1969); (with D. Alan Aycock) *Structuralist Interpretations of Biblical Myth* (1984); and his 'Fishing with Men at the Edge of the Wilderness' in *Literary Guide to the Bible*, ed. R. Alter and F. Kermode (1987), 579–99. Leach brings out the structural parallels, but fails to see that the fact that the echoes exist in a continuum is what is important about them. By draining the Bible of the element of time, and therefore denying the place of memory, he robs it of what is an essential, if not the essential, component. Leach's scientism has no room for speech or time, and so, far from being, as he suggests, about the 'real facts' of the Bible, it is in effect a play with shadows.

Chapter V

[1] John Freccero has suggested that St. Thomas's argument may explain Dante's mysterious reference, in *Inferno* ii. 108, to 'la fiumana ove'l mar non ha vanto [the river over which the sea has no boast]'. See Freccero, 'The River of Death: *Inferno* ii, 106–8', in *Dante: The Poetics of Conversion* (1985), 55–69. On the typology of baptism see Daniélou, *From Shadows to Reality*.

[2] David Damrosch, 'Leviticus', in *Lit-*

erary Guide to the Bible (ch. IV, n. 14), 66–77, esp. 68–9.

3 Ibid. 75–6.

4 Josephus, *Antiquities of the Jews*, in *Works*, vol. IV (Loeb edn., 1930), 403. Philo, *De Vita Moisi*, in *Works of Philo Judaeus* (Loeb edn., 1934–5), I. 483; see also III. 90–1.

5 Von Rad, *Old Testament Theology*, I. 235.

6 The fullest recent discussion of the Tabernacle is by Menaham Haran, *Temples and Temple-Service in Ancient Israel* (1978).

7 For details about the making of such objects see Umberto Cassuto, *A Commentary on the Book of Exodus* (1967), 420.

8 Damrosch is in no doubt about the relation of the death of Aaron's two sons to his making of the calf. See his article on Leviticus (n. 2), pp. 70–2.

9 Haran (n.6) takes recent scholars to task for holding this view, but it seems to me that he himself only provides a more nuanced version of it.

10 See Cassuto, *Commentary on... Exodus*, and any of the many good post-war studies of ancient Near Eastern culture, such as Henri Frankfort *et. al.*, *Before Philosophy* (1949).

11 Haran, *Temples and Temple-Service*, 150.

12 A. D. Nuttall first alerted me to the range of meaning in the Greek and Latin words.

Chapter VI

1 F. Petrie, *Tell El Hesy* (1891), 16–17; quoted in Robert G. Boling, *Judges*, Anchor Bible (1975), 2.

2 The theory was first proposed by George D. Mendenhall, *The Tenth Generation* (1973). It has been developed in Norman Gottwald, *The Tribes of Yahweh* (1980).

3 See Boling's edition of Judges (n. 1), and Barry G. Webb, *The Book of Judges* (1987).

4 Alter, *Biblical Narrative*, 37–41; Mieke Bal, *Femmes imaginaires* (1986), 88–131.

5 I owe this insight to David Pocock.

6 Boling, *Judges*, 276. It is interesting that both Boling and James Martin, in the *Cambridge Bible Commentary*, try to 'clean up' the text of Judges at a number of points, such as 1:14 and 3:22, where the MT reading seems too disgusting for modern tastes.

7 S. Lasine, 'Guest and Host in Judges 19: Lot's Hospitality in an Inverted World', *Journal for the Study of the Old Testament*, no. 29 (1984), 40.

8 Ibid., 49, 40–1.

9 Boling, *Judges*, 146.

10 R. de Vaux, *Ancient Israel, Its Life and Institutions* (1961), 467.

11 Bal, *Femmes imaginaires*, 105–25.

12 Gideon too seems to seek only personal revenge at 8:19. See Boling's note, *Judges*, 157.

13 Ulrich Simon, 'Samson and the Heroic', in *Ways of Reading the Bible* (ch. I. n. 18), 166.

14 Bal, *Femmes imaginaires*, 98–9.

15 Lasine contrasts her silence to Tamar's very vocal response to her rape in 2 Samuel 13. This suggests that David's own ability to speak what he feels in some sense releases speech in those around him.

Chapter VII

1 I use the edition of *The Passover Haggadah* illustrated by Arthur Szyk, ed. C. Roth (1980).

2 Brevard Childs, *Memory and Tradition in Israel* (1962), gives the figures and explores some of their implications.

3 Y. H. Yerushalmi, *Zakhor* (1982), 8, 6–7. Scholars have for some time now been questioning the simple opposition between Hebrew historiography and that of the rest of the ancient Near East, recognizing that there was such a thing as a historical tradition in Babylon, for example. The old picture does not, however, seem to me to have been substantially altered. See B. Albrektson, *History and the Gods* (1967); H. W. F. Saggs, *The Encounter with the Divine in Mesopotamia and Israel* (1978), ch. 3; John van Seters, *In*

Search of History (1983).

4 Yerushalmi, *Zakhor*, 8.

5 Herodotus, *The Histories* (ed. 1954), 13.

6 Just as there are 70 descendants of Noah, so there are 70 descendants of Abraham.

7 The close relation between the present and the future is what distinguishes prophecy from apocalyptic. In the latter it is simply a question of deciphering the future, there is no longer any possibility of altering it. But the two genres or attitudes cannot of course be neatly separated.

8 Von Rad, *Old Testament Theology*, I. 276.

9 J. Ackerman, 'Joseph, Judah and Jacob' (ch. IV, n. 7), 85–113.

10 The idea of the 'remnant' as it is elaborated in the prophets, and particularly in Isaiah, forms a crucial bridge between the two attitudes I am contrasting. The term itself, *she'ar, she'erit*, undergoes, from Genesis to Ezra, the kind of transformation which C. S. Lewis traced for a number of English words, such as 'kind', in his brilliant *Studies in Words*. In Genesis 45:7 Joseph says to his brothers: 'And God sent me before you to preserve you a posterity [*she'erit*] on earth, and to save your lives by a great deliverance', and it is as 'posterity' too that the woman of Tekoah uses the word in her story to David (2 Sam. 14:7). Isaiah seizes on the word and seems single-handedly to transform it. He calls his son Shearjashub ('A Remnant Is Escaped'), and he rings the changes on it in chapters 10 and 11: 'And it shall come to pass in that day, that the remnant of Israel [*she'ar Yisrael*], and such as are escaped of the house of Jacob...shall stay upon the Lord.... The remnant shall return, even the remnant of Jacob' (Isa: 10: 20–21). 'And there shall be an highway for the remnant of his people, which shall be left, from Assyria [*lish'ar amo asher yisha'er me'ashur*]' (11:16). Here he identifies the remnant with the exodus of long ago and puns brilliantly on the name of Assyria and the word for

'which' (*asher*). Clearly this nexus of associations helps him to formulate his vision, and the term recurs at 37:32 and 46:3, as well as in his speech to Hezekiah in 2 Kings 19:31.

Once the notion of a remnant is seen in this way it brings with it the idea of choice: do I follow the apostates or do I return to the true way and form a part of the remnant which will be saved? So the word moves from 'posterity' to 'surviving group' to 'those in the diaspora who have preserved their distinctiveness'. From there it is a small step to seeing the remnant as a life-giving force in the midst of an indifferent people: 'And the remnant of Jacob [*she'erit Ya'akov*] shall be in the midst of many people as a dew from the Lord, as the showers upon the grass' (Micah 5:7). The difference between this and the situation St. Paul describes is of course that the remnant here is that which has held on to its ancient traditions, whereas for Paul the congregation of the faithful has had to make the active choice of joining.

11 M. D. Johnson, *The Purpose of the Biblical Genealogies* (1969).

12 Michael Wyschogrod, 'A Theology of Jewish Unity', *L'Eylah*, no. 21 (1968), 28.

13 Ibid.

14 F. Nietzsche, 'On the Uses and Disadvantages of History for Life', *Untimely Meditations* (ed. 1983), 62.

15 This is why the structural anthropology which Edmund Leach, for example, seeks to apply to the Bible falsifies at the same time as it illuminates. See ch. IV, n. 14 above.

Chapter VIII

1 Moshe Greenberg, *Biblical Prose Prayer* (1983), 7.

2 J. L. Kugel, *Idea of Biblical Poetry*; see also Ruth Finnegan, *Oral Poetry* (1977), ch. I. Henri Meschonnic has devoted a number of works to this theme, esp. *Jona et le signifiant errant*.

3 See Jonathan Magonet, *Form and Meaning: Studies in the Literary Tech-*

niques of the Book of Jonah (1976), esp.
ch. 2, a detailed analysis of the prayer
of Jonah which examines its use of
quotations from other parts of the
Bible.

4 S. Kierkegaard, 'The Immediate Stages
of the Erotic or the Musical Erotic',
Either/Or (ed. 1959), I. 43–134.

5 Greenberg, Biblical Prose Prayer, 38;
F. Heiler quoted in ibid., 39.

6 Ibid., 43–4.

7 S. S. Blank, 'The Confessions of Jeremiah and the Meaning of Prayer',
Hebrew Union College Annual, XXI
(1948), 335–6.

8 H. U. von Balthasar, Prayer (1963); F.
Heiler, Prayer (1932), 358.

9 Greenberg, Biblical Prose Prayer, 35,
and ref.

10 Quoted in Timothy Hyman, Introduction to Ken Kiff: Paintings 1965–85
(1986).

11 George Herbert, 'Prayer'. For an interesting though to my mind misguided
exploration of this issue in Herbert, see
A. D. Nuttall, Overheard by God
(1980).

12 Jonathan Magonet, in his study of the
book of Jonah, points out that until
2 : 6a the author makes use of a number
of phrases from the Psalter, cunningly
woven together, but that 'at this point
both stylistically (the narrative form)
and from the point of view of what is
described, the author breaks into new
territory, where the terminology of his
tradition is no longer used, and perhaps
can no longer be used' (Form and
Meaning, 49). Though Magonet sees
the prayer in a slightly more ironic light
than I do, what he says here reinforces
my general argument in this chapter,
that it is through the familiar that we
can reach the unfamiliar. His book is
one of the best examples of the benefits,
for a full understanding of the Bible, of
a close literary reading.

13 I am indebted for my understanding of
this Psalm to B. Bayer, 'The Rivers of
Babylon', Ariel, no. 62 (1985), 43–56.

14 Harold Fisch points out an interesting
aspect of this theme in Ezekiel 33. The
prophet there castigates his audience

for listening to him as they would to a
bard or entertainer, and not as one who
is telling them an awful truth: 'And,
lo,' says Ezekiel, miming their speech,
'thou [i.e. himself] art unto them as a
very lovely song of one that hath a
pleasant voice, and can play well on an
instrument: for they hear thy words, but
they do them not' (33 : 32). See H.
Fisch, Poetry With a Purpose (1988),
ch. 4.

Chapter IX

1 Walter Benjamin, Understanding Brecht
(1977), 73.

2 John Jones, On Aristotle and Greek
Tragedy (1962), 84–96.

3 Jonathan Magonet points out that the
verb yarad, 'to go down', plays an
important role in the book: Jonah 'went
down' to Jaffa, found a boat and 'went
down' into it; when the storm broke he
'went down' into the innermost parts of
the boat. The verb recurs in the 'psalm'
of chapter 2. See Magonet, Form and
Meaning, 17.

4 Ezekiel, Exagoge, tr. R. G. Robertson,
in Old Testament Pseudepigrapha, ed.
J. H. Charlesworth (1985), II. 812–13.

5 Both Josephus and Pseudo-Philo suggest
that Nimrod was the builder of the
tower. The idea passed into Christian
tradition and is to be found in Augustine, Orosius and Isidore of Seville.

6 Sternberg, Poetics of Biblical Narrative, 88–90.

7 Fishbane, Biblical Interpretation, 508.

8 Anthony Hecht, The Hard Hours
(1967), 13.

9 Jorge Luis Borges, Labyrinths (1964),
74–5.

Chapter X

1 See Alter, Biblical Narrative, 127, for
a good analysis of the narrative possibilities inherent in such ways of describing characters: daughter of Saul, wife of
David, etc.

2 Auerbach, Mimesis, ch 1; Alter, Biblical Narrative, 126–30. Of course most
biblical names have some meaning, but

this usually relates to an incident connected with the character, not to a fixed moral quality. See my discussion of names and meaning in ch. VI above.

3 Alter, *Biblical Narrative*, 128–30.

4 Sternberg, *Poetics of Biblical Narrative*, esp. ch. 7; Kermode, *Genesis of Secrecy*, chs. 2 and 4.

5 *The Diaries of Franz Kafka* (ed. 1964), 394.

6 A book like Anne Banfield's *Impossible Sentences* (1982) brings out just what the style of the classic novel can do that other forms of narrative cannot. The present book, like those of Alter and Sternberg, presents the other side of the story: the things the classic novel cannot do and which are done by, for example, biblical narrative.

7 Note the echoes of Genesis 50:20, discussed in ch. IV above. The verbs are different here, though.

8 The emergence of Joab in the course of 1 and 2 Samuel is a central theme of Jan Fokkelman's massive *Narrative Art and Poetry in the Books of Samuel*, vol. I: *King David* (1981).

9 Sternberg, *Poetics of Biblical Narrative*, ch. 6. Joel Rosenberg, in an analysis of the episode, has argued that we have to see it in broader terms than the personal, that David's staying at home while the army fights is not just a sign of his new sloth or reluctance to face the enemy in person, but of his new status: the Israelites have decided to have a king like the surrounding nations, and not a charismatic leader like Joshua and the Judges, and a king has, in the interests of the kingdom at large, to protect his person. See Rosenberg, *King and Kin*, 99–199.

10 *Mishnah*, ed. Danby, Sot. 1. 8, 294.

11 *Franz Rosenzweig, His Life and Thought* (rev. ed. 1972), 245.

Chapter XI

1 A clear and useful summary of the early meanings of 'gospel' is to be found in *New Testament Apocrypha*, ed. E. Hennecke and W. Schneemelcher (1963), I. 71–80.

2 I am aware that scholars are prone to break up John 8, arguing that its different units were only put together at a late stage. However, I follow here the procedure I have been following throughout this book, which is to start from the assumption that the author or final redactor knew just what he was doing.

3 Since writing this chapter I have come across an essay which takes roughly the same line with regard to the interconnection of the evangelist and Jesus, though the argument is couched in trendy Bloomian terms: Donald Foster, 'John Come Lately: The Belated Evangelist', in *The Bible and the Narrative Tradition*, ed. F. McConnell (1986), 113–31.

4 Many of these other gospels are much later than the canonical gospels, so it could be argued that they failed to get in because the canon had already been closed. However, they have too much in common with OT apocrypha, much of which was being written at the time of Jesus, and with the fragments of Gnostic and other material of considerable antiquity which new archaeological finds are constantly bringing to light, to make this a telling argument. It is at any rate secondary to the argument I develop in this chapter about the radical internal differences between the apocryphal and the canonical gospels.

5 *The Apocryphal New Testament*, ed. M. R. James (1924; repr. 1985), cited in the text as 'James'. The book is so pleasant to handle and so well presented that I use it in preference to *New Testament Apocrypha* (n. 1), which is more recent, and so includes rather more material, but which is still not complete, since new fragments are constantly coming to light. For material not included in the Hennecke and Schneemelcher volume see *The Nag Hammadi Library in English*, ed. J. M. Robinson (1977). A work not included in any of these volumes, since it does not deal with the New Testament, but with which it is nevertheless useful to

compare the canonical gospels because
like them it deals with the life of a
miracle-working charismatic figure, is
Philostratus' *Life of Apollonius* (ed.
1970).

[6] On the Pharisees see Louis Finkelstein,
The Pharisees (1946); Jacob Neusner,
Judaism in the Beginning of Christianity
(1984); Geza Vermes, *Jesus and the
World of Judaism* (1983).

[7] Kermode, *Genesis of Secrecy*, ch. 4.

[8] Hennecke and Schneemelcher divide
their volume into ten sections, the
longest of which is entitled 'Gnostic
Gospels and Related Documents'; but
much of their classification seems arbitrary.

[9] Kermode, *Genesis of Secrecy*, ch. 1. But
note that Mark is only echoing Isaiah
6:9–10.

[10] A. Schweitzer, *The Quest of the Historical Jesus* (1926), 353–8.

[11] For a recent and valuable addition to
the enormous literature on the parables, which stresses their links with
the Hebrew scriptures, see John Drury,
The Parables in the Gospels (1985). He
discusses the Prodigal Son on pp. 139–
48.

[12] Bernard Harrison, 'Parable and Transcendence', in *Ways of Reading the
Bible* (ch. I. n. 18), 203–7.

[13] S. Kierkegaard, in *On Authority and
Revelation* (ed. 1983).

[14] See especially Kafka's story 'The Hun-
ter Gracchus', and his letter to Max
Brod of 5 July 1922.

[15] Kermode, *Genesis of Secrecy*, 66–71.

Chapter XII

[1] The literature on St. Paul is of course
extensive. Some interesting modern
reappraisals are contained in E. P. Sanders, *Paul and Palestinian Judaism*
(1977); John G. Gager, *The Origins of
Anti-Semitism* (1983); and Hyam Maccoby, *The Mythmaker* (1986). These
and other scholars are concerned to find
'the real St. Paul', and they therefore
sift the evidence to determine which
parts of the Gospels and Acts have been
influenced by Paul, which by the teach-

ing of the Jerusalem church, and so on.
My feeling is that we will never be able
to know, of Paul any more than of Jesus,
just what they said and what was added
later, and that such attempts are
doomed to circularity: you dismiss as
inauthentic what does not fit in with
your notion of the man, and then use
what is left to confirm your vision. This
naturally does not mean that there is
no advance in understanding, but it
does help to explain why scholars hold
with such passionate conviction to
quite different and incompatible visions
of 'the real Jesus' or 'the real St. Paul'.
Here, as elsewhere in this study, I have
stuck to what is before me, though
recognizing of course that there is no
such thing as 'the text itself'. But I deal
with that point in chs. I and II, and
below in ch. XV.

[2] Maccoby, *The Mythmaker*, 191.

[3] Poe called his story of a murderer who
cannot keep quiet, 'The Imp of the
Perverse'; Dostoevsky's is *Crime and
Punishment*. They are exploring the
same psychological tangle, only Dostoevsky feels that there can be no full
explanation without the use of Christian
concepts. In this he rejoins the Kierkegaard of *The Sickness Unto Death*. But
the depiction of the desire to do something which one knows is fatal to one is
not confined to Romantic and post-
Romantic literature. It is one of the
main subjects of Euripides and Virgil.
Many recent scholars have stressed the
decisive changes that occurred between
Homer and Virgil, and even between
Sophocles and Euripides, and it is over
a century now since Nietzsche analysed
the changes that occurred between
Homer and Plato. I hold, with Nietzsche, that such changes do not occur
once only in any civilization, and
would see these as largely parallel to the
ones I am arguing for in this book. Four
works in particular seem to me to offer
suggestive parallels: Bruno Snell, *The
Discovery of the Mind* (1953); E. R.
Dodds, *The Greeks and the Irrational*
(1951); Eric Havelock, *Preface to Plato*
(1963); and John Jones, *On Aristotle*

and Greek Tragedy (ch. IX, n. 2). Jones, in the preface to his book, promises a multi-volume survey of changes in the conception of personality in European culture, but so far only the Aristotle book has appeared at one end of the trajectory, with, at the other, his brilliant studies of Wordsworth, Keats and Dostoevsky. Curiously, he seems to want to keep clear of the Bible.

4 All quotations from St. Augustine, *Confessions* (ed. 1961), cited in the text as *'Conf.'* with the chapter and verse.

5 Some of the best recent work on Dante, notably that of Charles Singleton and John Freccero, has stressed the influence of Augustine on the *Commedia*. Freccero's recently collected essays (cited in ch. V, n. 1) are even entitled *Dante: The Poetics of Conversion*. However, much as I have learned from these two scholars, I have come to feel that the differences between the *Commedia* and the *Confessions* are more important than the similarities. It would take another essay to give detailed reasons for this, but some points are relevant to the present argument: the descent into Hell is undertaken with the help of a guide; the 'opening of the eyes' is gradual, not sudden, and is not even completed by the end of the poem, since its main result is the poem itself; when, before he is vouchsafed his final vision of the Rose, Dante is asked to 'confess', this does not mean to search out his sins and tell them, but to utter the creed; the very fact that this is a poem, and a highly wrought one at that, places it in quite a different category from that of the confession or the autobiography.

6 Patricia Caldwell, *The Puritan Conversion Narrative* (1983), 2, 163.

7 On the subject see Marthe Robert's *L'Ancien et le nouveau* (1963), tr. as *The Old and the New* (1967), and my own *The World and the Book*.

8 S. Kierkegaard, *Either/Or*, I. 141, 142.

9 Ibid., 153–4.

10 Ibid., 160–2.

11 See Peter Abbs, 'The Development of Autobiography in Western Culture from Augustine to Rousseau', D. Phil. diss. Univ. of Sussex (1987).

12 In 'The Apostle Paul and the Introspective Conscience of the West', *Harvard Theological Review*, no. 56 (1963), 199–215, Krister Stendahl tries to argue that there is no warrant for finding in Paul what we later find in St. Augustine and Luther. While sympathizing with his premise, that we should 'be suspicious of any "modernizing"', whether for apologetic, doctrinal, or psychological purposes' (p. 214), I do not feel that he makes out a convincing case.

Chapter XIII

1 Graham Hughes, *Hebrews and Hermeneutics* (1979), 3. Scholars cannot agree on whether the Epistle to the Hebrews is addressed to a tight community of recently converted Jews, a whole synagogue perhaps, or to a much looser group, perhaps even separate individuals; to a group of Christians disillusioned by the failure of Jesus to reappear; or to any group of Judaic Christians. They cannot even decide whether it pre-dates or post-dates the destruction of the Temple in 70 ACE. Since however it turns out in practice that what they think of the letter governs their choice of setting and date, and that their choice of setting and date is used to back up their arguments about its meaning, we are faced with a circular argument common to biblical scholarship, which is so often both meticulous and fantastical in about equal proportions. One can observe the process at work in, e.g. Hughes and Moule, n. 3 below.

2 See, e.g., Geza Vermes, *Jesus and the World of Judaism*, and his article in the *Cambridge History of the Bible*, vol. I, ed. P. R. Ackroyd and C. F. Evans (1970), 199–231, and the bibliographies in both works.

3 Hughes, *Hebrews and Hermeneutics*; C. F. D. Moule, *The Birth of the New*

Testament (2nd edn., 1966).

4 Hughes, *Hebrews and Hermeneutics*, 56, 93, 95.

5 Ibid., 58–9.

6 See Borges, 'Kafka and his Precursors', *Labyrinths*, 199–201; Eliot, 'Tradition and the Individual Talent', *Selected Essays* (1951), 13–22; Stephen Medcalf, 'Virgil's Aeneid' in *The Classical World*, ed. D. Daiches and A. K. Thorlby (1972), 297–326.

7 See F. L. Horton, Jr., *The Melchizedek Tradition* (1976).

8 Ibid., 122.

9 E. H. Gombrich, *Art and Illusion* (1968); Wallace Stevens, 'Anecdote of the Jar', *Collected Poems* (1955), 76.

10 Mary Douglas, *Natural Symbols* (1973), 40–1.

11 A. N. Wilder, *Jesus' Parables and the War of Myths* (1982), 151; Hughes, *Hebrews and Hermeneutics*, 133.

12 Moule, *Birth of the New Testament*, 17: Hughes, *Hebrews and Hermeneutics*, 89.

13 See esp. Peter Brown, *The Cult of the Saints* (1981), and *Society and the Holy* (1982); R. W. Southern, *Western Society and the Church in the Middle Ages* (1970).

14 Douglas, *Natural Symbols*, 19–20, 21.

15 On *berit* see Jon D. Levenson, *Sinai and Zion* (1985), 15–86; and D. J. McCarthy, *Treaty and Covenant* (2nd edn., 1978).

16 On apocalyptic, see *Apocalypse: The Morphology of a Genre*, ed. John J. Collins, *Semeia*, no. 14 (1979), and Collins's *The Apocalyptic Imagination* (1984): also *Apocalypticism in the Mediterranean World and the Near East*, ed. David Hellholm (1983). Fishbane has some valuable comments in *Biblical Interpretation*, Part Four.

17 Havelock, *Preface to Plato*. Nietzsche's most extended treatment is in *Twilight of the Idols* (ed. 1968), and in the third essay of *On the Genealogy of Morals* (ed. 1969); but there are many acute observations the rest of his voluminous writings. John Jones, *On Aristotle and Greek Tragedy*, has some relevant remarks on our misreading of Aeschylus

(see p. 293), and his central argument, that we misread the Greeks when we do not recognize how different they are from us, applies to my whole discussion of the Hebrew scriptures.

18 The literature on *figura* is extensive. Erich Auerbach's seminal essay is to be found in his *Scenes from the Drama of European Literature*. Jean Daniélou, in a dazzling sequence of books, has illuminated its role in the Christian liturgy: see esp. *From Shadows to Reality*, and *The Bible and the Liturgy* (1956). Yet there has been surprisingly little questioning of the implications of *figura*. For some scattered thoughts see my *The World and the Book*.

19 I am thinking particularly of the work of Edmund Leach.

Chapter XIV

1 Von Rad, *Genesis*, 347–8.

2 Speiser, *Genesis*, 290–4.

3 Louis Ginsberg, *The Legends of the Jews* (1913), II. 10.

4 The most convenient moderm compendium of traditional Jewish commentary on the Bible is to be found in the Artscroll Tanach Series. The examples here are from the 6-vol. *Bereshis* (1980), IV. 1628–37.

5 Christian commentary does not have much to say about the man in the field. Both Chrysostom and Augustine comment on Genesis 37, but only in order to draw out the parallels between Joseph, the beloved son sent out into the world by his father and falling into the hands of evil men, and Jesus. See Chrysostom, Homilia 7, Migne, *Patrologia Latina*, Supplementa 4, cols. 680–4, and (?) Augustine, Sermo XIV, *Patrologia Latina*, vol. XXXIX, cols. 1767–1770. I owe these references to James Shiel.

6 Kermode, *Genesis of Secrecy*, ch. 3, esp. p. 53.

7 Ibid., 58–9.

8 Ibid., 65, 72.

9 Thomas Mann, *Joseph and His Brothers* (1959), 359–67; cited in the text as 'Mann', with a page ref. to this edition

in the H. T. Lowe-Porter translation.

[10] Frye, *Anatomy of Criticism*, 184.

[11] Muriel Spark, *The Only Problem* (1984), 189.

[12] S. Kierkegaard, *Concluding Unscientific Postscript* (1971), 78.

[13] See Gillian Rose, *Encounter and Ethical Life: Essays in Kierkegaardian and Jewish Modernism*, forthcoming.

[14] Harold Fisch, *A Remembered Future* (1984), 90. The whole of his ch. 5 is relevant to my argument. Fisch's latest book, *Poetry With a Purpose* (ch. VIII, n. 14), is also close to my concerns here.

[15] Fisch, *A Remembered Future*, 90–2.

[16] S. Kierkegaard, *Fear and Trembling* (1954), 122.

[17] See my essay, 'The Balzac of M. Barthes and the Balzac of M. de Guermantes' (ch. II, n. 3), for further thoughts on the springs and implications of trust or doubt in the writer.

[18] See, for example, *Midrash and Literature*, ed. G. Hartman and S. Budick (1986).

Chapter XV

[1] Quoted in John S. Coolidge, *The Pauline Renaissance in England* (1970), 144–5.

[2] Midrash on Psalms to Psalm 90 : 3, in Ginsberg, *Legends of the Jews*, I. 3.

[3] P. Celan, *Collected Prose* (1986): 'The Meridian', 44–5; Introduction, vii–viii.

[4] Schneidau, *Sacred Discontent*, 215.

[5] Harold Bloom, 'From J to K, or the Uncanniness of the Yahwist', in *The Bible and the Narrative Tradition* (ch.

XI, n. 3), 19–35. See also Bloom's essay, '"Before Moses Was, I Am": The Original and the Belated Testaments', in *Notebooks in Cultural Analysis*, I (1984), 3–14.

[6] Sternberg, *Poetics of Biblical Narrative*, 437.

[7] Auerbach, *Mimesis*, 12.

[8] See Alter, *Biblical Narrative*, 24–7, and, for a quite different view, the works cited in ch. VII, n. 3 above.

[9] Havelock, *Preface to Plato*.

[10] Colin Davies, 'Soaring Aspirations', *RA*, no. 17 (Winter 1987), 30.

[11] John James, *Chartres: The Masons Who Built a Legend* (1982), is the best study known to me of the role of tradition in the work of the Gothic masons. It throws light on the working of *all* traditions.

[12] See Shemaryahu Talmon, 'The Textual Study of the Bible – A New Outlook', in *Qumran and the History of the Biblical Text*, ed. F. M. Cross and S. Talmon (1975), 321–400; and Fishbane, *Biblical Interpretation*.

[13] Howard Nemerov, *The Oak in the Acorn* (1987), 116, 120.

[14] I owe this example to Jonathan Wittenberg.

[15] On the Bible's unwillingness to resolve contradictions or remove repetitions, see Sternberg, *Poetics of Biblical Narrative*, 385–6.

[16] Thomas Nagel, 'Subjective and Objective', *Mortal Questions* (1979), 213.

[17] One of Nagel's other essays is called 'What Is It Like To Be a Bat?'.

[18] Fishbane, *Biblical Interpretation*, 401, quoting Huizinga; Brian Wicker, *The Story-Shaped World* (1975), 46–7.

BIBLIOGRAPHY

James S. Ackerman: 'Joseph, Judah and Jacob', in *Literary Interpretations of Biblical Narratives*, vol. II, ed. Kenneth R. R. Gros Louis (q. v.)

P. R. Ackroyd and C. F. Evans (eds.), *The Cambridge History of the Bible*: vol. I, *From the Beginnings to Jerome* (Cambridge, 1970)

B. Albrektson: *History and the Gods* (Lund, 1967)

Robert Alter: *The Art of Biblical Narrative* (London, 1981)

   and Frank Kermode (eds.): *The Literary Guide to the Bible* (London, 1987)

Brian Appleyard: *Richard Rogers* (London, 1986)

W. H. Auden: *The Dyer's Hand* (London, 1963)

Erich Auerbach: *Mimesis: The Representation of Reality in Western Literature*, tr. Willard Trask (Princeton, N. J., 1953)

   Scenes from the Drama of European Literature, tr. Ralph Manheim (New York, 1959)

St. Augustine: *Confessions*, tr. R. S. Pine-Coffin (Harmondsworth, 1961)

Mieke Bal: *Femmes imaginaires* (Paris, 1986)

Hans Urs von Balthasar: *Prayer*, tr. A. V. Littledale (London, 1963)

Anne Banfield: *Impossible Sentences* (London, 1982)

James Barr: *Biblical Words for Time* (London, 1962)

   Holy Scripture: Canon, Authority, Criticism (Oxford, 1983)

   'Reading the Bible as Literature', *Bulletin of the John Rylands Library*, LVI (1973–4), 10–33

B. Bayer: 'The Rivers of Babylon', *Ariel*, LXII (1985), 43–56

Samuel Beckett: *Not I* (London, 1973)

   Proust and Three Dialogues with Georges Duthuit (London, 1965)

Walter Benjamin: *Understanding Brecht*, tr. Anna Bostock (London, 1977)

Bereshis: A New Translation with a Commentary Anthologized from Talmudic, Midrashic and Rabbinic Sources, 6 vols., The Artscroll Tanach Series (New York, 1980)

W. Beyerlin (ed.): *Near Eastern Religious Texts* (London, 1978)

Sheldon S. Blank: 'The Confessions of Jeremiah and the Meaning of Prayer', *Hebrew Union College Annual*, XXII (1948), 331–54

Harold Bloom: ' "Before Moses Was, I Am"; The Original and the Belated Testaments', *Notebooks in Cultural Analysis* (Durham, N. C.), I (1984), 3–14

   'From J. to K, or the Uncanniness of the Yahwist', in *The Bible and the Narrative Tradition*, ed. Frank McConnell (q. v.)

Robert G. Boling: *Judges*, The Anchor Bible (New York, 1975)

Jorge Luis Borges: *Labyrinths*, ed. Donald D. Yates and James E. Irby (New York, 1964)

John Bossy: *Christianity and the West, 1400–1700* (Oxford, 1985)

Peter Brown: *The Cult of the Saints* (London, 1981)

   Society and the Holy (London, 1982)

Patricia Caldwell: *The Puritan Conversion Narrative: The Beginnings of American Expression* (Cambridge, 1983)

H. von Campenhausen: *The Formation of the Christian Bible*, tr. J. A. Baker (London, 1972)

Umberto Cassuto: *Biblical and Oriental Studies*, tr. Israel Abrahams (Jerusalem, 1973)
  A Commentary on the Book of Exodus, tr. Israel Abrahams (Jerusalem, 1967)
  A Commentary on the Book of Genesis, tr. Israel Abrahams, 2 vols. (Jerusalem, 1964)
  The Documentary Hypothesis, tr. Israel Abrahams (Jerusalem, 1961)

Paul Celan: *Collected Prose*, tr. Rosemary Waldrop (Manchester, 1986)

James H. Charlesworth (ed.): *The Old Testament Pseudepigrapha*, 2 vols. (London, 1985)

A. Cohen (ed.): *The Soncino Chumash* (London, 1983)

John J. Collins (ed.): *Apocalypse: The Morphology of a Genre, Semeia* (Missoula, Mont.), 14 (1970)
  The Apocalyptic Imagination: An Introduction to the Jewish Matrix of Christianity (New York, 1984)

John. S. Coolidge: *The Pauline Renaissance in England: Puritanism and the Bible* (Oxford, 1970)

David Damrosch: 'Leviticus', in *The Literary Guide to the Bible*, ed. Robert Alter and Frank Kermode (q. v.)

H. Danby (ed.): *The Mishnah* (Oxford, 1933)

Jean Daniélou: *The Bible and the Liturgy* (Notre Dame, Ind., 1956)
  From Shadows to Reality, tr. Dom W. Hibberd (London, 1960)

Dante Alighieri: *The Divine Comedy*, tr. with a Commentary by Charles S. Singleton, 6 vols. (London, 1970)

Colin Davies: 'Soaring Aspirations: Interview with Peter Rice', *RA: The Magazine for the Friends of the Royal Academy*, no. 17 (Winter 1987)

E. R. Dodds: *The Greeks and the Irrational* (Berkeley, Calif., and Los Angeles, 1951).

Mary Douglas: *Natural Symbols* (Harmondsworth, 1970)

John Drury: *The Parables in the Gospels* (London, 1985)

T. S. Eliot: *Essays Ancient and Modern* (London, 1936)
  Selected Essays (London, 1951)

I. Epstein (ed.): *The Babylonian Talmud*, The Soncino Press (London, 1948)

Louis Finkelstein: *The Pharisees: The Sociological Background of Their Faith* (Philadelphia, 1946)

Ruth Finnegan: *Oral Poetry: Its Nature, Significance and Social Context* (Cambridge, 1977)

Harold Fisch: *Poetry with a Purpose: Biblical Poetics and Interpretation* (Bloomington, Ind., 1988)
  A Remembered Future: A Study in Literary Mythology (Bloomington, Ind., 1984)

Michael Fishbane: *Biblical Interpretation in Ancient Israel* (Oxford, 1985)

Jan Fokkelman: *Narrative Art and Poetry in the Books of Samuel*. Vol. I: *King David* (Assen, 1981)

Donald Foster: 'John Come Lately: The Belated Evangelist', in *The Bible and the Narrative Tradition*, ed. Frank McConnell (q. v.)

H. and H. A. Frankfort, John A. Wilson, Thorkild Jacobsen: *Before Philosophy* (Harmondsworth, 1949).

John Freccero: *Dante: The Poetics of Conversion* (Cambridge, Mass., 1986)

Hans W. Frei: *The Eclipse of Biblical Narrative* (New Haven, Conn., and London, 1974)

Northrop Frye: *Anatomy of Criticism* (Princeton, N. J.,1957)
  The Great Code: The Bible and Literature (New York, 1982)

John G. Gager: *The Origins of Anti-Semitism* (New York, 1983)

Gérard Genette: *Figures III* (Paris, 1972)

Louis Ginsberg: *The Legends of the Jews*, tr. Henrietta Szold, 6 vols. (Philadelphia, 1911–13)

Norman Gottwald: *The Tribes of Yahweh* (London, 1980)

Moshe Greenberg: *Biblical Prose Prayer* (Berkeley, Calif., and Los Angeles, 1983)

Kenneth R. R. Gros Louis (ed.): *Literary Interpretations of Biblical Narratives*, vol. II (Nashville, Tenn., 1982)

Menahem Haran: *Temples and Temple-Service in Ancient Israel* (Oxford, 1978)

Bernard Harrison: 'Parable and Transcendence', in *Ways of Reading the Bible*, ed. M. Wadsworth (q. v.)

Geoffrey Hartman and Sanford Budick (eds.): *Midrash and Literature* (New Haven Conn., and London, 1986)

Eric Havelock: *Preface to Plato* (Oxford, 1963)

Anthony Hecht: *The Hard Hours* (Oxford, 1967)

Friedrich Heiler: *Prayer: A Study in the History and Psychology of Religion*, tr. Samuel McComb (New York, 1932)

Erich Heller: *The Disinherited Mind* (Harmondsworth, 1961)

David Hellholm (ed.): *Apocalypticism in the Mediterranean World and the Near East* (Tübingen, 1983)

E. Hennecke and W. Schneemelcher (eds.): *New Testament Apocrypha*, tr. R. McL. Wilson, 2 vols. (London, 1963)

George Herbert: *The Works of George Herbert*, ed. F. E. Hutchinson (Oxford, 1941)

Herodotus: *The Histories*, tr. A. de Selincourt (Harmondsworth, 1954)

Samson Raphael Hirsch (ed.): *Pentateuch*, tr. I. Levy, 5 vols. (London, 1958–62)

Homer: *The Iliad*, tr. A. T. Murray, 2 vols., Loeb Classical Library (London, 1924)
  The Odyssey, tr. A. T. Murray, 2 vols., Loeb Classical Library (London, 1919)

F. L. Horton: *The Melchizedek Tradition* (Cambridge, 1976)

Graham Hughes: *Hebrews and Hermeneutics: The Epistle to the Hebrews as a New Testament Example of Biblical Interpretation* (Cambridge, 1979)

Timothy Hyman: Introduction to *Ken Kiff: Paintings 1965–85*, Catalogue of the Serpentine Gallery Exhibition (London, 1986)

John James: *Chartres: The Masons Who Built a Legend* (London, 1982)

M. R. James (ed.): *The Apocryphal New Testament* (Oxford, 1924; repr. 1985)

Marshall D. Johnson: *The Purpose of the Biblical Genealogies* (Cambridge, 1969)

John Jones: *On Aristotle and Greek Tragedy* (London, 1962)

Josephus: *Works*, tr. H. St. John Thackeray, 6 vols., Loeb Classical Library (London, 1926)

Gabriel Josipovici: 'The Balzac of M. Barthes and the Balzac of M. de Guermantes', in *Reconstructing Literature*, ed. Laurence Lerner (Oxford, 1983)
  'Perec's Homage to Joyce (and Tradition)', *The Yearbook of English Studies: Anglo-French Literary Relations Special Number*, ed. Claude Rawson (London, 1985)
  The World and the Book (London, 1971)

Franz Kafka: *The Diaries of Franz Kafka, 1910–1923*, ed. Max Brod, tr. James and Tania Stern (Harmondsworth, 1964)

Frank Kermode: *The Genesis of Secrecy* (Cambridge, Mass., and London, 1979)
  (ed.) *The Literary Guide to the Bible* (see Alter, R.)

Sören Kierkegaard: *On Authority and Revelation*, tr. Walter Lowrie (Princeton, N. J., 1983)
  Concluding Unscientific Postscript, tr. D. F. Swenson and Walter Lowrie (Princeton, N. J., 1971)
  Either/Or, tr. D. F. and L. A. Swenson, 2 vols. (New York, 1959)
  Fear and Trembling, tr. Walter Lowrie (New York, 1954)

James L. Kugel: 'On the Bible and Literary Criticism', *Prooftexts*, I (1981), 217–36

'On the Bible as Literature', An Exchange with Adele Berlin, *Prooftexts*, II (1982), 323–32

The Idea of Biblical Poetry: Parallelism and Its History (New Haven, Conn., and London, 1981)

Stuart Lasine: 'Guest and Host in Judges 19: Lot's Hospitality in an Inverted World', *Journal for the Study of the Old Testament*, no. 29 (1984), 37–59

Edmund Leach: 'Fishing for Men on the Edge of the Wilderness', in *The Literary Guide to the Bible*, ed. R. Alter and F. Kermode (q. v.)

Genesis as Myth and Other Essays (London, 1969)

(with D. Alan Aycock): *Structuralist Interpretations of Biblical Myth* (Cambridge, 1984)

Sid Z. Leiman: *The Canonization of the Hebrew Scriptures* (Hamden, Conn., 1976)

Jon D. Levenson: *Sinai and Zion: An Entry into the Jewish Bible* (New York, 1985)

C. S. Lewis: *Reflections on the Psalms* (London, 1968)

Saul Lieberman: *Hellenism and Jewish Palestine* (New York, 1950)

Hyam Maccoby: *The Mythmaker: Paul and the Invention of Christianity* (London, 1986)

D. J. McCarthy: *Treaty and Covenant* (Rome, 1963; 2nd edn., 1978)

Frank McConnell (ed.): *The Bible and the Narrative Tradition* (Oxford, 1986)

Errol McGuire: 'The Joseph Story: A Tale of Son and Father', in *Images of Man and God: Old Testament Stories in Literary Focus*, ed. Burke Long (Sheffield, 1981)

Jonathan Magonet: 'Abraham and God', *Judaism*, XXXIII (1984), 160–70

Form and Meaning: Studies in the Literary Technique of the Book of Jonah (Bern and Frankfurt, 1976)

Thomas Mann: *Joseph and His Brothers*, tr. H. T. Lowe-Porter (London, 1956; repr. 1959)

Andrew Martin: *The Knowledge of Ignorance* (Cambridge, 1985)

S. Medcalf: 'Virgil's *Aeneid*', in *The Classical World*, ed. David Daiches and A. K. Thorlby (London, 1972)

George Mendenhall: *The Tenth Generation: The Origin of the Biblical Tradition* (Baltimore, 1973)

Henri Meschonnic: *Jona et le signifiant errant* (Paris, 1981)

Pour la poétique, II (Paris, 1980)

Migne: *Patrologia Latina*

C. F. D. Moule: *The Birth of the New Testament* (London, 1962; rev. edn., 1966)

Thomas Nagel: *Mortal Questions* (Cambridge, 1979)

Howard Nemerov: *The Oak in the Acorn* (Baton Rouge, La., and London, 1987)

Jacob Neusner: *Judaism in the Beginning of Christianity* (London, 1984)

Friedrich Nietzsche: *On the Genealogy of Morals*, tr. W. Kaufmann and R. J. Hollingdale (New York, 1969)

Twilight of the Idols, tr. R. J. Hollingdale (Harmondsworth, 1968)

Untimely Meditations, tr. R. J. Hollingdale (Cambridge, 1983)

A. D. Nuttall: *Overheard by God* (London, 1980)

Philo: *The Works of Philo Judaeus*, tr. G. D. Yonge, 4 vols., Loeb Classical Library (London, 1954–5)

Philostratus: *The Life of Apollonius*, tr. D. P. Jones (Harmondsworth, 1970)

Stephen Prickett: *Words and the Word: Language, Poetics and Biblical Interpretation* (Cambridge, 1986)

James B. Pritchard (ed.): *Ancient Near Eastern Texts Relating to the Old Testament*, 3rd. edn. (Princeton, N. J., 1969)

Marcel Proust: *Contre Sainte-Beuve*, ed. Bernard de Fallois (Paris, 1954)

A la recherche du temps perdu, ed. Pierre Clarac and André Ferré, Pléiade edn. (Paris, 1954)

Gerhard von Rad: *Genesis: A Commentary*, tr. John H. Marks, The Old Testament

Library (London, 1961)

Old Testament Theology, tr. D. M. G. Stalker, 2 vols. (Edinburgh, 1962)

Paul Ricoeur: *Essays on Biblical Interpretation*, ed. Louis S. Mudge (Philadelphia, 1980)

Marthe Robert: *The Old and the New*, tr. C. Cosman (Berkeley, Calif., and London, 1967)

Origins of the Novel, tr. Sacha Rabinovitch (Brighton, Sussex, 1980).

C. H. Roberts: 'Books in the Graeco-Roman World and the New Testament', in *The Cambridge History of the Bible*: Vol. I, ed. P. R. Ackroyd and C. F. Evans (q. v.)

James M. Robinson (ed.): *The Nag Hammadi Library in English* (New York, 1977)

Joel Rosenberg: *King and Kin: Political Allegory and the Hebrew Bible* (Bloomington, Ind., and Indianapolis, 1986)

Franz Rosenzweig: *Franz Rosenzweig: His Life and Thought*, presented by Nahum N. Glatzer, revised edn. (New York, 1972)

Cecil Roth (ed.): *The Passover Haggadah*, illus. Arthur Szyk (Jerusalem, 1980)

H. W. F. Saggs: *The Encounter with the Divine in Mesopotamia and Israel* (London, 1978)

E. P. Sanders: *Paul and Palestinian Judaism: A Comparison of Patterns of Religion* (London, 1977)

James S. Sanders: *Torah and Canon* (Philadelphia, 1972)

Nahum Sarna: 'The Bible: Canon, Text and Tradition', in *Encyclopedia Judaica* (Jerusalem, 1971), vol. II, cols. 815–32

J. F. A. Sawyer: *From Moses to Patmos* (London, 1977)

Herbert Schneidau: *Sacred Discontent: The Bible and Western Tradition* (Berkeley, Calif., 1977)

Gershom Scholem: *On Jews and Judaism in Crisis* (New York, 1976)

The Messianic Idea in Judaism (London, 1971)

Albert Schweitzer: *The Quest of the Historical Jesus*, tr. W. Montgomery (London, 1926)

Lou H. Silberman: 'Listening to the Text', *Journal of Biblical Literature*, CII (1983), 3–26

Ulrich Simon: 'Samson and the Heroic', in *Ways of Reading the Bible*, ed. M. Wadsworth (q. v.)

Bruno Snell: *The Discovery of the Mind: The Greek Origins of European Thought* (Cambridge, Mass., 1953)

Charles S. Singleton: *Commedia: Elements of Structure* (Cambridge, Mass., 1956)

R. W. Southern: *Western Society and the Church in the Middle Ages*, The Pelican History of the Church (Harmondsworth, 1970)

Muriel Spark: *The Only Problem* (London, 1984)

E. A. Speiser: *Genesis: Introduction, Translation and Notes*, The Anchor Bible (New York, 1964)

Krister Stendahl: 'The Apostle Paul and the Introspective Conscience of the West', *Harvard Theological Review* LVI (1963), 199–215

Meir Sternberg: *The Poetics of Biblical Narrative* (Bloomington, Ind., 1985)

Wallace Stevens: *Collected Poems* (London, 1955)

Opus Posthumous, ed. Samuel French Morse (New York, 1975)

Jonathan Swift: *A Tale of a Tub*, eds. A. G. Guthkelch and D. Nicholl Smith (Oxford, 1958)

Shemaryahu Talmon: 'The Textual Study of the Bible: A New Outlook', in *Qumran and the History of the Biblical Text*, ed. Frank Moore Cross and Shemaryahu Talmon (Cambridge, Mass., 1975)

Oliver Taplin: 'Homer Comes Home', *New York Review of Books*, XXXIII (1986), no. 4, 39–42

Tsvetan Todorov: *The Poetics of Prose*, tr. Richard Howard (Ithaca, N. Y., 1977)

Edward Ullendorf: 'Thought Categories in the Hebrew Bible', in *Sudies in Rationalism, Judaism and Universalism: Essays in Memory of Leon Roth*, ed. Raphael Loewe (London, 1966)

J. Van Seters: *In Search of History: Historiography, The Ancient World, and the Origins of Biblical History* (New Haven, Conn., and London, 1983)

Roland de Vaux: *Ancient Israel: Its Life and Institutions*, tr. John McHugh (London, 1961)

Geza Vermes: 'Bible and Midrash in Early Old Testament Exegesis', in *The Cambridge History of the Bible*, vol. I, ed. P. R. Ackroyd and C. F. Evans (q. v.)

Virgil: *The Aeneid*, tr. H. Rushton Fairclough, 2 vols., Loeb Classical Library (London, 1967)

Michael Wadsworth: 'Making and Interpreting Scripture', in *Ways of Reading the Bible*, ed. M. Wadsworth (Brighton, Sussex, 1981)

Barry G. Webb: *The Book of Judges: An Integrated Reading* (Sheffield, 1987)

J. Weingreen: 'Hotzetikha in Genesis 15:7', in *Words and Meanings: Essays Presented to D. Winton Thomas*, ed. Peter R. Ackroyd and Barnabas Lindars (Cambridge, 1968)

Brian Wicker: *The Story-Shaped World* (London, 1975)

Aharon Wiener: *The Prophet Elijah in the Development of Judaism* (London, 1978)

Amos N. Wilder: *Jesus' Parables and the War of Myths: Essays on Imagination in the Scriptures*, ed. with a preface by James Breech (London, 1982)

Alison Winton: *Proust's Additions: The Making of 'À la recherche du temps perdu'*, 2 vols. (Cambridge, 1977)

Ludwig Wittgenstein: *On Certainty*, tr. Denis Paul and G. E. M. Anscombe (Oxford, 1979)

   Culture and Value, tr. Peter Winch (Oxford, 1980)

   Philosophical Investigations, tr. G. E. M. Anscombe (Oxford, 1963)

Michael Wyschogrod: 'A Theology of Jewish Unity', *L'Eylah* (London), no. 21 (1986), 26–30

Yosef Hayim Yerushalmi: *Zakhor: Jewish History and Jewish Memory* (Seattle, Wash., and London, 1982)

INDEX OF NAMES

INDEX OF BIBLICAL PASSAGES

Old Testament

Apocrypha

New Testament